IF NOTHING CHANGES,
NOTHING CHANGES

IF NOTHING CHANGES, NOTHING CHANGES

THE NICK DONOFRIO STORY

NICK DONOFRIO
with **MICHAEL DeMARCO**

HOUNDSTOOTH
PRESS

IF NOTHING CHANGES, NOTHING CHANGES
The Nick Donofrio Story

ISBN   978-1-5445-3133-5   *Hardcover*
       978-1-5445-3134-2   *Paperback*
       978-1-5445-3135-9   *Ebook*

For my wife Anita, son Michael, and daughter Nicole.

*I am who I am in great measure because of your
love, your support, and your sacrifices.*

*And for my parents—Nick and Beatrice—who gave me
a work ethic that balanced ambition with the Golden
Rule and the opportunity to pursue my dreams.*

CONTENTS

Preface   ix

PART I. LESSONS FROM MY FATHER

1   My Father   3

PART II. A CAREER OF CHANGE AND INNOVATION AT IBM

2   Early Days   19

3   Managing   25

4   Taking Charge   43

5   Expanding Leadership   71

6   Moving into Top Management   95

7   Working with the Government   121

PART III. VALUES AND THEMES IN MY IBM CAREER

8   Fathers, Sons, and Values   149

9   Changing to a Market-Centric Focus   161

10   Leading for Change and Innovation   183

11   Encouraging, Engaging, and Mentoring   201

12   Changing IBM's Technology   235

13   Equity   265

14   My Way   281

PART IV. EXTENDING CHANGE AND INNOVATION TO SOCIETY

15   Serving on Boards of Directors   301

16   Significant Technology Shifts   341

17 The New World of Work   351

18 Innovation and Change   365

19 Leadership and Talent   387

20 New Frontiers in Innovation, Collaboration, and Education   395

21 On Life and Living   425

Acknowledgments   441

Contributor Chapter Index   443

Bibliography   445

References   447

PREFACE

My fifty-seven years as an engineer, technologist, and business leader have seen extraordinary developments in technology, paralleled by equally profound social and cultural changes. I was fortunate to work at the heart of many of these technological changes during my forty-four years at IBM (1964–2008) and always challenged myself to do my part in driving and enabling them.

I was well-prepared for IBM, having received a great education in engineering at Rensselaer Polytechnic Institute and Syracuse University, along with lasting instruction in life, change, and innovation at the hands of my father. Eventually, I was in a position to lead many of IBM's key decision-making efforts about existing and emerging technologies, forming the teams that developed and released those technologies, and enabling so many talented engineers, scientists, and businesspeople to innovate.

You will not find in these pages a year-by-year history of my career at IBM and beyond. Rather, I will tell stories about how my career unfolded, how change and innovation were such important parts of my career, and how the results of those changes and innovations transformed both IBM and our clients, and later in my life, other enterprises and entities that I have had the pleasure of serving. And transformed me as well.

In writing this book, I have been fortunate to reconnect with so many of my colleagues from across more than fifty years, and they have contributed their stories and memories to this effort. Indeed, they tell much of what happened.

As I have reviewed my career with colleagues both old and new, themes that have guided my work and me, both inside and outside of IBM, became evident:

- Always be willing to ask for help and always be willing to learn. Learn what you do not know with an open mind and as quickly as you can. Understand full well that in the future, you will be judged less by what you know and more by how you address what you do not know.

- Always fully understand what you are doing and why you are doing it. Technology matters, and you must get it right. Ultimately, what you are not doing may prove more important to your success than what you are doing. Technology for technology's sake benefits no one.

- Always listen to your clients. Value constantly migrates, and you do not control it—your clients do! They have the problems and needs that matter.

- Always start with the problem and not the answer. Innovation makes or breaks everything in the twenty-first century. Its drivers have become more global, interdisciplinary, and collaborative in nature, and you must adapt to its breakneck speed.

- Always remember that time is never your ally. We all have the same amount in a day, we can never get any back, and we will never have enough when we need it the most.

- Always understand and appreciate where you stand on the issue of change. Do you lead it, tolerate it, fight it, avoid it, or embrace it?

If I have done my job right, you will recognize these themes in the stories that follow. When you finish reading this book, I hope you will walk away with a few new ideas and a better understanding of both the history and the future of innovation and the impact that it has had and will continue to have on all of us.

—Nick Donofrio, December 2021

PART I

LESSONS FROM MY FATHER

The home where I was raised. My parents worked incredibly hard to give us a good childhood and to prepare us for life. On this very front porch, my father taught me a lesson that in many ways has defined my life until this day.

1

MY FATHER

hroughout my career, I have shared the story of my early life with colleagues at IBM, as well as the students, scientists, engineers, educators, government leaders, businesspeople, and others around the world whom I have been lucky enough to address. I tell them how fortunate I was to have had a father who believed in hard work, constant improvement, and change. This was how you got ahead in life, he believed, and I found him to be right. The lessons I learned from my father have served me well and continue to do so to this day.

Nicholas Joseph Donofrio was my strongest teacher, supporter, and enabler through his lessons. The mindset, the work ethic, the focus on results—these lessons were drilled into my head during childhood. My father taught me what I needed to know to succeed in my business career, and the lessons often came the hard way, for him and for me.

His story began in the Italian ghetto of Beacon, New York. His own father, Guiseppe D'Onofrio, had immigrated to New York in 1904 from the town of Arpaia in Campania, Italy. He had learned the shoemaking trade in Italy but became a hat maker upon reaching Beacon.

A decade later, on October 9, 1914, my father was born, the third of four sons to Guiseppe and his wife Elvira. Shortly after the birth of the fourth son, my grandmother passed away. My grandfather did what all good Italian fathers in America did in similar situations: he called his family in Italy and asked them to find a second wife for him. My grandmother Concetta soon arrived, played a crucial role in guiding the family, and helped life go forward for Guiseppe and his boys.

My grandfather, a serious, quiet man, spoke very little English, but I had a sense that he was very smart, with some cultural interests, though no time to pursue them. He had to work very hard to support his family. Life was a constant struggle to keep the family together and to put food on the table, and there was little time to be deeply involved with his children or to guide them toward any particular future.

Growing up, my father was outgoing and friendly and, lacking direction at home, looked to his friends for guidance. He was a smart kid, but impressionable, struggling to find his own way, while not forgetting his family roots. At the age of fourteen, he dropped out of school, partly to help support the family during the early years of the Great Depression and partly due to peer pressure. Sensing a need, he also stood up and assumed leadership of his family, becoming the kind of take-charge, go-to person that every family needs. From that day on, he was the one who always was there when his brothers and parents needed him.

After leaving school, my father went to work at a local factory, a hard environment that turned him into a tough, heavy-handed person. He had no far-reaching ambition or grand vision for the future, but he worked and made his contribution to the family. At the same time, he became part of the Italian social life in Beacon. He and his buddies loved partying and all that went with it. Even though this was the time of the Great Depression, they found ways to have fun. My father was young, physically fit, and good looking, and he had no problem finding a good time around town.

In the late 1930s, my father met Beatrice Fulvio, a Bronx-born Italian of strong intellect and faith, who had moved with her family to Beacon shortly after graduating from high school. Beatrice was a spirited character who worked at the same hat factory as Guiseppe, and before too long, she was dating his son Nicholas, and going, as she liked to say, "here, there, and everywhere."

They both worked hard and enjoyed dating and dancing. It was the Big Band Era, and Mom and Dad loved to dance, particularly the Lindy Hop. And they were very good at it! The Second World War soon came upon them, though, and Dad, along with several of his buddies, decided to enlist.

Dad and Mom kept dating and were eventually married while he remained in service to our country. Out of necessity, they first lived with my mother's parents, before later moving to the other side of Grandma and Grandpa's duplex house, where they would remain for over a decade.

My father served the country by joining the Army Air Force as an aircraft mechanic. He worked with his hands and brawn, never on the front lines, and his time in the Army made him tougher and more responsible.

After the War, my father became a guard at Matteawan State Hospital for the Criminally Insane in Beacon. It was a job that required his toughness on a daily basis. His buddies worked there, too, all of them sticking together. They even became volunteer firemen at the same time. For the next several decades, their lives followed a simple but meaningful routine: go to work, have a beer before heading home, fight fires when called upon, and help each other as needed. They took their responsibilities seriously, believing that they needed to give to get.

My father was not only smart, but tough—maybe by nature, maybe by habit, maybe by circumstance. He understood where he had taken himself in life thus far, but now he started to want new things. A house of his own for his family. A better way for his children—two boys and two girls—Francis, Nicholas, Gloria, Elvira.

He knew he needed more money to achieve these goals, so he began to work even harder. In addition to his work at Matteawan State Hospital, he took on multiple jobs such as night watchman, house painter, and janitor. It seemed as if he was always out of the house working. He had ambition for himself but knew that given the times and the choices he had made, his ambition would have limits.

As our family grew, my father and mother took on different roles, as they sought to turn their hopes and ambitions into reality. Mother was the homemaker and in charge of our education. Father was the brawn, the provider, and the one who taught us how to reach for a better way.

MY FATHER AS MY TEACHER

I cannot emphasize enough how seriously my father took his responsibility for pushing his children toward bright futures. His vision involved a lot of hard work, whether we liked it or not, particularly for his two sons. Even as very young boys, my older brother Fran and I had chores and responsibilities.

Fran, four years my senior, started with a long Monday-to-Saturday newspaper route—over one hundred daily deliveries to make—and I helped him. I also started my own smaller delivery routes before eventually taking over Fran's when he left for college.

Fran and I worked hard on our grandparents' duplex house, too, often alongside our father and beloved Uncle Dave. We did the gardening, cut the grass, painted the fence, and did the many other as-needed chores that never seemed to be done. My father had no tolerance for mistakes, even the ones that all kids naturally make, and we had to do the work until we got it right. We quickly learned how important it was to pay attention and to do our work well the first time.

Of course, I did not work all the time. I had my own group of buddies, and we always were getting in trouble. I always feared that my father would punish me when I did something stupid or crazy or caused damage, and he usually did.

Yet there also were times when I expected punishment but did not get it—like the time when I foolishly cut myself playing the knife-tossing game mumblety-peg, the time I badly damaged a friend's bicycle, or the time when I managed to get a very bad case of poison ivy. At such times, my father might help to bandage my wounds, fix what had been broken, or simply offer genuine understanding. I began to recognize that there was a complexity to my father, that maybe this tough guy had a depth of thinking I had not been able to see or understand in my earliest years. That didn't necessarily make things easier. In fact, things soon became much harder.

In 1955, when I was about ten, my father had saved enough money to buy his own house for our family, and we moved from the old neighborhood. The house needed a lot of work, but it was a source of great pride for him, and rightly so. My father, his buddies, my brother, and I worked hard together to make improvements and repairs, and we did the work at a high level of quality. Often my father had to figure out on his own how to fix something or make it work, and I admired him for that—there were no instant answers to be found on YouTube or a smartphone in those days. I was awed by how readily he could take something that was broken and turn it into something useful.

Naturally, my brother and I had to take care of our new house, but at the same time, we still were expected to take care of our grandparents' duplex. Even though I would have preferred not to work so hard, I did take pride in seeing improvements take shape, and this sense of accomplishment bonded me closer to both my father and brother. I realized that my father was forcing his work ethic on us even more than before, and that drove even greater satisfaction for me in seeing the results of my hard work. I also found ambition stirring within me. Like many young boys, I wanted to outdo my brother and be more successful than him, which would not be easy, as Fran had set the bar high.

I began to think more deeply about how I related to my father, too. I realized that I *feared* him, and that is why I did what he told me. Yes, I was taking more pride in my work, but I worked because I had to and because I feared him, not because I enjoyed it or *wanted* to please him. I was still pretty young, and all I really wanted was to be out playing sports with my friends. I needed to figure out a way to deal with what he wanted me to do, yet still have time for some fun, just like I had done in the old neighborhood.

This yearning led to a realization—a very important one—that I have since applied throughout every stage of my life and in many different situations, both personal and professional: I had to learn how to manage myself, and in turn, my father. By this I mean that instead of reacting emotionally to his hard-driving, critical approach, I learned to react logically. I would find myself thinking, *Even if you don't want to do what he says, why bother putting yourself in a position of fighting with him? Do what you need to do well, but do it as quickly as you can, and then go find where the guys are hanging out.*

As I moved more in this direction, I noticed that I was not getting in trouble or getting punished as much. I became aware that if I thought through my interactions with him, I would be in better shape than when I had just reacted emotionally to his heavy-handed style.

My siblings saw that something was different between my father and me, but when I tried to explain my ideas to them, they didn't buy in. They were still acting—and reacting—emotionally, while I was figuring out how to resolve conflict by thinking and acting differently.

As my relationship with my father matured, I started to see things as he did. I understood why quality—and the sense of pride that came with it— was so important. I learned that whatever job I was doing, I should do it well and with dedication. And as I saw the results of our work, I eventually realized that I was no longer working out of fear. I was adopting my father's work ethic, commitment to quality, and pride as my own. Instead of trying to outdo my brother, I was seeking excellence for its own sake. I was developing a crucial mindset I would need later in my career.

Slowly, fear of my father evolved into admiration. Here was a man who always found a way to get things done with the resources at hand, a trait that I too would need many times in the years to come. For example, most of the tools and equipment he had at home were hand-me-downs that he fixed after they were discarded by someone else.

The best example might have been our first power mower. What a mess of nuts and bolts, grease, and oil! Over the years, we had plenty of push mowers to use—he would sharpen his own blades, get his own honing done— but one day he brought home this horrible, old power mower he had gotten somewhere. I asked, "Dad, what are we going to do with that thing? The gas tank isn't even connected!"

Yet he made it work. He had no money for repairs, but he found some old copper tubing and started fiddling with it. He figured out that he could not just connect the tubing directly to the tank because it would vibrate and break, but if he arranged the tubing into a spiral form, it could hold. So, he took a big, fat saltshaker from the kitchen, wrapped the copper tubing around it like a spring, and connected it to the gas tank and the mower. He had to do it pretty precisely, because the tank and mower were on two different levels, but somehow, he figured it out. It looked ridiculous, but it worked.

I never forgot that spirit of creativity, that innovative mindset that enabled him to find a solution to any problem he faced. I did my best to not only bring that same spirit to major challenges I would face at IBM, but eventually to infuse it into the more than 200,000 technology professionals I would lead so that they could solve incredible leading-edge challenges in ways they never would have predicted. Of course, that remained decades into the future. I still had to get through high school with this complicated man.

While I now was delivering much better on his high expectations, he remained just as tough. My father never complimented me or my brother when we did high-quality work. He was trying to get us to understand that we should do work the right way because that was our responsibility, not because we might receive a compliment from him. We learned that when we did our work well, our sense of pride would be our own reward.

Even though he was just as tough as ever, my abilities to duck and weave within the systems that were presented to me were improving, too. Take report cards, for example. In grade school, our report cards had grades on the front along with comments about behavior on the back. While I always received good grades, I sometimes got into trouble at school. As a result, my father would look first at the back of the report card to check my behavior, and I frequently was punished for the things I had done at school.

As I had with the yard work, I changed to meet this dynamic. Rather than give up mischief, I learned to think about it more logically. I realized I could still be a bit of a jokester, but just not in school, where my behavior would become known to him as soon as the next report card was sent home.

Once I made that decision, I did not get into trouble *at school* anymore. I picked my moments for mischief more strategically. Through this type of nuanced thinking, I began to understand that if I could not change a system, I could change the way I operated *within* that system to my advantage, a trait I would use for the rest of my life.

As all of this played out over the course of a few years, it became obvious that my father was focusing differently and more intently on me than on my siblings. Perhaps he saw something in my work results or sensed the changes in me and thought that he could really make something out of me. Whatever the case, as I grew, rather than let up, he got *harder* with me. He obviously thought that if he pushed me harder, he would get more out of me and be of more help in preparing me for life. And I found myself up to each challenge that he threw at me.

We continued to work together all through my teen years. I not only was working at the family homes and delivering papers, I also worked at a local store. One time, my boss offered my father and me the opportunity to earn some money by putting in a new floor at the store. We worked all day and much of the evening together on the job. Everything went wrong, but we stuck with it, and eventually finished the job.

I just was glad to be done with the project, but he then surprised me first by noting aloud that I had worked harder on the floor than he did and then by rewarding my effort with a larger-than-expected share of the money. This was a great moment for me, because I saw that if I worked incredibly hard, I could earn not only a reward, but praise, too.

As I moved through high school, I could tell that my new approach toward my father was working better and better. Yes, I had to be good and do the things he expected, but we were getting along well. My father liked that I was excelling in high school by getting straight As and high marks on the New York State Regents exams. He liked that I was looking toward my future with ambition, too.

All the same, my father was stricter and more rigid with me than my friends' parents were with them, and this seemed to me like an injustice. I could not go out and have as much fun as others, and I did not have as much free time. Going into my junior year of high school, I decided to challenge my father about his system, though it took me some time to gather the courage to do so. What my father said in response to my challenge provided me with one of the most important lessons I would ever receive.

"IF NOTHING CHANGES, NOTHING CHANGES"

My father loved to sit on the front porch during summer nights after a hard day of work. He would have a few beers. He would sit there waving at friends who drove by, and they would beep their horns. Other friends walking past might come up onto the porch to visit, and he would sit there with them and hold court. Here, I knew, was where I had the best chance to catch him in the right mood for the conversation I had envisioned.

Finally, one night, I made my move. It was just the right time and the right moment. Maybe it was the cool of the summer evening. Maybe I just could not hold it inside anymore. Whatever it was, I went out onto the porch and said to my father, "Can we talk about something, Dad? I really need to talk to you."

"Sure," he said. "Sit down. Let's talk."

I can see this all as if it were yesterday, when after years of struggle, I finally asked my father, "Why do you push me so hard? Why is nothing ever good enough? Why do you have to be so controlling?"

He sat quietly for a few moments before saying, "Because if nothing changes, nothing changes."

He paused, letting that sink in a bit with me. Then he continued, "Son, if you are not happy with what you have been getting, then why keep doing what you have been doing, since all you will be getting is what you have been getting. If you want something different, then you have to do something different. You have to change."

This guidance was simple, yet so profound, and I admit that it would take me a long time to fully process the wisdom behind his words. But I understood them enough. I understood that he had a plan for me and was doing what he could do to build me into a better person, because he wanted me to have a better life than he did. I also realized that he thought that if I grew up in a strict home, I would learn how to achieve levels of success he could not even imagine. I would end up in a better place, because he had not taken the path of least resistance with me.

The conversation ended, and I went back inside the house, my dreams of freedom dashed. Eventually, I would come to fully understand just how much he contributed to everything I would go on to accomplish and experience. And I would never forget the way in which he explained himself to me that night on the porch.

MY MOTHER'S CONTRIBUTIONS

While I have focused extensively on my father's lessons, it is impossible to overstate my mother's contributions to shaping me, my childhood, and my life. My parents acted as a team, instilling their Old World values, training me, giving me my values, and shaping my success. I have a blended personality, a combination of how both my mother and my father brought me up. Both of my parents made sure I had the right set of experiences as a child, and they both made sacrifices so I could earn the fine education that led to my career.

In fact, my mother was the dominant parent in many ways, a behind-the-scenes leader, as tough as she needed to be with me, but gentle, too. My mother taught me to "be nice, be thoughtful, and don't be fresh, because people need each other."

My mother could bring out the good in almost anyone, and she taught me how to reach out to people to help them. I developed many of the qualities I eventually used as a manager and a leader from my mother.

As long as she lived, even at the age of ninety-eight, my mother remained as smart as a whip. She was my rock and a great influence in my life. While three years have passed since we lost her, I still miss her greatly.

WHAT I LEARNED FROM MY PARENTS

My father's style was to let us figure out the lessons he was imparting, not to explain them to us. He taught implicitly, a technique that I have applied throughout my life and career and sometimes will apply in these pages, too. However, since my father's lessons were so important, I want to lay them out clearly here:

- The way forward to a better life is through hard work.
- You need to pay attention to learn how to do things right.
- You can start with nothing and still figure out a way to make something.
- Whatever job you are doing, do it well and with pride.
- Make a commitment to quality and responsibility.
- Seek excellence for excellence's sake.
- When you do your work well and correctly, your sense of pride is your reward.
- You make many choices every day, often subconsciously. Use your free will to make the decisions that are right for you. If you give up your free will, that is your choice.
- And of course, if nothing changes, nothing changes.

These lessons served me well while building my career. They still do today, pushing me to keep seeking excellence in the things I choose to do rather than coast on past laurels.

When I became a manager and then a leader at IBM, I found that I had to learn how to adapt these lessons to whatever situation I found myself in at any given time. While the work ethic my father drilled into me has been a valuable gift, I came to learn that I could not use my father's control-and-command style with the highly skilled and often brilliant colleagues I was asked to work with and/or lead at IBM. Instead, I had to become collaborative, an enabler for my team—a lot more like my mother, in fact. As a leader,

I figured out that my real job was simply to listen to my team members and fight for them until they could bring our vision to fruition. I learned to be tough, but fair; flexible, but highly productive; and to always move quickly.

Still, the substance of his lessons always has guided me: Be willing to work hard, change, and deliver results without excuses. Figure out the culture you find yourself a part of, so you know how to promote your ideas and make a difference. *Always* accept the challenge.

And most important: change may be the harder road, but if nothing changes, nothing changes. Always keep changing.

I could not have had the career I did without these lessons or without the focus and push from my father. My father left us in April of 1999 at age eighty-five, his tough and hard life having caught up with him too soon. I forever am grateful to this tough, complicated, visionary man.

PART II

A CAREER OF CHANGE AND INNOVATION AT IBM

Early in my career, IBM featured me in this recruiting advertisement. There is no doubt that IBM gave me assignment after assignment that ran "technologically hot." (Reprint Courtesy of IBM Corporation©)

EARLY DAYS

A s soon as I arrived at Rensselaer Polytechnic Institute (RPI) in Troy, New York, during the fall of 1963, all those lessons from my father slipped right through my fingers, at least for a while. Like many kids, I struggled with my newfound independence. Given how limited my freedoms had been at home, I had to make a bigger adjustment than most kids starting college, and it did not take long before I was partying too much.

At the same time, my courses were harder than they had been in high school, and I was not ready to buckle down to the extent needed. Chemistry was just miserable for me. In those days, at the halfway point of a sixteen-week semester, RPI would send your grades home if you had any Ds or Fs. I had a D in chemistry, so the note went home to my parents. Right away my father said, "What's going on here? Too much partying?"

I denied the accusation, but there was truth in what he had said. I knew that he was disappointed. As a kid, I feared him as an authority. By now, I feared disappointing him as a person, and that drove me to correct course. Reality had struck, and I had to regroup quickly. I called upon the work ethic he had built in me, put my newfound freedoms aside, hit the books hard, and aced the chemistry final to salvage a B for the semester. I *earned* that B, and after that, I took my grades seriously enough that I brought my overall grade point average up to a 3.5 out of 4.0 for my freshman year.

While most kids go through a similar maturation process in college, the speed in which I made this turnaround turned out to have lifelong ramifications for me, because in doing so, I had made myself eligible to compete for a co-op assignment during the spring of my freshman year. RPI had steep criteria that had to be met before you could even apply to compete, and relative to the size of my freshman class, the number of co-op positions was very small. Having met those criteria, however, I applied, and I won opportunities with a few companies, including IBM.

Little did I know, but my timing was eerily perfect. Over the next three years, I would complete three co-op assignments for IBM, all hovering around the IBM System/360 mainframe computing system—which in time would be known to people around the world simply as the mainframe—which just had been announced in April 1964, and shipped the following year.

Needless to say, I was in awe of System/360. It was an engineering wonder that *Fortune* called at the time, "IBM's $5,000,000,000 Gamble...the most crucial and portentous—as well as perhaps the riskiest—business judgment of recent times." Of course, that gamble paid off, and System/360 established IBM as *the* leading information technology company for the next quarter century.

The IBM co-op assignment also altered my college experience significantly, because I would be working during the fall of 1964 rather than completing a typical academic semester. To compensate, I spent that summer at RPI doing the first semester of sophomore year with the other co-op students in my class. While the IBM opportunity was very helpful and great in many ways (the money I earned made the cost of my education much more manageable), it also meant I was out-of-phase with my class, basically alone for at least one semester, and clearly off stride.

As my classmates began their sophomore year in Troy, I was further down the river in Poughkeepsie, working in IBM's Ferrite Core Exploratory Group. Ferrite cores were the devices used to build memory subsystems for IBM's computers as late as the mid-1960s. Our group "specced" the cores and designed the planes containing the cores so they could be integrated into the memory subsystem.

These ferrite core memories were state of the art. Current in one direction magnetized as a "1" and in the other direction as a "0." With or without power, they remembered their contents, since the written magnetic direction remained in the core. Amazing devices indeed.

After a few quick lessons and courses, I learned the systems and wrote a technical report that allowed others to quickly spec and design their own memory planes based on system needs. This technical work was accepted by the IBM technical community and was documented officially as an IBM Technical Report (TR). Boy, was I ever proud! I worked with so many bright people who were so incredibly experienced in what they did that I felt very fortunate. (Ironically, a few years later, I worked on and eventually led the Semiconductor Memory Program that ultimately replaced the Ferrite Memory Program at IBM.)

In June 1965, I received an assignment that complemented the ferrite core memory plane work in that it focused on the drive and sensing circuitry associated with the memory subsystems. I learned about transistor design and IBM's Automated Logic Design System. The experience was vital to me, as a few years later the very first custom integrated chips I designed at IBM were driver and sensing chips for semiconductor memory chip arrays.

My last co-op assignment, during the summer of 1966, was in system design. At the time, IBM was doing a great deal of work on an associative memory computer that would allow much faster access to data by interrogating memory by content instead of by address. This work taught us a lot about how to design and architect these systems, and while in many ways these content addressable memories were years ahead of their time, we did make a few exclusive placements for systems that were built.

For an ambitious young student, each of these assignments was simply amazing, exciting, and stimulating. I was literally and figuratively in the center of the computing universe, fittingly enough, as the incredible System/360 name referred to the 360 degrees in a circle. It was a symbol of IBM's audacious ambition to meet every need of every user in both the business and the scientific world with this offering. For several decades, that audacious ambition was at the heart of the IBM culture.

Inherent in that desire to meet every need of every user was a promise and commitment to compatibility. System/360 was the first product family that allowed business data-processing operations to grow from the smallest machine to the largest *without* the enormous expense of rewriting vital programs. It went down in company lore that IBM CEO Thomas Watson, Jr. said at the time, "We will remain compatible with ourselves and serve you, your company, your applications, and your data. If you elect to change, the choice will be yours, dear customer, and not ours."

Dick Linton (*Forty-year IBM Veteran and Early Donofrio Manager*): It was a time when IBM felt they could do anything and everything. If it wasn't aggressive and if it wasn't on the cutting edge, they didn't want anything to do with it! It had to be over and above what anybody could even think about.

Dick Gladu (*Thirty-five-year IBM Veteran and Early Donofrio Manager*): It was a phenomenal time to join the company. Talk about transition! When I joined in 1961, I had not had any real coursework in semiconductors or semiconductor theory. The first system I worked on was a vacuum tube system in Kingston. These were systems! They took up an acre of space. They had their own vacuum tube circuit cards. They had their own cooling and power system. They had a display panel that was half the size of a nice-sized living room.

But we were on the cusp of major technology breakthroughs. There was a lot of excellent work being done in IBM Research on semiconductors. The key movers and shakers like Lew Terman and Bob Dennard and Dale Critchlow were really making the initial strides in the semiconductor business. The first time that I had an opportunity to work with the Research guys was when they were doing some experimental work on tunneled diodes called Esaki diodes. This was really one of the first attempts to try to get a memory built out of semiconductors for a major IBM product.

We were at the Poughkeepsie and Fishkill sites, doing hand-and-glove work with the guys in Yorktown, the Westchester County headquarters of IBM Research. We ended up putting together this crazy-looking card of tunneled diodes. The card was 72 bits by 1,000 words, and lo and behold, it was shipped as a product.

There was a lot of cooperative work between East Fishkill and Germany, and with the Poughkeepsie team, and then ultimately, the Burlington team. So it was an incredible period to be on the cusp of such a major technological revolution as we were in the early to mid 1960s.

I experienced that excitement and energy, too, even though at the same time, in those early days, I felt like a nobody. This was the first real job I had, and I could barely grasp the scale of what I was working on or the history of the company I had joined. I knew who Thomas Watson, Jr. was, and I certainly knew what IBM was becoming, and how it was growing by leaps and bounds, but otherwise, I was a complete neophyte. I understood the basics of the engineering, but everything I was learning mattered, because I was working in a very critical area. As the System/360 was coming together, I was right in the middle of the action designing core memory planes. Even now, I shake my head and think, *Yes, I did that! I was part of history!*

As a college student in the mid-1960s, I could never have imagined that one day I not only would oversee the mainframe business, but that during Lou Gerstner's well-chronicled turnaround of IBM in the mid-1990s, I actually would lead the incredible team that "saved the mainframe," kept Watson, Jr.'s promise, and made a major contribution to saving the company. Remarkably, the mainframe business remains vital for IBM and the world to this day.

My RPI years flew by until graduation day arrived. And I will never forget that day, because that was when my father first said to me, "You did a good job, son."

It was incredibly hot, humid, and uncomfortable that day in my gown and mortarboard, but I could have cared less, because my father had paid me this rare and very meaningful compliment. More than fifty years later, I am amazed at just how much of an impact his words made on me.

And I had done a good enough job at RPI that following graduation, I received several job offers, some from companies with whom I had never interviewed. Job offers simply slipped under the door to my room. A California-based government contractor was offering the most money, so naturally, I was leaning toward that opportunity.

And then, very much to my surprise, I went to work for IBM.

Two factors contributed to my decision. First, I was planning to marry Anita Berner, my high school sweetheart, so working for nearby IBM would allow me to live at home and save money. Second, moving to California was not going to go over well with my wife-to-be, her family, or my family, especially my mother.

My mother's family was very close-knit, typical of Italian families at the time, and no one had ever moved a great distance away. She looked me in the eyes and said, "Nicky, you are going to go out there to California? We are never going to see you. Why not accept IBM's offer and see what happens?"

How could I say no?

I took her advice—and she never let me forget it! In June 1967, the week after I graduated from RPI, I began working for IBM in Poughkeepsie, New York, about a half hour from my parents' home in Beacon. I started my career as a circuit designer on a competitive task force to determine what technology IBM would use to replace ferrite core memories.

By 1969, the competing options were reviewed and analyzed, and decisions were made that would alter the course of history for IBM and the world. Semiconductors were here to stay, while both bipolar transistor technology and FET (field-effect transistor) technology would also be pursued for different reasons.

Very briefly, the bipolar process was a technology for integrated circuit fabrication. Bipolar transistors were used because of their advantages in high-speed operations, such as communication systems, and because of their high-current drive capability for power applications, such as can be found in the automotive sector. For years, the bipolar process was the only viable semiconductor technology available for integrated circuit fabrication. And yes, they remain in use today. There are three terminal devices that utilize current flow in two different planes in the semiconductor to enable the transistor to act as an amplifier and/or switch. These devices typically dissipate more power-per-unit of semiconductor and are more complex to fabricate, generally requiring more semiconductor material per device, and thus are more expensive.

Field effect transistors, meanwhile, are a type of transistor that uses an electric field to control the flow of current. FETs also have three terminals—source, gate, and drain—and control the flow of current by the application of a voltage to the gate, which in turn alters conductivity between the drain and source. Sometimes known as unipolar transistors since they involve single-carrier-type operation, FETs use either electrons or holes as charge carriers in their operation, depending on the polarity of the semiconductor material. FETs are in general simpler semiconductor structures to build and thus, less expensive.

Most of what we needed to know about design rules for FET devices in their early life at IBM, we could fit on a single sheet of paper. At the same time, the design rules for bipolar devices filled a large three-ring binder.

I initially became a bipolar circuit designer for the sensing and driver chips needed by FET arrays. Little did I know that these technologies would follow me throughout my entire career.

After completing these chips, I was given the opportunity of designing the FET array, which I did under the guidance of Dick Linton, who in turn, reported to Dick Gladu.

Dick Linton: In the late 1960s, IBM Research was starting to look into using field-effect transistors (FETs) as memory components.

This was met with skepticism in a lot of technical areas, as people didn't think you could put thousands of transistors on a chip and have a reliable operating chip. We put together a technical report detailing how we could build the memory using FETs and make it a practical thing that the systems guys could use—it would have the right power, could be cooled and packaged, and so forth. You needed a lot of other circuitry, as well. Nick was in the department that was working on these peripheral circuits that were necessary to make the array operate correctly and to be able to package it on modules and boards and put it in the computer itself. So, Nick and I met at that time. He was one of the bright engineers in that group. At some point, I became the Manager of the Array Design Group, and Nick wound up working for me.

I was no deep thinker at the time, nor a philosopher. I was about executing and delivering. As Nike would famously say two decades later, "Just do it." That was me. I was in a just-do-it mode.

Dick Linton: I think we were all aggressive. We all thought we were part of something big, something that was going to change the computer industry, and by the way, make a lot of profit for IBM. We had some figures at one time about what a small fraction of a penny it cost to make these memory bits, and how many dollars that IBM could charge for them, so we knew that if we could make it work, we were going to be part of something that was historic, would change the industry, and also would make a lot of money for IBM.

I was doing all kinds of challenging and ambitious technical work at IBM, and given the growth of the company, opportunity was everywhere. Before long, I would start my rise up the ladder of management.

3

MANAGING

B y 1970, IBM decided to transfer the entire FET memory mission from East Fishkill to Burlington, Vermont. Given my work on all three chips involved, I was asked to be part of the move. Not only that, IBM was offering me my first opportunity to manage, a role I had never envisioned for myself before.

Dick Gladu: I was looking for a First Line Manager for a circuit design group to support this FET activity. I had been watching Nick over the last few years, and he was an interesting guy, fully dressed in his leisure suit and his pointed boots. And while he was a little rough around the edges, he just reeked potential. So we sat down and talked. I said, "Hey Nick, I'd like you to come to Burlington to be the manager of this group." Nick said, "Manager? I'll never be a manager." I said, "Well, give it a try. We'll work on it. Come on up."

I told Dick that I was an engineer, not a manager. What did I know about managing people? Furthermore, there were other factors in play. I had to finish the master's degree in Electrical Engineering I had begun through the IBM Syracuse University Extension Program. My wife and I just had our first child, Michael. And we had just bought our first house. Add to that the fact that Anita was not very keen on moving to Burlington, Vermont, wondering just how many days of sunshine there would be up north and the fact that she knew her parents would not be thrilled with me taking their daughter into the far reaches of the North Country.

Nonetheless, Anita and I talked it out and agreed to take the chance. With a healthy nervousness in the pit of my stomach and stars in my eyes, I gave Dick the answer he wanted, along with a few conditions that made it work for Anita, me, and our family.

> **Dick Gladu:** I think Nick had a bit of fear of the unknown. He wasn't that many years out of school at the time, and he was a technical guy. He hadn't been working for IBM for that long before he joined my group, so he was just getting comfortable with the work environment. He had a strong technical background, so he was comfortable there, but I think the thought of stepping into everything that would go with being a First Line Manager at that point in time was a little unnerving. But he did, and we all headed to Burlington.

Being so young, I could not help but think that both my life and likely my career would be changed forever if I made this move. Yet with the decision made and the opportunity obvious, I now had to explain it to my family, particularly my mother.

As we sat at the kitchen table in Beacon one evening, she challenged me, "Where is Burlington, Vermont? Is it light or dark up there? What's it like?"

She wanted me to fully think through the implications of the move. I was breaking with tradition and the Italian values my parents both knew. The family stayed together. *Always.* You did not leave. If an employer asked you to relocate, you found a new job instead. But that was the old model. My parents—*including* my mother—raised their children to find jobs. They had raised us to pursue careers.

I am sure my parents had discussed the fact that this day would come. They had not raised me to stay. They had raised me to go. Now it was time for my mother to accept, "If nothing changes, nothing changes." She did just that, though not without feeling profound pain.

Of course, it was not just me who would be leaving home. I had to transfer my entire team from the Mid-Hudson Valley to Burlington. They were a bunch of designers, working on different kinds of chips, and they were great people.

> **Dick Gladu:** We were all very close, probably a dozen-and-a-half people spread across three small first-line groups. One was looking at static cells. One was looking at dynamic cells. The other was looking at actually applying those to some kind of a product design. So we would meet all the time. We'd see each other every day.

These were friends, colleagues, and really good people. They had roots in the community. We played golf together and socialized together, and now we were heading off into the far reaches of the frozen north together. It was going to be a journey. It helped ease my mind that we would be doing this together, as a team, but it was going to be different, that was for sure. Because the dynamic was about to change. We had been peers, we were most certainly friends, and suddenly, I was their manager.

I could not help but wonder if that would change how we thought of each other, or if it would disrupt the flow of work. In my mind, I was just one of the guys. Would I be accepted as an authority figure?

> **Dick Gladu:** People liked Nick and respected him. He had the ability to make people feel at ease, and he worked well with a bunch of different people. In the group that he joined, there were older folks and more experienced folks—there probably wasn't anyone younger than him—but he had the ability to work with these people, make them feel comfortable, make suggestions, do a very respectable job, and present himself in a fashion that made people feel comfortable with him. I knew he was the man for the job.

Dick Linton: When we moved to Burlington, I became the Second Level Manager, with two first-time First Level Managers reporting to me, one of whom was Nick. They each had a team of about six or eight people. Nick was managing the people who were doing designs. You always try to challenge people. You want to make sure that their designs are well-studied and well-simulated before you turn them over to manufacturing. It's very painful to build something. It takes a lot of energy and a lot of time. Nick understood this type of pressure. And of course, all of these things were scheduled to go into various IBM systems on a precise schedule. If your design was not ready, if you couldn't get it manufactured and tested, that meant that some IBM system was not going to ship on a schedule, and IBM could not make the profits it anticipated. So you were always under pressure to have your designers do things right so that things went along according to plan so that IBM systems could roll out of the factory on schedule to keep the profits coming. This was a new pressure for Nick to handle.

We were building chips that were different and edgy, further out, and it was not an easy task at all. I was not sure what I was doing as a manager either, so that made it even harder. I was feeling my way. I went to IBM's management school to learn, but of course, you still have to cut your teeth on the job, and that was a process for me.

One of the men who worked for me at the time was Luis Arzubi. I had first come to know Luis in the '60s when we both were designers. At that time, I still was in East Fishkill, while Luis already was in Burlington. Luis was a very gifted design engineer, so when we consolidated operations in Burlington, I wanted him on my team. He saw both the good and the bad during my earliest days as a manager.

Luis Arzubi (*Thirty-year IBM Veteran in Engineering, Management, and Executive Roles*): Nick was very nice and engaged people's

families. He would invite me to his house, introduce his family, and
we would have dinner. I had been in the car industry working in
Argentina prior to joining IBM, and I was not used to that degree
of friendliness, and that impressed me as a very nice thing to do. So,
he came across as being, first, nice. Second, hyperactive. And third,
very eloquent. He communicated intensively and extensively. A First
Line Manager usually is a glorified Team Leader. As a Team Leader,
you had to pay attention to detail and provide technical and financial
guidance directly to each individual that worked for you. Nick paid
great attention to detail, and I think that's the way it should be, but
in terms of providing guidance, you can get into details and provide
help and advice without being controlling. I think very early on, as
a First Line Manager, Nick was controlling. He tried to tell people
what to do in every sense, and with his hyperactivity, in spite of the
fact of being eloquent, if you wanted to talk with him, your time was
limited. He was in a hurry.

Dick Linton: Nick was a very good engineer and when you're
as good as Nick, there can be a tendency to not be patient with
others. Instead of trying to guide them in terms of how to do
their work better, you can get rigid and say, "You gotta do it this
way!" That was Nick at the time. Nick was very straightforward
and demanding—"This is the way you do it"—and I'm sure some
people could take offense to that. They'd say, "You're not giving me a
chance," or "You're not listening to my view." He could lose patience
with people who didn't quite see it his way. He had to learn, as many
of us did, that his role as a manager was not to do the job of his eight
employees—which he likely could have done—but to get his eight
employees to each do their jobs as well as they could.

It was not long before I was feeling lousy about this new role of mine.
The transition was so tough that everything almost came unraveled

completely, which was brought to full light when it came time for my first
IBM Opinion Survey.

Opinion Surveys were departmental surveys through which the people you managed—in my case, the same friends and colleagues that I had
brought north with me—could comment on their manager's performance
without attribution. So, they felt free to say what they really thought. And
what my team really thought about me could not have been made clearer:
I was a disaster. On a rating scale with "5" being the best and "1" being horrible, I think I averaged a 1.08. Someone must have tossed me a "2" out of
sympathy, just to bump the average up a little bit, but the message remained
the same.

I was miserable. I figured that my IBM career was over. How could I possibly recover from this failure?

When I dug deeper into the feedback, it was clear that in the eyes of my
team, I thought I knew how to do their jobs better than they did. To be fair,
I had grown up with the department, so I did know a lot about the different
jobs. However, constantly telling everyone *what* they should be doing and
how they should be doing it was not managing—it was me dictating to them
and me limiting their contributions and growth.

> **Dick Gladu:** He was a very strong guy—strong technically
> and hands-on. Part of the learning process to managing highly
> technical people is to give them a sense of ownership of what
> they're doing and let them do their job. You help them solve their
> problems, but otherwise you give them some room. That was a
> work in progress for Nick.

In those days, Opinion Surveys were defining moments, because every
department was expected to *do* something with the survey results. Every
department was expected to put a patch-up plan together to try to improve
themselves. Well, the problem in my department seemed to be *me*, and I
knew I was in for punishment. In those days, it was very hard to get fired or

demoted at IBM, but I was worried that my days as an up-and-coming performer who was looked at for choice opportunities might be finished almost before it started.

> **Dick Linton:** Those surveys could be hard on you sometimes! You had to do some soul searching and ask yourself, "Okay, what am I doing that could make somebody feel that way about me and my performance?"

I went in to see my team after receiving the feedback from them and said, "Look, there is no real reason for us to even talk about this Opinion Survey. It does not matter. It was terrible. I clearly offended you. I clearly screwed up. I have clearly not been the manager you wanted me to be. I do not know if I will remain as your manager, or even if I will remain with IBM. But I need your help. I need you to tell me what I need to do to change, because clearly this is not working."

And remarkably, they did help me, to a person. They told me that they did not even know what their individual responsibilities were, because I was making all the commitments and simply assuming the role of supreme leader. I was doing all the jobs. These were my friends, but here they stood up and told me what a jerk I had been, how domineering I had been, and how uncoordinated and controlling I had been. I wanted—*needed*—to do everything. After listening to them, however, I was ready to adapt. I was ready to change.

When I look back on that first managerial stint of mine, it was absolutely a case of me managing the way my father had managed me. With my father, it had always been, "I'm in charge. Do what I say. We've got to move fast, and this is the best way."

While that worked with a little kid who did not know any better, it did not work with this group of well-educated professionals I was managing in Burlington. They did not need a dictator. They wanted a collaborator. Luckily, I had a template for that, too—my mother. My mother had been a tough but fair enabler when I was a kid, always there to give praise, always there to urge me on and to push me to be my best. Perhaps that was where I needed to turn for inspiration.

> **Dick Gladu:** As far as change goes, the first thing he did was to get rid of his leisure suits and started wearing Armani. He shaved. He lost weight. He exercised. But more important, he developed a level of openness. He turned into a people-type person. I'd like to think I helped in that, but regardless, rather than overpowering people, he started working with them to understand better how they might contribute and to help them through any rough spots they might experience. He became a stickler on Performance Planning and Appraisals, and I think a lot of that evolved from the initial feedback that he received from his group.

As soon as I understood my job as being less about doing and more about enabling, my career took off like a rocket. The technology world was changing rapidly, and in an era of frequent change, I learned that the best management style is one that is adaptable, one that is flexible. When you move from job to job within a company as I did, you have to constantly adapt. But even within the context of a single job, a rigid management style did not make any sense, because just when you think one way about something, along comes a jolt to the system that requires you to go another way. That was how the real world was beginning to work, and that has only intensified in the time since then.

When I became flexible and adaptable with my team, I gave them a chance to shine. I enabled their greatness, which in turn made me look good.

> **Luis Arzubi:** Nick was very driven with regard to his own career, and that drive led him to become politically astute about the structure of IBM. In other words, because he was so driven, the significance and the priorities of his outlook on life moved him to

modify his behavior. Whether he became less controlling for Nick or for the team, he still did the right thing. And I suspect that many things in Nick's life didn't happen naturally. I think he decided many things that happened to him. But because he's also a great person, he did not do these things at the expense of others. In fact, he helped others, in part because he was politically astute.

These changes did not mean that my father's influences were now obsolete. Far from it. In fact, I began to recognize another synergy. I realized that the work ethic he had instilled in me really could come to bear within IBM—that this company did recognize people who were focused not just on working hard but on *achieving*. Results mattered at IBM, just as they had with my father.

That was the mindset my father had drilled into me. It was not just effort. Obviously, he had wanted me to apply effort on the lawn, the hedges, the garden, my schoolwork. But what he wanted even more were *results*. He either rewarded or punished me based on results, not process, so going to work for a company with a culture steeped in a similar results-oriented tradition was in a sense perfect for me, once I understood it. I was not trimming the hedges or delivering newspapers or weeding the garden anymore. The stakes were much higher. This was IBM, and I was driven to succeed, so I wanted to understand what mattered within this company.

Once I understood that my upbringing aligned with what IBM believed in, I was off and running. In today's corporate-speak, we might say that my values were aligned with IBM's values. While I was not thinking in those terms in those days, that's essentially what I came to understand.

At this time, the world was in the early years of what became known as Moore's Law. Introduced by Intel co-founder Gordon Moore in 1965, the "law" observed that the performance of electronic chips would double every eighteen months or so. This law largely accounts for the blistering pace of change that defined my entire career and continues to drive the pace of technological change today.

As Moore's Law took hold, there were broader changes happening in society. With the counterculture movement of the late '60s and early '70s underway, even IBM loosened up—a bit, anyway.

Some of IBM's transformation reflected that the company was no longer a "family business." In 1971, Thomas Watson, Jr., the namesake son of IBM's founder and first CEO, and also the man who had championed the market-changing System/360 mainframe I had cut my teeth on, passed the baton to T. Vincent Learson. While IBM had had two visionary CEOs in its first six decades—the father and the son—Learson was more of an operations guy.

A math major at Harvard, Learson had been at IBM since 1935. He rose through the sales and marketing ranks: he became vice president in 1954, senior vice president in 1964, and president in 1966. He was also elected to the board of directors in 1966. He remains an IBM legend to this day because he was, without a doubt, the driving force on the ground for the System/360.

However, by the time he took the CEO role, he was nearly sixty, so his time at the helm proved more transitional than anything. As a First Line Manager, I did not interact with Learson directly, but he understood the importance of our work in Burlington and made sure that we had the investment and resources to carry through on our mission.

By early 1973, and after only eighteen months running the company, Learson passed the baton to Frank Cary. Cary served as CEO for more than eight years, providing stability and steering IBM through an unprecedented period of rapid growth in products, revenue, and profit. While others resisted, Cary recognized the emerging threat of the personal computer and spearheaded our push in that direction.

Under Cary's leadership, IBM became a little kinder and gentler, a little more thoughtful, a little less bureaucratic, a little less structured, and a little less locked into existing ways of thinking. This shift enabled our massive company to move more nimbly while maintaining our market leadership.

I became more nimble, too.

Once I became more adaptable and gave my teams more room to move—while remaining just as focused on delivering results—opportunities kept coming my way. During my first 10 years with IBM, I held five or six jobs. I was exposed to a lot, and I saw a lot. It was a very fast-paced lifestyle: *go, go, go, do, do, do, challenge, challenge, challenge, problem, problem, problem.*

I found this all exhilarating. Each time I solved a problem or met a challenge, I was given another more important assignment, which also meant moving my family around the country. At one point, we moved four times in three years.

Dick Linton: Eventually, Nick went off to work for Ed Davis, who was leading Burlington at the time. Nick became his right-hand man. You could see in that time period that he was good at putting together plans—"Here's the division plan. Here's how much we're going to spend on this technology and that technology. Here are the expense dollars that it's going to take. Here's where we're going to invest. Here's what manufacturing is going to do and how much they're going to charge for their product." It became clear that Nick was very good at seeing the big picture and putting together those plans and reviewing them with the corporate people and the division people who were there to inspect the plans. After a few years with Ed, Nick was assigned to General Technology Division Headquarters, where he became Director of Planning. He continued to show the kind of business acumen and technical assessment skill IBM needed—"What are the technologies we should invest in? What's valuable? What are the things that we should be doing? What are the things that we shouldn't do?"

During these years, as I moved into my thirties, I began to think differently about who I was, what I was doing, and where I was going. The drive always had been there—that was just who I had been raised to be—but up to this point, there had been no master plan. But now, as I began to have some success at IBM, I started to wonder if I could keep this momentum going or if it would prove to be a fluke.

As I continued to grasp at a visceral level that what IBM wanted from me was the same thing that my hard-nosed Italian father of mine had wanted—the willingness to work hard, the willingness to change, the willingness to deliver results without excuses—my confidence continued to grow. I came to see that there literally was no difference for me between working for the Watsons and the Carys of the world and working for my father. Results mattered, whether within the moment or over the long term. Once that insight fully sank in, I knew that I could keep the momentum going, whereas others might burn out or prove to be flashes in the pan.

I realized that my career at IBM could really turn into something big. Things were moving fast, and the problems thrown at me were getting bigger and tougher. There were benefits, like more money, but there also was more pressure. I saw the stakes as being too high for me to fail, and to keep going, I had to keep moving.

Every chance I got, I very deliberately took a different road, the harder road, the change road. Instead of staying where I was, I constantly challenged myself to take the next big swing. Every decision led back to my father's mantra: If nothing changes, nothing changes.

I could not say no.

In fact, I adopted a mantra of my own: Always accept the challenge.

As with many young executives before and after me, accepting the challenge came at a cost. While I had joined IBM to *avoid* moving away from the family, it seemed as though all I did in these early years was keep moving and moving and moving and moving. I could not have done it without the constant support of my wife Anita and our young children. Their flexibility allowed me to realize my full professional potential, even as they, no doubt, sometimes suffered from the constant uprootings.

In the early 1980s, while we were living in Manassas, Virginia, I was asked to return to Vermont, this time as the Director of the IBM Burlington Development Laboratory. This was a huge development for my career, and greatly broadened my responsibilities, not just in terms of technologies that were critical to IBM's success, but also in terms of the hundreds of talented people that comprised the lab, for whom I was now responsible.

As Lab Director, I brought in not only new designs, but new ideas. I was not brought there to preserve the status quo, but rather to instill change and to shake up the culture. One of the most important innovations we brought was thinking in terms of leveraging logic, not just memory. Rather than just continuing to pursue modest, incremental improvements in our current FET technology, we began to get very excited about what was known as CMOS FET technology.

Dick Gladu: CMOS stood for Complimentary Metal-Oxide-Semiconductor, and it really defined the process that was used to make these FET devices. It was a rather straightforward process, less costly and less expensive to manufacture than its alternative, which was a bipolar process that resulted in faster, but more expensive devices. So it was a tradeoff. We had been focusing on Metal-Oxide Semiconductor (MOS) FET devices, and that was the basis for a whole string of things we put together in Burlington along with IBM colleagues in Germany, but now we pondered a major change.

Luis Arzubi: Even in the early 1970s, IBM understood the merits of CMOS. Simply put, in all the systems, you have the "stuff" that remembers and the "stuff" that makes the decisions on the data that is remembered—the memory and the logic. When I tell you that the world discovered the value of CMOS in the early '70s, it was mostly in the logic. And IBM, being the technology behemoth that it was, with the resources it had, launched a gigantic program to get years ahead of everybody else on CMOS logic technology. At first, however, the technology was half-baked. It was not there yet.

This was an ill-fated CMOS effort on the part of East Fishkill that simply was not reliable or manufacturable. But they kept at it, and over the years, they developed a great deal of trade craft, knowledge, and expertise on CMOS, along with a patent and technology know-how portfolio.

In this context, IBM was trying to be more flexible and adaptable in the early days of Moore's Law. The CMOS technology improved, and as with all technologies, especially semiconductor technologies, there are lots of little things that need to go right before breakthroughs occur. Each has physics to deal with, and often trade craft is not skillful enough to make it happen. As the work was being done with CMOS for logic in East Fishkill, and we saw from Burlington the progress they were making, we wanted to use the technology—but for memory.

Still, I can remember being in meetings with all the big muckety-mucks and feeling like this sort of rebel-without-a-cause wacko. I saw myself as a young guy coming to them with a lot of wild-and-crazy ideas, and nobody quite knew what to do with me or with the ideas. But I was not going to stop pushing no matter how crazy they thought I might be, because I believed without hesitation in my people, and I believed in our ideas. I did everything I could to represent those people and their ideas to the big shots so that we could move IBM Burlington in this new, CMOS-driven direction.

Luis Arzubi: During this time, he always impressed me as a steady, consistent person, both in terms of driving the plans and his personality. One of his leadership traits that I admired, that I probably didn't see in any other person at IBM at the time, was his demeanor. He would get upset, but he would never get mad or lose control or show bad temper. It was very unusual for a guy to never really have a tantrum—there were so many problems that frustration was available in every corner—but Nick was always very steady. If he would get in a confrontation with me or anybody else, he always would defuse the whole thing by smiling, either by design or by nature. He would just smile, things would calm down, and we'd just keep pushing.

It was not always easy for me, but I believed that Luis and the rest of my team could make this happen. Finally, while I was stuck in the middle of one of these endless meetings defending my colleagues and our work, I had an epiphany. I already had realized that my results-orientation was well-suited for IBM. Now, I took a next step.

I began to see myself less as a rebel defending wild ideas, and more as someone with a unique role to play within IBM. I thought to myself, *There's more to life than all of this, Nick. You have to have a philosophy. You have to have a culture. IBM has a philosophy and a culture, and if you want to make your crazy ideas happen at IBM, then you have to be able to fit them into that philosophy and culture. You have to be able to speak to that culture.*

It was much like the realization I had as a kid when I decided to duck and weave *within* my father's system rather than rail against it. It was another freedom-through-integration type of thought, and it hit me all at once sitting in that meeting.

Then and there, I started to think about my career in a different context.

Then and there, I started to think of myself truly as part of IBM.

Then and there, I realized that working for IBM was more than just working for any company.

For the first time, I internalized the notion that I need to have a coherent, unwavering philosophy about working for IBM. If I'm going to make a difference here, I have to understand the culture, and I have to become part of that culture.

I started to become a student of Thomas Watson, Sr. and Thomas Watson, Jr., reading everything I could about their management styles and the values that they established for the company. I studied the once groundbreaking book *A Business and Its Beliefs*, which Watson, Jr. published in 1963, which remains relevant to this day, almost six decades later. I read their speeches and their memos to employees and every article I could find. I became enamored with the Watson family, what they had achieved, and the culture they had created. And in large part, because I learned to synergize myself and our ideas into that distinctive IBM culture, I was able to sell my team's ideas more effectively and persuasively. Within three years, the move to CMOS in Burlington was solidified and became the foundation of our work.

> **Luis Arzubi:** He was always a very good communicator, and I think Nick was always quite clear of where we were going and what was going on. We kept pushing, and eventually we achieved the 4-megabit CMOS. We got it qualified, I won a few awards, and CMOS was used in all the IBM systems going forward.

Meeting that technological milestone was a turning point for the Burlington lab. While we measure the outer limits of performance in petabytes and terabytes today, four megabits was huge at the time and represented years of hard work! And we were free to make that move only because IBM leadership had given us the opportunity to take action—to drive change. That milestone was a turning point for me, as well. I was graduating from being a manager to being a leader who could synchronize the courage of my convictions with the broader IBM culture.

> **Mark Papermaster** (*CTO and EVP, Advanced Micro Devices (AMD); Former IBM Executive*): Nick always was very supportive of innovation. When he saw bright people who had different ways of doing things, he got behind them. Over the course of his career, you can find any number of examples where he personally supported an innovator, who in the normal processes, where managers are worried about tomorrow, and not necessarily next month, next year, or even the next decade, might have been overlooked, Nick has always been that supporter and that champion of innovation.

Now I could go home at night and say to myself, "Gosh, look at who you are becoming. They are actually listening to you! You are influencing the leaders of IBM and giving voice to some of its top innovators. You are changing the course of the company."

That Burlington team had produced a string of FET memory products that established their leadership in the industry. They were literally changing IBM and changing our entire industry in its wake.

Now, almost overnight, the Burlington facility became a world leader in CMOS FET Logic. It went from a leading dynamic random access (DRAM) memory chip developer and manufacturer, enabling computers and devices to store and remember what is wanted and needed, to a leading-edge logic chip developer and manufacturer, enabling computers and devices to actually *know* what to do with all the data that had been found, seen, and saved. This transformation was a long time in the making, and not without issue and challenge, but so right for the times and the needs of IBM and its customers.

IBM was not about to let the grass grow under my feet in Burlington, though. My eyes were about to be opened in even more remarkable ways.

4

TAKING CHARGE

B y the early 1980s, I was establishing myself within IBM as someone who fixed problems and always accepted the toughest challenges. Coming off a series of successful assignments in White Plains, Manassas, and my latest successes in Burlington, I was asked to serve a year as Secretary of the Corporate Management Board at IBM's headquarters in Armonk, New York. Here, I was given a front-row seat to the inner workings of the corporation by attending the semimonthly Management Committee Meetings.

I orchestrated them.

I organized them.

I put the agendas together.

I took the very few notes allowed.

I did the follow up.

I did the briefings and debriefings, as appropriate.

I saw the problems. And of course, I saw the successes.

In short, I was in the room where it happened!

That is what being the Secretary of the Corporate Management Board was all about. I came to understand the company, how it worked, what went on, and the personalities in charge. While I was not responsible for any decisions that were made, I saw the decision-making process of IBM's leaders up close and personal.

And they saw me. It was increasingly evident that the leadership team was personally engaged in my development, with clear plans in mind if and as I progressed. They had seen what I had done over the course of two decades, understood my basic raw capabilities, and were building on that foundation by giving me exposure to the upper echelons of the company. I give IBM credit for deliberately shaping me—and by IBM, I especially mean such influential executives as John Akers (who had become CEO in 1985), Jack Kuehler (a technology whiz who was later named President and Vice Chairman of IBM), and Terry Lautenbach (a future member of IBM's Management Committee).

They saw the potential in me, as did Jerry Haddad and Bob Evans, the man who invented the System/360. They were all IBM icons, and somehow, they had seen something in this kid from Beacon, and to their credit, nurtured it.

I spent that time in Armonk on my own. Anita stayed in Burlington with our children, Michael and Nicole, and I commuted back and forth on weekends. It was challenging, but together we were a team, and knowing that IBM's top brass saw potential in me made it easier on us all.

But one never stood still for long in the old IBM.

In less than a year, IBM assigned me *back* to the Burlington facility, this time as the Site General Manager. Anita, the kids, and I were all relieved. Michael had made it clear he was finishing high school where he started at South Burlington High. He was on track to graduate in June of 1987.

All things CMOS were happening in Burlington at this time. Luis Arzubi and his team had designed, developed, and were qualifying a very powerful CMOS DRAM chip to go along with the CMOS Logic chips that were already in process.

The team succeeded, Michael graduated, and almost on cue, IBM asked me to move back to headquarters to contribute to a very important project. After much back and forth with the family, I accepted the assignment, and in September of 1987, we moved for basically the last time, this time to Ridgefield, CT. Michael was not impacted much, because he was going off to college that very month, but Nicole did not agree until she had extracted the same commitment out of us that Michael had earlier—that no matter where I went or what I did, she would start at and graduate from Ridgefield High School. We all acclimated during the final months of 1987, and then we turned the page to a new year.

And what a year it was. The year 1988 was simply amazing for me. My head still spins when I think of it. IBM was struggling to keep pace and stay relevant in a rapidly changing technology world. John Akers was at the helm, and he believed that the company needed to be reorganized to give us our best chance to compete. He gave the task to Terry Lautenbach, and my job—the important one I had moved to Connecticut to take on—was to help him.

I worked for Terry directly for the last six months of 1987 and the first three months of 1988. We successfully completed our reorganization work, and during this time, I happily renewed old relationships and made new ones.

Following the reorg task, I was named the IBM Head of Corporate Development, a true dream job for me. Here, I was worrying about technical strategy and the vitality of the technical workforce, exercises I greatly enjoyed that relied on both my tech and business savvy. I was one of several folks in roles like this at headquarters. I loved it. Terry was responsible for an incredibly large piece of IBM, and I was one of his key players. Life was good. But then, more change.

In April of 1988, Terry assigned me to the former IBM PC Company, now called the Entry Systems Division (ESD). They recently had lost their development leader after announcing PS/2 and OS/2, and they needed help. I blinked twice and gulped three times when he told me I was going to work for Bill Lowe as his development lead. I remember telling Terry, "My expertise is semiconductor technology and chip design, not computer design."

Terry looked at me, smiled, and said, "Nick, you learn fast and have sound judgment. We need you there now."

While I had other ideas and options for him to consider, I knew he had his mind made up, so I simply smiled and accepted the challenge. I was dropped into the middle of IBM PC Company and its newest commitments aimed at turning its fortunes around. We had a lot riding on the new top-to-bottom line of PS/2s, with the latest and greatest 3½-inch diskettes versus the industry-standard 5¼-inch diskettes, our Micro Channel bus versus the industry-standard bus, and our OS/2 versus Windows.

It was all out warfare, and I was replacing a key general who had just walked off the battlefield in a space where I had no experience. Ugh! I put my head down and drove forward as hard as I could and as fast as I could. I was responsible for IBM's efforts in Austin, Raleigh, Boca Raton, Hursley (England), and, of course, Redmond, Washington (near Microsoft's headquarters).

The development plan was aggressive and rich with content and contention. Trying to balance the two was not going to be an easy task, but again, I jumped in feet first. As an engineer, I immediately looked for the hardest and worst problems to solve and then proceeded to do everything I could to solve them. I learned as fast as I could. I visited everywhere I could. I dealt with the issues front and center and worked to create a new product plan and to build new relationships that would work.

I had taken everything apart and was just starting to feel good about putting it all back together again when, in December of that same amazing year of 1988, Terry called me into his office at Armonk, where I found him waiting with John Akers and Jack Kuehler.

I knew immediately that, once again, something was about to change. After the usual pleasantries, Terry explained that he was about to announce a series of changes and that he wanted me to take on a new role. Along with Akers, he had concluded that it was time for me to become a Division President and that the newly-formed Advanced Workstation Division (AWD) was going to be mine to lead.

As I had only months earlier under similar circumstances, I began to explain the many reasons why I should stay put, not the least of which was all of the unfinished work I would be leaving behind with the PC Company. They smiled and said, "We know all about what you have been doing and where things are in the IBM PC Company, but we need you in Austin immediately."

Right about then, Jack Kuehler added, "You do not have to move your family to Austin, Nick. You just have to find a way to manage AWD from wherever you choose to be."

They made it all sound so nice, but of course, I knew better. I knew that my mission was to fix the RS/6000 workstation project. RS/6000 was going to be our entry into the already highly competitive, high-performance advanced workstation and open-software marketplace, but we had been struggling with it, as evidenced by a long backstory that dates to 1975.

That was when IBM began pioneering work at the Thomas J. Watson Research Center that led to the invention of a computer architecture called RISC—Reduced Instruction Set Computing. It was envisioned as the successor to the then-current architecture preference known as CISC, or Complex Instruction Set Computing, and ultimately enabled the global advanced workstation computing market I was about to personally enter. But as with a number of its critical innovations in the IT industry, IBM had failed to capitalize on it.

RISC and CISC refer to the architecture of the computer itself. *How does the computer actually move information around? What instructions does the computer respond to?* That is called an architecture—the basic blueprint for how the computer works—and the instruction set is very important as it relates to what commands are sent and how the computer responds. And the number of instructions per cycle matters, too.

With CISC, as the name suggests, instructions per cycle were complex, and therefore time-consuming for the computer to process. The thinking behind RISC was to simplify the instructions given to run a computer, making it much faster.

IBM made RISC work and had the patents to prove it, but to be honest, we just could never get a grip on the RISC market in those early days. For our first market entry, we decided to put a RISC card inside a Personal Computer and gave it to Bill Lowe and the Entry System Division to push. We called it the RT PC. The effort turned out to be half-baked, not surprisingly, because Bill and his team already had enough on their plates with fighting off all of the rival PC makers and addressing the vast and rapidly growing CISC-based PC market.

The incentives just were not there. A RISC-based PC not only was a distraction to ESD, it was a product they thought they could beat out and bury with their own systems. I had just spent the last six months leading these guys, so I had a very good understanding of their plans and their mindset, and it was no surprise to me that the RT PC failed when we went to market. We just made far too many mistakes with it, including shipping a number of RISC cards that we found out later did not always do what they were supposed to do. I eventually would have to deal with these problems as the President of AWD.

We were not the only company struggling to get its arms around the RISC market. While Intel's instruction set at that time was CISC (complex) and our own System/390 was CISC (complex), the landscape was shifting. A lot of RISC architectures were beginning to emerge, and the market was pulling away, making itself into what became known as the High-Performance Workstations market. Digital was very good in this space. HP was getting better. Sun was dominating. These were the big winners, and they were just cleaning up in the market. There were others around, too.

But IBM was not around. Here we had created the technology, but we were not capitalizing on it. We were barely in the race.

Back in Armonk, John Akers and his team were thinking, "Why aren't we getting this right? Come on. Why are we taking so long to bring this to market?"

Finally, they decided, "We are done with the people in Austin who are running this program. We are moving Nick there to see what he can do, because we are not getting it done."

So that is how I had ended up in Terry's office that day, with John Akers summing it all up in saying, "RISC-based architecture. We invented it. We developed it. We created it. We never deployed it. Now it's the workstation marketplace. It's UNIX über alles, and here we are stumbling and fumbling over and over again. Nick, you need to fix this, and ASAP. We are counting on an AWD product set for revenue *next year.*"

My head was spinning, as Terry reached across the table, extended his hand, and said, "Congratulations, Nick. We need you to pull this off, and we will help you in any way we can."

If I had already stepped up for IBM a few times before, I really was going to have to step up this time. We all shook hands, and within days, I was announced as the President of the Advanced Workstation Division.

On the one hand, this was a great opportunity for me. The RS/6000 was IBM's hope for the future and intended to replace the mainframe as our primary profit engine. Yet the pressure was enormous because the project had been slipping and slipping, with IBM's revenues slipping right along with it. So as my dream year of 1988 neared completion, my mission and mandate for 1989 could not have been any clearer. I had to stop the slippage in Austin and get an IBM workstation into the market that year.

Well, when I arrived in Texas, it did not take long to determine that John had told the truth that day in Terry's office. We *were* indeed stumbling and fumbling, and now here I was, in charge of the biggest challenge I had ever seen.

David Carlucci (*Twenty-six-year IBM Veteran and Former Leader of the Mainframe Division*): Nick inherited a mess. He replaced an extremely bright engineer and PhD who prided himself on being an expert in RISC technology, but who wasn't well organized, was a bit of a loose cannon, and didn't work well with others. He had been kept on board in that capacity because he was the guy who had ushered the technology through, which was no small task, but he simply didn't have the skills to bring a finished product to market in a timely fashion. We had invented the technology, but then had fallen woefully behind our competitors in implementing it.

If I was going to have any chance of straightening out this situation, I was going to need an incredibly strong Chief Technology Officer, because there were so many things left that needed to be worked on for our initial release, both from a software perspective as well as an application perspective. But I also needed somebody with credibility who could see ahead and envision the future of the RS/6000 beyond our immediate deadlines: *Where are we going to go? Can we get to these more powerful workstations?*

I was pretty sure the man for the job was a young theorist and researcher by the name of Tilak Agerwala. He had been a professor at the University of Texas at Austin, before becoming a researcher with IBM Research, where he was pushing very hard on this whole RISC-based architecture.

His interest and belief in RISC obviously were important to me, but so was the fact that he came out of the research labs. IBM Research had invented RISC, and the people running the program before I went down to Austin had come out of Research. They were better researchers than they were operators, but I still was going to need their help. In Tilak, I saw some-one who could both have credibility and maintain a strong relationship with Research.

Tilak Agerwala (*Thirty-five-year IBM Veteran with Executive Positions in Research, Strategy, Advanced Development, and Business Development*): At that point, IBM was placing a huge, big bet on the technology and on Nick. While in Research, I had been part of the team that did the early architecture work for what would become the RS/6000. All of this is a team sport, and that team even included John Cocke, a legendary IBM Fellow who later won the Turing Award, the National Medal of Technology, and the National Medal of Science. I also had been a member of the Corporate Technical Committee at one time, and I had written a paper on how everything in the future—from workstations all the way up to supercomputers— was going to move toward parallel computing and clustering, and that even workstations were going to use symmetric multiprocessing.

I asked Tilak if he would dare to help me get the RS/6000 right, to always be honest with me, and to keep me connected to the primordial ooze.

I knew this was no small decision for him to make—leaving the prestige of Research for the Wild West atmosphere of Austin—but I believed that just maybe, *together*, we could help the team get this done.

> **Tilak Agerwala:** Given my background, Nick decided that he
> wanted me to be his Director of Advanced Technology Development.
> My very first impressions of Nick were, "Here's a person who's an
> outstanding individual. I can trust him. He's going to make all the
> right decisions." He seemed very honest and very, very personable.
> It was a big decision for me, but I felt I could totally trust Nick to do
> the right things.

So Tilak became my closest advisor as we set out to tackle this sizable challenge. It was essential for me to complement my skills with someone who brought new capabilities to the table. I knew my own shortcomings. What I did not have, I looked for in others who did. To me, that was part of being self-aware and self-assured, two elements I believe are essential in every leader.

Tilak proved as good as I had hoped. He was very technical. He was very thoughtful. He had taught architecture. He had taught computers. He understood how they worked. He was not an operator; he was a theorist. He could paint the future. That is pretty much how he spent his entire career at IBM. He was deep into high-performance computing as it evolved, and he was a big contributor to that evolution.

> **Tilak Agerwala:** I sensed in the first few months that I met Nick that
> he just had a way of being very straightforward and very honest, that
> he recognized the technical capabilities of people, and that I could
> take this risk with him at the helm. I was moving from Research to
> a team in Austin that was under real development time pressures,
> but I went down there feeling that this was going to be a very good
> opportunity. It was a little weird to get out of the lab and go to a

place like that. I was quite hopeful that I would be part of getting some of the really key technologies that I had been talking about in my research career—like the multiprocessing technology—into the product plan, if not in the first go-round, then in the second.

While Tilak was already thinking about future iterations of the technology, I quickly had to deal with a problem stemming from the original RT PC and those theoretically-flawed RISC processors that had been shipped to customers. For example, we had to take back all the computers we sold to Boeing, because the RT PC had a rounding error in the floating-point unit in the RISC-based processor. We could not guarantee the accuracy. You should have heard them when I made that call—my ears still are ringing!

We ultimately took back 65,000 RT PCs because there was a chance that they could produce an error, even though the chances were limited. We could not put our customers at risk, even if it meant that the RS/6000 program had to go still further into debt before we could push forward.

Still, I felt good with Tilak and several others from our team at my side and with a partner that was hungry to succeed. While we developed the equipment for the RS/6000, France's Dassault Systèmes was supplying us with their design software, known as CATIA. My contact with Dassault was a young executive by the name of Bernard Charles, who understood the challenges I was facing. And I understood his.

Dassault Systèmes was an IBM Trusted Partner. In the past, they had made contributions to the mainframe, so we knew them well. And they needed us. In fact, at that time, we were the *only* sales channel that they had. In other words, Dassault only sold their software through IBM. Bernard and I became best of friends during this timeframe, because he understood the power of what IBM was trying to do with the RS/6000, and he also understood Dassault's role in our plan.

Bernard Charles *(Vice Chairman of the Board of Directors and Chief Executive Officer of Dassault Systèmes)*: This was a very delicate time

for IBM. When Nick was asked to go to Austin, it was really the
transition between what was a marginal success—the first release
of the RISC technology called the RT PC, which basically was not
competitive on the market—and what would become the RS/6000.
So, the RS/6000 was a massive mission. The mission was to make
IBM competitive in the workstation market that was not only
emerging, but was accelerating and becoming a very, very important
higher-margin business segment.

While the margins were not as high as those of the mainframe,
the segment was very critical for IBM's future. Nonetheless, the
RS/6000 project was in trouble when Nick first arrived in Austin.
The biggest issue was the reliability of the machine, but there were a
whole number of problems. The workstation does not exist without
the integration of computing power and graphic power. You cannot
have a workstation recognized if you do not have a symbiotic
integration between the two, and we were not there yet.

It is true that we were not there yet, but Bernard and his colleagues at
Dassault typified what we needed to release the RS/6000 platform with
AIX, our version of UNIX. We needed applications. As the name suggested,
workstations were intended to do work, but very few people were writing
new code on them. They were not development platforms, as much as they
were operational platforms—design this wing, design this car, design this
chemical formula, operate this part of my business, run my pharmacy—and
we needed applications to do that. We needed databases to do that. We
needed transaction systems. We needed a whole bunch of things. And to be
credible in that operative space, we needed Dassault Systèmes, CATIA, and
their programs running on our workstation computers.

I tried to hit the ground running, because John Akers had said that we
should be announcing products in 1989. I started to get my hands dirty and talk
to people to understand the true status of the RS/6000 so that I could offer John
my estimations of when we could announce and ship our first workstations.

Tilak Agerwala: Nick got right down there into the guts of the RS/6000 development effort. In the early stages, he set the tone by saying, "Look, we're in this together. And I'm here to be the bridge between Jack Kuehler and our team. I'm here to help, but you've got to be open with me."

So initially, it was really about Nick getting engaged with the details. In the beginning, Nick kept telling us, "Look, we don't have time to fool around. We're with you. Let's get going."

Once I had a handle on what was going on, I was mortified. After a few months, I realized that there really was nothing. I said to myself many times, "Oh my God! How could they ever have thought that this could be done within a year?"

I had to go back to John and the Management Committee at IBM as soon as I could figure out what I had and what was possible. It took a few months, but finally, during the first quarter of 1989, I informed John, "The RS/6000 is not going to happen in '89. It is just not possible. It is nowhere near where you think it is or where anybody has told you it is. We will be lucky if we can get the job done sometime in '90."

IBM had a lot riding on the system shipping in '89, so when I told John and the management team what was happening, I was expecting them to be disappointed. I was not expecting them to initiate an audit on the project, though, but that is exactly what Akers did.

As if I did not already have enough problems, over the next two months, the skies darkened, the IBM planes flew into Austin, and we were audited day in and day out. The folks in dark suits eyeballed the development schedule, the software schedule, the manufacturing schedule, the release schedule, the marketing schedule, and the sales schedule. They reviewed everything and then went back and told John, "Nick is right. He'll be lucky if he gets this done in 1990. Forget about 1989."

John did not like that at all. In fact, in a highly unusual move, he came personally to the last audit review in Austin, listened, and then clearly expressed his disappointment. I said to him, "Nobody is more disappointed than me, but I cannot do what I cannot do. This is the best we are going to do, John, and it will take all that we can do to hold it together."

As all this was going on, I had to let my team know just how hard it was going to be before we saw daylight. I would to say to people all the time, "If you do not want to be here, leave now. If you are not enjoying what you are doing, I don't need you here, because it is going to get tougher. I am never going to pay you all that you think you deserve, and I am never going to thank you all the times you think I should thank you, even though I want you, need you, and want to reward you. You have to be here for some other reason—and that reason is that you believe in what we're doing. And if you do not, then please leave now."

A lot of people quit that team because they thought it was going to be a disaster. I had to replace four big desertions, but even so, we started turning it around. I put the team back together again with people who believed in miracles—or at least liked adventure. These were people who I could motivate, and who in turn, could inspire me further. These were people who accepted the challenge.

And I accepted the challenge, too, right there with them. A leader must be willing to roll up his or her sleeves and be a true part of the team. There can be no hiding in an office or off at a faraway headquarters. The team in Austin quickly understood that they would see plenty of me.

David Carlucci: Nick had pressure on his shoulders, getting things back on schedule and staying to schedule to get it out the door as a successful launch. He had an incredible energy, and that was a motivator. He wasn't viewing things from the sidelines or from the top. He was in it. He was always in it.

It helped that we had chips on our shoulder (no pun intended). Back then, Austin was a relatively new site with a bad reputation. People would look at Austin and say, "They are the Wild West. Nobody cares about them.

They never get it right. They are always wrong. All they do is embarrass us. They say they are going to do one thing, then they do nothing."

It was very obvious to me—and eventually we made it obvious to the entire IBM company and world—that this was an incredibly talented and committed and capable team of product developers, manufacturers, sellers, marketers, and partners. Furthermore, we had the RS/6000 chip set from Burlington, a must-have if we were going to create a high-performing, competitively-priced system with staying power. This team held the winning hand, and we were going to play it for the world to see.

I would tell them, "We are building an amazing price-performance product offering here! It is going to hit DEC and Sun where it will hurt the most and the longest! We are going to put ourselves on the map as every client's system of choice. We will simply outperform the competition and earn our way because we are better."

At the same time, I was trying to improve the whole Austin reputation with the rest of IBM. The best way to improve our reputation, I thought, was to enable an open, collaborative environment where everybody could simply say what was on their mind. I would say, "If you tell me the truth, we will get to it. We will work on these problems, and we will get them done. If you are forthright, I will be forthcoming!"

We would have these meetings every Friday. Everybody was welcome. I asked them for their candor and honesty. No problem was too big or too small. Anybody who had a gripe could come in. I would say, "I want to hear what you've been talking about. What are your concerns? What don't we have? Why don't we have it?"

We ran a very open process that allowed people to have their say. It was this idea of, "We are not closed. We are not hunkered down here in Austin." It was during these days that I really solidified my ideas around the power of collaboration.

Tilak Agerwala: I saw him do this throughout his career. He encouraged everyone to attend these meetings. It was supposed to be an absolutely open discussion. Afterwards, he would take all the action items and actually implement them.[1]

Bernard Charles: I was meeting with Nick every six to eight weeks, flying from Paris to Dallas, and then driving to Austin to review the project. It was not a one-shot review. Nick has this incredible capacity to follow up with drive and to inspire people. He loves people. And he loves technology. He loves both, and he put them together. He brought people together to take on challenges and reach goals. The first thing that I learned from Nick is that you had better make sure that everyone involved on the project understands what the goal is and what is important. It's not one formulation. It's a formulation adapted to the role of the people and what each has to accomplish to get to the end result. That's Nick. This is what I learned from him, and I apply this technique to this day.

Over time, what we needed to do came into focus. We had to write an *entire* operating system—only 1.5 million lines of code. (Nothing serious!) We had to develop, announce, build, organize, and supply-chain something like twelve models of this RS/6000 family.

I had fixed plenty of problems before, but this was an entirely different ballgame altogether. The pressure on the team was just unbelievable.

This required me to base my thinking on a practical plane: *What are my assessments of the organization's capabilities? What can it do?*

I knew there would be nothing gained in asking the team to do things that it was not capable of doing.

Of course, that went for Bernard and the Dassault Systèmes guys, too. As far as I was concerned, there was no "us" and "them." There was only "we." We all needed to be one.

So, I tried to define success for this team, based upon what I believed they were capable of doing. We would discuss what I defined as success, and once they said "yes" to something we could all get behind, then I could begin to measure whether we were actually getting there. And of course, they were measuring me, too, based upon my ability to create an atmosphere for them in which they could succeed.

> **Tilak Agerwala:** I saw somebody who created an environment where people were going to be open and accept the challenge, and I saw an executive who was going to make decisions. I saw an executive who needed the team to be with him, got the team to be with him, and in return, was protective of the team. When the development timeline was going to move, he tried to understand why that was the case. He brought all the facts together. And then he would go back to Jack Kuehler and explain why things were going to be delayed. I saw somebody that had a deep understanding of people and at the same time had a deep understanding of the details of what needed to be done and was making the decisions.

> **Bernard Charles:** I remember this meeting where we had to explain why the graphic architecture connected to the RS/6000 was leading to noncompetitive results. Our program could not perform properly. So, Nick invited us to a meeting and gave us the entire day—listening to us, looking at our demonstration, looking at our presentation—to really understand all aspects of the issues. He was the boss, but he spent the whole day together with us and his team, listening to us present the issues.
>
> And of course, it's human nature: his team wanted to defend themselves and explain why something was not an issue, but he would nicely say, "Hey guys, listen. This has to work. Don't you think that what you see is not working properly?" He was, in a decisive way, opening the eyes of the people to let them see what we were seeing, and then say, "Do we agree, all of us, that there's a problem?"

Tilak Agerwala: He tended to sit down and calmly understand what the real technical issues were, whether they were in Research, Development, Hardware, or Software, and he tried to get to the bottom of those technical issues. He tried to understand where people were coming from with their issues. I saw him make decisions, including very gut-wrenching decisions, always on a sound technology basis. Today we would call that Evidence-Based Decision Making, but Nick was doing that 30 years ago.

Bernard Charles: He would work with each of us and say, "Okay, what's the action plan? How are we going to address that?" He would not let a meeting conclude without having the date for the next review and without having each of us commit to take our next step forward. It is not common for top executives to do that. Nick was giving us his full attention and making sure that there was joint agreement on the problem and joint agreement to have one plan forward. And he would say, "I don't care if Dassault Systèmes is just a partner. They are with us for the journey, and we are going to consider us together as one team."

For so long, we did not have anything to offer anybody, so I could not get anybody on the East Coast to pay attention to us. But we had a plan, and we kept working the plan. Finally, we started to hit the ball hard, and people started to believe that we knew what we were doing from a technological standpoint.

Tilak Agerwala: Nick is the type of leader who doesn't get frantic in a crisis. In fact, he ends up being the calming influence and the voice of reason, and he always gives the technology and the technical aspect huge importance. One of the things that sticks with me is Nick saying, "Tilak, no matter what you do, no matter what negotiations you are in, whatever decisions you are trying to make, never lose your technical integrity. Be bold enough to say the technical truth as you see it."

As the technical teams and Dassault began to hit their stride, we had to get ready to market the RS/6000. This required a big effort on my part, because IBM was entering new and, to many, unwelcome territory. We needed a specialized sales force, a whole new marketing campaign, and maybe most importantly, the ability to break through *internal* resistance at IBM to the RS/6000 and AIX, which was the name for our proprietary UNIX operating system.

> **Sam Palmisano** (*IBM CEO, 2002–2012, and forty-year IBM Veteran*): Nick's a very strong technical leader, as well as a very inspirational leader, so he could be very persuasive. He made a lot of strong arguments as to what we needed to do to participate in the UNIX market, which was a bit contrary to our more traditional proprietary approaches like the mainframe. Nick had the ability to see the market as it was, as opposed to how we wanted it to be. The UNIX market was emerging. There wasn't a standard at that point in time. There were multiple versions of the operating system going.

There were important people within IBM who actually believed that if we were successful with the RS/6000, IBM literally would be ruined. They did not want to step outside of the proprietary world that we had built our success upon. But the world was changing, and fast.

John Akers was with me. He had shown his hand very clearly. But others, from the most senior executives to the most junior professionals, were not sold.

> **Sam Palmisano:** To see the market the way Nick did, you had to be willing to participate in a non-IBM world versus the total proprietary world that we were accustomed to historically. Everything we did

on software was oriented and architected to optimize our hardware business—so the databases, the transaction managers, all those sorts of things—the stack was all optimized for the mainframe or the AS/400, where it was totally integrated. The databases were totally integrated into the operating system.

Bob Samson (*Thirty-six-year IBM Veteran and Former IBM General Manager, Global Public Sector*): The RS/6000 was a very different computing architecture and a very different computing paradigm. And a lot of people in IBM were saying, "What the heck is this thing? I mean, really? We're selling mainframes; the world's a happy place." But Nick became this cheerleader for a technology that was emerging in the industry and selling it in a way that ties into his idea of "If nothing changes, nothing changes," because what it required was someone who saw the power of it before anyone else. That's what Nick did.

Bernard Charles: IBM was making so much money with the mainframe. The mainframe was the king inside IBM, but there was Nick having the incredible energy to drive people to believe that the RS/6000 would be core and would be the future of IBM.

To give you an idea of just how much resistance we were facing, consider the fact that the database that we had running on the RS/6000 was Oracle's! IBM would not give us DB2! It was not until years later that they decided to support our workstations, because for the longest time, we were viewed as the enemy. UNIX was seen as the enemy of IBM. From within! So many people within IBM thought we were going to kill the company with UNIX, it made my head spin. This is what we were up against.

Sam Palmisano: I think sometimes the harder piece, the more complicated piece, is taking on the culture. Everybody in the organization was focused around proprietary approaches, and Nick had to make the argument for the more open approach. To me, that's more stress—having to fight the internal system—than actually making the products work. With the RS/6000, Nick was doing both.

As I was fighting the internal machinery, my Development team in Austin continued to make remarkable progress. My job was to keep them moving forward to bring the product to life, and at the same time, prepare the Sales & Marketing team to make it a success in the marketplace.

David Carlucci: Nick is a very disciplined individual. He has a great sense of humor, but serious. He has an affable style, and friendly, but very tough. He's just basically a no-B.S. guy: "There's a job to get done. Let's go do it. And let's do it as a team."

He was not the kind of person who was a Development Executive and pointed his fingers at Sales & Marketing, which sometimes happened within the company. He was very oriented to getting a team of the best people to get whatever he was working on done, and that RS/6000 team gelled well.

Nick had a respect for people's opinions and people's viewpoints, but he knew the goal and didn't accept a lot of excuses or platitudes or anything around not meeting the goal. We were with him quite frequently in Austin, and I saw how disciplined he was at the time. He was very supportive of his Development team, but very demanding as well. And he expected that Sales and Marketing would be engaged hand-in-glove with them.

Bob Samson: And we did work hand-in-glove with the Development guys. We needed to really understand this product, because Nick was building a specialized RS/6000 sales force to sell it. That was his vision. He believed that once it got into the market, it would gain traction, because the value proposition was so strong.

Now, that is a term that is more in the vernacular today than it was then, but that was one of Nick's terms. He would characterize the RS/6000 as "a new value proposition for the industry." We'd all look at each other and think, *What the heck's a value proposition?* It just was not in the vernacular, but now we've got this new thing, with a very different set of technical characteristics, and a very different value proposition, to take to the market with a specialized sales force.

The key to this significant shift in how IBM viewed the market was that I enabled a lot of people who made a lot of wonderful things happen. People listened to me, and we turned the RS/6000 around. There were amazingly talented people in Austin who simply needed to be led differently, and my job was to enable them so that they could be successful. It was a great honor to have been able to do so. I was so proud of them as that initial RS/6000 neared completion.

As we prepared to announce, we still were not perfect, but we had a lot of the right stuff, and we had a good view of the future. We had enough to blow out the current competition while Tilak and the team were already working through the shortcomings for future releases.

Tilak Agerwala: The main thing was that Nick was there. As always, it's not the words that count; it's the actions, and you could see that Nick was doing what he said he was going to do, and most of the team was doing what they said they were going to do. I was very happy to be part of the executive team that eventually brought the RS/6000 to market, but it was an intense journey for Nick, me, and everyone involved.

Bernard Charles: He had the ability to look at the best of every team member. He looked at the good of people before looking at the limits of people. He also gave extreme attention to assembling the right people together. It's not putting the same people together. It's putting incredibly complementary people together. Another thing, when Nick was there, he was good with everyone. Even if people did not notice their own behavioral changes, when the meeting was over, they'd have a positive smile, no matter how hard our problems were to resolve. I've never seen a meeting, in a very hard situation, where we would leave being upset with each other, which is not often the case when you have big crises. That's how Nick got everyone through as a team.

We announced our first product offering on February 14, 1990. Akers had us demonstrate it at his Annual Leadership Kickoff Meeting in Rye, New York, and we blew it out! The workstations were great. Everybody loved them, and they loved us. I will never forget it. This was the first time IBM ever did anything like this at a meeting, and we built off of that energy.

To demonstrate our technical superiority, we ran many face-offs and competitions against other products and companies. We had a DEC machine on the right. We had a Sun machine on the left. We had an HP machine, too. And we ran circles around them.

Our first shipments were made less than three months later, in May 1990. We promised we would deliver everything by the end of May that year, that all products would be ready to ship. And they were, and history was made.

The RS/6000 was able to outperform expectations at every turn in the road because we had those applications in place. That is why everything took off like a rocket. There still was resistance to overcome, but once we had such a great product, the marketing teams loved us, and the sales teams loved us even more.

Sam Palmisano: Nick would say to me, "You've got to sell the heck out of them." That was our role. He promised, "Look, I'll make this thing work. You go sell it." So, we did, and we did for years.

Bob Samson: It ended up being one of the most successful platforms IBM ever introduced.

You might think this successful launch would have made me a hero to many within IBM, but that cultural resistance remained strong—and from very high up. Not long after we shipped, I went back to Armonk for a meeting with the IBM Advisory Committee, which was made up of all ex-IBM CEOs. This was an old IBM technique. They met two or three times per year, and they wanted to see me during their summer meeting.

These were the people in the room: John Opel, Frank Cary, Vince Learson, and, for good measure, Thomas Watson, Jr. Can you imagine that? John Akers was not there, because the sitting CEO was never asked to attend.

Now, this was the *old* IBM. The *old* Armonk. The *old* board room. Big horseshoe table, dark brown leather, and ringed with steel. I am standing in the middle, all alone, and I am talking to them about the RS/6000. I am trying to explain to them what it is going to do, why it took so long, and where we were going to go next.

These were the old-schoolers who had built IBM into a behemoth on the strength of the mainframe, and they were very protective of that still-powerful business line and what it meant to the Company. They were concerned that the RS/6000 might cannibalize the mainframe and mid-range business and destabilize the company. One of these men even stood up, looked me in the eye, and said, "You're the guy who is going to ruin IBM."

I held my ground and replied, "With all due respect, I'm not that guy. I'm the guy who's trying to figure out how to get the IBM Company into new markets that are growing very rapidly and are not serviced by anything we're doing. I have no intention of undoing the Mainframe System/390 or our AS/400 mid-range computer."

I continued, "I have no intention of harming those franchises. I have no intention of going after their market. We're going after a market where we have nothing. So you're giving me far too much credit for being the person who's going to undo the IBM Company. I'm a person who is trying to help the IBM Company."

I will never forget saying that, because it had the merit of being true. From May to December, we actually created a billion-dollar business—even *after* crediting customers for those returned RT PCs which had not worked exactly as promised. In seven months, the revenue for the Advanced Workstation Division went from something like negative $250 million to more than $1 billion.

The IBM RS/6000 workstation and server family, including the AIX operating system, proved to be a highly-successful line of products with a lasting and profound impact on the future of IBM and the information technology industry itself. It began with that flying start. It felt amazing.

> **Bob Samson:** You cannot understand the degree of difficulty of getting to that first billion. You look at it and think, *Ah, what's a billion dollars? You went from zero to a billion dollars? Big deal.* It actually is a big deal, because it was a hardware platform. It was a new paradigm. It was a whole different way to get work done. Hardware market share—hardware gains—are hard-wired, so you always need people that are cheering you on, keeping the faith, moving it ahead, being insightful, and understanding the customer. And that's what Nick did. This was a fiercely competitive industry with a lot of players already there. The degree of difficulty was astounding. And that's why this whole idea of a value proposition that Nick pushed so hard was so important.

Our approach to the RS/6000 helped illuminate a core tenet of my philosophy of innovation—*"How do you create more value?"* In many ways the RS/6000 and AIX are very good examples of technological innovation that did not deliver value until we did the more mundane things.

I did not invent the architecture. I did not invent RISC. But I got the *value* out of it. In effect, we created the whole pSeries for IBM, because for those three years that I was the leader of the IBM team in Austin, we focused, executed, and shipped things out the door fast enough to ensure that we could establish ourselves in a market that we had invented but until then had failed to capitalize on.

Smarter people than me had tried and failed. So, what was the difference? I think because I have an inquisitive mind, I push a little further and a little harder. I always want to know not just what is going on, but why it is going on, and why it cannot be better.

So as the developers wrote the 1.5 million lines of code, as we worked together with Dassault, I did not settle. I was not afraid to ask questions big and small. I was not afraid to ask, "What could be better? What more could we do? Why is it going wrong? What did we do wrong? How do we learn from that?"

Luckily, the team in Austin fed off of that energy and that prodding. An added benefit in this victory was the solid footing it provided for our partner Dassault Systèmes, whom we continued to do business with for decades to come.

Bernard Charles: It was a survival question for Dassault Systèmes, and Nick understood that. And I think that's why he had this special interest in us. It was very simple. There was a double-responsibility that Nick understood well. He knew that without success with the RS/6000, not only would IBM suffer, but my entire company would not survive. Our competitors were already on other workstations. They were not necessarily in the kind of struggle-for-life mode. They were gaining market share being on non-IBM equipment. I think that made my relationship with Nick a very special relationship, and he was very sensitive to my situation. Thirty years later, Dassault Systèmes is a world leader in its elite sector for design, simulation, and modeling, serving 350,000 companies around the world. The culture in my company was influenced by Nick, and I'm not saying that to be nice. I owe him.

Tilak Agerwala: Overall, the RS/6000 was an exhilarating experience. It wasn't that long a timeframe. Nick went down there in '88, and by 1990 we had already built the Advanced Workstation

Division into a billion-dollar business. So, we're talking about a very short period of time, but it was intense. Then, when things started coming together, Nick also was there with the team celebrating successes.

David Carlucci: We all felt pretty proud when we got the thing launched to good reviews, but we were well behind in the marketplace, so there were a lot of challenges coming to the market as late as we did. But I think it was viewed as a strong success for Nick and for those of us who were associated with it.

In the end, we gave IBM something brand new and squeaky clean that worked and that solved the problems that mattered. That made the RS/6000 easy to sell. And when you have got one of those things, people will love you to death.

So I figured I was positioned pretty well for my next move within IBM. I was feeling very good. I had fixed a *really* big problem this time. I figured I was going to get promoted, and that all the sacrifice—the stress and the time away from my wife and teenage kids—would prove worthwhile.

I was thinking that Akers and his team would make me a Corporate Vice President. At that time, if you were a Corporate VP, you had more or less made the IBM big time. I was not there yet, but I was an ambitious guy, and I wanted to get there.

So, when I was called back to Armonk, I figured they were going to tell me something great. And guess what? I was wrong. They did not promote me.

Even worse, they said, "We need you to do it again."

What?

I can hear John Akers in my head to this day, saying, "We need you to go to Poughkeepsie to fix the mainframe business. You're going to become the President of the Mainframe Division."

My jaw just about hit the table. Here I just had put a computer in the marketplace that was being likened to the mainframe as IBM's premier product line—my Austin team and much of the press believed this—and now the leaders of the IBM Company were telling me that they want me to go to Poughkeepsie to fix the business that many thought had served its time and was ready to be replaced. I am thinking, *Are you crazy? This is first prize for what I just did?*

I was not happy. They did not promote me, and they asked me to take an assignment that did not make sense to me at all.

But I was a company man. I had made that leap years before. So, I kept a stiff upper lip, I told John Akers, "Okay," and I headed to Poughkeepsie, New York.

At least my mother was happy that I was coming home.

5

EXPANDING LEADERSHIP

took charge of the struggling mainframe business, by then branded as the System/390, in December 1991. I was far from ecstatic about the job, but I knew what John Akers wanted from me, and I was going to do my best to get it done. I also knew that this could be a sinking ship, and I had been tasked with not only keeping it afloat, but with finding a way to turn it into a sleek cruiser.

Despite the breakout success of the RS/6000, IBM, as a whole, was having problems. CEO John Akers was feeling the heat, even though he truly was an icon and one of the builders of the modern IBM. As a salesman and executive, he helped make the System/360 and its successor System/370 huge successes. As CEO, he faced the rise of the personal computer by building our own successful PC business. Unfortunately, that business was being chipped away by rivals with clone machines and by Microsoft's increasingly dominant Windows software, against which our OS/2 software struggled to compete.

John, along with IBM's US General Manager Terry Lautenbach and IBM President Jack Kuehler, the company's highest-ranking technologist, understood the severity of our problems. The board and the investment community wanted to know how they intended to fix the problems. The business press was highly critical of IBM at the time, too.

Among the so-called experts, consensus was building that in an increasingly-competitive global economy, IBM had to be more nimble and that our size—once the hallmark of our greatness—now was the problem. As John, Terry, and Jack considered IBM's options, they began to discuss dividing the company into a number of independent businesses, some that actually would compete against one another.

Within the company, gossip grew, as IBMers from all walks of the company attempted to understand whether their part of the business was in favor or not. Lingo started to circulate such as "good company/bad company," "new company/old company," and even "remain co/go co."

With the mainframe, I definitely was in a "bad company" part of IBM. Only months removed from creating a key piece of the "new company" with the RS/6000 in Austin, I now found myself heading up a part of the company that was seen as part of the past and potentially even up for sale. IBM was thinking that it would keep "new company" entities like the PC business, the RS/6000, and some software and services, with the rest going on the market.

Having been part of IBM throughout twenty-five years of success and market leadership, this was a new environment for me. These were new problems. Of course, nothing was official yet, so despite the mounting tension, I had to do the best that I could to stay motivated and to keep my team motivated around revitalizing the mainframe business.

And the fact of the matter was, when I thought about the situation, there were some positives about my new role. For one thing, I was back home. Poughkeepsie was not far from where I had grown up in nearby Beacon. I was back home professionally, too. I had cut my teeth on the mainframe when I was a kid just starting back in 1964, and the mainframe remained the symbol of what had made the modern IBM great. Now, more than twenty-five years later, I was back as president of the division. In a company as big as IBM, with so many divisions and products, to end up in the same place where I had started—and as the leader—seemed symbolic. I was back home.

Sure, the mainframe had fallen from grace, but it still was *the* mainframe, and it was up to my new team and me to see if we could restore some luster to IBM's most iconic diamond. I rolled up my sleeves and got started. As I had done three years earlier in Austin, my first move simply was to listen.

Linda Sanford (*Thirty-nine-year IBM Veteran and Former SVP of Enterprise Transformation; Member of the Women in Technology Hall of Fame*): Nick had a way of creating very, very open dialogue. He was a very unusual type of leader for that time. Back then the leadership style still was more command-and-control. But Nick was very collaborative. Collaboration starts with listening. And he did that. He listened to employees: "What do you think?" And in listening, he actively helped them to bring out their own thoughts and ideas. He encouraged them that nothing was off the table. Nothing. Nick would say, "Don't think you can't. If you think you can't, put it on the table; we'll figure out a way to do it if it makes sense."

At first, as it had in Austin, my head was spinning, and I was thinking, *What's going on here?* I listened to everybody, learned the culture, and learned what people thought might be the way forward for the mainframe. As I reflected on all that I heard and saw, I thought to myself, *I don't know if Watson could make heads or tails of this, but there are some great people here!*

So even as I was stunned by the accelerating pace of the mainframe's business decline, I was profoundly struck by the candor of the people in Poughkeepsie. They had very bold ideas. When I asked, "What are we doing here?" people always responded, "We are using bipolar process technology, but if we could have our way, we would move the mainframe to CMOS."

CMOS? They were preaching to the choir. I had just done the RS/6000 in CMOS. Before that, I had led the team that brought CMOS to Burlington and first qualified it in the 1980s. Back home in Poughkeepsie, my technology dreams were catching up with me. I was steeped in CMOS and my new team was *thinking* CMOS.

The idea of moving the mainframe to CMOS had a lot going for it. For years, the bipolar process was the only technology available for truly high-speed performance integrated circuit fabrication, but the bipolar process did not allow for the high levels of integration and low-power operation that could be achieved with CMOS.

Here I was, with a chance of saving all of IBM by bringing so much of what I had learned together in one bold move. This role that I had not wanted now seemed to offer the chance of a lifetime! We had a long, long, long way to go, however. I had to carefully marshal my facts, so I kept listening and learning, and needed to craft a true strategy before I could get too excited.

Luckily, I had a great partner to help me do just that. I had first gotten to know Linda Sanford during my time as Secretary to the Corporate Management Committee, before I went to Austin. She had come up through our typewriter, printer, and copier ranks, which were about as far removed from the aura of the mainframe as possible, but Linda also had software experience that would prove incredibly critical on the mainframe journey we were about to charter.

> **Linda Sanford:** Nick brought me in to help reinvent the mainframe after we hit the proverbial brick wall. To bring in somebody to the hallowed halls of Poughkeepsie and "Mainframe God-land" was very, very unusual. Nick wanted a new pair of eyes for the organization, someone who would ask the questions that the old guard would assume they already knew the answers to. He knew that the answers may be different, or that they needed to be different.

I knew Linda had a brilliant mind, and I also knew that, thanks to her diverse IBM experiences, she would not be overly burdened by the way things had always been in Poughkeepsie. While she played a different role for me than Tilak had in Austin, she gave me that complementary person I needed to think through the mainframe strategy.

> **Linda Sanford:** He wanted me first to help him rethink and rewrite the strategy. He wanted to know, "What did we miss?" And though he was a brilliant engineer, he wasn't just looking for us to invent our way out of the problem. He'd say to me, "What do our clients

want? What do our customers need? What are their business challenges?" And so, when we talked about resetting the strategy for the mainframe, the first thing he told me was, "Go out and talk to customers. What happened?" That was a great way to step into this new role.

Nick let me be me. I could meet with clients, ask questions, and then come back and meet with the senior team at the mainframe organization to give them perspective about what I was hearing from clients. Nick made me feel like that brought added value to the organization, and so I worked on our transformation strategy for the mainframe for about a year, helping him to lay out a new strategy.

I went out and met with dozens of clients as well. These were some of the biggest and most demanding companies in the world. I needed to hear first-hand what they wanted and then make sure we would be responsive.

The stories Linda and I were hearing centered around the rise of the mini-computer. Companies like Digital, Data General, and Wang Laboratories had made a dent in the marketplace in recent years with these minis, claiming that they could do the work of much larger mainframes, but at a much lower cost.

While sophisticated CIOs who needed the processing power and capacity of the mainframe understood the ruse, they were struggling to defend their needs in their conference rooms. They needed our help and quickly.

As I listened to clients, as I listened to Linda, and as I listened to the team as they discussed and debated everything we had heard and knew, a strategy began to take shape in my mind. And you guessed it: it was centered upon CMOS.

I said to myself, *CMOS is our path forward! We are not going to do what we have been doing. We are going to do something entirely different. We are going to go to CMOS. We are going to make this a parallel system. We are going to rewrite our software, including the operating environment, and we are going to turn this thing around.*

Now we began to run our thinking past key clients. We brought in Client Advisory Teams. We explained CMOS to them, including the pros and cons as they related to bipolar, and we asked for their input.

Linda Sanford: At the time, we had a different set of competitors who were coming in with different, lower-cost technologies, and that's what our clients were looking for from us. We had to explain to them, "Look, CMOS is not quite as powerful as bipolar, but let me tell you how we're going to bridge the gap between here and there," and we would ask them for their input. You just couldn't do this in a silo up in Poughkeepsie all by yourself and then just—poof!—push it out the door one day and say, "Here it is world, come get it." That would have been very, very risky. Nick knew we needed to engage with clients as we became more and more serious about making the leap to CMOS.

The shift to CMOS was a big idea, fraught with risk, and it would require a powerful change agent to get it through the chain of command at IBM. I had been through that wringer with the RS/6000, but this was the mainframe. Was I up to the task?

And was my team? To recast the iconic IBM mainframe as a parallel system would require a team with thick skin that could endure incredible uncertainty. You have heard the expression trying to turn around an aircraft carrier? I had been around long enough to know that this was not going to be easy, even with the current mainframe spiraling down and taking all of IBM with it.

Why? For one thing, many of our clients still loved the System/390 the way it was, and I understood that IBM loved happy clients. For another, the fact remained that the mainframe was not actually losing money at the time. We were making money. And in big, bureaucratic companies, where change usually comes much too slowly, shouting, "The sky is falling!" while talking about an iconic money-maker that clients love is usually a losing play.

Just the same, many of us knew that the mainframe was hurting the company. If I was going to get the approval to make the switch to CMOS, I was going to have to formulate my thoughts and opinions into a compelling pitch to management that was sensitive to these realities.

My approach was to connect the dots between the fact that the mainframe, while admittedly still profitable, undeniably was making *less* money, and that reduction in income was increasingly problematic for IBM, because every last cent of mainframe revenue was needed to fund the "new company" initiatives that John, Terry, and Jack were organizing their strategy around. If they wanted to keep spending on "new company," they were going to need more revenue from "old company," and a CMOS mainframe, as I saw it, was a way to do just that.

This need gave my pitch some bite, because IBM's business model was failing, and failing fast, and nobody understood that better than John Akers. I started telling John, Terry, and Jack, "Look, our problem with the mainframe is that we're doing it all wrong in today's market. We haven't been able to fight well in this lower-cost space, because we haven't been built to fight in this space. We're in a foot race, but we're clad in armor. We can't compete."

That much they understood, but what I told them next ran counter to principles they had long espoused: "The first thing we have to do is start dropping the price."

Now, at IBM at that time, the idea of cutting mainframe pricing was heresy. Price was determined by something esoteric known as "million instructions per second," or MIPS, and all of the strategic planners and finance people would tell me over and over again why MIPS were not "elastic," and why every nickel I took away through reduced price was a nickel lost. They did not believe that lower prices could spark higher volume. They had multiple studies "proving" their points, including studies that somehow tied our MIPS price to the country's GDP!

Well, I believed they were wrong, just flat-out wrong, and I wanted the chance to prove that there *was* elasticity to that curve. I do not profess to be the smartest businessperson in the world, but I am not stupid, and I knew in my guts that they were just plain wrong. We all knew that P(rice) $\times$ Q(uantity) = R(evenue), but only I believed that we would get more R if we lowered P, because it would grow Q to a great enough extent.

I did not mince words or hide from a fight. I would say, "You guys don't know what you're talking about. You are thinking after-the-fact, rather than generating the leading-edge thinking that this company *needs* right now!"

I now was going directly against some of the principles that people who had mentored me espoused. But I knew they were wrong. I reminded them of my work on the RS/6000 in Austin and how we knew that the world was headed in a lower-cost direction. I warned them that we would be dead if we didn't lower the price.

Mark Papermaster: The industry was transitioning from the old technology—bipolar transistors—into the new technology of CMOS. I was on the team that began that new approach, leveraging that new technology in chip design, and I heard about Nick as the lead executive that called out the need for that change. At the time, mainframe computing dominated IBM's revenues and was the big kahuna with the proven bipolar technology, so he had a tough sell on his hands.

It was a gut-wrenching time. These were great people who had educated, trained, and invested in me. And it is not like they had totally cut me loose or totally forgotten me. They were concerned for me and trying to give me support, but my team and I were in a different world, so there were fewer and fewer people to turn to for help.

Furthermore, the fact remains that as much as John and his team cared about me as a person, professionally speaking, I was leading the piece of the company that everyone thought was taking the company down and that they seriously were considering selling. We were expendable, and I had to keep that in mind, even as I worked to give my team the opportunity to prove that we had a plan for the mainframe that could make everyone happy, and as I worked to get leadership to hear what I was telling them.

During these difficult days, my best and strongest partner was Mike Attardo, who was the head of IBM's General Technology Division and responsible for all semiconductor and packaging technologies including those of East Fishkill. If we were to make the switch to CMOS, he would be the leader taking the responsibility for what would become the sunk bipolar semiconductor and packaging investments in East Fishkill.

At the same time, Mike was responsible for delivering all the CMOS technology we would need then and for the foreseeable future. Mike and I discussed this switch at great length and agonized over it, and he got on board. Mike and I knew exactly what we were doing and why.

Perhaps just through sheer tenacity and saying the same things over and over and over, the company started to get comfortable with the switch to CMOS. In fact, I will never forget an infamous early morning meeting that Mike and I had with John Akers in old Armonk where we finally brought him over the top and received the go-ahead.

Mark Papermaster: When we understood at our outpost in Burlington that the mainframes would need this new technology, it was very exciting for us. It was a very big challenge.

Vijay Lund (*Thirty-year IBM Veteran and VP of Systems & Development*): It took great leadership and thinking to say the time was right to cut over to CMOS and to have the confidence in Team IBM to get through the chasm from bipolar to CMOS in a finite amount of time. That's because if it wasn't done right, we could have lost the entire business. The competition was ready to exploit any dents in the armor with IBM's transition.

My team had a vision. We understood where we were going. We understood that it was doable. Now we had to get heads-down committed to make it happen.

As we ramped up our efforts in 1992, there were a lot of moving parts to our plan, but essentially, we had to do three things in the course of about three years. First, we had to release one final bipolar mainframe while development of the CMOS machine took place. Then, roughly eighteen months later, we needed to release an early version of the CMOS mainframe. Finally, in 1994, we would introduce the fully-transitioned CMOS mainframe.

It was not a fun time by any stretch of the imagination, because it was so intense. Even with logic on our side, the resistance to technology change—coupled with the rate of change that needed to happen—was huge in a large company such as IBM. If I thought resistance to the RS/6000 had been great, resistance to the CMOS mainframe was on another level altogether.

We were doing all of the things people told me not to do. We were moving to CMOS. We were dropping the price. There is no doubt that I understood the consequences of failure, but I also understood the consequences of *not* acting. By moving to CMOS, we were improving the cost base for the mainframe so that we could compete with the other price performance computing options in the marketplace that were all CMOS based. That was the way forward.

> **Mark Papermaster:** Nick drove the change. It's very hard. When people choose technologies, it's almost like religion.

I believed in my abilities as a problem solver and engineer. All throughout my career at IBM, I fixed problems. I believed my team could get the job done. These were incredible people. We all took the challenge seriously, tearing everything apart.

There is no doubt, though, that I was under tremendous pressure. I was making life-changing decisions every day. Luckily, John Akers gave me an advisor to be my sounding board—a longtime IBMer named Dick Gerstner, whom I knew, liked, and respected. In fact, Dick had been my manager when I first started working on the RS/6000, and we had a good rapport. Dick helped me to stay grounded and to hold onto my beliefs during many grueling days and nights. I am grateful to have had him by my side, because it was a very complicated transformation.

We were not just replacing bipolar with CMOS on the hardware; we had to change the whole software package, too. We had to take what was not a parallel system and make it into one. The mainframe operating environment relied on big uniprocessors, and the bigger the uniprocessor, the happier the mainframe, and the more work it could get done. We could divide the uniprocessors into pieces, and we also could put these uniprocessors together into tightly-coupled symmetric multiprocessors (SMPs) to make four, eight, or even sixteen processors act like one.

Now we were breaking that model. We were going to break everything into small pieces and make them parallel. In the new CMOS environment, we could go up to 512 processors, which was a lot then, and we could do it with no application change. What this means is that our clients would not have to change anything when they switched over from the bipolar mainframe to the CMOS mainframe. Naturally, this was very attractive to them. They could simply add or subtract processors, depending on their needs. They could modify or modulate or adjust or grow or shrink their mainframe workload on their own terms and conditions.

It is worth pointing out that my aspiration here was consistent with the original promise that Thomas Watson, Jr. made when he announced System/360 on April 7, 1964. The team was committed and bought-in and on target to protect his now decades-old "no application change" promise. They knew full well that what we were about to undertake was something that had never been done before!

I knew we could be successful in the mainframe space with this approach, and we started to make significant progress. We began proving to people that we knew what we were talking about. But we were far from out of the woods, and the clock was ticking, because even as the mainframe team was gaining some momentum, many were sounding the death knell for IBM, and those "old company"/"new company" breakup talks were growing louder and louder.

Ross Mauri (*Forty-one-year IBM Veteran and Current GM of IBM's Z and LinuxONE Server Division*)**:** When I joined IBM, John Opel was on the cover of TIME, and we were going to be a $100 billion company and were building manufacturing sites all over the world. You couldn't speak higher praise than what we were getting. Then things really turned in the early '90s, the dark years. Now we were reading that we were the dinosaurs and that we were going to go out of business.

Linda Sanford: I can still see the cover of Fortune magazine where we were the dinosaur on the way to extinction. It was a tough time for everybody. We were worried that we would not be able to make payroll and that we would lose our jobs!

One of my most difficult jobs was to keep the CMOS mainframe team focused and motivated as local, business, and national media began to circle IBM like vultures. Even more difficult, I had to conduct IBM's first-ever layoff, and right there on my own home turf.

Working in conjunction with Mike Attardo, my partner in this decision, we had to shut down major parts of East Fishkill and Poughkeepsie and Endicott to ensure that Burlington could handle our CMOS demand and drive progress on the roadmap of technology success fast enough to make everything work. There was a cost to what we had to do—emotional as well as financial. We had to let good people go.

Vijay Lund: Nick is a gentle soul, but he had to do tough things. He was asked to do IBM's first layoff. We had to take a lot of cost out of the bipolar organization as the technology was phased out, so a large number of jobs left Poughkeepsie and Fishkill. During that time frame, Nick received death threats on his family. There were lots of lives that were affected in Poughkeepsie and Fishkill, predominantly, and of course, there were second-order effects in sales and marketing and manufacturing and everything else. He really took on so much, and yet he did it with style, grace, and a gentle hand.

Corporations across America were making similar decisions through-out the 1990s, as downsizing and reengineering became commonplace, but that did not make it any easier. You need to understand—IBM had *never* let people go in its entire history. Lifelong employment was assumed. But as we made the transition from bipolar to CMOS, we just were not in a position to carry as many people, especially those who did not have the skills we needed going forward.

Working with Mike, we sadly laid off nearly 35,000 people in the Mid-Hudson Valley and cued up most of the $8.9 billion in extraordinary charges against revenue in 1994 against the bipolar chip and packaging technology that we no longer needed. It was gut-wrenching because even as large as the plants were in Poughkeepsie, Kingston, and Fishkill, I knew these people, and they knew me. We ate at the same restaurants. We shopped at the same stores. Our families played tennis and swam together at IBM facilities. We were a community, and it was horrible knowing that so many lives would change. But it literally was the only way that IBM could survive.

I was trying to focus on the future and on those people who would remain, but at the same time, I felt terribly for those people who had to leave through layoffs and early retirements. And yes, there were death threats, and yes, I had bodyguards at work and at home. Local police officers were stationed 24/7 at my house. Believe me, I knew just how serious everything had become.

I tried very hard not to take everything personally. I try to never use that expression because business *is* personal to me, but during these days, I had to find a way not to dwell on the negative or else it would have consumed me. Instead—and maybe the engineer in me saved me this way—I was keeping my eyes on where we were making progress and where we were having successes.

Ross Mauri: After we got over the shock of the first round or two of layoffs, Nick got everybody focused and believing that we could bring the mainframe back. He'd say, "We can do this, and only we can do this. There's no team on the planet better than this IBM Mainframe Team. We can resurrect the mainframe. We can save the company." He just gave such clear direction and hope that everyone believed him. Everyone worked seven days a week. Nobody was telling us we had to work; we just knew. Everyone worked phenomenal, long hours for years to bring out these machines.

We literally blocked out the rest of the world to just focus on doing the job that we needed to do. Through those years, we had hope, because our leader convinced all of us, "We can do this." We could see the technology, so we agreed with him. Nobody was doubting the technology, but he helped us see that with that technology we could save the mainframe and save the company.

I was so busy. My mind was occupied. My body was occupied. But busy or not, I never lost sight of what was going on around me, and a little less than a year into our mainframe turnaround efforts, even more dramatic changes came. For the first time ever, IBM brought in a CEO from the out-side. That CEO, of course, was Louis V. Gerstner, the well-regarded CEO of RJR Nabisco who also had led major pieces of American Express.

And yes, Lou was Dick's brother.

When Lou Gerstner took over on April 1, 1993, we were the first business unit he visited. By this time, I am sure, Dick had already explained to his brother what was going on with the mainframe and how we were trying to fix the problems. But now he was coming to size us up as people and as a team for himself.

As Lou described in his book *Who Says Elephants Can't Dance?*, my team and I began to give him a detailed presentation, complete with the requisite "foils"—clear 8" × 11" transparencies that would be magnified and illuminated from clunky projectors that occupied every conference room in the entire company. This approach represented standard IBM protocol for the time.

No more than a few minutes after we started, and just as I placed my second foil on the projector, Lou got up and turned it off. We all stood in silence. I had no idea what was happening! But then he broke the silence, saying, "Let's just talk about your business."

IBMers called it "The Click Heard 'Round the World," because within twenty-four hours, literally everyone in the company knew what the new CEO had done! To me!

But he had made his point. He did not care about transparencies. He just wanted to talk—about where we were, what we needed, and where we saw the mainframe business going. We must have talked for three hours. It was a fantastic meeting.

The net result was that Lou understood from the start the transition we wanted to make. I told him it would be costly, because we had to divest of assets that we did not need anymore. I told him we had to make a different technology choice, too, explaining why CMOS was the way forward. I also explained the marketplace consequences of our plan to him. We believed that our competitors—the Japanese manufacturers of that era—would likely stay in the old technology longer, build bigger things sooner, and be more successful than us in the short run until we could bring ourselves up to equivalency with our new CMOS mainframe offering, which was still well more than a year out. We needed him to stick with us through these challenging times, because once we created our solution, we believed that we would simply outdistance the competition.

Lou understood and appreciated everything I told him. I had been an "old company" outcast, but now, with Lou, the whole equation had been turned upside down. As is well known, he made up his mind very early not to break up the company. He was going to hold IBM together, and not only that, the mainframe division was back in the fold. We were no longer part of the "old company," on our way out the door. In fact, Lou actually placed our plan for fixing the mainframe at the center of his turnaround strategy.

Sam Palmisano: When it was all going south, Lou came in and took a lot of cost out, which we had to do, but that wasn't enough. I certainly was aware of what was going on with the mainframe. If those guys hadn't figured out technically how to move that platform off of this technology called bipolar to a more cost-competitive semiconductor product called CMOS and have it perform, I don't think the transformation would have been as successful. Lou needed Nick's team to come up with a product roadmap that could save that high-end line so that there would be enough cash to pull everything else off. That was the way to a happy ending.

Lou Gerstner was not a man afraid of change, and he was tough. Things were going to be different at IBM; things could not stay the same. As Lou began to make the moves he had to make, my team and I kept grinding.

Lou backed our plan just as he said he would, but he would become concerned and angry when things would go wrong. I could not help but be reminded of my early life in Beacon and the lessons about change that I had learned from my tough-as-nails father. That life experience gave me the fortitude to hang in there whenever Lou would bark, "Why did this happen?"

I would stay calm, and remind him, "Remember, I told you that our competitors would do that, but we are not doing that; we are doing this instead. This is how we are going to compete."

He would nod, and to his credit, he stayed with us all the way. He put a lot of pressure on us, but at the same time, he was under unbelievable pressure, too.

To a large extent, the fate of the company was hanging on my ability to pull everything together to make this profound shift in technology, system, and business strategy successful. Arguably, no company had ever attempted to transform its flagship product at this scale while remaining true to their clients and their investments and Watson, Jr.'s original promise.

We were changing the operating model of the system without changing the application model to the client. We were doing it all under the covers. The client's code and data would not have to change. To take all of the old code and data into the new world without changing it was a pretty powerful value proposition. Tech companies just do not do that.

With just about any company you can name, when something goes out of cycle, that is the end of it. It is history. But we did not do that. We did not put our legacy out of service. We took it forward. That was a powerful statement emotionally, as well as technically.

Yet even as we worked to build this new, cost-competitive CMOS mainframe for the future, we had to stem our revenue decline now, which takes me back again to the controversies around mainframe pricing.

Remember, my strategy all along was to succeed in stages. While we were working to overcome all the technological challenges that the transition brought with it, we had to develop and bring to market our final bipolar mainframe. We had told our engineers that the future was in CMOS, but still somebody had to develop this last machine. Who would want to do that?

Amazingly, Vijay Lund stepped up and said he wanted the job. He had been with IBM for a decade or so up to that point, but his career was about to get very interesting.

Vijay Lund: When Nick announced the move to CMOS, I was watching. I was getting ready to put my hand up and say, "I want to be a part of this new technology wave that you folks have decided we're going to ride." Why not? Every person that I knew in the mainframe division was eager and excited to move onto the CMOS mainframe product line. But then I thought to myself, *Maybe there is an opportunity to prove myself on the last bipolar system that IBM would develop*, which was being called the President's Ten-Way.

I put my hand up, volunteered, and they said, "You got it. You've got the whole thing from chips to systems to everything. You're in charge. You're the Program Manager for this whole President's Ten-Way system."

Vijay was the man. He built the last bipolar mainframe. And he did it without a full understanding of how his role truly fit into the overall picture. But he figured it out.

Vijay Lund: The CMOS team was pretty bullish and aggressive with their schedules, and the plan was that by 1997 they would have a CMOS system in the marketplace with as much processing power as the bipolar machines. They were running quickly to the finish line, and of course, Nick was very active with product development and systems development.

Meanwhile, here I was working on the final bipolar mainframe with inexperienced engineers brought in to backfill for the experienced engineers who had been let go as part of the phase-out of the bipolar infrastructure. I didn't know if the leadership really even cared much about what we were doing, but I was enjoying every bit of the President's Ten-Way experience. Finally, I got my first opportunity to present the status of my program to Nick in Poughkeepsie as part of an all-day review of the CMOS program. I was coached very strongly by Nick's people that I would get about five minutes to review the President's Ten-Way, really, as a courtesy. I said, "Okay. That's fine with me. If you want me to walk in there with two charts, I'll walk in there with two charts."

Well, Vijay laid out his schedule, some issues that needed to be closed before release, and some marketing thoughts that were on his mind. So far, so good. But then he said, "You know, Nick, I really don't know why we're doing this product, because every financial person in the company tells me that I'll be the first program manager in IBM's history to lose money on a product line. I don't want to be the first to lose money. I don't understand why we would ever want to lose money on this. There's no glamour left on this product line, but we have a game plan, and we are on track."

I told Vijay, "Listen, I want you to keep your head down. I want you to finish this thing. I don't want you to debate anyone in the company about the need for this product or the financials of this product. I've looked it all over and it makes good sense to me. I just want you to go do it. But before you release the design to manufacturing, I want you to come see me and tell me what the issues are and what we need to do."

> **Vijay Lund:** That first presentation stuck in my mind. It was a very gentle discussion, very businesslike. And then of course, when we were getting ready to get this product to manufacturing, I scheduled a meeting with Nick. I gave him an update, we had a discussion along with a few of his people, and Nick said, "Proceed. Go into manufacturing. We're going to go ship this thing. Go get this thing done on time." I said, "Okay, it's going to be on the floor and out the door in 1994, Nick. Just remember that." He said, "Okay, let's do it."

And right about that time, when we built the last bipolar mainframe, we started to know we were going to be successful with our first, small, stopgap CMOS mainframe, too. We had to get it out and over with, and then there would be a gap until our CMOS product rolled out. The Japanese companies had fun with us during that year, as they continued down the bipolar path. But I actually knew during that timeframe that in the long game, we were going to be the winner.

I also knew I had a winner on my hands with Vijay Lund, who had run the program nobody wanted on schedule and on performance. Not only that, but he also helped me carry the day on the price elasticity debate.

> **Vijay Lund:** The bottom line is that IBM made a lot of money on that machine. The financial guys were looking at things with doom and gloom and not understanding what we were doing from a customer perspective. They were looking at it from a straight-line, competitive, cost takedown perspective. They were saying, "Don't take the price down; just milk the cow and get out of it." But Nick was very aggressive on pricing with the President's Ten-Way as the precursor to both the "baby" CMOS release scheduled for 1996 and the full release slated for 1997. He was thinking strategically. He was thinking

long term. He wasn't thinking short term. This goes to Nick's judgment in business, and I think he played his cards extremely well.

Vijay had played his cards well, too, whether he knew it or not at the time. After finishing his work for us, he was getting ready to head to Austin where the workstation business kept growing and wanted his skills. Just before he left, though, I decided I needed him in Fishkill instead.

Vijay Lund: I was getting ready to go to Austin to join the workstation division, but literally the night before I was to leave, I got a phone call from Tony Befi, Nick's Executive Assistant and also the Lab Director in Poughkeepsie.

He said, "Hey, Vijay, I just want you to know that tomorrow morning we're going to announce that you're responsible for our 1997 CMOS system that we're getting ready to take on. The 1996 release is coming along well, but as you know, that's a small effort. The 1997 effort will be the brand-new CMOS technology that's truly going to replace your last bipolar system in the marketplace. The 1996 release is just a stopgap to bring some CMOS out there and see what our customers say, but 1997 is the big bet."

I don't know why Nick chose me, to be honest. I had been successful once on a "low-profile" project, so my guess is he made a bet that I could make the next leap. I think he was just banking on my having won that first game of the World Series, so why not use me for the final game, too.

The next morning, we announced that Vijay would lead the CMOS chip design effort that would prove very pivotal to the IBM Company. I stayed on top of Vijay, and it took everything he had, but we shipped the CMOS '97 System on time, and in the end, we were highly successful. Along the way, though, we suffered a lot of short-term defeats and faced sorrow, anguish, and concern.

Ross Mauri: We started to bring the new releases. We were bringing out a new generation of mainframe every year. That's how fast we were turning the technology and trying to get it to be robust enough to run the world's biggest banks and businesses like that. There was always something every year that we'd put out as our goal to drive to the next system—one year Linda Sanford dubbed it the "Run for the Roses"—and we just kind of blocked the world out around us.

Lou remained in our corner the entire time. He listened, he understood where value was to be found, and though impatient, he stuck with us until we delivered that value.

Everything I told Lou on the day of our first meeting came true, though it was a long and hard journey to get there. But sure enough, when we delivered, our competition was gone, and the IBM 390 System Z (today known as z System) stood by itself.

Lou delivered on his game plan, too. Against serious odds, Lou held the company together, focused on customer needs, and took out a lot of costs, all while under intense scrutiny from Wall Street, the financial media, and even the mainstream media. IBM had been saved, and my team had done its part.

Sam Palmisano: Nick's team—and it was a team effort; it always is—was incredible. Nick had Vijay Lund, who was the guy who figured out how to go from bipolar to CMOS from a technology perspective, and Linda Sanford, who actually was running the mainframe business for him. I would argue that they are one of the main reasons that IBM survived.

This is the story that hasn't been told. I have read all the books, and I participated in elements of the turnaround story—the growth of business services, the cultural changes—and they all were important. I'm not trying to diminish any of it. But there's another story within the story, one that saved the company financially, and that's the mainframe story.

Lou was a great leader, but if Nick and his team hadn't pulled off the mainframe, we would not have had the financial capacity to get through the crisis. I understand that none of the books are written that way, quite honestly, but the mainframe team saved the company. If you understand the economics of the IBM Company back then, they were able to come up with a technological path that saved not just the mainframe but all the software, services, and financing on top of that box. And at that point in time, I bet you that probably was 60 or 70 percent of the income statement. So, it wasn't trivial what they did. They created the technological road maps for Lou to pull the whole thing off.

A lot of people give me credit for saving the mainframe, but this was a real team effort. As the leader, my real job was to simply listen to everybody and fight for the team until they could bring their vision to reality. These were smart people, and when we had problems to solve, we would lock ourselves in a room until we could talk our way to the right answer.

We did a lot of that.

Call it innovation. Call it adaptation. Call it change. We were a team, and we lived and died together in those sessions.

When I think about what we did with the mainframe, I feel happy for all those who came after me and continued to run the business successfully. When all was said and done, the lion's share of the publicity and fanfare for IBM's turnaround went to Lou, and that is as it should be. He was the CEO; he did an amazing job taking out costs, right-sizing the company, and refocusing all of Big Blue on the customer. He also made that pivotal decision to hold the company together, and as a lifelong IBMer, I thank him for that. But it was our team, with our daring move from bipolar to CMOS and a new system structure, who made all that possible.

Our success had another very welcomed outcome, this time personal: I was finally named Corporate Vice President. Not only that, Lou created an opening that allowed me to enter a new phase of my career just as IBM entered a new phase of its storied history. Always take the challenge, right?

*   *   *

These two "chapters" in my career—helping to create the "new" IBM by turning the much-troubled RS/6000 into a game-changing product that eventually led to IBM's supercomputing successes, and saving and revitalizing the "old" IBM mainframe so that it became one of the most critical elements of the Gerstner turnaround (not to mention a major contributor to both IBM and the globally-integrated economy's success over the last twenty-five-plus years)—represented leadership under extremely stressful circumstances.

Why was I the right leader for both of those situations? I am not perfect. I am flawed. And yet I got through both of those chapters of my life successfully.

When I consider that question, I do not believe there is a single answer, but a lot of key ingredients went into the mix.

First, my Italian upbringing, my Catholic upbringing, and what my mother and father taught me mattered. I am not an overly religious person, but I am a practicing Catholic. I believe, and I try to do right. I strive to be honest, candid, and open at all times. I try to look for the greater good, and I try to have faith that there are answers to the problems that I face. Thanks to my mother and father, I have always been focused on my free will and ability to make choices. I am bound and determined to exercise my free will to improve the common good.

Adding to this sort of "Old World" tool kit is my training as an engineer. I never let the technical upset me, and even though the myriad technical challenges we faced with CMOS, the RS/6000, and the mainframe were enormous, the engineer in me always believed there were answers to the problems that confronted us.

As an engineer, I could take big problems and break them into smaller pieces that I could more easily solve. I think that is what some people at IBM saw in me early on and why I kept getting important challenges one right after another.

While this problem-solving demeanor worked for me, I do not know if it existed in a lot of others at the time. Importantly, it gave me the courage of my convictions and the ability to say to a John Akers or a Lou Gerstner, "I know that this isn't the answer you were looking for, but it's the truth."

By the time my work on the mainframe was finished, I had been with IBM for over thirty years. My early years had been marked by diverse, challenging experiences that leaders like John Akers had thoughtfully found for me. I had good business training. I had gotten got to see a lot of the inner workings of the company up close. So by the time I was an operational leader charged with solving some of IBM's biggest challenges, I was not flying blind. I had a tool kit to call upon. I am forever grateful to the IBM Company for adding that tool kit to the raw materials I brought to them.

6

MOVING INTO
TOP MANAGEMENT

H ere is something that might surprise you: *IBM is the most successful technology company in history.* And arguably the most innovative.

IBM either invented or had a hand in just about every seminal computing technology of the past seventy years. The hard disk drive? IBM. DRAM Memory chips? IBM. Relational databases? IBM The floppy disk? IBM. The personal computer? You know who.

Or at least now you do.

It has always bothered me that IBM never received the credit it deserved for its leading-edge technology, its inventions, its record number of patents, or its culture of innovation.

And in June 1997, Lou Gerstner was steaming mad about this very real perception problem that dogged us. *BusinessWeek* magazine had just done a huge cover story on "The World's Greatest Labs." Its editors and reporters had spent entire days at IBM Research facilities in New York, California, and Switzerland, getting previews of everything in the pipeline and on the horizon. Our public relations people spent months working with them.

When the issue came out, across twenty-four pages, there was just one mention of IBM: "Still a research bulwark."

I remember reading the article and thinking, *Bulwark? Are you kidding me?*

But if I was mad, Lou Gerstner was livid. He called me down to his office that Friday morning and said, "Nick, this has to change. We have all this great stuff, and we're either not moving fast enough to get it into market, or we're not getting credit where credit is due. I need you to fix that."

Lou was asking me to take on an entirely new challenge, one that would span the entirety of the company. Lou's idea was to create a new role that would give me executive leadership of, among other things, IBM Research and our entire global technology community of more than 220,000 professionals.

In this new role, I would not be running a business anymore. I was graduating from the operational phase of my career. What Lou was envisioning for me was a more strategic and innovation-based role, and over the course of my final decade with IBM, this role evolved to allow me to venture far beyond anything I had already done in terms of creating value for the business.

And no, Lou did not create this role for me simply out of frustration over the *BusinessWeek* feature, although that may have been the final catalyst. As he began to think about the post-turnaround IBM, he understood that if the right person could be situated at the intersection of the business and the technology functions, he or she could play a key role for the company going forward.

Lou knew me as an engineer, a technologist, and an operational leader, but I had developed a reputation for sound business judgment, too. I had seen a lot in my IBM career and had the bona fides so that people thought, "He may not be hands-on anymore, but he actually understands things. He understands the value proposition. He understands how to solve problems. He understands that you start with the problem and not the answer."

Sam Palmisano: There are so many dimensions to running IBM—marketplace dimensions, geographic dimensions, portfolio dimensions. When you got into the portfolio or marketplace dimensions, Lou Gerstner was world class, but in the technology space, where all those things interact and we had to bring it all together, Nick had all those skills, which was very rare. A lot of people might have great engineering skills or great product skills, and sometimes they're right and sometimes they're wrong, but they're not as facile when it comes to the broader contexts of these things. Nick saw the big picture.

While it would take time for the role to fully evolve—nothing changes if nothing changes, after all—Lou's decision proved remarkably prescient as IBM emerged from its turnaround. My ability to see the big picture would prove valuable at this juncture in IBM's history.

The role went far beyond technology. I was participating in strategic conversations about every aspect of the IBM Company. Whether it was Services, Software, Hardware, Technology, or the PC business—even Corporate Communications and Human Resources—I began to provide guidance and direction to operational leaders and to senior management about where I saw the world going and how I thought each, by themselves and by working together, could best position IBM to win in that world.

In particular, I clicked with Sam Palmisano. We had worked together in John Akers's office years earlier, and we had continually bumped into each other as we both were rising in the company. Even though we came from different places and different spaces, we seemed to constantly end up in client situations together. We never saw each other as competition, but rather as colleagues and collaborators.

Sam Palmisano: Back in those days, I ran Services, then the PC business, and then I went back to Services. Then they put me in charge of the Hardware business, which was Servers, Storage, and Semiconductors. During this time, Nick had gone to work for Lou on strategy and integrating all the technical teams, which Nick did so well. In any of these roles, if I had an important meeting coming up, I'd often go to Nick and say, "I need you in here with me. I'm not a technologist. I can't do this without you."

And he was phenomenally helpful to me. We'd sit in the meetings together, and people would come in with whatever technological point of view that they might have. We were making massive investments in those days—billions of dollars—between semiconductors, storage, servers, and the businesses themselves, and Nick was a great partner of mine in my decision-making. He really steered me in the right direction. Nick and I just worked well together.

The reason it worked so well with Sam was that he knew his own strengths and weaknesses, I knew my own strengths and weaknesses, and we knew each other's strengths and weaknesses. It allowed for a very synergistic relationship.

It also could prove surprising at times. More than once, I found myself in client meetings with Sam trying to figure out what he had just committed us to and whether anybody could possibly deliver it! But usually, our different skill sets allowed us to come up with new and better ideas.

We began to collaborate even more when he took over the Server group several generations after I had run it. From time to time, I helped him make decisions, such as whether or not we should get into Linux. If he did not understand a technology matter, he would be on the phone with me saying, "What the heck am I doing, Nick? This doesn't make any sense."

I enjoyed my new role with Lou, and as he approached retirement, all of our business metrics—from revenue to net income to cash flow to earnings-per-share and return-on-equity—were at or near all-time highs. We were cranking out patents at truly unprecedented and historic rates. We expanded our Research and Development footprint to new countries and markets. Even our employee headcount was back to where it had been before the downsizing took place.

Lou had done a great job bringing IBM back from the brink, but there was still so much to be done. As the first "outsider" to ever lead IBM, Lou deeply believed that the path to IBM's future would need to be tightly linked to IBM's past. To build on all that we had accomplished over the previous decade—including literally saving the company—the torch needed to be passed back to an IBM "lifer," and that lifer turned out to be Sam Palmisano.

Lou succinctly captured the logic in his 2003 autobiography: "I was always an outsider. But that was my job. I know Sam Palmisano has an opportunity to make the connections to the past as I could never do. His challenge will be to make them without going backward."

I could not have been more excited about the opportunity that lay ahead of us.

Sam Palmisano: Lou understood that he needed people like Nick, Paul Horn (Research), Bill Zeitler (Servers), Steve Mills (Software), me, and a lot of other IBM veterans to succeed. He actually said to me one day, "Look, you guys are the natives with the maps. This place is a jungle. I have no idea where I am in this jungle. You have the map. I need your help to get me out of this jungle."

Lou fixed the place and cleaned it up and did what he needed to do as far as downsizing the company and then rightsizing it by building it back up again in different spaces. He was brilliant at doing it, but when it came to the day-to-day work, he pretty much let us do it.

He was a tough guy. There was never an easy day working for Lou Gerstner, but we all liked working for him. I know I did. Nick would say the same thing.

But now it was my turn, and I did intend in some ways to take us back to IBM's roots. And I knew if I was going to be successful, I needed Nick.

When Sam became CEO, there was some discussion about whether I should leave IBM. I was in my late fifties, had been Blue for nearly four decades, and let's face it—I was not getting the top job. Perhaps I could have been CEO for any number of major companies. Sam and I were very candid with each other, talked things through, and decided mutually that the best course for me was to stay and help him. I told him what role I could play.

He liked that. He knew what I was good at, and he knew that I would solve problems for him.

Almost immediately, he started giving me more and more responsibilities. I soon was named Executive Vice President—rarely used by IBM and with me becoming the only one in the company at the time—and my role within top management expanded in ways no one had considered previously.

> **Vijay Lund:** It wasn't that Lou didn't value Nick, but I just saw a different level of collaboration with Sam. They were different personalities, of course, but to Sam, Nick was an equal. Before he'd make a big decision, he'd tell his team, "Let's ask Nick what he thinks. Nick knows technology. Let's go talk to him."

> **Sam Palmisano:** Our partnership continued when I became CEO, and it continued until the day he retired. Even as CEO, I never went to a deep technical meeting without Nick. I wouldn't do it. I could handle the financial side and the marketing and sales sides, along with what I thought IBM should be versus what it had become because of our financial problems before Lou had come in and led the turnaround.
>
> But at the end of the day, we were a technology company. We were building the Services business and our Software business, but we were still fundamentally at the core a technology company driven off our hardware platform. And Nick was a great partner. He helped keep me straight as far as where I should invest or not invest, and what deals we should do or not do. He was at every meeting when it came to the technology side of IBM. I never went to one without Nick. I wouldn't do it. I would have been crazy to go alone.

> **Vijay Lund:** Nick started to provide guidance and direction to the company at large under Sam. Sam was a very intense leader, but even so, I saw Nick exercise his gentle hand even more than he had back

when I was with him in the mainframe days. He was engaged in big
conversations about products and services, and the stakes were high,
but I never saw Nick get angry. I saw him get frustrated a few times,
but never angry. He never pounded his fists or threw things around.
He was always a consummate professional.

Sam's working relationship with me was different from the ways in which
he interacted with everybody else because we knew each other so well. He
trusted me. I would describe things to him and make complex technological issues simple for him, and he would say, "Yes, that's what we'll do. Let's
do that, Nick."

There was another side to it, too. As Sam took control of the business, my
role at the intersection between business and technology took on greater
importance. I could create tremendous value for IBM if I could instill more
of a market mindset with the technical community and help them understand and better align around the needs of the business.

And that mindset required us to not only make decisions about where to
invest resources but also the really hard decisions about which parts of the
portfolio to jettison. These decisions would have huge implications financially, technologically, and emotionally for IBM and IBMers. They would
inform and impact our entire corporate culture.

The first major decision that Sam and I partnered on concerned the hard
drive business. IBM had invented the technology and were basically responsible for every major industry improvement in performance for four decades,
mirroring or even outpacing Moore's Law. But the market was becoming
increasingly commoditized. Sam knew what he wanted to do to solve the
problem, but he wanted to talk to me about it first, because of our tech community's emotional attachment to this business.

Sam Palmisano: We decided that we wanted to be in storage
systems but not in the drive business, because the drive business was
totally commoditizing. Before I did anything, though, I went to Nick

and said, "Look at the numbers. You can see where the business is headed. We can all see where it's headed. We've got to persuade the engineering community that we've got to get out of this business, because we can't do it without their buy-in."

Nick, of course, understood the economics of the business. Even if we had wanted to be one of the two or three survivors in that space, we'd still have a low-margin business by IBM terms. At the end of the day, we had to drive higher margins than our competitors. Nick agreed that getting out was the right thing to do, and it became his job to convince the people who had invented these incredible things.

I knew that this would be a decision that many within and around IBM would find stunning. I needed to carefully communicate our decision to sell the business to the people who had not only created the business, but who, only a few years earlier, had been awarded the US National Medal of Technology by President Clinton for doing so.

I knew they were thinking, "Nick, we invented the very first Winchester File Hard Disk Drive! We invented the entire business. The president had honored us for our achievements. And now you want to *sell* it?"

But it was very clear where the business was going, and there just were not going to be the margins that our business model demanded. Because I spoke the language of the technical community, and because I had their trust, I could help them understand why the deal was necessary. I could, and hopefully did, soften the blow.

Sam and I negotiated a deal directly with Etsuhiko Shoyama, who was then president of Hitachi. We worked with our leaders in Human Resources and Corporate Communications to ease the transition for the people who would be moving to Hitachi and for those who would remain in IBM. The day the deal was announced, we arranged for senior leaders, myself included, to visit every lab and facility that touched the disk drive business to talk directly to the employees. Hugs were given out and tears were shed, but at the end of the day, the employees thanked us for the candor, the empathy, and the human touch.

> **Sam Palmisano:** Our shareholders didn't want us to be in that business. They wanted us to drive up the value-chain with the stack to get to the higher-profitability kinds of things. But before we could do anything, Nick really had to bring along the technology teams and the research teams who had invented all these things and convince them that this was the right thing to do. And he did it. He had to do this sort of thing quite a bit.

> **Vijay Lund:** Nick had seen and done it all, and he loved technology so much that the entire technical community believed in him. If he told them something, they believed him. They had faith in him.

These were massive deals, and I valued this new role, even when I had to be the bearer of tough news. What I loved even more, though, was having the ability to be a mentor writ large for the entire IBM technical community—all 220,000 of them. Sam really encouraged me in this role, because he understood the power of a broad-based technical community that was energized by a common philosophy and commitment to creating value.

> **Vijay Lund:** There's no doubt that Nick was in his glory mentoring. People from all parts of the IBM Company wanted to be mentored by him, because the word had spread that Nick was someone you wanted to be mentored by. He was, and is, a genuine person who cares about who you are, and that makes a difference. But he was more than just a nice guy. Nick was very influential, too. People would sometimes refer to Nick as "The Godfather" because of how he wielded quiet influence, and that was even more true under Sam.

I took great pride in the fact that anyone would turn to me as a mentor, as someone trusted who could work with them on their problems, their careers, or any issues they faced. I always made the time to talk to the technical team—whether in large settings, small settings, or one-on-one. It was important to me. It was important for the individuals that I met. It was important for morale, particularly as Sam and I began to shape our vision for where IBM could go next.

GLOBAL INTEGRATION AND THE INNOVATION AGENDA

By 2004, I was in a position that allowed me to go far beyond anything I had done before in terms of impact, including the RS/6000 and the mainframe. My ideas around innovation were really gelling—it was all about delivering value. Innovation was becoming increasingly global in nature, increasingly multidisciplinary and collaborative—and I was in my element.

Around this time, Sam and I were starting to believe that the next step after what Lou had achieved was to integrate IBM on a global scale. Sam would eventually coin the phrase "The Globally Integrated Enterprise" to describe what we had in mind, and it was going to be a massive challenge to pull off with a company as large and complex as IBM.

This was not just about being "multinational" or even "international." This was about having one way of doing things, from technology to HR practices to marketing and sales, and everything in between—across more than 170 countries on six continents.

> **Sam Palmisano:** You can argue that Nick and I shared a point of view because we grew up in an IBM that was integrated at one point in time. Call it déjà vu if you want, because if you go back to the late 1960s and early 1970s when we were getting started, that's how IBM worked. People noticed where we were coming from and thought, These guys are going back to the past, but that was only part of it. What really drove us was a point of view that the way we could

differentiate ourselves and be unique in enterprise computing was through an integrated IBM.

With Sam at the helm, my job would be to integrate the technological side of the business, but we would need another player to reinvent the operational infrastructure of IBM. That job was about to fall to someone who had my unmitigated trust, and that was Linda Sanford, who had been so critical to saving the mainframe.

Linda Sanford: I was pulled out by Sam Palmisano. I had run the mainframe business after Nick, then I went to storage, and I was running sales when Palmisano pulled me out to lead the transformation of the workings of IBM.

Sam Palmisano: We had to persuade her to come and do this. She was making a lot of money and happy, and I told her, "I need you to do this big transformational job." She thought I was crazy, but I got her to buy into the vision.

The three of us began to meet to fine-tune the vision. Each of us believed that the idea of the Globally Integrated Enterprise was the way forward.

Sam Palmisano: We wanted to be the best there was at "Enterprise Computing." We weren't trying to be the coolest brand. We weren't trying to be like the iPhone in today's world, or the iPod back then. We weren't trying to be "cool." We wanted to solve large, complicated technology problems that no one else really could tackle. That was the driving vision, and we all bought into that, and I guess it was the IBM gene pool. Linda, Nick, and I all grew up in that world, and I think that's why we made a great team.

If integrating the company was not a big enough challenge in and of itself, it was further complicated by another hurdle that only longtime IBMers like the three of us could appreciate. Dating back to 1969, when Thomas J. Watson, Jr., was still at the helm, the United States government had launched what would become a thirteen-year-long antitrust suit against IBM.

We prevailed, but the experience left deep scars and forced us into ways of doing things that were less than optimal structurally, culturally, and financially for decades to come.

> **Sam Palmisano:** With the Justice Department suit, we created all these siloed businesses, because we knew that if we lost the suit, we were going to have to spin things off. So, Tom Watson and Frank Cary and all those guys created all these different lines of business. You had the AS/400 division. You had the Mainframe business. You had the RS/6000 business. Storage was a business. Printers was a business. You had the product-related services, and then later, professional services. And within each business, you had all these redundant functions.

The entire antitrust experience was very draining, and even when the government finally dropped its suit in 1982, we really never unraveled the distinct business lines. At the time, we were running on all cylinders and the most admired company in the world, thanks primarily to the System/360 and its successors. So, the urgency was not there.

But our tremendous margins and profitability masked the underlying inefficiencies from the silos, and that started to catch up with us in the late '80s and then especially during the near-death experience of the early '90s. Even with all that Lou Gerstner did to reshape IBM, we had never dealt with reintegrating the business operationally. We still had these lines of business—and even some new ones—built around their own self-contained business models. Sure, they were larger and more consolidated, but they were still self-contained in how they went to market and still supported their own development organizations and support staff. We needed to tear down the silos and become one IBM again.

> **Sam Palmisano:** We just felt that if you had a belief that the technology would continue to commoditize, and that you had to be in the solutions space, then the only way that we could uniquely differentiate ourselves was to integrate IBM—to put the best talent we had and all of our solutions in front of the client and the marketplace. That was the belief that led to the Globally Integrated Enterprise. We had to integrate IBM on a global scale. That was the strategic point of view and the driving principle that Nick, Linda, and I believed.

My primary role in activating this vision was through what I called the Innovation Agenda. My title had even been expanded to Executive Vice President, Innovation and Technology in order to deliberately and meaningfully emphasize what I was trying to accomplish.

If we were going to pull the IBM Company together, we had to help everyone understand that there was more to life than just technology and there was more to life than just inventing things. We had to demonstrate to every IBMer, regardless of role or level, that they had the ability to *innovate*. We were not going to just be a technology-based company, but a company that was creating value across the board.

An integrated IBM, focused on market-driven innovation, would be a value-creating powerhouse, and there were myriad ways to create that value. But to do so, we had to unleash the innovator in everyone, and to do that, we had a lot of reorganizing work to do.

> **Sam Palmisano:** Even though she thought I was crazy, Linda started to drive the cultural transformation of what we needed to do internally. I think she realizes today that that was much more impactful than just running the mainframe business or sales, but at the time, she had her work cut out for her.

Linda Sanford: How did our processes need to change? How could we enable people to come together—not just the technical guys coming up with the solutions, but working with our sales teams, working with our customers? How could we become horizontal? It required breaking down the vertical silos that all businesses were built on way back when, and enabling a much more horizontal, end-to-end, "through the eyes of the customer" engagement process. You could say things to people like, "You've got to work across the silos," but that's hard to do if you aren't organized to enable it. We literally needed to re-lay out our processes so that they were much more seamless and horizontal end-to-end.

Product, Software, and Hardware had to come closer together because we had to optimize around the platform, not optimize around the hardware or the pieces of software. We had to bring them together to come up with optimized solutions.

At the same time, we needed our team in Services—both consulting and technology services—to articulate and differentiate these hardware- and software-based solutions. We had to build and then bring all those capabilities together.

We also had to develop a go-to market model in which we no longer had dedicated specialists who only sold discrete offerings such as storage, databases, workstations, or mainframes. Instead, our people had to develop the skills needed to listen to clients and to understand their business in great detail so that we could deliver the right solutions to meet their needs.

Behind all of this, our management systems had to change. For example, we still did not have one global platform to support all of IBM in the back office. Our financial systems were all fragmented and segmented. We had to create a common back office to support and drive efficiencies and productivity. All of that fell on Linda.

Linda Sanford: As in the mainframe days, Nick and I again had to work very closely together. We started to look at the processes of the company, understand how they had worked for all these years, and then identify what needed to change. Our development processes were one of them, and that's where Nick and his unique and evolving take on innovation really took hold.

We had to rethink all the technology offerings we were creating around innovation and value, and nothing else. I can name any number of innovative things that have very little technology in them, that have almost no new thinking in them, that had very little discovery associated with them, but are true innovations because of the value they created by solving problems. There is no value in creating technology for technology's sake—it needs to create value to matter. That was the way the Watsons saw the world from the 1930s into the 1970s. That was the way my father saw the world, too. That was the way I saw the world. And that was how IBM was going to see the world again.

> **Bob Samson:** Nick created an agenda that forced the company to think horizontally. It sounds simple, but it was enormously complex, because the company was highly siloed. You've got the Hardware Group, the Software Group, Services, and even within those groups you've got subgroups. And your measurements always drove you back to your silo, and where the measurement goes, so goes the culture.
>
> Nick understood that better than anybody. He began illustrating for people that the power of IBM is not a vertical silo. It's a horizontal play.
>
> In other words, how do we stitch together multiple different components from different organizations to create a more profound Value Proposition for a client? How do you stitch together work in IBM Research, which was also siloed, and get people to think and share ideas horizontally? That's where real innovation occurred. At the core of what he was doing, that was it—forcing organizations

inside the company to think horizontally—because that's what would unlock the value of IBM.

Sam Palmisano: This was Nick's gift—he could see all facets of this massive undertaking. Many people with technology or engineering backgrounds are great product guys. You see them in industry today—young entrepreneurs who are phenomenal product guys— but they need to partner with someone. For every Steve Jobs, Bill Gates, or Mark Zuckerberg, you have, respectively, a Tim Cook, Steve Ballmer, and Sheryl Sandberg to complement their technical genius. Nick was one of the few guys who could see the engineering, product, and business sides with great clarity and communicate that vision clearly in his own unique way. Nick could see the total picture.

When everyone is working together around a shared understanding of what success looks like, you start to look at problems differently. You are better positioned to look deeply into the issues and then engage horizontally—leveraging your abilities, your underlying technologies, your understanding of the marketplace, your people—to see how you can unlock new and hidden value. That is how you solve problems. That is what I called innovation.

I had seen this approach work repeatedly throughout my career, but I still had to prove it to the IBM community. I had to prove it to the technical community. I had to convince them that innovation was more than being inventive, discovering things, or even creating new categories.

Linda Sanford: It was Nick who distinguished "invention" versus "innovation." He would make a point that we need both, but invention was coming up with a brand-new idea, something no one had ever thought of before. Innovation was also about newness, but it was about: how do you use this to solve problems you've never been able to solve before? And that distinction is very important.

In today's world, you need both, but more and more it's about innovating new solutions to problems that we haven't solved yet.

He was very articulate about the distinction between the two. He would say, "We need both. We need the PhD researchers who are the brilliant minds creating the next Einstein kind of a thing. But we equally and arguably more importantly need people who are using those inventions to solve some of the problems of the world."

That requires a collaborative approach, because you need a businessperson, a marketing person, and an everyday user all coming together to give their perspective on a particular problem and how you apply technology to solve it in an innovative way.

In later chapters, I write much more about how we shaped this innovative and collaborative mindset at IBM. For now, suffice to say that it was *the* key to creating the enterprise computing company we envisioned.

Sam Palmisano: Because Nick had that broad perspective, he could see these shifts in technology, and he could see the implications and the economics and its impact on IBM. So he went out to Research and he went to the product side of the business. He'd get all these people to buy in on why something was the right thing to do and not just for financial reasons. He had ways of getting them to collaborate, of forcing them to collaborate.

Much as Linda and I were mutually dependent, we needed the same mindset to be true for all IBMers. Innovation takes off like a rocket when nobody thinks that they can do it all by themselves. By partnering with colleagues to solve problems, with more minds at work, better solutions are created.

That became the Innovation Agenda in a nutshell. It became about integration. It became about bringing people together. It became about teamwork across all of IBM. And we drove that into the company piece by piece.

Sometimes very visible shifts in direction can be a powerful tool for sending strong signals to skeptical audiences—especially when it comes to rewards and recognition systems. With Sam's approval, Linda and I took a long, hard look at how we chose IBM Fellows, who are the very top of our technical community and a rare breed.

At the time, there were no more than fifty active IBM Fellows; people who had won Nobel Prizes, Turing Awards, and other distinctions for technological excellence. But truth be told, some of these people liked working in isolation. Some wanted little to do with the marketplace or customers, but this was not at all consistent with our understanding of innovation or our plans for a Globally Integrated Enterprise.

So, we looked at the selection criteria and the nomination process and asked ourselves whether the people that we were anointing as "the best of the best" were truly our best collaborators as well. It was no longer about coming up with a new invention, but more about the innovative impact that the technology was having on the world.

Word got out quickly. People saw which of their peers were being honored, and behaviors changed. And that allowed us to rethink everything from our development processes, our research priorities, our approach to engaging clients, and yes, our technical recognition programs.

We were better positioned to now drive that mindset—and the processes needed to enable that mindset—into the entire company so that we could solve problems that *only* IBM could solve. We did that by going horizontal, by becoming a globally integrated enterprise. None of us could have done it alone.

> **Sam Palmisano:** In technology, it's always been about the team. I know that when books are written it's always about the individual, because you can't sell books about a team. Nobody cares about a team in a book, so it has to be a Gates or a Jobs or Mark. That's what it seems to take to sell books. But the fact of the matter is, if you observe the industry, it always has been a team, because those skills

rarely exist in one person (although Nick had the ability to close that gap as much as anyone).

I did understand teamwork, and by this point, I had been managing and leading people for a long time, whether they be the small teams in Burlington or the turnround teams of the RS/6000 and mainframe. I had a reputation for being a collaborative leader, but now we were trying to create one truly global team of some 400,000 diverse people from around the world and to get them collaborating as much as possible while truly feeling a part of IBM. This was an entirely different ballgame that would require some new tools and approaches.

Sam Palmisano: And that led to all sorts of things like the ValuesJam, the InnovationJam, and other efforts we dreamed up to get everyone involved in enterprise-oriented innovation.

VALUES AND JAMMING

One of the things that really helped Sam, Linda, and me during this time-frame was an internal tool—really a methodology—that IBM had pioneered to engage our entire employee base in decision-making and direction-setting. Based on the concept of jazz musicians who may not even know each other coming together, playing their respective instruments, and creating something entirely new, we had started investing in "Jamming" back in July 1998, about a year after I took on the responsibility for corporate technology under Lou.

Our first "Jam" took place at IBM Research, with all seven of our global labs connected by videoconference technology. Everyone in Research, from interns to IBM Fellows, was asked to simultaneously brainstorm around the future of technology. Everyone was on equal footing, including Lou Gerstner, who surprised everyone by showing up and sitting in a conference room with startled interns!

By 2003, driven in large part by influential leaders on our Corporate Communications team such as Jon Iwata, Mike Wing, and David Yaun, seventy-two-hour Jams were taking place on IBM's corporate intranet and literally open to every employee in the company.

Shortly after he became CEO, Sam started asking his leadership team, "What does it mean to be an IBMer in the early 2000s? What are our values? What do we stand for?" The essence of IBM was deep in Sam's blood, in Linda's blood, and in my blood, but what about the blood of the new Big Blue talent spread all around the globe?

> **Sam Palmisano:** A bunch of us were sitting around one day, when I began to share that I felt that we needed to revisit the Value System of IBM. We couldn't go back to the Basic Beliefs (a pioneering code of ethics established by Thomas J Watson, Sr. in the 1930s). They were very simple principles—best service to the customer, be nice to your colleagues, etc. If we were moving forward by embracing our past, the idea was that we needed to at least recreate that value system, though not with me writing a book like Watson did. We decided that if we were going to try to reintegrate IBM, we needed values to integrate around.

I understood Sam's point, and in fact, there was precedence. Shortly before I spent my first summer at IBM, Watson Jr. had published a groundbreaking management book called *A Business and Its Beliefs* derived from a speech he had given. He took his father's values into the mid-'60s, and they became a mantra; something every IBMer from that era could recite unprompted:

- Have respect for the individual.
- Give the best customer service of any company in the world.
- Pursue all tasks with the idea that they can be accomplished in a superior fashion.

While I did not fully understand in my co-op days, these values, handed out by titans of industry, spoke directly to me, because they put into words my father's humble, hardworking approach to life. While he had never experienced the high-tech work environment where I would spend my career, he certainly did prepare me for it, and that was no accident.

Of course, the world had changed dramatically since my summers with my father and my early days with IBM. And just as Watson, Jr. had modified his father's original value statement, Sam now wanted to modify it again for the 2000s.

One of Sam's profound insights at the time was that the values could no longer be dictated from the top. People were just too smart and too cynical. For the new set of values to stick and take hold, they had to come from the bottom up and from IBMers the world over. The Jam approach was perfect for the task.

Sam sponsored it. Ginni Rometty, who headed our consulting business and who would later succeed Sam as IBM's CEO, played a key role. Paul Horn from Research and our technology team had to figure out how to make it all work. Jon Iwata, our senior vice president from Corporate Communications, had to free up resources, educate employees about what we were about to do, and drive participation from hundreds of thousands of people, many of whom did not speak English.

Sam Palmisano: We were in the early days of what we now call social media, and we had these online forums, and Nick was in there guiding the discussion and making sure the thing didn't spin too far out of control. It was classic Nick. I was in there responding. We were all in there. But Nick was just battling, making sure things didn't get headed too far down the wrong paths.

It was kind of a madhouse at first—I mean, hundreds of thousands of IBMers, 24/7 for three days, posting every minute in hundreds of different discussion threads. *Anyone* could start a discussion—and we encouraged them to do so. That said, we could not just let it turn into some glorified gripe session or a platform for someone advancing a pet project, and that is why, with the help of Linda, Jon, David, and others, I steered the Jam. It became a personal passion of mine to see this through, and in the end, it was a very constructive platform that led to a very clear and meaningful set of values.

As the Jam progressed, it became obvious that we would end up with three values to align with the three basic beliefs that we were replacing. It is almost wired into our DNA as IBMers: the power of threes! In the end, the new values emerged: Dedication to Every Client's Success, Innovation that Matters (for the Company and the World), and Trust and Personal Responsibility in all Relationships.

> **Sam Palmisano:** Nick literally was in there banging away, using his personal persuasion again. He was passionate about these things we had to do, and he would not let it go down a rat-hole of irrelevant commentary. That mattered because not only had we successfully created our new values, but the Executive Team was now sold on the value of Jams.

The great thing about these values, largely because of the way they were created, is that they were more than just corporate lip service. They were real. And while they linked us to our past by echoing the values the Watsons had articulated, these new values were aimed into our global future.

Still, the hard work around values was only beginning. Linda and her team now had to drive this value system down into every operation of IBM on a global scale. We had to instill it into everything we did and make it part of the behavior of every IBMer.

> **Sam Palmisano:** You could go anywhere in the world and employees knew our values. In fact, Harvard's Rosabeth Moss Kantor wanted to figure out, "Is this real or not?" She suspected it was just a typical quality campaign or something like that. So she went all over the

world and talked to IBMers, and they could rattle off their role in the value system, and she thought, *This is unbelievable. I've never seen anything like this before.*

There were a lot of people involved, and we worked hard on that first Jam. Sam's tales of our madcap adventures are true, but it ended up working great, even though for a while the train appeared to be headed off of the tracks.

One of the most powerful outcomes from ValuesJam was how it instilled a company-wide mandate around innovation. It wasn't just me and a small team talking about innovation alone now—it was 400,000-plus IBMers. We still had a lot of work to do to change the culture and instill confidence in every IBM innovator, but we were on our way. I loved the fact that our next global Jam, in 2006, was "InnovationJam."

> **Sam Palmisano:** I used to go to Research at least once a year, and this one particular time, I said, "Show me the things you're working on in the laboratories that will have the biggest impact on IBM and society." So they went through all this stuff that they had, and I left there all fired up and all excited. I came back to my office and found Nick. I said, "This is incredible stuff. We've got to get all of IBM to participate in how we should apply this stuff."

It was remarkable—the chairman of IBM was so engaged that he set this decree—we were going to do another Jam. "What we'll do is set aside this pot of money, and our employees can give us ideas about what we can do with all this great technology that we have in our labs. It's going to be great!"

For once, I was the voice of caution: "Sam, we've got to think about this. First of all, we never disclose our emerging technology to anybody—including employees."

"Yup. That's true, Nick."

"Second of all, these things aren't ready for people to understand. They have to understand it to apply it in any way that's meaningful."

Sam was not deterred. "That's the point, Nick. We're going to have to train them. This is what they're going to learn. We're going to teach them about what we have and why it matters."

By that point, Sam literally was jumping up and down. He is a big man—probably 6′ 4″—so it was quite the picture. He was all wired up, and I remember him exclaiming, "That's the whole thing, Nick. We're going to be open with our approach, figure this thing out, and play with this stuff. Let's even invite clients to join us. We have to do this ASAP because we can't figure out how to apply all this great stuff until everyone plays with it. If everyone Jams, they'll come back with these great ideas."

And, just to make it more daunting, he asked me to sponsor the Jam, chair a committee with the finance guys, and manage our investment in the best ideas.

He then asked me, "How much do we need to invest for people to take me seriously here?"

I replied, "I don't know. Maybe $100 million?"

He said, "You got it. Go do it."

He did not pause for a second.

So, the idea for InnovationJam was born, and I sponsored it. My role was to figure out, along with Paul Horn, how to run it from a technology and operational perspective, and Jon Iwata and David Yaun did an amazing job designing it and getting people—including people from dozens of external client organizations—to participate. And Sam gave us something like eight weeks to pull it off.

More than 40,000 new ideas later, we used a combination of natural language processing and good old-fashioned conversation to narrow in on a Top 10 list of potential innovations. I managed their development, funded them with Sam's $100,000,000, and resolved them into the company's business flow over the next twelve to eighteen months.

Within three years, we had over $1 billion in incremental revenues from these ideas alone. The momentum continued even after I graduated from IBM in 2008.

Sam Palmisano: To Nick's credit, since I'm sure he thought I was completely whacked out that first day, he figured out how to do it all. We had to figure out how to present the technology so that people actually could work with it, figure out what it did, and then create proposals and prototypes and a business case for why we should invest in some of these ideas. We did Smarter Traffic in Stockholm. There was an idea around micro-banking in the emerging countries. A third idea focused on diagnostic systems in healthcare.

I'm sure there were some ideas in there that were bombs, but nonetheless, the InnovationJam solutions that Nick drove led to a lot of the solutions that we later launched with Smarter Planet, the most successful marketing campaign we had ever run in the history of IBM. It won every award the following year, and in the terrible economic environment of 2009–2010, we actually were growing. It's hard to imagine. Everybody was getting killed, but we were having record years.

David Yaun (*Former IBM Vice President, Technology and Innovation Communications*)**:** Sam Palmisano was the right leader for the post-Gerstner IBM. But he needed a wingman. He needed someone to handle cultural transformation, to handle policy and the folks in DC, and to drive this whole concept of innovation day-to-day. What was really interesting is that he let Nick play "good cop." This partnership drove a renaissance for IBM from 2006 to 2012. Our financial performance was great, but we were also showing up not just on lists of the "World's Most Innovative Companies," but topping them. The best technology people in the world wanted to work with IBM—and at IBM—in a way that we hadn't seen in decades.

In these years, Nick had free rein to reestablish IBM as an innovation powerhouse—not just a technological innovator, but a cultural innovator, a policy innovator, and a place where people could innovate regardless of their role. Sam gave Nick the longest possible leash imaginable, and Nick ran with it. Nick and Jon Iwata did the same with me. IBM would not have hit that renaissance if Nick hadn't been the visionary and driving force behind our culture of innovation. And I'm grateful that I got a chance to work so closely with him on these projects and that I was able leave my own little mark on IBM history, too.

Sam Palmisano: Nick and I were a great partnership, there's no doubt about it. I think people underestimate the amount of effort that went into creating this enterprise-tech company. We went back to our roots. We had created the modern banking system. We invented the UPC and point-of-sale devices. Go back in time, and all those things that we did were all enterprise tech, and so we believed, "That's how we'll differentiate ourselves again." It worked. It clearly worked for a long time. And I could never have been successful— and I'll be the first to admit it—without Nick.

I was there for about half of Sam's tenure, before graduating in late 2008. It is difficult for me to say, but I think history backs me up here: the balance of power in decision making changed around that time.

Maybe I should not have left. Maybe I should have stayed. Maybe things could have been different. Did I do all the right things and put all the right people in place before I left? Maybe I did, maybe I did not. I know I did not get everything right. No one ever does.

But Sam and I were a great team in those years. I respected him, he respected me. I trusted him, he trusted me. I could not have asked for more.

7

WORKING WITH THE GOVERNMENT

THE BEGINNINGS OF ARTIFICIAL INTELLIGENCE

While IBM's first name is, indeed, "International," and over the past two decades it has operated as a Globally Integrated Enterprise, it is also, obviously, a US-based company headquartered in New York State. Not surprisingly, the US federal government has been one of IBM's largest clients for decades, and the relationship between the two is crucial to both parties.

Over the past century, many of the most significant government accomplishments were undertaken with IBM as a technology partner. When the US Social Security Act was passed in 1935, government record-keeping skyrocketed in terms of volume and complexity. The Roosevelt administration turned to Thomas Watson, Sr. and the IBM Corporation to undertake what was then considered the "biggest bookkeeping job" ever.

IBM's punch card equipment was used to create and maintain employment records for an employee population of 27 million Americans, a major moment in IBM history. Three decades later, IBM computing technology helped NASA safely and accurately land astronauts on the moon.

My positions at IBM afforded me the opportunity to work with the US government on numerous rewarding projects, both large and small. As with every aspect of my IBM career, things started small and ramped up over time.

Chris Caine (*Twenty-four-year IBM Veteran, Former IBM Vice President, Governmental Programs*): In 1984, I came to work for IBM in the Governmental Programs Office. I entered doing state government relations, and around the 1987-88 timeframe, I went to Nick and asked him—given his Vermont experience—to work with members of Congress from the Vermont delegation, and a couple of others, and he willingly agreed. Nick played a role in a program that was basically a grassroots lobbying network of IBM executives from around the country. Essentially there was a desire to have one voice, or a personification of the company, so the company could better relate to elected officials at all levels of government, and Nick was the Senior State Executive for the State of Vermont.

I knew our relationship with the government mattered greatly to the bottom line, but I also truly believed IBM had a role and responsibility to help make the country and the world a better place in ways that transcended any short-term profit considerations. To me, it was not just the right way to do business, it was the only way. I wanted to do whatever I could to ensure that IBM was seen as a commercial partner that the government could trust, particularly as the pace of technological change accelerated.

Chris Caine: Nick's initial role was about explaining the IBM Company and our values to the outside world and getting elected officials to be partners with us on distinct public policy issues that mattered. He was always very open, acceptable, and agreeable to helping in any way he could. I think that just typifies his personality. After that first Vermont-oriented experience, our relationship grew more extensive and deeper and broader, including, but not limited

to, a period of time when he led IBM Government Programs, and I
reported to him.

Anne Altman (*Thirty-five-year IBM Veteran, GM Global Public Sector,
GM Mainframe/System Z, GM US Federal & Government Industries*):
Perhaps more than any other senior executive, Nick's commitment
to our nation was most visible through his engagement. He's very
proud of his Italian heritage, and there is no question that he is so
proud of being an American. That includes service to his country,
being active in political issues that matter, and supporting the good
work of our government, military, and civil servants. He's just very
passionate about that.

Chris Caine: By definition, Nick personified IBM's technical
excellence. It was very important for the company to have somebody
who could personify that with unquestioned credentials and judgment
and decision-making capabilities with the outside world, whether
it was universities, the government as a customer, the government
as a policy maker, the government as an investor, or economic
development officials trying to figure out how to invest and create
value in the future for the betterment of a community's members, as
well as for economic growth. Nick really typified all of that.

My efforts with the federal government really accelerated in the years
following the successful launch of the RS/6000 and the evolution of the
underlying technology. Of all the work that I eventually did with government partners, perhaps none was as important as the efforts I initiated in
this area.

As we entered the 1990s, a global race to dominate what was being chris-
tened as "supercomputing"—massively powerful computers that would
provide any country or business with an incredible competitive advantage
over others—had begun. My passion to advance IBM's leadership in this

realm, especially in partnership with the US government, earned me the nickname "Godfather of the Supercomputer" with many of my colleagues. As with all of my IBM accomplishments, it was less me than it was a team effort, but I am very proud of our supercomputing work, which is still paying off for the country—and for IBM—to this day.

In particular, I am referring to work that we did to help define and advance the Department of Energy's Accelerated Strategic Computing Initiative, better known as ASCI. The ASCI story began one day for me with a phone call I received from a man named Vic Reis.

As I would soon learn, Vic had some serious bona fides. An undergraduate from my alma mater, RPI, Vic also had earned an MS from Yale and a PhD from Princeton before launching his career. After early success at MIT's Lincoln Lab, he became Assistant Director for National Security and Space in the Office of Science and Technology Policy in the Executive Office of the President during President Reagan's first term. Later, he enjoyed stints as Senior Vice President with Science Applications International Corporation (SAIC), as Director of Defense Advanced Research Projects Agency (DARPA) during the George H. W. Bush Administration, and as Director of Defense Research and Engineering at the US Department of Defense.

By 1993, Vic was serving as Assistant Secretary for Defense Programs in the US Department of Energy, which is when I first spoke with him. Vic had an incredible challenge he needed to solve, literally for the good of humankind.

Vic Reis *(Technologist and Former US Government Official; Architect and Sponsor of the US Nuclear Stockpile Stewardship Program)*: When the administration changed from George H. W. Bush to Bill Clinton, I suddenly ended up in the Department of Energy running their Nuclear Weapons Program. President Clinton had said that he would seek a Comprehensive Test Ban Treaty, continue a moratorium on nuclear underground testing, and, "To assure that our nuclear deterrent remains unquestioned under a test ban, we will explore other means of maintaining our confidence in the safety, the reliability, and the performance of our own weapons." The "other means" was left to DOE and the National Labs to figure out, and it seemed to us that the only way to do this was experimentally-validated predictive simulation. We did some analysis, and the big unknown was in computing power. I had some understanding of parallel computing dating back to my time leading DARPA, and I knew that we had to get about a factor of 100,000 more computer power in about ten years if we were to meet the president's goal.

Well, at that point, I really felt we had to get IBM involved. They were the big computer guys. I felt we needed a company that was the big gorilla in computing. The only person I knew who had connections into the highest levels of IBM was former Secretary of Defense Harold Brown, who was on their board. I went to see him, gave him the backstory, and he said, "Oh, you should call Nick Donofrio."

At around the time Vic called, we had just created our first supercomputer, the Scalable POWERparallel system, better-known as the SP1. Emerging directly out of the RS/6000 effort, SP1 was a parallel supercomputer—essentially a cluster of RS/6000s—introduced in February 1993.

Naturally, at IBM, we knew we were going to enter the supercomputing business. We knew that we needed to be in this market and making these systems. We knew what these systems were going to be capable of doing, with SP1 being only the beginning. What we lacked at that point in time was the right opportunity and the right real-world problem to show the world what IBM could do.

Well, when Vic called, it seemed like he was putting that opportunity right in my lap. Right from the get-go, my immediate thought was, *You have got to be kidding me—that is a great problem! We are going to do this!*

We decided to meet in person to discuss it in more detail. When we got together, Vic had himself all pumped up. He knew what he needed. He explained how the idea of a very specialized computer that is only useful for the military did not work, because for one, they could not afford it. But if a partner who saw commercial potential in parallel computing could team with them, then perhaps it could be a win-win.

He showed me their roadmap. They had mapped out the amount of computing power they would need to be able to do the simulation work, and Vic was no slouch. He knew what was going on, but he could not get it done without a partner.

I immediately thought, *Of course we can do this. This makes so much sense. Why would we explode nuclear weapons if there is a better way?*

Vic Reis: I explained my idea that we could work on this military problem together, develop this computer that met my needs and that of the United States, but then leave IBM with all of this parallel computing experience to pursue their own goals. We weren't interested in telling them how to do the commercial work, but we needed them for the nuclear stockpile. And I think that's where Nick's leadership really came in to play. He really believed in my idea.

When Vic finished his pitch, I said, "Okay. What do you really need here? What kind of a partnership are you looking for with us?"

He explained that they wanted to create three procurements, in each case teaming a computer company with one of their labs, each of which had been developing different codes and different experimental devices with which they were going to test the codes.

In Vic's mind, they would not be pitting the corporate/lab teams against one another, but instead, would be hoping that we each would succeed and create applications to not only solve the challenge of nuclear simulations, but other military applications, as well. He envisioned that IBM, along with Intel and Silicon Graphics, would be the commercial players.

I told him I did not have any desire to do anything with the others, but Vic said, "I can't do it just with IBM. I have to do it with others, too." I understood his position and appreciated his transparency.

After the meeting, I went back to Armonk and briefed Lou Gerstner. At this point, I was not asking him to commit IBM, but he sensed my enthusiasm. At the same time, I could tell from what Lou was saying that Harold Brown already had talked to him and that he understood the potential opportunity without me having to say too much.

The next step was for Vic and me to circle back and talk with Harold directly. I will never forget this meeting—we sat and waited for Harold in the uncomfortable chairs of an indoor swimming pool waiting area, sweating through our suits and ties while he did laps! He finally got out of the pool and gave us a pep talk. There was no doubt in his mind that Vic's plan was the right approach. Harold turned to me and said, "Nick, you have to do this. You have to help us. We've got to get IBM behind this."

This time when I went back to Lou, I said, "We're going to have to step up here. We don't need to spend any more money than we normally might spend, but we have to commit ourselves to the Nuclear Stockpile Stewardship. And they're not just asking for work now, but for a real commitment. They have a ten-year roadmap, and once we start, we can't back out."

Lou was kind of reluctant to do that. Nobody in business likes to make multi-year commitments. I promised him that this commitment would not scorch the Earth for us, so he gave me the go-ahead, though not without warning me, "Just don't lose a lot of money."

To this point, high-performance computing was notorious for losing money, but Lou and I both knew this was our way forward. He knew that we were going to make ASCI part of our business model and that we were going to make sense out of supercomputing in ways that we had not in the past.

I set up a meeting for Vic and his team to come to IBM Headquarters, where maybe a half dozen or so people from IBM Research gathered to hear his thoughts. Given the importance of this effort, Lou agreed to attend as well.

Vic Reis: By the time I went up to New York for the meeting, I had been able to pull about $80 million out of the budget to build a machine. We were going to have a competitive bid for the beginning stage. I took two or three people from my labs, and we waited to begin. I think some of Nick's researchers were pretty skeptical about the whole thing.

Finally, Gerstner walks in, and people are respectful, and I gave him this little pitch about what we were trying to do with nuclear weapons and the level of our computing needs, and why we think parallel computing is the way to go. Gerstner looks around, and he very colorfully says, "IBM is a big iron business. And this is the biggest iron around. This could be our Apollo program. You guys win this."

And then he walked out. There was this somewhat stunned silence. Frankly, I think Nick had figured all that out ahead of time and planted it with Gerstner. I never talked to Nick about it, but I think it was somewhat staged. Either way, by God, Lou Gerstner had made himself clear.

I understood the bottom line, and I knew as well as anyone that Lou Gerstner was a bottom-line guy like few others. But I understood the bigger picture, too, and obviously so did Lou.

Here we had the opportunity to help the United States and others eliminate the need for actual tests of their nuclear stockpiles through simulation. We also had the opportunity to validate the efforts in parallel computing that we had been making by leveraging "clusters" of RS/6000s. God bless Harold Brown for having seen the potential, because once again, not everyone within IBM could see the big picture at the time.

Bob Samson: This was a national imperative, but inside IBM, there were a lot of forces suggesting that we not even be involved in that business. They'd ask, "Why on earth are we doing that?" It was analogous to the RS/6000 in its early stages. Nick was the cheerleader, because he saw where we could go with this thing, and once again, he worked to fend off the naysayers.

Nick always looked at the federal team as a place where you really could create an agenda of innovation, because the federal government had money, and in the right situations, you could build scale quickly, since that's what they typically needed. Given the opportunity to scale, you could test different ideas, new paradigms, and new solutions in that world first. It gave Nick a chance to have a little sandbox for innovation.

While I had absolute clarity on how this was all going to work, the fact of the matter is, I did not have immediate line control over a particular product group to make this happen. I had to influence others to do what needed to be done, whether they sat in Research or on my former RS/6000 team, which by this time was known as the System P team.

Bob Samson: It wasn't the normal paradigm of, "Let's have this division work on that." This was not a traditional product development paradigm. For this project, Nick was engaging technical people and researchers at a level that no one else had the credibility to do. He was stitching together people that he knew who were brilliant, taking them from other parts of the company, and bringing them together to work on IBM's High-Performance Computing initiative. Nick just knew the people.

I not only knew the people, I knew *the* person—Tilak Agerwala, my trusted partner from the RS/6000 days—I needed to help me pull this off. Thankfully I was able to bring him on board.

Up until this point in time, supercomputing had been dominated by what was known as vector machines. A vector processor is a central processing unit (CPU) that implements an instruction set where its instructions are designed to operate efficiently and effectively on large one-dimensional arrays of data called vectors. Vector machines had appeared in the early 1970s and dominated supercomputer design through the 1970s and into the 1990s, most notably the various Cray platforms.

For years, however, Tilak had been advocating a different way forward. He believed that everything—from the RS/6000 workstation he helped create all the way up to supercomputers—was going to move away from vectors and toward parallel computing. The SP1 had been a first step toward this vision, but we had a long way to go before we could solve problems of the scale and scope Vic required.

> **Tilak Agerwala:** My team believed that collections of clusters of RS/6000 nodes could, in fact, handle the vast majority of workloads that a Cray Supercomputer could if they were run in a throughput kind of manner, since capacity was important in addition to just capability.

We set Tilak and his team up, almost as a skunkworks, in Kingston, New York, to see what they could do with their ideas. By 1994, they had delivered the SP2 supercomputer, which was a paradigm changer, because it represented the transition point from vector supercomputers to parallel cluster supercomputers, which is exactly what Vic had in mind for the ASCI supercomputer and why I had been so excited when I received his initial phone call.

To give some perspective, in 1994, we placed an SP2 capable of performing 136 billion calculations per second with The Cornell Theory Center. At the time, it was the world's fastest and most powerful general-purpose supercomputer. Vic's challenge, which we officially committed to only two years later in 1996, was to build a supercomputer capable of performing more than three trillion calculations per second. So while we were on our way with our parallel cluster supercomputers, the journey would be long.

> **Tilak Agerwala:** We committed to the Department of Energy's Lawrence Livermore National Laboratory to build a supercomputer which would be a massive 100 teraflops. That's what it was going to take to ensure the reliability of their simulated tests of the nuclear stockpile, given the Nuclear Test Ban.

Vic gave us the problem, and as we started to understand it better, we designed a general-purpose computer that could solve for his needs. We had an approach that made sense, and we started to get a rhythm and flow.

Anne Altman: Nick knew all the people who were developing this system. He knew the people who were developing the code and the computing capability. He knew the architects on my team and in Research. He knew the leadership and the pioneering talent in the national labs. He knew everyone! There were times when the entire team would seem to lock horns, and Nick would step in to say, "I know you can do this, so just do it. Don't tell me all the problems around it. Just do it. You can do this."

I had to keep my team focused, because the national labs always thought they had better ideas. They thought they could build better computers than we could. While we needed their problem to build our systems and welcomed their ideas and thoughts about systems, it ultimately was our job to build the supercomputer, and my job to ensure that was understood.

Working out a partnership between very, very bright and intense people is never easy. I tried hard to define the roles we should and would play as members of the same team.

In effect, I had to be a diplomat and try to keep both teams on an even keel. I would listen to my team and then go spar with Vic. I kept saying to Vic, "Do me a favor—promise me you won't tell me how to design computers, and I promise you I won't try to tell you how to design bombs. I'll build you the computers you need; just don't tell me how to build them."

Vic Reis: Nick would come to me and say, "Well, you've got some really talented computer people working at Livermore, but at some point, I'm going to have to tell them, 'We're not going to tell you how to build nuclear weapons. Don't tell us how to build the computer.'"

That was a good line, but in truth, there really was a developmental partnership that grew between Livermore and IBM. And the main guy in developing all of that from the IBM perspective was Nick. I think his ability to put the right type of people from IBM on to interface with the Livermore guys over time is the story.

We knew we could do it, but that did not mean it would be easy. It was a difficult project, and it was not long before we were behind schedule.

Anne Altman: For Nick, failure was not an option, as the saying goes, and that's the way he led our team. We had regular updates on our progress, which sometimes meant saying, "We're having difficulties with this or that," and at one point, we were having some sticky problems and had fallen well behind schedule. Among our concerns was how to communicate our schedule slippage to Lawrence Livermore National Laboratory. We were anticipating a volcanic reaction once this was exposed.

I took a few deep breaths, briefed Nick, and waited. And Nick, like only Nick can do, gave me his unambiguous response. He said, "This program is not a purchase of a system. It is not a purchase of hardware. It is a partnership between the United States Government, with a critical mission, and an industry partner that's willing to elevate the success of the partnership above any individual success."

That was his passion. He was looking well beyond our concerns of the moment toward the incredible mission we had undertaken, which I think gave him the perspective to see things differently. I remember him saying, "It may be unpleasant, but we're going to talk to the client. We're going to do it. We're going to be fast. We're going to be open. And we're going to work with them to develop a Recovery Plan in the best interests of both of us." And that's what he did.

Vic Reis: Nick was easy to work with, and part of it was he was very straightforward on things. You always knew where you stood. He also had tremendous character. I never heard Nick say anything bad about anybody else. I had dealt with many contractors in the past, and there always was a certain tendency for each to tell me bad things about the other company. I never heard any of that from Nick. We just happened to get along very well, and I had great trust in his leadership.

I would say to Vic, "I am not building anything special for you. I am not going to build you $50,000 toilet bowl seats or $25,000 wrenches. That's not who we are. I am going to build you a general-purpose computer that solves your problems, and then I am going to go elsewhere and commercialize it. It's going to solve problems other than just the ones that you're talking about. I'll be the honest broker, and tell you, 'No, we're not doing that. We can't put that instruction in because nobody else wants it that way.'"

At the same time, Lou was greatly worried that I would fall victim to these pressures and make all sorts of special promises to keep us in business with them. There was a lot of tension to balance in these situations, but it was something Vic and I worked on constantly. We had open lines of communication between us, and that fostered trust.

Vic Reis: We didn't just say, "Here's a spec. Design the spec. Here's the money." There was a lot of real partnership in terms of development.

Tilak Agerwala: It was an iterative process, and it required very powerful people like Nick and Vic to keep things going. We entered into this partnership with Livermore, and we pushed that original SP2 technology until we could solve their mission-critical problem for how to certify the safety of the nuclear stockpile. It was a balancing act between staying in scope while changing the paradigm for the future, and taking that risk is where a lot of the innovation actually lies.

Together, we were able to make it all happen. IBM signed up for a huge challenge, and in the end, history was made. In all honesty, I do not know how it would have worked out without IBM's involvement. I am not saying it couldn't have gotten done without us, but it is dubious.

We have every reason to be proud of what we achieved. We have a history there. I am proud that I was able to be part of it. I am proud of the work we did, and the people whom we worked with on ASCI. Clearly with the origins of my work in this arena, with Vic, who is a national icon, and Harold Brown, who was a national icon, why would I not be?

Vic Reis: I gave a talk when we celebrated achieving our goal and said that getting IBM and Livermore to work together was sort of like film critic Pauline Kael's description of Ginger Rogers and Fred Astaire getting together in movies: "He brought her class, and she brought him glamour." That got a little bit of a laugh—but I didn't say who was who!

But it was a question of two very different styles of operation and two very different cultures. How we came to work together and deliver a product of this importance was no small task, and the guy who sat on top of that was Nick. Frankly, I had confidence that he could deliver. IBM delivered, of course, but Nick was the right person for that role.

Anne Altman: Nick was always committed. He listened. He didn't cut us short. And as a result, I think he made many other great leaders within that team, because people wanted to emulate his leadership style. It was perhaps for Nick his finest hour with the program, and a few years later, Nick received the United States National Nuclear Security Administration's Gold Medal. It was the first time that the Gold Medal has ever been presented to a non-government employee. It just doesn't happen, and he got the Gold Medal from the Department of Energy!

I take particular pride in that award, given to me by Secretary of Energy Samuel Bodman, because the Department of Energy had never before recognized the contributions of a civilian in that way. To be the first—me, that little kid from Beacon who was told, "If nothing changes, nothing changes"—well, it meant a lot, and I still take the medal out every once in a while to look at it just to be sure it really happened.

I know exactly what it says: "For distinguished service, awarded to Nicholas M. Donofrio. September 2009." And on its back is the National Nuclear Security Administration symbol.

I believe the ASCI achievement was just as important for IBM. To me, our collaboration with Vic and the NNSA truly encapsulates IBM's core value of "Innovation that matters—for our company and for the world." I have nothing but the greatest admiration for Vic and Harold for their commitment to IBM, the opportunity that they provided to us, and the vision that we shared.

Chris Caine: I would think everybody would agree that it was in the world's interest not to have the Soviet Union and the United States doing physical nuclear tests. That would have an effect on the environment and all kinds of other things, and that's what the High-Performance Computing Initiative was all about. It was able to achieve that societal objective, yet at the same time, not abandon the national security needs and imperatives of our country. Not very many Americans knew about that nor understood it if they knew it, of what the reach or the implications of that were. And it was really done by these two guys—one named Vic Reis and one named Nick Donofrio—bringing their respective organizations together to achieve this objective.

Sam Palmisano: This willingness to take big risks with IBM's reputation to help friendly governments is what drove the whole thing. Nick worked very, very closely with governments around the world, especially in this space they call "the Friendly Nations"— basically NATO and Japan—and fundamentally, he drove a lot of these projects that created all these very, very advanced systems for scientific laboratories like the Lawrence Livermore Labs. He was the IBM person who worked with government entities to create these technologies.

Anne Altman: As a senior leader, especially with the government, he had three principles with which he led: (1) Is it the right thing to do for IBM? (2) Is it the right thing to do for the client? (3) Is this in America's national interest?

Following our initial effort, we continued to work with the Department of Energy on subsequent versions of ASCI, and we continued to evolve our supercomputing offerings. And just as Vic had anticipated, we continued to push further into the supercomputing business.

Our researchers had a million ideas. The problem was, I was not interested in an idea a minute. That is not how you make money. That is not what real innovation is about. But Tilak was a good partner. He understood that if you could clearly define the problem that actually needed to be solved, we could take on any one of these massive challenges.

Tilak Agerwala: As it had been with the RS/6000, within a couple of years, we had built our supercomputing efforts into a billion-dollar business. And then late in 1999, we realized that we needed another paradigm shift.

We began to reach out to other sectors with massive data-intensive challenges, because we knew that we could apply what we had learned working with the national labs. It was just another manifestation of innovation—putting together the right pieces to solve real-world problems.

A natural focus area was medicine, pharmaceuticals, and healthcare. We began a dialogue with leaders in this space and convinced them that we knew what we were talking about and that we could help them. But we didn't want to play small ball.

Consistent with Lou's colorful Apollo analogy around ASCI and our vision of taking on grand challenges and doing big things that only we could do, IBM announced in December 1999 a $100-million research initiative to build a massively parallel computer that could be used in the study of bio-molecular phenomena such as protein folding. And to show just how serious we were about the initiative, we gave ourselves a five-year timetable to build this computer.

The project was named Blue Gene, given its initial goal of helping biologists understand the processes of protein folding and gene development. In addition to the biological application, we wanted to keep developing our massively parallel machine architecture and software, just as we had been doing with the ASCI program. And we wanted to do it in a cost-effective way.

That is what Blue Gene was all about. We were going to solve real problems—really difficult ones—and we would learn as we solved those real problems. That is value creation.

Taking such leaps of faith came down to understanding the problems at their core, aligning the right talent around them, and asking that talent to do things better than they had ever been done before.

Tilak Agerwala: Around 2000, I returned to Research, where the Blue Gene Project was taking shape. I was leading all of the Systems "Advanced Technology Development" at that point. I remember very distinctly Nick telling me, "Tilak, I want us to be the first to get to a petaflop. I don't know if Blue Gene is the right answer or not. You decide. If it's the right thing, we'll build it. If it's the wrong thing, tell

me what the right thing is, but you've got to get us to a petaflop. I
want to be the first in the world to get there.

While it is a rather esoteric concept outside of deep computing circles,
"flop" refers to the number of floating-point operations that a computer can
process in one second. "Peta" is basically ten to the power of fifteen, which
is a heck of a lot of zeroes, and at the time, was a heck of a lot more than
any computer could handle. At the time that Blue Gene was announced, the
best performance was roughly two teraflops, or about 1/500th of the capacity that we were looking for in this computer. And yet we told the world we
would close the gap in five years! I knew it was possible. I knew it would be
difficult, but I knew that we could get there.

As with the Stockpile Stewardship Program, I understood the prestige,
profit opportunities, and mission-critical elements of getting to a petaflop.
The United States had fallen behind Japan in supercomputing, and I believed
that IBM had a responsibility to help the country take the title back.

Sam Palmisano: Today you've got all these technologies and all
of this capacity given away for free on clouds, but in those days
you didn't. We were proposing these massive machines that were
probably going to cost us $50 to $60 million to build, and we didn't
know if they were going to work. And even if we could get them to
work, we didn't know if the five-year roadmap could get us there.
But Nick was passionate in this area, because (a) he believed this
was the future of computing, and (b) if we could create this capacity
at a low enough price point, we could solve a lot of problems that
nobody had been able to solve before, not just in terms of modeling
and engineering design, but healthcare. It's just beginning to come
to fruition today, with the mapping of the genome and personalized
medicine, but none of that was possible without massive computing
capacity, and Nick wanted to see it happen.

Tilak Agerwala: Blue Gene was a complete paradigm shift. Remember, we had just achieved 100 teraflops. Now we were trying to get to a petaflop, but Nick's words were enough ammunition for me! This machine was based on the paradigm that we are going to gang together very cost-effective, power-efficient processors and actually go down to the embedded-processor technology.

Paul Horn (*Former IBM Senior Vice President, Executive Director of Research, 1995–2007*): What Nick did so well was help create the culture—the freedom and protection for the Research Division— that allowed us to do wacky stuff that sometimes worked and sometimes didn't. He helped create a culture that let Research do both incremental development as well as "far out" projects. With Blue Gene, we connected on a home run.

Despite Blue Gene's genesis in computational biology, remember my original thesis—we did not want to build computers for the sake of building computers. That is not a great idea. Building computers because you have a problem to solve is a better idea. That thinking really stuck with me from the ASCI program—we take real problems, and we solve them.

To me, that is innovation, and as the years went on, I would teach the IBM technical community to think this way. This is how we did Blue Gene. This is how we started doing all these High-Performance Computing projects. We were getting more and more out of our research investment, and always with the goal of solving real problems in mind.

Tilak Agerwala: We started with the Blue Gene/L, which shipped in 2005. It brought supercomputing leadership back to the United States from Japan. It was another major paradigm shift, and IBM won the National Medal of Technology and Innovation in 2009 for the Blue Gene development and its application.

I wanted to beat the world to this milestone, and when we finally got to a petaflop in May of 2008, it was a great feeling. We had outperformed our competitors in other computational segments, and I knew that in time, we would here, too. With incredibly capable talent growing at an accelerating pace everywhere on this planet, global leadership in anything is an increasingly daunting task, but we went for it, and we were successful.

Leadership here matters greatly to me. Of course, it does—it is a matter of national pride. I care about my country, which is why I invested so much energy into supporting IBM's government business.

While the ASCI program, Blue Gene, and related supercomputing initiatives drew directly on my engineering and technical background, my senior positions at the time required me to be ambidextrous in my approach. In addition to these special projects that were alluring and exciting, I also needed to invest years of effort in helping IBM strengthen and grow its federal business and relationships because of unresolved wounds that remained from IBM's near-death experience in the 1990s.

Back in 1994, during the early years of Lou Gerstner's tenure, he made the difficult decision to sell our Federal Systems Division to provide a necessary cash infusion that would keep the rest of the company together. Frankly, this decision, however essential, was a shock to both parties, given the historical relationship we had enjoyed with government for so many decades.

As IBM stabilized and returned to growth, we began to refocus on Washington, DC. The problem was that the federal government still was upset with us for "abandoning" them.

Because I had been so active inside the Beltway over the years, executive responsibility for reenergizing the business fell to me. I needed a dynamic on-the-ground leader to fix the situation, and I turned to Anne Altman, who had done such a good job on the ASCI project.

Anne Altman: Nick was deeply engaged with a number of federal government clients. He spent his time and energy earning the trust and respect of agencies whose mission was to protect national interests. The senior leaders within the defense and intelligence community always left their doors open to Nick. Within IBM, Nick was the sponsor of the Federal business. He spent time not just on the very advanced technological challenges like ASCI, but across our entire Federal business.

While I could support Anne from the senior level, she was going to have to figure this out. She had to determine how to reengage this market, regain their trust and confidence, and explain why the new and better-integrated capabilities of IBM deserved their attention.

Anne Altman: Nick gave me the permission to create a strategy to grow our business, which at the time, was quite small. We had sold the business, and here we were knocking on their door again. The first thing that I experienced was a client base that was still very angry with IBM. Their mindset was, "You sold the business. You abandoned us." The memory fibers were visceral and long-standing.

While we understood their frustration with us, we also understood that the new, integrated IBM would be the ideal enterprise computing partner for large, complex government agencies. They just needed to be willing to take a good-faith look at this "new" IBM.

Anne was the perfect leader to make this happen. She was able to step back, see the big picture from the standpoint of IBM, and then see how to creatively relate our value proposition into the very specific needs of the Federal government.

Anne Altman: What I was hearing from government leaders was, "We need help rearchitecting our business systems and reimagining how we do the business of the people." It was a phenomenal period, and Nick was very helpful in taking the time to listen to what I was thinking about and understanding the corporate investments necessary to accomplish our turnaround. It was during this time where our relationship really took flight. I felt empowered.

Anne had the perfect attributes of a rising young executive. She was very open to ideas and to being coached. She also was willing to roll up her sleeves and take action. She had the respect of her team and a true devotion to the client and their needs. She was ready to go.

Anne Altman: In 2001, I presented our strategy to IBM's Operating Team. Lou Gerstner, of course, was still running the company. Sam Palmisano was there. That was my first opportunity to come in at the highest level of the company and say, "I'm going to show you how we can be a $3 billion business in this market space."

As Anne was beginning to implement her strategy, we pulled off a strategic maneuver that had particular ramifications for our Federal business. When we acquired PwC Consulting from PricewaterhouseCoopers, Anne received a strategic shot in the arm that would prove game-changing in terms of the breadth of our capabilities: an army of consultants who had deep knowledge of how the federal government worked, and how to best address their unique needs in an integrated fashion.

Anne Altman: Overnight, I had 3,000 new employees. So, for me it was, "How do I work with this and integrate it?" And it was fantastic because that was the turning point for so many of us. For the Federal business, suddenly, I could think, "I have a ton to work with here, and an opportunity to bring a different set of value to the market beyond just hardware and software. Now we can do it end-to-end, but we're going to do it end-to-end differently than a systems' integrator like Lockheed Martin or Northrup. We're going to do it as a commercial integrator, which is where the federal government had told me they most needed help."

From there, Anne and the Federal business were off to the races. I stayed very involved with the senior leadership in many agencies during these years, becoming a frequent visitor to the top brass of the Department of Defense, the NSA, the CIA, and several others that I cannot mention publicly. Suffice to say, I had my clearances—these people knew more about me than I knew myself!

I put in the time to understand their needs and goals, not only because I cared about helping the US government, but because the partnership between the government and businesses such as IBM has always been a hotbed of innovation. I was proud of Anne and everyone on her team for reenergizing the business line.

Anne Altman: Nick knew that IBM always had been essential to the United States as a partner. It was essential to technology and it was essential to the human capital efforts that supported these programs. IBM was essential to supporting space exploration and putting a man on the moon. He believed IBM needed to be part of these technology-driven historical efforts, and he was passionate about that. Nick recognized the immense import of being involved, and it's hard to balance that in a company like IBM, because we weren't just a government contractor. We were a huge commercial enterprise with clients around the globe. And yet somehow, he was drawn to serve his country in this unique way.

Chris Caine: This "helpfulness DNA" so much defines Nick. His DNA is really about helping others but doing so with a discipline and a dedication to outcomes, as opposed to just helping others without any measured outcome. So, he really personified the IBM brand as a technology leader in a shifting marketplace and a shifting world.

From a policy perspective, Nick and I were a tag-team in integrating and addressing and interacting with officials all around the world to explain the technology shifts that were taking place,

their impact on society and economics, what IBM had to bring to
the table, and why we could be trusted as a partner to government as
they tried to do important things to make the future better.

There was—and of course still is—a lot of untapped potential to innovate
in partnership with the government. One idea that Chris and I came up with,
along with other colleagues, was a concept that we call the "Trusted Foundry."

For example, I saw no reason why the government had to manufacture
semiconductors, even for the intelligence community. Why not rely on
leaders such as IBM to do that for them in a way that was as secure, or arguably more secure, than they could themselves?

The idea was that we would take a portion of our Burlington facility
and convert it into an almost quasi-government entity. The Department
of Defense could give IBM their requirements, and we could produce the
integrated circuits and technology needed to do the advanced intelligence
mission of the country.

That was not a business concept the government had used or understood
at that time, but it created a business model for IBM that was quite unique.
Eventually, it was broadened to include other microelectronics suppliers to
increase competition and ensure the entire supply chain could be trusted,
which was fine with me. As long as the country is advancing in a cost-effective way and working with suppliers of high integrity, the idea works.

Anne Altman: It's not very polite, but people would say, "Oh
yeah, senior executives from IBM just kind of fly over everything
and then leave." Not Nick. Nick became deeply involved with the
senior leadership of these agencies. He developed the same kind
of relationship that he did with colleagues. He was authentic. He
listened. He kept in mind their critical concerns, and he mobilized
around them. And he held people accountable. People both inside
and outside of IBM didn't want to disappoint Nick. So government
executives always took his call. They responded positively because

he was investing his personal time, energy, and talent, not just tasking others to follow up. He was investing himself in the effort.

Tilak Agerwala: Until the day he retired, Nick was our champion. No matter where he was, he had government relationships, which meant a big focus on the national labs and a big focus on the intelligence community. He was constantly helping us, protecting us, and fighting for us, even when he had moved on to the Executive Vice President role and wasn't directly responsible anymore. He was constantly there as the champion.

While working with our government came naturally to me, no one had to tell me to do it. I grew up during the Vietnam War era, but for a variety of reasons my number was never called to serve in the military. Ironically, late in my career I was asked by our business in Vietnam to meet with the country's leadership to share my thoughts on creating a national innovation policy. It was a moving experience that led me to think deeply about the futility of war, about my friends and peers who served, and about how profoundly things can change over a generation or two.

Projects such as ASCI, Blue Gene, and the Trusted Foundry proved to be some of the most rewarding and gratifying work of my career. I was able to contribute to the advancement of my country in tangible ways, while also elevating IBM's prominence in key segments of the information technology industry.

Sure, there were tremendous ups and downs, and moments of elation and great doubt, but I had constant exposure to incredible technologies and even better people. As hard as I worked, it was never lost on me that I was also a lucky man to be born into a particular time and place that positioned me to make a meaningful impact on our nation and our world.

PART III

VALUES AND THEMES IN MY IBM CAREER

TOP: The RS/6000, which paved the way for IBM to enter the Workstation marketplace and became a billion-dollar business within a year.

RIGHT: The System/390, which used CMOS technology to save the mainframe business and in some ways, IBM itself.

BOTTOM: ASCI White. a computer cluster based on IBM's commercial RS/6000 SP, which enabled the Department of Energy to simulate testing of the nuclear stockpile rather than conduct live testing.

8

FATHERS, SONS, AND VALUES

A s a spiritual person, I always have had a sense that greater powers were at work throughout my IBM career. My journey could not have been scripted nor predicted, but looking back, it is impossible for me not to think, *Something made it go that way.*

Some people may suggest that I was "lucky," while others might ascribe my trajectory to "skill" and "hard work." And while elements of luck, skill, and hard work all played a role, I do not believe they alone tell the entire story.

So many things could have gone one way or another. I might have accepted the West Coast offer coming out of RPI. I could have left IBM for other opportunities several times over the years. Management could have assigned any number of highly qualified people to those leadership roles that did fall to me. None of those things occurred.

Then there was my performance. I could have screwed up at any point, and truth be told, I sometimes *did* screw up, even within the high-pressure RS/6000 and mainframe efforts.

Somehow, over the course of more than four decades, things always fell into place for me. And while I do attribute some of my success to those greater powers, I firmly believe that a primary reason I thrived within IBM comes down to one word: *values.* I had an ethos instilled in me early in my life by my parents, and it turns out that ethos aligned perfectly with that of my employer of forty-four years.

Looking back, I realize that my parents gave me the right set of experiences as a child, making sacrifices they did not have to make. These experiences and their sacrifices allowed me to earn engineering degrees at RPI and Syracuse, which in turn enabled me to get my start at IBM. And as I have indicated, in a very real way, they gave me my managerial and leadership training, too. Their values became my values.

My father gave me my fighting spirit and the drive to do a job well and to be successful. Once that sense of pride is instilled in you, you cannot leave anything half-done. You cannot leave it alone. Because of him, I am just wired this way.

But unlike when I was a kid working all those odd jobs for him, I could not do it alone as an adult—either at work or at home. Very early in my IBM career, I realized that to succeed, I needed others to see things through with me. I learned this lesson the hard way during those tough early days in Burlington, but I only had to learn it once. After that, my life became all about enablement, bringing the good and the best out of people, which is where my mother had shaped me most.

So in retrospect, it is clear that I inherited the drive to see things through from my father and the desire to see other people succeed from my mother. That balanced combination was powerful, because it enabled me to get results while building strong, sustainable relationships.

But there was more. While I was learning to become a strong, collaborative manager of my teams, I initially perceived myself as a rebel with senior leaders, boldly pushing wild ideas on overly-cautious minds who were safeguarding the status quo. But during that meeting in Burlington, as I fought to advance the CMOS cause, I had the epiphany that I could drive change better within this innovative company if I *aligned* myself with the IBM culture and philosophy rather than rail against it.

It was the same epiphany I had while working for my father as a kid. I succeeded within his system by giving him the results he demanded while still staying true to myself. Now as I was making this deep, emotional, and abiding decision to truly *join* IBM, the same dynamics were in play.

While I carried my father's legacy with me as my career blossomed, it became increasingly clear to me that similar values not only were already a part of IBM's DNA, but that the DNA came directly from another father and son team. Of course, I am talking about the Watsons, those two complicated giants upon whose shoulders all IBMers built their careers.

Their combined legacy traces back to 1914, when an unemployed, forty-year-old Thomas Watson, Sr., a one-time star salesman for National Cash Register, interviewed with sixty-four-year-old Charles R. Flint, leader of Flint & Co. Flint specialized in pulling together companies into trusts, including one he formed in 1911 called the Computing-Tabulating-Recording Company, or CTR. CTR manufactured time clocks used by factories to track the time of employees who "punched the clock" in and out each day; scales for weighing and pricing items sold by the pound; and tabulating machines, which added up and sorted information recorded as punch holes on rectangular cards.

Though the trust had potential, by 1914, CTR was flailing, and Flint needed someone to run it, which was just what Watson aspired to do. He understood the products and believed he could make something of the trust. Through force of personality, he built a culture that valued integrity, optimism, and reaching goals, which for salesmen meant joining what he called the Hundred Percent Club by meeting or beating ambitious quotas.

Over his first few years with CTR, Watson grew revenues from $4.2 million in 1914 to $14 million in 1920, largely through leadership of the tabulating machine market. However, a competitor named Powers Accounting Machine, with more innovative and user-friendly tabulating machines than CTR, was on its heels. In a maneuver that would be repeated often in the years to come, Watson funded a lab full of the best engineers he could find in order to fend off the upstart. He created groups in the lab, offered each the same challenge, and watched as rivalries developed that sparked urgency and invention.

His tactics worked, and CTR's new technologies blew past Powers, securing for Watson the leadership in tabulating machines and punch cards he desired. Even at this early stage of what would become IBM, Watson embraced research as a means for meeting marketplace needs, and not for any grander purposes. In other words, from the very first days of IBM, results mattered—solving customer problems mattered—and results to Thomas Watson were measured by sales. He was known to say, "Everything starts with a sale. If there's no sale, there's no commerce in the whole of America." Almost ninety years later, I adhered to that same general principal: IBM's Innovation Agenda was designed to invest research dollars to address marketplace needs, and not just to show how clever we could be.

While CTR struggled through a recession in the early '20s, Watson continued to build what he believed would become a powerhouse, symbolized by his changing of the company name in 1924 to the more aspirational-sounding International Business Machines. By 1927, Watson fully understood the potential of the tabulating machine, the new concept of data processing, and the excitement with which the public saw these "thinking machines." He pushed his team hard to translate that potential into sales.

According to Watson, Sr. biographer Kevin Maney, in September of 1928, even as the tabulating division thrived, Watson drove his sales executives harder, telling them, "You men don't know what you are trying to do. Why is the tabulating division in such an awful condition? Because you fellows don't know what you want to do. Last month was the biggest month we had, over a half-million dollars net for August. That ought to have been a million dollars. And you should have gone after it. It's right out there waiting for you."

Reading that passage, in which even a record month brought about a berating, I heard echoes of my father hovering over me in the yard:

"You're doing that all wrong!"

"That's all? You can't do better than that?"

That said, outside the office, Watson's dynamic with his own young son was very different than my father's with me. Thomas Watson, Jr. was a poor student, constantly in trouble, and not his father's favorite among the four Watson children. Aloof and consumed with business matters,

Watson, Sr. for the most part still praised his son and told him what a success he was going to be, although no doubt he wondered if that was going to prove true.

At the same time, Junior would contrast his failings with the successes of his powerful father: "Everything he did left me feeling inconsequential by comparison." By the time he was fourteen or so, he began to suffer debilitating bouts of depression.

Of course, the elder Watson had an optimistic streak that bordered on delusional, as he would display throughout the Great Depression, when he again counterpunched by increasing production and continuing to hire salesmen, even as the stock market and economy collapsed.

Whether by insight or luck, his optimism paid off with the passing of the New Deal's National Recovery Act of 1933. The act required businesses to provide the government with huge amounts of data. The government had to manage this data, as well as the data demands from Franklin D. Roosevelt's welfare, price control, and public works programs. Not surprisingly, the demand for IBM tabulating machines skyrocketed, especially with the passing of the 1935 Social Security Act. Without IBM punch cards, business and government alike could not have met the challenges of the era.

While Watson's star rose to the point that, by 1936, he had the largest salary in America, that of his son continued to sink. Ever the optimist, the elder Watson never gave up on the boy, and used his persistence and influence to find an Ivy League college to accept him. Lucky to gain admission to Brown, the younger Watson continued to drift and to party, seemingly destined to become an underachieving playboy.

Then something happened to Watson, Jr. akin to the transformation that I underwent with my own father at a much earlier age when we moved into the home he bought, which I helped to repair and maintain. As Watson, Jr. recounted in his autobiography, "Somehow, through his moralizing, his example, and his impressive tolerance for my misbehavior, the old gentleman got to me. Sometime around my sophomore year at Brown I started learning how to police myself...My father began to exercise a profound influence on me...Maybe he was four thousand miles away, but I'd feel him like the keel of a boat, pulling me back upright again."

In many ways, the dynamic between the two Watsons was not all that unusual, but of course, their story was only getting started. After graduating from Brown, Watson, Jr. joined IBM as a salesman. The father treated his own son no differently than his own executives and salesmen. The younger Watson recalled, "My father never praised me for my work as a salesman. It was so easy for him to deprive me of my self-confidence with just a word."

World War II intervened, changing the fates of the United States, IBM, and equally profoundly, Thomas Watson, Jr. Already a passionate amateur pilot, the younger Watson joined the Air Force, and his confidence swelled. He wrote, "Finally I felt in a position to do something that counted...For the first time in my life, I wasn't worried about being overshadowed by Dad." The younger Watson returned to IBM after the war a new man, full of confidence in himself and his abilities for the first time in his life.

Not that the challenges wouldn't be intense: IBM had to switch back to peacetime production, and in order to retain its full wartime workforce and not let anyone go, sales of tabulating machines would need to *triple*.

As it turned out, and as Watson, Sr. foresaw, the pace of technological change was about to accelerate. At the same time, pent-up postwar demand for consumer goods exploded, creating a growing need for tabulation and data processing. While IBM was sitting pretty in the immediate aftermath of the war, by the early 1950s, the company not only was ensnared in a federal antitrust suit, but also was facing a dawning computer age that some believed had the potential to make IBM's tabulation machines obsolete.

Father and son fought ferociously over both the antitrust suit and the future of computing. The younger Watson wanted to settle the suit and put it behind the company, but the father wanted to fight the charges. As for computers, not surprisingly, the elder Watson did not see them as posing a serious threat to the tabulating machine empire for a long time. The son, younger and more in touch with the times, knew that the tremendous speed of electronic circuits might eventually prove irresistible to data-hungry customers.

Much as his father had done in response to the Powers threat years earlier, the younger Watson believed "that the smart way to protect our future would be to hire electronics engineers—large numbers of electronics engineers. Whether we ended up trying to commercialize computers and magnetic tape or not, IBM needed to understand what was going on; the field of electronics was advancing so fast, on so many fronts, that I thought a small group would never keep up. We needed a critical mass. But this was before Dad made me executive vice president, and nobody in his research and development operation would listen to me."

Not until the Korean War, when the younger Watson and his team hatched an idea to finance and build computers known as the "Defense Calculator" (eventually the IBM 701) for the federal government to aid the war effort—the largest project in the company's history up to that point—did the father truly allow the son to be his own man within the corridors of power at IBM.

What Watson, Jr. describes next, I would experience myself a decade later, and echoes the stories shared earlier by Dick Linton and Dick Gladu: "You only had to visit Poughkeepsie to get a sense of the fundamental change taking place in engineering...Poughkeepsie was wide open—the ideas seemed as abundant as air, and you had the impression of a limitless future...everybody believed that collaboration was the only way to move a complicated electronics project along. There was tremendous imagination and inventiveness everywhere you looked."

As this transition was taking place, and the IBM 701 remained in development, father and son continued to fight like crazy. For a time, Remington Rand took the lead in the dawning computer age with their UNIVAC, which correctly forecast the 1952 presidential victory of Dwight Eisenhower and became something of a synonym for computers and the technology age. By 1954, though, IBM's next-iteration 702 computer had caught up to UNIVAC, a testimony to the younger Watson's growing leadership skills, as well as the cultural DNA built into IBM by his father. By the 1956 election, it was *IBM's* computers that delivered Eisenhower's reelection forecasts, not Remington Rand's.

By this time, the elder Watson had made his son IBM's president, the company was about to break the half-billion-dollar mark in sales, and the company was growing at a scale never before seen in American business. The son wisely began to establish a modern corporate structure to replace the one-man show that his father always had more or less been, putting the company in a much better position to manage so much growth.

At the same time that the forty-one-year-old Thomas Watson, Jr. was maturing into his role as president of the most incredible growth machine of the era *and* stepping out of the shadow of his powerful father, my own maturation process was beginning, as I more willingly stepped *into* the shadow of my hard-driving father. Over the next decade, he would mold me as a change agent, finally releasing me from *his* shadow, first to RPI and then, at the strong suggestion of my mother, to IBM.

Within a few years, I was a tiny part of Watson, Jr.'s $5,000,000,000 gamble on the mainframe that established IBM as the greatest force in technology. And within a few decades, it would fall to a team I led to save that very mainframe business and the company these two men had willed forward with their leadership, capacity to take risk, and results-oriented values.

Fathers and sons. It is not always easy territory; the father pushing the son to mature, to work hard, and to do more. And yet all of this happened—for the Watsons and for the Donofrios. In neither case were there any guarantees.

What there were, though, were values. Recall the values my father taught me, as detailed at the end of Chapter 1:

- The way forward to a better life is through hard work.
- You need to pay attention to learn how to do things right.
- You can start with nothing and still figure out a way to make something.

- Whatever job you are doing, do it well and with pride.
- Make a commitment to quality and responsibility.
- Seek excellence for excellence's sake.
- When you do your work well and correctly, your sense of pride is your reward.
- You make many choices every day, often subconsciously. Use your free will to make the decisions that are right for you. If you give up your free will, that is your choice.
- If nothing changes, nothing changes.

Compare these with the values articulated by Thomas Watson, Jr. in *A Business and Its Beliefs*:

- Have respect for the individual.
- Give the best company service of any company in the world.
- Pursue all tasks with the idea that they can be accomplished in a superior fashion.

It is easy to see how I could synergize the values of my father—along with my mother's encouraging, collaborative approach—into the IBM culture articulated by the Watsons. From that point forward, though it would take me years to connect these dots, IBM gave to me, and I gave back. They challenged me over and over, and I always accepted the challenge. IBM benefited me, and I benefited IBM.

I was able to play a team role for IBM, and at the same time, develop into the unique leader that my father envisioned I could become, as he hinted at that night on the porch. If I was the right man in the right place at the right time on multiple occasions, it was because I was steeped in a set of values that meshed so perfectly with those of the Watsons and IBM.

By the time I became IBM's Executive Vice President of Innovation and Technology, I was drawing upon these values to enable even more and even bigger transformations at IBM against a backdrop of dizzying global and technological competition. Leading from these values came naturally to me, because they meshed perfectly with the Italian immigrant values that I had been raised with in Beacon, New York.

I led. IBMers innovated.

I led. IBMers changed.

I like to think my tale is unique, but truth be told, the people who succeed within the complex, diverse organization that was IBM before and during my career generally tended to share these values. When colleagues frame their recollections and observations in terms of these shared values, I cannot help but feel good.

> **Tilak Agerwala:** IBM truly is a values-based company. We are not a company based on an individual personality. We are not like an Oracle. We are not like a Microsoft. We are not like Apple. Building a company that's based on values—and not a company that's based on a single individual—and then actually living those values is challenging. But that's what has kept the company alive.

> **Ross Mauri:** People come here, and it gets under your skin. It grows in you. You work for a great company; you know you are solving some of the toughest problems in the world and for mankind. The reason to be in IBM is to do great things, so it's the type of people not only that we attract, but the ones that stick around, like me. Nick just embodied that wholly, and because of his leadership ability, rose above the hundreds of thousands of IBMers who were cut from the same cloth to be our leader. Nick knew the core fabric of most IBMers, and every day, he reinforced that fabric. It comes from the 1940s and the 1950s, but especially was highlighted by the birth of the first mainframe in 1964. The seeds were sown before then through an ability to step back and say, "Oh boy, we have to do this a different way. The world's changing." Nick embodied that culture, and because he knew that

the majority of the people of IBM were of that same culture, he knew how to guide us very well.

Anne Altman: One of the greatest attributes of IBM, and the reason Nick stayed and the reason I stayed, was that it was this amazing culture of great leaders and leadership. We did have terrible times, and there obviously were moments in our history where we had to have courageous leaders like Nick to right the ship and keep us going, but the culture was one where there was an expectation that you'd be open to ideas and you'd be able to work collaboratively in teams. Nick was given permission to be the leader that he was, and he in turn did the same for me and for so many others.

Isn't it interesting? Even while my father's mantra of "If nothing changes, nothing changes" has never been more true, IBM's values have remained more or less the same for over 100 years. The ability to change and to respond to change are built into the values. Certainly, they have evolved over time to reflect a more global and more inclusive mindset, but their essence remains in place. Some things do remain the same.

We all feel it and know it—thanks to a global marketplace for ideas, intense competition, better education, and a host of other factors, the pace of change has never been greater. We will keep being knocked about by change, whether we like it or not. Why not choose to like it? The Watsons and my father understood that values oriented around change can help us to do just that.

My father sometimes added a second part to his porch quote that clearly drove home the logic and need for change. He would say, "If you don't like what you have been getting, why are you doing what you are doing, since all you will get is what you have been getting?"

He understood that it actually is easier to embrace change—to actively seek it—rather than sit back and let the world chip away at you. We all have to keep changing ourselves, regardless of how old we are, where we work, what we want to accomplish, or whatever obstacles we perceive ahead of us.

I strongly believe that the key to navigating these changes remains collaboration—within our companies, our families, and our societies. If Parts I and II of this book told the story of *what* happened in my life and career at IBM and *when* it happened, over the coming chapters, I will explain *how* and *why* I learned to embrace, apply, and benefit from constant change, and I will share a broader perspective of values-driven leadership, management, and organization.

In closing, I would like to add that I derived the quotes and information for my historical summaries found in this chapter from two fine books: Kevin Maney's excellent *The Maverick and His Machine: Thomas Watson, Sr. and the Making of IBM*, published in 2003 by Wiley, and Thomas Waston, Jr.'s *Father Son & Co.: My Life at IBM and Beyond*, published in 1990 by Bantam. Both books have much to offer readers wanting to learn more about IBM and technology history.

9

CHANGING TO A MARKET-CENTRIC FOCUS

F or the two decades after I joined IBM in the mid-1960s, the market-place rewarded companies that could provide total, integrated systems for their customers. This was known as vertical integration, and IBM was the leader throughout this entire time.

By the mid-1980s, however, smaller players had emerged and were succeeding by providing niche, horizontal pieces of the overall solution. While there were advantages for the customer, there were disadvantages, too. The primary disadvantage was that the customer now had to play the integrator role for their overall technology infrastructure.

During this transition, as the number of our competitors grew and marketplace expectations changed, I came to see that IBM needed to focus more on the *needs* of our customers and prospective customers. We needed to see them more as *"clients"* by thinking more holistically about their needs and their businesses and less about transactional relationships. And we had to do it rapidly.

Don't get me wrong. IBMers were working hard, creating amazing technologies, and earning patent after patent, but our overall orientation—from product development to delivery—was out of touch with the times. Our decades-long market leadership had enabled a long, slow, drift, and we were no longer as close to our "clients" as new realities and the pace of change dictated that we needed to be. Nor were we as close to our clients as our values should have driven us to be.

We had to refocus on their needs, learn to talk with them again, and build products that solved their actual problems. While I believe that I had always taken the customer into consideration, I understood that I had to take my game to a higher level. This personal evolution took place first as we stabilized and then grew during the Gerstner days, and after, as Sam gave me free reign to implement IBM's Innovation Agenda, which began and ended with meeting client needs.

My position, bolstered by the credibility I had earned leading tough transformation initiatives, gave me a bully pulpit to encourage IBMers to focus externally and to talk with clients. It came naturally to me. Whether inside of IBM or out, whether with employees, clients, the media, or other marketplace observers, I enjoyed sharing the IBM point of view.

But whenever I would speak, I would spend a lot of time listening, too. And observing. And thinking. It was all part of a process around building a market-centric focus.

In my mind, "market-centric" represented three pillars:

- Understanding client needs and how IBM could meet those needs both through existing products and services as well as new innovations.

- Having a point of view about the state of the industries that we served, future trends, and how our products and services were evolving alongside—and in fact enabling—those trends.

- Making relationships *personal* by helping not only our client entities to succeed, but by truly teaming with the flesh-and-blood people working for those entities.

UNDERSTANDING CLIENT NEEDS

Consider a perfect case in point—the mainframe turnaround detailed earlier—but this time from the perspective of IBM's traditional multinational Fortune 500 and government clients.

We typically interacted with the Chief Information Officers (CIOs) of these organizations. They had depended on IBM and the mainframe to meet the growing complexities of their operations with an integrated solution since the 1960s. While to some degree they may have balked a little at our prices and our market power, they also understood that what we sold them worked, that we stood by our products, and that we provided superior service.

But when niche players such as Digital, Data General, and Wang Laboratories emerged, they threw confusion into the marketplace, particularly with mini-computers—or minis, as they were known—which were smaller and sold for much less than the mainframe. Minis grew to have relatively high processing power and capacity, and for a while, they were all the rage.

Sophisticated CIOs understood that minis were hardly a substitute for an IBM mainframe, but nonetheless, a narrative took hold in the marketplace that the mainframe could be replaced. While many within IBM waited for the mini-computer fad to blow over, some of our most important customers saw the dangerous game we were playing, not only with our future, but with *their* futures, too. They needed the mainframe. But they needed the mainframe to adapt to the world they now lived in, too.

Larry Kittelberger, CIO of the then-*Fortune* 100 Tenneco, understood it better than most. He was one of quite a few CIOs who began voicing their concerns.

Larry Kittelberger (*Former CIO, Tenneco, Allied Signal, and Lucent Technologies*): On the margins, at first, little companies came along and started creating mini-computers. The mini-computers were falsely advertised as being able to do the same things as the mainframe, and a lot of CIOs replaced mainframes with mini-computers. The CIOs of the big companies knew better, but many boards didn't want to hear from them, and many were fired. They'd say, "Why are we spending all of this money with IBM on these mainframes when we can do the same thing on these mini-computers and they cost a tenth of the amount? Why would we do that?"

Not surprisingly, when other CIOs watched their peers losing their jobs, they opted for the minis. You have to understand that most CIOs in business at that time were people who came out of either finance or engineering and had no computer background at all. They were saying, "We'll get five of those minis and get rid of the mainframes." They did it, and they failed. There were banks that failed as a result. There were industrials that couldn't ship anymore. It was a disaster. So these CIOs lost their jobs, too! It became a joke that CIO stood for "Career Is Over," and that was because of what was going on with these mini-computers.

While Larry was watching these developments from his offices in Texas, Linda Sanford, myself, and others were reaching the same conclusions as we crafted our strategy to revive the mainframe franchise.

Larry Kittelberger: IBM was struggling. Akers was really big on the mainframe, because that's where they made all their money. IBM was used to the orders just coming in naturally every year. It kept growing, and they would replace our old systems, and the money kept flowing. It's easy to get lulled to sleep with that type of thing. The mindset was that mainframes are the answer, but their stock had dropped down to maybe the high-30s from a few hundred dollars a share, and they were not listening to people who were saying, "Mainframes aren't going to make it."

They weren't tied into their customers. They weren't listening to their customers. They weren't paying any attention. They really weren't. They thought the mini-computer was just a flash in the pan, because they knew that it couldn't do what a mainframe could do, but they thought that the people out in industry would be smart enough to know that, and they weren't.

I saw all this happening, and I started elevating the issue within Tenneco, saying, "These mini-computers aren't going to work," and at the same time, I was watching what was happening to IBM, and saying, "Oh my God! This can't happen!" Luckily for me, the presidents of my company all trusted me when I said, "Believe me, this is going to be a disaster!"

Linda and I believed CMOS was the key to changing the fortunes of the mainframe, and as already discussed, I was trying to push this vision within the same IBM that Larry was observing from the outside. As our annual losses mounted into the billions in 1991 and 1992, I was getting traction on the CMOS switchover, and that is when Lou Gertsner took over as CEO for John Akers.

Linda Sanford: Lou Gerstner had much more of a client perspective. He reinforced in all of us that we needed to go back to the client, talk to the client, listen to the client, bring back what they're telling us, and have it inform our strategy going forward.

Larry Kittelberger: When Lou Gerstner took over, I flew up with a few of my team to Poughkeepsie for a briefing with them. Nick was there. I'd never met him before. When we got started, I said at the top of my voice, "People, you need to understand that we cannot live without you! Because if IBM goes under, we can't operate. All this mini-computer stuff is a farce! You need to get out there and lead instead of crawling back into a shell and sitting back here and doing nothing!" The people said, "No, no, no, no, Larry. You're wrong." I said, "Okay, tell me why I'm wrong."

So they bring in this industrial psychologist they had used, and he stands in front of the room and says, "We went to the CEOs of businesses and asked, 'When you hear mainframe and IBM, what do you think?' They said, 'Slow. Dinosaur. Very expensive. We'll fire our CIO if he ever puts another one of these things in. We hate IBM. They're just sucking money out of the company.'" I said, "Well, that sounds about right."

I had never met Larry at that point, but he was making an impression, that's for sure. Here was a guy with some fire. Here was a guy who wanted to see change. Here was a guy very colorfully telling everyone the pain we were causing him. And just as I had experienced over and over when trying to sell my mainframe vision within the company, Larry heard the pushback.

Larry Kittelberger: The industrial psychologist tried to turn the tables back on me. He said, "It's not right, because we went back and said to these CEOs, 'Do you realize that with IBM, you can do multitasking, you can handle big databases, and you can do all these things that these mini-computers can't do? What do you think now?' And the CEOs said, 'Well, I guess they're okay.'"

Now, the psychologist says to me, "See? They think mainframes are okay." I said, "Buddy, you just tried to reprogram a CEO. He doesn't believe what you told him. He listened to you. He was being polite." Now, I was really wound up, and I started to yell, "You need to change your color! You need to change your name! You need to change everything about what you're doing because we can't live without you, but we can't live with what you're doing. You're killing the company!"

Our biggest clients needed us, but we needed to help them deal with the mini-computer problem that their own leaders were throwing in their faces on price, performance, and perception.

Larry Kittelberger: Immediately after the briefing, I sat down with Nick. We're both technology people, and Nick and I hit it right off. He said, "Larry, let's go back over this again. What do we need to be doing?" I said, "Well, I don't know. But I know one thing. You've got to get rid of the word 'mainframe.' Call it anything else. You need to change your color! You've got to get your costs down somehow. You've got to compete with these mini-computers."

Linda Sanford: The message we heard from Larry was a message we heard over and over from others. They needed this mainframe to stay alive. This needed to be fixed. It could not stay the way it was. It had to be transformed, not just for IBM, but for the world. This was a do or die. We had to get this thing right.

In some ways the mission was simple. In order to meet the needs of the client and the IBM Company, the mainframe had to change. As was detailed in Chapter 5, we used CMOS to get the full instruction set onto a much smaller, much less expensive machine with newly-designed chips and circuitry. The minis did not have the full instruction set required to run big corporate applications, but now we did, and at a price point the market would embrace, because we were using the same parallel computing concepts we had used with the RS/6000. I was excited to begin showing our first prototypes to clients. In fact, about six months after that first meeting with Larry, I called him in for another visit.

Larry Kittelberger: I jumped on a plane, flew up to Poughkeepsie, and walked in to the atrium of this building. All around the atrium there were places where IBM would display pieces of new equipment. They'd be off to the left and right with little steps going up to them.

This day, I noticed off to the left there was a dark blue curtain hanging down, and I thought, *That's kind of strange.* Nick finally came down, and he said, "Larry, I've got to show you this." He goes over to that curtain, and he pulls it back, and there are these ugly black machines there. I said, "Nick? Black?" He said, "Yeah. Black, because you told us the color was bad, and black is the absence of color! Now nobody can associate us with a color anymore." I said, "Wow. What a sight. There you go."

Okay, so I had made a good first impression with Larry, but he was going to want to know if it worked, of course.

Larry Kittelberger: Now, I said, "Nick, we also talked about how mini-computers have a reduced instruction set. Does this have the full instruction set that big businesses need?" Well, Nick had worked on this, and he had managed to get the full operating system into one of these machines. So I said, "Nick, what are you calling this thing?" He said, "We're going to call it a server." I said, "A server? That sounds pretty good, because that's what we're doing. We're moving data around." These were big technological changes, because they went to a mini-computer-type structure, but they were able to get the full instruction set into this thing. It was really a mainframe in a small machine, and the price went way down. The chips and the circuitry and everything else were newly designed.

Linda Sanford: Key clients like Larry, who were leaders in leveraging this technology, gave us positive reactions to what they were seeing happening. We were always testing with them and demonstrating early prototypes with them, and they were giving us feedback. We weren't just looking in the mirror and telling ourselves we were good, we were hearing it from different perspectives.

It all came down to understanding the client's needs. IBM was no longer in a position to tell them how things were going to be. We had to listen. And we did.

Larry Kittelberger: Nick was listening, and when this came out, it just turned the whole market. The price point caught everybody's eye, first of all. Then they went to the CIOs, and since IBM was embedded into every Fortune 500 company in the world, they could go in and say, "Look, we can run the full instruction set. We can run the big database applications on these new File Servers. They'll look like one big mainframe to you, but there will be separate machines hooked together and running parallel. The CIOs said, "You just saved my life, because now I can go in to my boss and say, 'I just cut my budget in half because I can go with these new machines.'" And IBM took off like crazy at that point.

From that first day, listening to Larry scream at us, I never forgot that he brought home viscerally just how much we were letting our clients down through our overall reluctance to change after twenty-five years of smooth sailing. I was never going to make that mistake again.

Larry Kittelberger: So many times in the years that followed, if Nick was introducing me to somebody, he'd say, "Here's a guy, when nobody would talk to us, he was screaming at us." And I was, but he was listening, and it saved IBM. Nick and his team came up with the concepts that changed the entire industry and made mini-computers a flash in the pan. They disappeared when the File Servers hit.

I am proud of the way not only my team, but IBM as a whole, responded to the threats we faced in those days of high drama as Lou took over. I believe one of the reasons he made the elephant dance again, so to speak, is that our market-centric genes were there all along. They just had gone a little dormant.

Of course, it is not enough for this market-centric mindset to only take center stage during a crisis or during a major turnaround of a major product line. A market-centric mindset involves understanding the markets each client competes within, what those clients are trying to accomplish today, what they need to be thinking about in order to stay out in front tomorrow, and finally, how we can help them. I loved doing business this way.

Sam Palmisano: He was the lead executive on I don't know how many accounts—many more than he probably should have been from a time perspective—because clients would never let go of him. They knew they could trust him. If they had a problem, he'd fix the thing. Nick was like a dog with a bone. He was not going to let go. He'd assemble a team. He'd be all over everyone. He'd deploy them to the client. He had daily or weekly checkpoints with the team on the issue, whether it was technology or support or whatever it might have been.

Lauren States *(Former IBM Vice President of Strategy and Transformation, Software Group Division)*: When I was Nick's Executive Assistant, he was client executive for maybe thirty-eight clients. I remember that one day I sat down and segmented his client portfolio by high, medium, and low importance and told him, "You have to give up the ones that are not worth your time. I will not compromise on that." I forgot what he said, but I know that my plan didn't go into effect.

Nick would always make himself available whether it was a client team or an individual. Obviously, he got assigned to the most important clients, but the most competent and engaging and aggressive client teams used Nick most effectively. It wasn't as though Nick, with his thirty-plus clients, divided them up equally. He made himself available to all of them, and really anybody else who needed help, but the ones who had the wherewithal and the need at the time to leverage him did so, and he fully engaged.

Jim Onalfo *(Former International CIO, General Foods; Former CIO, New York Police Department)*: I ran all IT activities for General Foods across thirty countries throughout the world. I had responsibility for about 46,000 people, so it was a fairly big job, and I was very demanding. To me, there was only one company that could provide all of my needs, and that was IBM. With IBM, I was able to migrate from the country support teams to the country managers up to area managers and right up to the top of IBM to make sure my needs were known, and that was Nick. I don't like to use the word "demanded," but I wanted to know everybody at my vendor companies, including CEOs, CIOs, and CFOs. That was one of my tactics for getting the kind of support I needed. Nick was a truly great representative of IBM, and a very honest individual who always tried to help me accomplish what I needed to do in my IT shops.

As a trusted advisor to a diverse client set, I loved not only the problem-solving and trouble-shooting, but the brainstorming about how IBM could help a customer create sustainable competitive or operational advantages. A great example comes from my valued Morgan Stanley client, Guy Chiarello, with whom I would look for what we called "FOAKs," which stood for First-of-a-Kind.

Guy Chiarello (*Chief Operating Officer at Fiserv, Inc.; Former President of First Data; Former CIO at JPMorgan Chase*)**:** There were always tactical and strategic issues going on for Morgan Stanley, and these conversations would include dialogue about the day, the month, the quarter. It was all about growing the business on the mainframe environment, and the pressures of that growth and the cost that went with it.

When Nick and I would get together, we would ask each other, "What FOAK ideas do we have today?" We'd discuss them, and then ask, "How do we go forward?" That was our approach, and I guess the reason we hit it off so well. Nick and I would often talk about how to use new ideas, new technologies, and new approaches to solve a problem.

Guy and I both wanted to be proactive. The race was never won for either of us, so we were always looking for these FOAKs.

Guy Chiarello: With Nick and I, it was always about how to blaze the next frontier. How do we take the mainframe environment to the next level? These "first of its kind" things really helped Morgan Stanley improve its business. For instance, we built disaster recovery zones for the business that were ahead of the times and at price points that were really terrific. We built testing facilities to mirror Morgan Stanley's environment with IBM. It really allowed us to stay on the mainframe a lot longer, because during this period there was tremendous pressure to move to open systems and LINUX and really move away from the mainframe world. Nick was really instrumental in keeping all of that in balance.

Larry Kittelberger: Nick listened extremely well. The thing you learn after years of working is that there are people out there who seem to have all the answers, because they think they know everything. The really smart people realize how much they don't know, so they listen very carefully, and they pick up and learn from everybody else. That's your brain trust. That's what you need in a company. People who know how to fit everything into a box are blockers and hurt your company. Nick is one of the people who realized that no matter how smart you are, there's other people who have good ideas, and you need to listen. That's why he's one of the smartest guys I've ever worked with.

Larry's point is well-taken, and while I always wanted to be open-minded to ideas I might hear, I also went to great lengths to bring a formal Point of View (POV) to my clients that reflected where IBM saw technologies, industries, and economies headed.

HAVING A POINT OF VIEW

In fact, one of the things that differentiated IBM from the competition is that we invested in developing and constantly updating detailed reports on where the world and more than a dozen industries were headed. Based on facts, data, and insights gleaned from clients, academics, and other partners around the world, these findings would often lead to the give-and-take conversations that fostered breakthrough thinking.

As a result, clients trusted that we could collaborate so that we *both* remained viable in a future that kept arriving faster and faster every day.

Larry Kittelberger: Every year, Nick would ask me to bring in my CIOs. I had about ten CIOs around the world, and we'd go to Poughkeepsie or Armonk, and Nick would host us there. He would speak to everybody about where IBM was going, and about all the technology they were developing. He would take us to the Watson Labs, and we would get a smattering of everything that was going on inside IBM. That kept us close to everything. When you're a CIO, you want to make sure when you're looking out there that you don't make a left-hand turn when the rest of the market makes a right-hand turn.

Ross Mauri: Nick would always say, "Innovation just doesn't come from the chip guys in Burlington. You have to have innovation across the entire stack, across all of what we do." We were helping businesses understand that they needed to reinvent themselves and giving them a context through IBM's view on how to do that.

Having a Point of View was not just slick marketing-speak. When I shared a Point of View, you can bet I believed it. In many cases, I was the one who had to fight to bring IBMers around to my worldview and had to personally *create* that Point of View to then take to the world. For instance, in the late 1980s and early 1990s, I was responsible for bringing the RS/6000 to market (as detailed in Chapter 4). I was championing a Point of View that not everyone within IBM wanted to hear, but that a new market of clients could not wait to hear.

I understood the rise of UNIX, as well as the internal resistance to the open operating environment it represented and how it flew in the face of IBM's closed-system traditions. But if nothing changes, nothing changes. IBM had to change, and I saw what we—along with Dassault Systèmes—could bring to the emerging marketplace of workstations.

> **Bernard Charles:** The mainframe was the king inside IBM, but there was Nick having the incredible energy to drive people to believe that the RS/6000 would be core and would be the future of IBM. I remember companies like Honda, BMW in Europe, and companies in the aerospace sector, including Boeing, adopting the RISC workstation from the IBM solutions as a progressive replacement of the mainframe, which was the proper architecture for what they were doing.

So what does all of this mean? A passion for innovation and change. If you believe in what you are doing, you will stand up for it, because you care enough to push for that better future. You care enough about your clients. You care enough about your company. And you care enough about everyone with whom you interact and work, because after all, these are people just like yourself. Some people say, "It's just business. It's not personal."

To me, it *is* personal. It always has been.

MAKE IT PERSONAL

I like to think that my IBM clients and my fellow IBMers saw that I cared for technology and its ability to be a positive force in the world and for the IBM Company. I believed in IBM's ability to be a force in creating and delivering that technology to the world, for the clients that entrusted us with helping them succeed—whether in business, government, or nonprofit—and for people themselves. IBM was and is a huge enterprise, as were most of our clients and partners. And yet all of those enterprises consist of *people* whom I had the utmost respect for and enjoyed supporting. I tried to never lose sight of that.

I am glad that clients like Larry, Jim, Guy, and Terry Milholland of Boeing understood this about me. It enabled us to work toward solutions in which everyone could win and to do so in an atmosphere of trust, mutual respect, and ultimately, even friendship.

Larry Kittelberger: Nick has the ability to bring people close to him. He was IBM to the user community. When we thought of IBM, we thought of Nick. We weren't thinking about their machines. We were thinking about Nick. Nick was IBM. Nick is the one who had the brains to really lead the technology side and had the personality to bring all the people who were the customers along with him.

Terry Milholland (*Former Boeing CIO, 1978–1999*): Nick is not at all what I would call a classic IBMer, in the dark suit, the white shirt, the classic tie. He was far more laid back. A greeting with him was warm and cordial. So many others I'll call salespeople—whether from IBM or other corporations at the time—were thin on deep personal relationships. They had one thing on their mind and one thing only, and that was to sell gear to you. Nick was not that way. He was far more interested in the success of the mission, which in our case was to see that a new airplane product—the 777—was done digitally, and that IBM technology supported that without any lingering issues. It was key from his point of view that he would marshal the resources necessary to see that the customer was successful irrespective of how much profit came IBM's way. His drive was the customer.

Guy Chiarello: He really cared about the client-first concept. That doesn't mean that he didn't care about the business, and that doesn't mean that he didn't care about the financials, but his philosophy always was, "If I can get the client to accomplish their goals, and be happy with IBM along the way, the revenue will only increase, the penetration of products will only grow, and the satisfaction will make it a long-term partnership." That was the way he brought himself to the table in every conversation right up to the present day.

To me it was not just good business, it was the way I wanted to live my life. Because I made things personal, and because people knew I cared, they would sometimes go the extra mile for me, just as I would for them.

This chapter began with the story of Tenneco CIO Larry Kittelberger coming to Poughkeepsie to read IBM the riot act for ignoring his needs, as well as the needs of his peer CIOs. I am going to tell another story about Larry that came years later, as it exemplifies the way I felt about putting the client first and making business personal.

Following his twenty-five-year run with Tenneco, Larry joined well-known CEO Larry Bossidy of Allied Signal for a whirlwind four-and-a-half years. Larry loved working for Bossidy, but following the Allied Signal merger with Honeywell, he was looking for a new opportunity. I had an idea.

Lucent had been established in the fall of 1996 when AT&T divested their technologies business unit. During the late '90s, as the bull market in stocks roared, Lucent was a darling of investors, and they also happened to be IBM's largest customer. I thought the situation would be perfect for Larry, and I set the wheels in motion.

Some friend I turned out to be! My timing could not have been worse. When Larry joined Lucent, their stock was trading around $75 per share and on its way to an eventual high of $82. Then the problems began. Sales began to plummet, and Larry ended up spending two years at Lucent restructuring the entire company.

They went from $57 billion in sales down to $20 billion in nine months, and he had to cut the business from 155,000 employees to 85,000 during that same timeframe. Bankruptcy was very much a possibility, but through a few strategic spinoffs, they managed to do what they had to do to stay alive.

When you think of a relationship between vendor and client, you typically envision the vendor supporting the client in a growth initiative aimed at upgrading for the future. But in this case, Larry needed to downsize, which is very difficult to do well. It was critical that I help Larry downsize his tech spend with IBM to fit the new needs of a much smaller Lucent.

Larry Kittelberger: During this time, Nick and I would meet, and we'd talk, and we'd commiserate. It had looked like a great job, but it turned out to be a tough one. But Nick and I worked together and got all of the computer technologies straight inside of Lucent. We did a lot of good work for Lucent, and we ended up saving the company. Lucent eventually was bought by Alcatel. So the fact is, we saved it, and Nick worked with me the whole time on this thing. If it wouldn't have been for Nick, I'm not sure we would have made it, because he really cut some corners with IBM to keep us afloat. It was Nick.

A good client is like a good friend. Anyone can be there when the going is good. When the going gets tough, you have to stand up. Lucent was an important client. Larry was an important client and friend. The market was shifting. My job was to help them shift along with it.

Larry Kittelberger: When I went to Lucent, we were IBM's largest customer in the world, so it behooved IBM to step up. It's harder to downsize a company than it is to upsize one. When you're surgically cutting a company, you have to be careful you don't break all the processes while you're doing so. So we used a very structured methodology to bring down things without breaking our main processes.

But in doing this, we ended up not needing all the computer equipment that we had. We had tons of equipment we'd leased from IBM sitting in the computer room that was idle, and the expense was going to sink us if we didn't do something about it. Well, Nick worked with us. He worked with us when we grew, and he worked with us when we came back down. Nick worked with us to be able to break leases and come up with new types of equipment so that we could downsize in an orderly way. He worked the technology side to bring down the machinery, consolidate, and bring in new equipment that was more powerful for the same price. He was an integral part of what was going on there.

I took great pride in helping Lucent and Larry manage their reversal as best as possible. Their market had changed, and I was personally vested in helping find the best solution possible for everyone. I believe that we did just that.

I will close with another story that worked out better from the get-go than Larry's time at Lucent. Ray Kelly, the Police Commissioner of the New York Police Department, who would become well-known for his willingness to use technology and data analytics to effectively and efficiently fight crime, approached Lou Gerstner looking for someone to run his IT department. When Lou asked me if I thought of anyone up for the job, my mind turned to my friend Jim Onalfo, who had been CIO for General Foods and other major companies as well as a valued IBM client and friend.

Jim Onalfo: Commissioner Kelly was a very smart man, and he knew that their current IT processes would not work for his police officers. So he talked to Lou Gerstner first. Lou Gerstner called Nick, who knew I was retired and home. So one day I get a call from Nick. He said, "Jim, how would you like to come out of retirement and work for the NYPD?" I asked, "What's the job?" Nick said, "You've got to build them a Real-Time Crime Center." I said, "Okay. I have no idea what that is, but I promise to deliver it for you." With that, Lou and Nick recommended me to go to work for the NYPD.

I knew Jim was the man for the job, because he was bright, well-organized, and bold. I had seen him push us at IBM many times to deliver for him exactly what he needed, and I knew he would do the same with Chief Kelly and Mayor Michael Bloomberg.

Jim Onalfo: If you're a CIO, the first thing you have to do is look at the current business processes that are in place and the current support for IT. That's what I did at the NYPD. I spent the first six months building an IT plan. It was very expensive. I presented it to Kelly and Mayor Michael Bloomberg, and I said, "Do you want to do it? If you are serious, here is the plan. Here are the resources I'm going to need. Here's the cost. Do you want to do it? If you don't want to fix it, send me home."

We were talking multimillions, but IBM, and Nick particularly, helped bless this plan. I was very arrogant with them, but I'd been a CIO for a long time, so I knew what I was talking about. And so did Nick. Kelly and Bloomberg both agreed, and from that point on, nobody would disagree with anything I said.

Kelly had a vision for what he needed, and I think he knew immediately that Jim was the perfect character to help him make it happen. As for Mayor Bloomberg, he obviously had a great grasp of the power of centralized data dating back to his business career and the very successful Bloomberg Terminals his company designed, so he was excited, too.

Jim Onalfo: The first thing I did was put together an integrated database that went back forty-five years, with any arrest and any criminal that existed. Well, with the ability for every cop in the city to access it, that alone was a major improvement for arresting. We have 100 precincts, so there were 100 databases that the precincts managed that literally didn't talk to each other. So the guy in precinct one had no clue what the guy in precinct two had in his database. I integrated everything in the first year and that changed the whole nature of how to access police records. That was the biggest improvement, giving the cops the ability to see who's who, and to check things out in a single database that went across every arrest and every criminal over forty-five years.

My belief in the magic combination of passionate people and leading-edge technology was perhaps never better displayed than in the important work Jim did for the NYPD in the high-pressure years following 9/11.

Jim Onalfo: The Real-Time Crime Center was Kelly's brainchild, and I designed it and implemented it. Some eighteen months after I presented my plan to him, he had the first Real-Time Crime Center, with cops, centralized databases, and access to all criminal records that went back several decades. It was primarily, first and foremost, an IBM mainframe with satellite computers in different places. It was networked with all the 911 data and all the things needed for a Real-Time Crime Center. What we had was this huge TV screen and forty cops with access to databases, and that's where the crime center started solving all the problems for New York City. Commissioner Kelly and his staff and precinct commanders said things like, "We've been in the desert for years and now you're bringing us some water."

The system was the envy of the global police community. Soon, officers were coming from all over the world for tutorials on what Jim had done for the NYPD. Sometimes you wonder if you are doing the right thing when you ask somebody to come out of retirement. I am very glad I did not let that stop me from calling Jim and encouraging him to take this opportunity.

Jim Onalfo: That was probably the best thing that I ever did in my life, to go to work for the NYPD, because it was a situation where I basically taught the cops how to catch criminals with technology. Until that job, it was not a predominant activity that supported the cops. So when we did it there, then the whole world followed. My wife even said to me, "Jim, I think you've been working your whole life for this job." And I think she was right. I did a lot of good work in IT, but nothing as significant as this, that helped keep people in New York City safe and then was spun out to different countries all over the world to do the same for them.

We lost Jim late in 2019 when he passed away at the age of eighty. He had a tremendous career, and I am glad that he saved the best for last. Our nation and the world owe him a debt of gratitude.

10

LEADING FOR CHANGE AND INNOVATION

A s a young manager in Burlington, confident in my abilities as an engineer, but less so in my abilities to oversee others, I struggled mightily
to give people the room to succeed in their own way. Self-confident
as an engineer, but not as a team lead, I micromanaged and bullied
my team, leaving them with the feeling that I believed I could do their jobs
better than they could.

After a horrible review, I adjusted course and began to encourage and
enable the very same people I had micromanaged to spread their wings. I
did that by creating an atmosphere that prized open communication, idea-
sharing, and collaboration in the name of delivering the results that our in-
house customers and the IBM Company demanded.

While that change did not happen overnight, it did happen quickly. Over
time, the challenge for me became less how to change my managerial style
and more how to scale it, since the challenges I faced, and the number of
people I was responsible for, only grew. Eventually, it became my job to create these same conditions for open communication, collaboration, innovation, and client-driven results for IBM's entire 200,000-plus global technical workforce.

While creating this atmosphere required a lot of thought and persistence at every stop in my career, I truly loved this challenge, because I loved seeing IBMers grow just as much as I love seeing technology advance.

I brought my engineering mindset to leadership and management, and I brought *me*. As a leader, I always talked openly to my team about my life. I wanted them to know that I was not some entitled executive who did not understand them. It was important that they knew that I was one of them, and that I was willing to lay myself out there for them, because I knew that in return, they were laying themselves out there for IBM and for me. It made for a powerful combination.

Collectively, what I wanted to see in any team, including the entire 200,000-plus members of the IBM Technical Community, was the understanding that—you guessed it—if nothing changes, nothing changes. I am not kidding. That was my touchstone.

Change is the operative word for all leaders. Everything always is changing, to either aid you or to hinder you. You simply cannot control it. Count on it and use it to enable yourself—and your team—to move faster to become more enabled for innovation.

And to move faster toward innovation, you need to have a deep-seated commitment to being:

- Problem-focused
- Open and collaborative
- Multi-disciplined
- Global-thinking and inclusive

By the time I was leading the entire IBM technical workforce, I had a clear vision for how we would accomplish our goals. It would represent a major change for IBM to orient itself to meet these four commitments, but in doing so, we brought the Innovation Agenda to life and positioned the company for years of strong growth.

PROBLEM-FOCUSED

As an engineer, I could always identify a problem and then break it into smaller pieces to be solved. I would take complex problems, break them into smaller problems, and then put them back together again to see if that answer worked.

From a business perspective, identifying a client's problem is an appropriate parallel. When I think about what IBM did with System/360 back in the 1960s, as much as it was about technology and leadership, it was even more about addressing the clients' issues, problems, and challenges.

Starting with the problem is *always* better than simply starting with the answer, but over time, and for various reasons, IBM had become too focused upon what we could make, rather than what our clients needed. And heading into the 2000s, we believed that after years of purchasing technology solutions a la carte, our clients once again wanted a single enterprise to solve their large, complicated technology problems.

> **Sam Palmisano:** Dell might create great PCs, HP might create great low-end servers, and SAP might create great application software, but IBM was going to solve complicated problems, whether it was in healthcare or finance or any other industry where we could integrate and bring all of our capabilities to the table. We weren't going to create just one piece of the solution. We were going to create the entire solution, which no one else really could do, but which IBM had been doing from the earliest days of Thomas Watson, Sr.

As Sam says, we believed that the future of IBM lay in applying the best of IBM's roots—providing comprehensive solutions for business clients—in new and innovative ways. But Sam's "if"—if we could integrate and bring all of those capabilities to the table—was a big if, and the starting point for that integration was IBM Research.

To be fair, that is a great starting point, one that any company or business executive would envy. IBM Research was doing amazing work at the time, advancing core technologies at a stunning pace—and for the first time get-ting mass acclaim for their work. Led by Paul Horn, Research was on a high following the success of Deep Blue, the high-performance computer that took on a reigning chess world champion in a match—and won!

Over a decade in the making, Deep Blue debuted in February 1996, win-ning its first game against world champion Garry Kasparov in game one of a six-game match. From there, Kasparov won three and drew two of the fol-lowing five games to defeat Deep Blue by a score of 4–2.

Seeing how close we had come to victory—stunning the world in that first game—Research went back to work on improving Deep Blue, and in May 1997, the computer won a six-game rematch with Kasparov. No computer system had ever defeated a reigning world champion in a match under standard chess tournament time controls. The publicity certainly served IBM well—*The Wall Street Journal* went so far as to estimate that Deep Blue received more than 6 billion "impressions" globally within twenty-four hours of the match ending. It even garnered a top twenty "Q rating" that suggested it was as well-known as, and seen as favorably as, many top celebrities.

As thrilling as the Deep Blue victory was for IBMers, there remained a bigger question: was the team as focused on the problem—providing comprehensive solutions for business clients—as they needed to be? Lou Gerstner did not think so. He turned to his leaders, me included, to make that happen.

> **David Yaun:** Paul Horn and his predecessor Jim McGroddy were both very strong Research leaders, focused on elevating the science taking place in the labs to greater relevance—but they grew up in the labs. Those labs, for the longest time, were isolated from clients and even from most IBMers. They really were ivory towers up on hills. Yes, they yielded technologies that became fundamental, game-changing products. Some the business capitalized on, some the business didn't capitalize on, and I think what Lou saw missing

in all this was the deep connection across IBM. Lou believed that Research needed someone with a little bit more business discipline and a track record to oversee it, so he named Nick as Paul's boss.

Paul Horn: Lou saw a more important strategic role for Nick than just running a division. As part of that role, he assumed oversight for the Research Division, which at the time was one of the major IBM sources of innovation. So Nick took over as my boss to better tie us into the rest of IBM.

Linda Sanford: It's one thing to tell the researchers or the engineers that they should be more innovative, but to innovate, you need to understand what the business problem is, and that means you need to interact with people. Well, the development processes really didn't allow that to happen, so we had to reinvent it. That was big at the time, and Nick was a big leader of a lot of that work that enabled much more of a collaborative exchange of ideas and testing of what was going on.

The problem was even more difficult than you might think. The Research Division and the Development Division at IBM had been highly segregated for decades. Together, Paul and I started to change that because we could not truly be problem-focused without becoming more open and collaborative.

OPEN AND COLLABORATIVE

Lou's "outsider" perspective helped to shine a bright light on the fact that we sometimes were our own worst enemies, worried more about winning inter-divisional competitions than in the marketplace, where the real game was being played. As he pointed out in his book, "Research-and-development units would hide projects they were working on, so other parts of the company would not learn of them and try to take advantage of their knowledge.

It went on and on in a staggering array of internal competitions. Teamwork was not valued, sought, or rewarded."

While IBM as a whole may not have been working collaboratively, I had been leading that way with every team I oversaw, whether a handful of people or an entire division. Now my job was to drive teamwork into these closed units and get them to open up, collaborate, and see the bigger picture.

David Yaun: At the time that Nick came over, he brought this focus on tightening the connection between Research and Development. Nick—with his legacy, track record, and heritage more than anything—was probably the only person at the time who could forcefully but also convincingly drive that integration. He could both see the value of this vision, but also kind of force the business into accepting, or yielding, to the benefit. He had the clout, he had the influence, and he had the gravitas to get the various divisions to work much more closely with Research.

Sam Palmisano: Nick was authentic, and he was passionate. If you're authentic and you're passionate, people are going to give you a lot of space, and they're going to listen more carefully. I think you can be more persuasive because of it. There wasn't Nick as a public speaker versus Nick in his office. Nick was Nick. And that's why I think he was so good in this role.

Now, it's more than being some sort of good guy. He also was deep on the subject matter. If he was making some statement, then it was factual, and probably no one was going to challenge him on it, because they knew he had done his homework. That combination of authenticity, passion, and subject-matter expertise, communicated in Nick's own unique way, could get people to do things. It's not that easy.

How could I get the ball rolling? How could I begin the difficult process of opening the doors to get these amazing people to work together? As I was searching for the message I wanted to communicate, I started to see myself from a different perspective for the first time in a long time. From the time of that first Burlington debacle where I nearly domineered myself out of a job, I was always relating to my mother and her more nurturing style of leadership.

Now, as I sought to motivate the technical community, I increasingly began to use my father and the story of that night on the porch—when he first said "If nothing changes, nothing changes"—to reach them. It was ironic—I could best communicate my vision for IBM's success in the early years of the twenty-first century by talking about my father, that tough Italian character from mid-twentieth century, post-World War II America.

There was a risk, of course, that this folksy anecdote, with its simple message, would at first glance, seem odd for this deeply analytical technical community. But the benefits that I inherited from him—the drive, the focus, the commitment not only to do better, but to be different, and to embrace change—resonated quite powerfully with a new and increasingly global group of IBMers. In particular, it resonated with our growing talent pool in so-called "emerging economies" such as India, China, Brazil, southeast Asia, and parts of Africa, where they were so eager to advance in a world in which opportunity had not been readily available to *their* fathers and mothers. Despite barriers of geography, culture, and even language, these smart and ambitious people could relate to the origin story of someone whose parents had pushed him hard into an unknown world of opportunity—one that had not been open to them and that they could only partially understand.

Above all, they could relate to my father's philosophy, because *everything* was changing in their worlds. The change they were embracing in every aspect of their lives mirrored what I was saying about IBM—what we needed to do and where we needed to go—so this "old school" philosophy all kind of clicked in a very interesting way. As it had been between my father and me in the early '60s, it now was between me and more than 200,000 IBMers from all over the world. *Do not run from change. Embrace it. Own it. Learn to love it. It is the only way.*

That said, I could not do the work of 200,000 technical employees. For our vision to become reality, we had to play as a team. We began to make some progress, and as Lou passed the baton to Sam, I was given even more freedom to push.

> **Sam Palmisano:** There were 200,000 people who were mathematicians, scientists, or engineers at IBM. I was sensitive to the culture, and I knew that they'd be respectful to me, because I was the CEO with a $6 billion R&D budget. But the truth of the matter is that they needed their own leader who could stand up and articulate the technology strategy within the business strategy and get everyone to buy in—the IBM Academy (of Technology), the Distinguished Engineers, the IBM Fellows. There was a whole system built around the technology workforce, and they needed a leader. All these guys in the engineering community are very smart with strong points of view, and you just can't tell them what to do. I could cajole them and persuade them and nudge them, but Nick could actually spar with them intellectually. And he was very persuasive.

Persuasive or not, we sometimes had to *force* change, too, particularly in the earliest days of the effort. That was a challenge at the organizational level, the team level, and the individual level. There were no shortcuts. Before we achieved true collaboration, we created codependency.

> **Paul Horn:** We had to get the Development labs to trust us enough to know that their products depended on us now. They weren't just going to take ideas from Research; Research was going to have a piece of the action. We had to be trustworthy, and that was an evolutionary process which I'm proud of having helped create, and Nick was behind it all the time making sure it worked.
>
> How did we do it? There were things we did to manage Research that were specifically designed to create "incremental innovation."

That might seem slightly derogatory, but I don't mean it that way. What I mean is that we were trying to ensure that each generation is better in an evolving product line. So you're making semiconductors. How do you make the next generation better? And the next generation after that? Or you've got a database. How do you make sure that DB2 evolves with speed and function in a way that keeps it the best database?

The implementation of incremental innovation involved a financial system, a management system, and a metrics system all designed to build partnerships between the Research Division (the more exploratory work) and the Development and Product Programs (go-to market). That evolution into a model—with a management and measurement system aimed at making sure we did a good job—was a process that took place over a number of years.

I talked about the difficulty of managing change with regard to the RS/6000 and the System/390, and it is no different when managing people. Especially in long-established cultures, like those that existed in the Research labs and Development labs, respectively, there is a tendency to backslide to old habits, unless someone keeps saying, "No, we're not doing it that way anymore." I had no problem playing that role.

Paul Horn: Whenever Research had an issue with the Development labs, Nick would step in. While generally Research was very good at what we did, there understandably were problems. Occasionally a product division would want to go off on its own. They would say, "The heck with having Research do that. Let's build up the program ourselves. Why give them money to do it? We'll keep the money here." Nick would not let those things happen. Nick was always there to make sure the new process would work. As soon as we had any glitch or there were any issues, he was connected to the rest of the company at a level and a way that always protected the concept. He was essential to our process reinvention being such an important ongoing success.

As we worked to nudge the internal relationships from codependent to collaborative, we made Research open up to the clients, too.

Linda Sanford: Nick had to get them to think differently—not just to be hovering in the holds of the Research Centers around the world—to get out and talk to our clients across all industries, to our end-users, so we would have a better understanding of what the issues really were and how to solve them and how to bring technology to bear in ways that had not been possible before.

Before that, we would have the engineers in the product laboratories working with clients, but researchers were kind of on their own doing their own thing. We had many patents on many things that were never applicable to IBM or IBM's clients, because we had brilliant men and women. But we had to say, "You guys have got to get out there in the real world, real time, innovating as well as inventing." Now we were opening the doors. We were driving the more collaborative approach to innovation, and Nick was the perfect leader in this setting, because he was able to get the engineers and researchers to work closely side by side, literally, with clients.

Sam Palmisano: That's the link that Nick created. He wanted to help the client, figure out what they needed to do, fix their problems if they had an issue with IBM, but also drive it into the product plans to get the fixes embedded into the technology itself. He didn't just fix tactical problems that might have occurred with clients. If there was something within the product itself that was causing issues, he'd get it into the product plan and drive it through the whole development cycle for the future releases.

Call it "Change Management." Call it "Execution." Whatever management gurus want to call it, we were doing it. We forced and forced and forced these historically siloed functions to collaborate. Finally, the changes began to take hold.

Not only did we drive this change to Research and Development, we always came in on a budget. One of Lou Gerstner's first major decisions when he came to the IBM Company in April 1993 was to cut the Research and Development budget by almost 40 percent, to roughly $6 billion annually. At that time, it was necessary for our survival. Yet as we recovered, that budget stayed at $6 billion. We took four billion out and we did not die! Cynics—including many of the people I was now leading—had said we would die, wondering aloud how we would get away with a cut that large.

We did it by refocusing. We did it by truly collaborating. We constantly worked on the efficiency and the effectiveness of our Research and Development spending.

Remember the story of my father creating that power mower with copper tubing? He had no money, but he got some copper tubing and figured out that if he could arrange the tubing into a spiral form it could hold, and he used a saltshaker to do that. It looked ridiculous, but it worked! If something was broken, he would fix it. He could get results even without enough money. He could innovate.

Research and Development at IBM was no different. For any good R&D organization, there is never enough money, even one with a $6 billion budget! Given how incredibly talented all these technical people are, they are never out of ideas, and therefore, in their minds, there is never enough money.

So setting the budget for R&D became more than just a financial issue, it became an art form. I had to feel the pulse of the organization. I had to know what was right for the organization. I had to start to develop a sixth sense for it, so that we did not spend too much money.

We were problem-focused now. We were not chasing every wild idea coming out of the labs. We were solving problems, constantly learning, always asking questions, always getting better. We were unlocking new and hidden value. We were measuring our progress and our expenses against what our clients needed and if we were making their lives better.

Even though we kept budgets tight, nobody doing important work ever ran aground. If someone needed more money, I would find them what they needed. I always could find a way to move funds around without actually increasing the top line. And $6 billion still was a lot of money.

Of course, I would hear from my teams all the time, "You're cutting me to the bone. You've reduced muscle mass."

Of course, you *can* get to a point where you have cut someone too thin.

You *can* get to a point where they are totally dysfunctional.

You *can* get to a point where you actually might destroy your organization.

But true leaders develop a sense for gauging the true health of a function. You cannot get that from a spreadsheet or from a finance team. You cannot get that from Wall Street analysts.

I got that from myself, with the help and insights of my colleagues. I developed that sense over time. I knew the teams, I knew the organization, and I had developed a sense for what was right and what was wrong in terms of allocating funds.

And IBM Research still was able to take big swings, believe me. Blue Gene, The Genographic Project, and Watson all emerged out of this supposedly constrained environment.

Paul Horn: We did a lot of "playing" still, but we made sure that we were connected to the product divisions. There's a spectrum of what went on in Research, and probably appropriately, Research is more famous for exploratory work like Blue Gene and Watson and programs like that on the exploratory edge of the spectrum. The important thing we did was create a full spectrum, so that the people who were working there really understood what it took to make the next-generation product that could go out the door on time and on budget, too. They really understood manufacturability and they understood the client, so when new ideas bubbled up, they could be more readily utilized. It's not as if the whole division suddenly became a development lab. It's just that we put in the interfaces and the measurement system to gradually change the culture.

I was and remain a big believer that sometimes the answer is less, not more. When we went from $10 billion to $6 billion, less turned out to be more. We produced so much more value for the IBM Company, our clients, and society at large. The constraints worked in our favor as we forced ourselves to collaborate and to work smarter and better.

Paul Horn: The way he connected to people and the way he projected his excitement and caring about what we could become is no doubt unique. He was able to take that ability and help the IBM Company transition in a way that I think very few people could have accomplished. I'm personally as proud about how the Research Division was managed to be innovative as I am of any individual piece of technology or technological innovation.

Having reinvented the processes and created new means that brought about openness and collaboration, I still was not completely happy. Because we had been so siloed for so long, collaboration often was far more difficult than it needed to be. Too many IBMers had deep, world-class expertise in a particular discipline, but they lacked the ability to understand how their discipline fit in with the other disciplines that made the whole machine come together.

If we truly were going to maximize our ability to provide comprehensive solutions to our customers' problems, we needed to think with a multi-disciplined mindset. I began to think about this next challenge deeply, and it led me in some interesting directions.

MULTI-DISCIPLINED

Your best business teams, like your best sports teams, thrive when you put a group of people together with complementary skills. Collaboration—and innovation—is a team sport. While the first baseman of your baseball or softball team likely could not take over as pitcher or center fielder with any degree of success, he or she will be a better player by having a solid understanding of those roles, and how what he or she does can and must mesh with what others are doing. Your best sports teams often include a wide variety of personalities, too, and the manager's challenge is to allow those personalities to shine in ways that help the team, not hinder it.

It is no different in technology, and I loved leading the various personalities I encountered along the way. Most of them, anyway!

> **Lisa Su** (*CEO, Advanced Micro Devices (AMD), 2014–Present; Former IBM VP*): Nick is very passionate about innovation. He's very passionate about technical talent and how you nurture technical talent, and he holds the belief that you can nurture, teach, and create an environment such that innovation is more applicable and more successful. I've learned that from him. As an engineer and as a leader, many, many people that I've met in my career very much focus on parts of the equation—"Do you have enough money?" "Do you have enough people?"—but Nick believes, "Yeah, those are prerequisites, but it's the people that you choose, the environment that you choose to put them in and foster for them, and the diversity of that talent that will get you the best results."

When I led business divisions and drove products like the RS/6000 and System/390 out the door, I actually knew most, if not all, of the people doing the work. I could fill an entire book with the adventures and misadventures of these IBMers, but one anecdote in particular might suffice.

Bob Samson: I'll never forget this one meeting in the Research Lab in California. This is the first time that some of these IBM researchers are meeting with an IBM sales guy, and I'm a fairly animated sales guy. I run around and jump on chairs. I'm kind of a crazy man. I go there and I'm presenting to this group, and there's a guy sitting in the front row with sandals on with hair down the middle of his back. And he's cleaning his nails while I'm sitting there.

Now you have to understand the juxtaposition of this, because I'm wearing a blue suit and a red tie, and I'm the IBM sales guy, meeting with the researchers. Nick's in the room, and he sort of detects this scene and thinks, *Oh boy, poor Bob.* Afterwards, he comes up to me and says, "Do you have any idea who that guy was who was cleaning his nails?" I said, "No. I don't know anything about him." He says, "He is one of the co-inventors of the hard disk drive, and he has bona fides that nobody in the world can measure up to."

These were two characters from two entirely different worlds. What could they possibly have in common? Well, they were IBMers. They were both among the best at what they did. I did not need to ask Bob to stop jumping on chairs if that is what worked for Bob. And I did not need to ask the researchers to wear suits and ties to make Bob more comfortable. What I did need from both of them was to understand and respect each other's strengths in order to best collaborate.

Bob Samson: It was just another example of how his mind is wired differently and with such a level of insight that you can't help but adjust to it. Who allows a guy to cut his nails in a meeting, and then doesn't denigrate him, but raises him up? He says, "Hey Bob, do you know what this guy did?" He didn't even think about the nail cleaning!

And I did not think about Bob jumping on chairs, either. There are limits to what people can do, of course, and those limits vary by company, by industry, and by region, but the goal is to leverage your talent so that $1 + 1 = 3$, not to put the squeeze on anyone's individuality.

Bernard Charles: Nick pays extreme attention to assembling the right people together. Not the same people, but complementary people. It's not putting the same people together. No, no. It's putting incredibly complementary people together. The second thing is, he will look at the best of every team member. He looks at the good of people before looking at the limits of people, and he looks so well that he makes people even better at what they are good at.

Bob Samson: When he built the team to sell the RS/6000, the lens he viewed it through was what he always called "the bona fides"—the different skills and capabilities—of the people who were going to help put this thing together with him. I'm just a sales guy. I run around and wave my hands. And yet Nick seemed to understand the value I happened to have, to tap into it, and to ask me questions in a profound way that helped get the RS/6000 where he wanted it to go. Whether you were the guy cleaning your nails in the front row of a meeting, an administrative assistant, or the Chairman of the Board, he valued who you were, what you did, what you knew, and appreciated everything about you. That was just a very unique quality.

It is not always so extreme as the story Bob tells, but I like to think that both my experience and my eye for people and their particular talents allowed me to make decisions that might have seemed unorthodox some-times, but in the end, proved successful. I made mistakes—plenty of them—but I think the net was positive in terms of the teams we built.

Lisa Su: I think he is very good at matching the right person for the right problem to solve. He has an incredible Rolodex from many,

many years, and so he is a great connector of talent and of people who should know each other.

Bob Samson: I think he kind of looked at me like a biology experiment. I'm standing on chairs and getting people going, and he noticed that, kind of kept me in his back pocket, and when he needed to tap into my type of energy or approach to selling, he'd play that card. That's how he built such organizational capability. He didn't do it around org charts or titles, but around skills and talents and personalities that he knew could work together in the right way. He's kind of like a chef. A chef never measures anything. They throw things in a pot and say, "A little bit of this, a little bit of that." All of a sudden you have something magical. That's what I think he did so masterfully. He knew when to call me for a thought or a comment, and he did the same thing with who knows how many people. He just knew how to play it to get the most out of everybody.

The key word from Bob is *everybody*—which is where global thinking and inclusiveness come in—and I will return to that idea in detail in coming chapters.

11

ENCOURAGING, ENGAGING, AND MENTORING

So much of good management and strong leadership is about driving results and getting the work done—and done well. To do that consistently over time, you have to invest in developing and motivating people, not just for the task at hand, but with an eye on the future, often without knowing exactly what your imperatives may be three, five, or even more years out. Overcoming that uncertainty is exactly why people are the most important part of making innovation and change happen.

I have always been interested in people and in figuring out how to help them get the best out of themselves. I spent a lot of my time at IBM, across all of my years there, encouraging, engaging, and mentoring.

It is gratifying to this day to know that the mentoring I did was a critical factor in the success of many talented people. It also helped me get the right people in the right places to get the work of innovation and change done.

I served throughout my career as a mentor to IBM's Technical Community, both collectively and at the individual level. These were not necessarily official mentoring roles, and I did not mentor only technologists or even only IBMers. If I could help someone—a client, a partner, an IBM employee, a former IBM employee—I tried to do so.

FOR IBM AND THE IBM TECHNICAL COMMUNITY

We all mentor by the example we set. I knew that people looked to me as a role model, most particularly within the IBM Technical Community, and at all times, I tried to act accordingly.

At the same time, I was comfortable in my own skin, so I always was just myself. I wanted the Technical Community to know that I was on their side and fighting for them and for their careers, and I also wanted them to know why I was so excited about the Innovation Agenda and what we could accomplish together if they were willing to embrace change.

> **David Yaun:** One of Nick's greatest assets is just his sheer force of personality, his sheer energy. When Nick would speak to members of the Technical Community, it wasn't necessarily the depth of the technical expertise that he was sharing or even the novelty of the insight that he was sharing, but it was the combination of the passion with which he delivered it and his unique ability to make them feel that they were part of the conversation. And he insisted on making everything simple for people to understand. So I think there's a unique skill there, and it was a great asset for IBM that we could put a knowledgeable, informed person out there who had the ability to explain things simply, to make the Technical Community feel included, and to just charm them.

> **Linda Sanford:** Nick became the mentor; he was the technical advocate for all of the technical people. We always referred to him as "The Godfather" of the technical community, and that was widespread. It first started in the hardware space, because that was most of our business, but then he rapidly moved, as we moved into software technologies and other spaces and places. He was encouraging engineers to think broader, to think higher, and to do better. And that was the reputation that was out there. It was his nature.

To me, truly supporting more than 200,000 talented people meant more than just being able to fire them up with a speech from time to time. I really wanted to be of assistance to each of them. Now, obviously, I didn't know most of those people, I could not name most of them, and I never met most of them face-to-face. But I valued each of them, I saw myself in each of them, and from a mentoring standpoint, I made myself available to each of them to the extent possible.

David Yaun: Nick would travel around the world and meet IBMers, whether it was an internal townhall-type meeting or an external type of meeting with IBMers in the audience. Quite often, very junior people would come up to Nick and ask, "Can I get some time for a mentoring meeting?" He invariably said, "Yes."

Now, for a while, I kind of viewed myself almost as his chief of staff, and I would think, *I've got to protect his calendar. He's the number two executive at IBM. He's a busy guy. He's got important things to do.* I'd see these meetings show up on his calendar with an entry-level engineer from Austin or Tucson or Boulder, and I'd cringe a little bit. One afternoon, I thought to myself, *I'm going to do something about this.* I went to see him, and I said, "Nick, you're the number two executive at IBM. You do not need to take these meetings. Why do you do this?"

He very earnestly looked at me and said, "David, they asked." He didn't say much more, and he shut down the conversation. It struck me that this was the way that leaders and mentors should be thinking about requests for their time. He wasn't making a value judgment of "this person's more important than that person" or "I can only give my time to someone in this category." Anyone that was looking for guidance and looking to improve themselves, he realized that there was value in making time available. I'll never forget that line—"David, they asked."

It never hurt to hear what was going on with younger talent. Was my message reaching them? Did they feel empowered? Did they feel enabled? In many of these meetings, I am sure I learned more from them than they did from me. And consider it this way: if your talent feels like they cannot ask you for help or advice, you have got much bigger problems than slotting a few half-hour meetings here and there.

INDIVIDUAL TALENT MANAGEMENT AND INDIVIDUAL MENTORING WITHIN IBM

Managing talent and mentoring, while related, are two very different things. In an organization large or small, you must constantly look at your talent, and place them into roles where they can help the company. That is talent management.

But there is more to it. Yes, you are looking to leverage their unique skills within the particular team situation you bring them into. At the same time, you need to ensure that they are developing new skills that will make them even more valuable in their next role and over time. When done well, both the short-term needs and long-term health of the company are met.

It is part science and part feel, and not every decision works. As my experience and network deepened and broadened, I often could see situations where I could shift talent around in a way that benefited the business and the individual.

I believe that when people are in roles in which they can engage their passion, build their skills, and be part of something larger than themselves, all of society is made better. Easily said, but not always easily done, especially in the era of rapid change that began in the 1980s.

> **Tilak Agerwala:** Nick was always passionate about developing the technical community, even in the early years. He knew instinctively that he couldn't get somebody on board with his project if he didn't take care of their development needs. He was always helping

individuals become IBM Fellows and developing technical executives under him. Eventually, he became the ombudsman for the technical community and this role was a big part of Nick's career. I am very grateful for his mentoring me throughout my career at IBM.

Each role is part of an overall journey for that individual. In a few examples below, we will hear from some incredible IBMers whom I identified for challenging roles. Next, they will explain how I went beyond just placing them in those roles, but mentored them for those roles, for their careers, and sometimes, for their lives. Each story has its own twists and bends in the road.

Linda Sanford

You have met Linda at several points already. She is a person I enjoy talking about. I got to know her during a time in which she was one of the assistants in the office of the then-CEO, John Akers. She was incredibly bright and had a different way of looking at things, and I could see she had tremendous potential. I brought her onto the mainframe team as we were beginning to try to turn it around, and in one way or another, we have been together ever since. Linda would go on to an incredibly impactful career at IBM and became one of *Fortune* Magazine's 50 Most Influential Women in Business along the way. As important, though, she has remained just as wonderful a person, even with all of her success.

> **Linda Sanford:** He brought me into an organization where many would have thought, *Oh my God, typewriters to mainframes?* But I could feel right away that he was supportive of me being there to bring in new ideas and observations. And yet he was not overly protective. That's what I appreciated an awful lot. He let me be me. He let me steer the ship at that point.

There were not a lot of women in technology leadership roles in the late 1980s and early 1990s, but I believed in Linda. That said, I never would have treated her with kid gloves or given the impression that she needed to be handled with kid gloves. That would have defeated the purpose. She would have to prove herself to this traditionally male workforce.

Linda Sanford: Nick introduced me to the organization with an email, and then he said to me, "You're going to meet with your whole management team. You go there and you introduce yourself." He believed in me and just said, "Go." And I did. I remember sitting there looking at an auditorium of all men—not one woman—all looking at me with their arms crossed thinking, *Hmmmm.*

I never thought it was because I was a woman, because what they said to me was, "You came from typewriters; what do you know about mainframes?" I said, "I really don't know much. But you know what? Together we're going to learn. I'm going to figure out what the customer needs, so let's get started." And we did!

But the fact that Nick sent me out there told me that he trusted me. I thought, *Oh God. I'm not going to let him down.* I'm sure he had played it all through in his mind already, and it all worked out.

I knew enough about Linda to believe she would be fine. Like me, she had an immigrant work ethic and mindset. She had an authenticity about her that won the men over almost immediately.

Linda Sanford: I came from an immigrant Polish family, and I grew up on a farm with four sisters. My grandfather would say, "Girls, if you don't get your fingernails dirty pulling out those weeds, you didn't get to the root of that problem, and that weed's going to grow back!" I grew up working with the guys on the farm and talking to them in that same sort of way, and I never changed. When you allow yourself to talk to people that way, it makes you authentic as a person.

Years later, after I'd joined Nick, I would walk the manufacturing floor every night before I went home, and the guys would say, "Hey, Linda!" and throw me a baseball that they'd been tossing around. It was no different than the dynamic on the farm. But as we played catch, I also would hear about how everything had gone that day—"Man, the orders are starting to come in," or "We're having a hard time manufacturing this part." I'd take what I heard, go back to engineering, and ask, "Guys, how can we change some things so that it's more manufacturable?"

I am a big fan of Dr. Seuss, and he was known to say, "Why fit in when you were born to stand out?" That is how I felt about Linda.

Linda Sanford: The fact that he let me go out on my own—"Do it the way you think you should do it"—had a profound impact on me, on my confidence, and on my personality. I could be who I was, and I have to tell you, especially for women in the engineering space back then, and even today, they believe that when they walk out of their home in the morning, they have to put on a different face to go into that environment. I never felt that way. First of all, that would have been horrible. I am who I am. Why do I have to put on a new face? Nick never expected that of me. He allowed me to be me and to succeed in my own way. That was very impactful on me—very, very impactful.

When someone's stretching, they are going to make mistakes. Linda was no exception.

Linda Sanford: He let me steer, and yes, I made mistakes. That's how you learn, and he would help me learn what I had missed. But he'd be supportive, and he would always set a higher bar. You don't realize how much confidence that builds in an individual—that it is okay to make a mistake. Now, you don't want to make a catastrophic mistake, but it's okay to make mistakes if you learn from them. The way he would handle mistakes was to ask, "Why didn't you think about this?" Or "What caused you not to go and explore that?" So he turned mistakes into a teaching moment.

He didn't say, "Oh, that was horrible. I'll go fix it myself." Instead, his way was to ask, "What did you learn? Why did you do what you did? Go make it better." I think a lot of engineers think this way—you want to understand why things happen the way they do and how it occurs. You keep asking yourself, "Why, why, why, why, why?" You keep peeling the onion back, and that's very important. We're not all going to be engineers, but to some extent, we all need to know what happened either right or wrong that caused an outcome to be something different than had been anticipated. While I felt bad that I might have messed up and disappointed him, he never made me feel like I was a failure. It was a totally different feeling. I would think, *Okay, now let me think. That didn't work, but let me test this,* and off I'd go. So that was a positive motivation, not a negative, where I'd think, *Oh God, I might as well leave now.* Instead, I could pick myself up and move forward, and he always was there.

When you see someone develop, they have got the values and the drive, and they care about the company and results, then as their leader, you do not want to leave their future to chance. You find yourself constantly looking for their next opportunity and the one after that.

Linda Sanford: I worked for him for five years in the mainframe world. He brought me in to do strategy, then had me go run the software development organization. Then he added the hardware development to the software development for me to lead. Finally, when he himself moved on to a bigger role, I ran all of the mainframe business. It was quite a five-year run for me.

Later, as has been discussed, we teamed at the strategic level to help Sam Palmisano build the Globally Integrated Enterprise. We were together until I retired, and really, until this day. My idea of mentorship is that at some point there is a sort of graduation, but the relationship never really has to end.

> **Linda Sanford:** It is family in many ways. That may sound trite. But it is family. I still consider him my mentor, even though I'm retired. We meet periodically, and our paths cross through different organizations, and I'm happy that we are still doing that. I know his family, he knows my family, and I think that's one of the core reasons why companies like IBM will stay together. I still talk to lots of IBMers. Nick does, too. We ask, "How are you doing? What can we help with?" It's in our blood.
>
> But I owe him so much. I think in all those dimensions—leader, mentor, friend—he believed in me, he set the bar high for me, and having that strong belief in me, it made me feel that I never wanted to disappoint him. That is very inspiring. That is very motivational for people. I think everybody feels that way about Nick. You never want to let him down. You never want to disappoint him. So you're going to do all you can in every aspect—work, life—in order to be who you can be. I think that's so important. He just believed in me. He didn't even have to say it in those words, but I knew he did. He was going to be there to support me. If I needed help, he'd always be there, so I didn't want to let him down. And as a result, I never let myself down, and I feel like a better person because of that.

It is great when a mentee stays with me for life like Linda has done. I tell them over and over, down the years, the same mantra I had accepted for myself: "*Always* take the challenge."

Of course, they have their own free will and have to live their own lives, so that idea of "always" gets tested, as I learned with Ross Mauri. Like Linda before him, Ross eventually ran IBM's mainframe business, and as of 2021, he remains a vital executive at IBM.

Ross Mauri

Ross, a big part of the mainframe turnaround, was a young man I had been mentoring for some time, even by then. His story reflects both my approach to talent management and to mentoring, particularly the ability to know when to push, and when to briefly let up.

> **Ross Mauri:** I got to know Nick when I was a First or Second Line Manager, and he was a Division President and then later a Group Executive. He always had been one of those "Big Names in the Sky," so to speak, that you see on org charts, but who almost don't seem real. Then in the early '90s, as Nick became directly involved with Poughkeepsie, where I worked, I got to hear Nick, see Nick, and participate in meetings with him in which I was either a listener or a presenter. So Nick went from this mythical figure—a person that you'd see on billboards or posters—to someone that was real.

I took notice of Ross in a few of these sessions, because I liked the things he had to say. He was young and a bit raw, but he was bright, communicative, and open-minded. Pretty soon I took an interest in him and his career.

> **Ross Mauri:** Going back almost thirty years now, if I knew I was going to interact with someone like Nick, I'd be a little scared— maybe a lot scared—and then how things unfolded in those meetings really formed your opinion of that person. I remember being scared meeting with Nick in different contexts in the '91–'92 timeframe, but he never made me feel uncomfortable. So my first impressions of him were of this wildly smart high-ranking executive that I felt I could actually relate to. I think that's one of the things

that stuck with me as I got to know him better and better and as he actually started to mentor me. I realized, "He's this really smart senior leader, but wow, he interacts with me like I'm a normal person."

I would watch and listen to Ross during this timeframe when we were developing our strategy for reinventing the mainframe. It was a very fast-paced project that encompassed not just Poughkeepsie but all the important IBM mainframe labs. He held his own in meetings with other more senior managers, and I could see that he had leadership potential.

Ross Mauri: I always felt like the little kid in the room, but Nick always treated me as if I were an IBM Fellow. Over that timeframe, he was asking more and more for me to come to meetings. I think he saw someone who had great potential but didn't realize it. I think he saw someone who could understand technology but wasn't so enamored with it that it was my whole life or that it was the only thing I could do. He saw someone who was open to new ideas, made reasoned decisions, and could communicate in a style that he felt was appropriate. His interest in me wasn't for my IQ, I know that, and it wasn't for my deep technical knowledge either. I think he picked me for my balance. I was a balanced individual, and I think he felt he could trust me in navigating waters that would be, sometimes, very rough.

In Part IV, I will explain the concept of the "T-Shaped Individual," or someone who combines both deep subject matter expertise with broader areas of knowledge in a way that lends itself to innovation and collaboration. Ross was just that sort of person. Many great individual performers are not cut out to be managers or leaders because their focus is too narrow, but Ross had potential because of his balanced and broad makeup. He just needed grooming.

I decided to send him to France, where we were starting a client server unit. With his youth, I knew he would take a bit of a beating from some of the more senior executives there, but I also believed he was ready for the challenge.

> **Ross Mauri:** In March of 1993, Nick called me out of the blue. He said, "Are you sitting down?" I said, "Yeah, I am." He said, "I want you to go to Paris." And like the naïve person I was, I said, "Texas?" He said, "Ross, please! France." I said, "I didn't think there was a development lab in France. I'm just a pure software developer." He said, "I know what you are. We're starting a client server unit there, and we need an executive to lead it. I want you to go do that."

He was ready, although he did not know that or fully believe that just yet. Would he accept the challenge?

> **Ross Mauri:** I was totally shocked, because I always viewed myself as a lab rat, but a week later, I was literally announced in the job in Paris, and flying back and forth. The relationship with Nick—I didn't do anything overt—but he was drawing me in more and more. I guess he could trust me and trust the things I was doing, and our bond had started to form during that time. So before he sent to me to Europe, I asked him, "Will you be my career manager, Nick? I'm going to Europe, but you're going to be the one to bring me back." He said, "Absolutely. I am going to oversee your career."
>
> His saying that was really life-changing for me. He probably was doing it anyway, I just didn't know it, but that was a real discussion between the two of us. So I went off to Europe, and I was there for two and a half years. He always stayed in touch with me. If he was there, he always made sure he saw me, and we just formed this relationship where if he wanted to know what was going on, he wouldn't hesitate to call me or send me an email or see me in person when our paths could cross.

As Ross succeeded in Europe, I started to envision him working directly with Linda on the mainframe, but the timing was not quite right yet. That happens in talent management all the time. In the meantime, I had to find him some good developmental challenges.

Ross Mauri: When I came back from Europe, I was in a holding pattern waiting for this one particular job to open. Then one day Nick came back from Lou Gerstner's staff meeting and said he wanted to talk to me. I went into his office with my notepad and my pencil in hand, and he looked at me and said, "You won't need those." I said, "Oh, man. Now what, Nick?" He said, "We talked about you today, and tomorrow, you're going to go meet Lou Gerstner, because you're going to be his next Technical Assistant." I proceeded to tell Nick why I didn't think that was a good idea, that I really wanted to go back to the lab, and that I'd had enough of headquarters. He let me talk for about two minutes, and then he just said, "You didn't hear me, Ross. I said that tomorrow you're going to go down and meet Lou Gerstner. He just wants to make sure that you two can communicate, because you're going to be his next Technical Assistant." Again, I'm a young kid. I was probably thirty-five years old at the time. I'm still wide-eyed. Well, I became Lou's Technical Assistant for the next nine months, and then Nick brought me back and put me in the role of VP of Mainframe Hardware, a role that he'd already earmarked me for at an earlier time.

Working for Linda, Ross was a huge part of the mainframe turnaround, and I continued to look for ways to build his career. He also was watching me and the example I was setting as a leader.

Ross Mauri: By this time, Nick had shown again and again that he was just the ultimate role model for me. I would always observe him in how he dealt with extreme stress, or people yelling at him, or all these different things that happen in business. I was just a sponge soaking it up, because to me, it was just a master class in leadership from Nick. Anytime I could learn things just by observing, I did that.

I saw that Ross was dedicated, a fast learner, and a collaborator at heart. As he matured, we established a relationship of great candor.

Ross Mauri: As a mentor, he was always there for me. If I ever wanted to talk for two minutes or a half hour, he was always there. He'd make time. And I know I wasn't the only one. I always felt that I could go get a straight answer, even though sometimes it was not necessarily the answer that I was hoping to get or thinking I would get. But in the long run, it was a good answer, because he was really thinking about me, not just in the moment, or the day, or the current job.

And then a funny thing happened. Ross did not accept the challenge.

Ross Mauri: After two years as VP of Hardware, he offered me my first General Manager job, but I would have to move to Raleigh, North Carolina. It was only two years after I had moved back from Paris, and I decided to turn him down. The reason I turned him down was not because the job was terrible, but because we had just moved back from France, I had two kids, all four grandparents were alive, and all four grandparents lived within a half hour or less of us. I was worried that if I moved us away again that one or more of those grandparents wouldn't be here when we moved back. I really wanted my kids to get to know their grandparents, a luxury I never had as a child. So I turned him down for a very important executive role, which I did not want to do. He took it amazingly. He empathized with what I was talking about. He obviously wanted me to go to Raleigh, because he was moving chess pieces for a reason, but he understood.

I certainly could have pushed Ross harder, and no one would have questioned me. In the mid-'90s, younger employees basically still did what they were told and went where they were asked to go. Pushback was rare, because ambitious talent worried very much about making "career-limiting moves."

I know that Ross agonized over his choice, and I understood well the tradeoffs that young people had to make. Obviously, I had made them myself, and obviously, he had heard from me many times, "Always accept the challenge." And yet, he had given me all I had asked for a long time, and now it was my turn to give to him something in return that was important to him.

> **Ross Mauri:** He always coached me, "You always take on the
> challenges, because that's what the company needs you to do," and
> I knew that's what he always did, so I knew this was going against
> his mantra. I was worried about disappointing Nick, but the way
> he handled it was amazing. It showed the character of the man. I
> think he saw that prior to that, and then after that, I took on every
> challenge he offered. It didn't hurt my career. He could have put
> pressure on me to take it, which is what a lot of people would do.
> He didn't say, "Oh, no, Ross. I want you to go back home and think
> about this again." He read in the moment that the right thing to do
> was to back off and to go find somebody else. I think that's part of his
> ability to judge people. He's an extraordinary judge of character and
> truthfulness. He reads people very, very well.

Every situation is different, and in that particular moment, I sensed that I needed to bend with Ross. More than twenty years later, Ross remains one of IBM's best executives, so I think I made the right call. It can be easy to let ego get in the way, or to demand total loyalty from someone, but true mentoring should not work that way. True mentors recognize when to push and when to let up, as the Anne Altman story will help to show.

Anne Altman

Anne had joined IBM in 1981 and had spent most of her career in and around the federal space. I first met Anne when she was in sales during the days leading up to the RS/6000 launch. My initial impression was positive, and I followed her career evolution from a distance as she began to be groomed within the Federal Systems Division and then as the head of a Services team in Manassas focused on building capabilities that were implemented for the Navy. When IBM sold that business, Anne helped to divest the division and then headed to Software, where she eventually ran a sales organization. Eventually, she came back home, when she was asked to go to DC to run Federal Government Sales.

> **Anne Altman:** Coming back in '99 to run Federal Government Sales, I was immediately thrown into this deep relationship with Nick, and that's when we became very close. He became that person who was my mentor, my partner, and my avenue within the IBM Company to represent the potential for growth within the federal business.

By this time, I was deeply involved in our Federal activities across many channels, so I reached out to Anne and said, "I'm really delighted and proud that you are in this role running the Federal business. I'm here to help you."

> **Anne Altman:** Right away he said to me, "Now it's up to you, Anne, to engage me when you need me, because I will show up."
> So in some respects, I thought, *This is amazing. I have somebody who understands the client, who will listen to me, and who is open to coaching me or evaluating what I'm putting together.* And then, he did it. He actually did it.

You will recall that Anne was facing a federal government that was extremely upset with IBM for having divested our federal business during the turnaround, and five years' time had not been enough to erase those bad feelings. It was up to Anne to rebuild this now small business, and she did a great job selling our integrated capabilities. She made major contributions to the Nuclear Stockpile successes with the Department of Energy and across the board.

> **Anne Altman:** I think he recognized that I was able to step back and understand the challenges that we were facing and that I would be creative in how I approached navigating those challenges. I became one of his people, and that's when he became more than a mentor of mine: he became my sponsor. There's a big distinction.
>
> In small meeting rooms, with very senior people and very frank conversations, the question comes up, "Who should we put in this job? Why should we do that?" A mentor can be very passive, but a sponsor puts themselves at risk by vouching for you and saying, "I think this person can do this job." Nick is willing to be a sponsor. He put his reputation on the line to advance people who he thought could do the job.

As she met the challenges she had been given, we looked for new opportunities for her. With Anne, though, she loved what she was doing so much that she did not want to change.

> **Anne Altman:** I was a Managing Director. I was running the Federal Government business. We were growing by leaps and bounds. We had at this point sixteen or seventeen consecutive double-digit quarters of growth. The marketplace was saying, "Wow, IBM is back in a huge way." Life was really exciting for me. And then I would get a call. At IBM, calls always came between Thanksgiving and Christmas, and they would say, "Okay, we want you to go do something else."
>
> But I loved what I was doing. It was the best job I'd ever had. So I called Nick and said, "Do I have to take this job? I just need to know.

If I do, I'll salute and go do it, but I don't want to. I have more work to do right here." So he told me, "No. I'll manage this. We'll take you out of that, and you'll be fine." I think having Nick cover my back was important for many years after that, and I continued to love that job.

As a mentor you can sometimes take your foot off the accelerator, as I did in this case with Anne, because she was still growing in her role. But the worst thing that you can do is let that growth plateau for too long.

> **Anne Altman:** A few years later, I get the call right around Christmas again, and it was, "We want you to go run the mainframe business." So I called Nick, and I said, "Do I need to do this?" He said, "Well, Anne, everything's a choice. You don't have to do it. However, if you want to continue to grow in your career, you will do this."
>
> So I thought to myself, *Okay, that's that.* Deep down I knew he was right, but still I was thinking, "Why me? Why not Ross Mauri?" It was Sam who said, "I want somebody who always is thinking about the client, who has the voice of the client, who has lived their life out in front of the clients." So that's when I moved to run the mainframe business and ultimately the successful launch of the Z-10. It was very helpful to get that nudge from Nick and have him say, "You have to go do this." It was what was best for me, and that's what makes Nick a phenomenal mentor. He listens, but if you ask, he advises.

I always advised from a place that balanced the needs of the individual with the needs of IBM. I had made a career out of IBM, it had worked very nicely for me, and I wanted the same for our top talent. But the times were changing, IBM was changing, and with those changes came a difficult adjustment period for me, as the dual story of Lisa Su and Mark Papermaster will show.

Lisa Su and Mark Papermaster

I first became aware of Lisa in the mid to late 1990s. She had joined IBM in 1995 and made her mark in semiconductor research and development.

> **Lisa Su:** Nick was someone who was many, many levels above me when I first joined IBM, so I knew him from afar, and because of the Technical Resources Program that IBM had, he knew me maybe before I really knew him! At that time, IBM had a very structured and regimented way of saying, "These are the people we want to keep an eye on," and somehow given Nick's hardware background and his semiconductor background, he was aware of me.

As with Ross Mauri, I saw beyond Lisa's technical brilliance to her leadership potential, and I took a similar approach as I had taken with Ross.

> **Lisa Su:** One day, after I had been with IBM for about five years, I received a call from Nick's office asking if I would go down and visit with him. I was a Second Level Manager who was working on an important project, but not somebody that I imagined would need to go see Nick Donofrio. So I went down to his office in Armonk, and he said, "Look, we've been tracking your career, and we want to help you develop. Would you want to be the Technical Assistant to Mr. Gerstner?" I thought, *Wow!* It was just an incredible opportunity.
>
> Nick said, "My goal is to help you through this," because typically they had chosen more senior people for that particular developmental responsibility, but they gave me a shot at it. I think Nick was very instrumental in saying, "Hey, we have some really top technical talent. Let's figure out how to help grow them faster."

As with Ross, I did not just place Lisa and forget about her. We got to know each other better.

Lisa Su: When Nick identified me to spend a year in the Chairman and CEO's office, that's when he really became my mentor. I was a PhD only five years out of school. I had no idea what to do or what to expect in this new role, but Nick said, "Look, my office is right downstairs; come see me whenever you want." And I really did go see him. We had regular meetings once a week to talk through any dumb questions that I had about how to work in that environment and how to be useful and how to learn. It was my first opportunity to interact with Mr. Gerstner. It was my first opportunity to really get to know Nick. I also had the chance to participate on some of the larger technology strategy councils that IBM had at the time, where they'd be talking about large strategy items for the company. It definitely was the best developmental opportunity of my career, and I owe that to Nick for somehow picking me out of a crowd as someone who was deserving of that kind of challenge.

Lisa did a great job working for Lou, and we continued to find challenging opportunities for her within IBM in the early 2000s. During these same years, I also was mentoring a young man by the name of Mark Papermaster, with whom I had first crossed paths in Burlington many years before.

Mark Papermaster: I had started with IBM as an intern in 1980 at the Space Center in Houston, but my real love was chip design and computers. I looked at what was going on at IBM in Burlington, and they were really at the forefront of chip design. I managed to get myself transferred onto the team that began leveraging the new CMOS technology in chip design.

Nick was an electrical engineer. He had been a circuit designer, and that's how I had chosen to start my own career, and when I first heard Nick speak, it was incredibly inspirational. Most anyone that worked closely with Nick will probably tell you that he inspired them, but I felt that more than most, because I looked at his background of circuit design and how he had been able to be so influential in driving IBM and the industry. After my first time hearing him speak, I decided that was my model; that I'd be served very well if I set my goal to try to achieve any of the kind of success that Nick clearly already was achieving and would go on to have over the course of his career. He was that inspirational. When you heard him speak, and he talked about taking on adversity and enacting change, you believed you could do it, too.

I came to know Mark much better a few years later, when he moved to Austin to be part of the POWER Design Team.

Mark Papermaster: I joined the microprocessor design team in 1990. This would be the first single chip implementation of the first RISC architecture for IBM, called POWER. Within a few years, I was the Director of the POWER4 Design Team. POWER4 at IBM was a transformational design. It was intended to leapfrog IBM back to the forefront in CPU design. We were marching it to market, and it had tremendous revenue at stake. I remember we ran into solvable but tough challenges, but if we didn't solve them maniacally, we could have been late to market. I ended up giving Nick updates weekly by telephone. By then, Nick had risen to the Senior Vice President level, reporting directly to the CEO. He had the ability to take important projects like the POWER4 and reach down into the organization to someone at my level and say, "Look, this is important. I need a weekly update."

As with the others, I saw the broad and deep qualities in Mark that I prized. And I saw a quality young man whom I could count on for candid answers.

Mark Papermaster: That's when I really got to know Nick well. I already had immense respect for him as the technical leader and management leader he was at IBM, but during that period when we were really under the gun, and we knew what we were doing was so critical for IBM, I really got to know him as an individual. That was incredible because I really understood then how much he deeply and personally cared for individuals.

I would never meet with him where he didn't ask about my wife. She was an engineer at IBM at the time, and he knew my wife, so it was always first about my family, and then about IBM family. When I say IBM family, I mean colleagues, so the discussions often then went to, "How is the team doing?" He would inquire about other leaders, too. For me, that was incredibly inspirational to see that he was so balanced across both business and the human side of innovation and engineering.

The sky was the limit at IBM for both Lisa and Mark, but it was not to be. Without a doubt, they both believed in the idea of always accepting challenges, but as the technology market evolved, and competition for talent intensified, they both chose to leave IBM in the prime of their respective careers. Lisa left first, and Mark followed about a year later.

Lisa Su: One of the larger recognitions that you can receive as a Vice President was to get elected to IBM's Senior Leadership Team. That was a group of the top 300 executives or so that are selected by the senior vice presidents and CEO, and Nick got me there, and then in 2007 I decide to leave. It was a very, very difficult decision for me and a difficult discussion with Nick. IBM was a wonderful company, and is a wonderful company, and I will always believe that IBM shaped me as an engineer, as a manager, as a leader, and as a technologist. The thing that I always appreciate about IBM is that not only was it a great Research & Development organization, but it truly was a great People Development organization. There were a lot of resources and attention paid to Talent Development. I learned everything I know because I had that opportunity for fourteen years.

I was not happy about losing Lisa, especially to a smaller company. Inherent in what she articulates—how IBM shaped her as engineer, manager, leader, technologist—is the very ideal of the broad and deep T-Shaped Individual. It had taken years of well-planned development and advocacy to create that breadth and depth, and now she wanted to leave?

Lisa Su: The only issue that I had with IBM, frankly, was that I was a semiconductor person, and semiconductors was a $3 billion business within an $80 billion company. We were relevant, but we weren't the most important thing at IBM, and I had this idea that I wanted to someday lead a semiconductor company. I didn't see how that was going to happen within IBM.

While I could understand her desire to go deep in semiconductors, and I admired her ambition, I believed that over time, she would miss out on the opportunity to experience the full breadth of the evolving technology map. That was the opportunity that IBM represented and that was the opportunity I had mentored her to be ready to experience.

Lisa Su: That was a very difficult conversation to have with Nick, because he viewed the world much more broadly than I did at the time. He viewed the whole world of hardware and software systems, and he fully believed I would have a great career at IBM. In hindsight, I think he's completely right. I would have had a great career at IBM. But when you're young and you're ambitious, and you think you know exactly what you want to do, which in my case was go deeper in semiconductors, then you have to go for it. So it was a very difficult decision, and I was quite sure that Nick was very upset with me for some time, because he had invested so much in me, the company had invested in me, and he wanted me to stay and see it through.

When you lose someone of Lisa's caliber, it stings. I was not used to losing top talent. My own retirement date was approaching, and I wanted my mentees positioned to represent my values after I departed, because we had such great momentum with the Innovation Agenda. And then I lost Mark, too!

Mark Papermaster: Nick retired in 2008, as did Bill Zietler, who had been heading up our Server Division. I run very much on personal conviction, and at that time, when Nick and Bill retired, and the direction of IBM was going more toward services and less to hardware development, I chose to leave IBM. It was a tough call, and one I know Nick was not happy about. He was disappointed, but I think he had enough understanding of what I was going through. At the time, it became very acrimonious between IBM and me when I left, because I left for Apple. I went to Apple because they were investing a lot in hardware, but it was not the kind of hardware IBM was doing. I went to work on iPods and iPhones.

In life, as in football, there is a long game and a short game, and for an IBM lifer like me, it felt like my short game had failed me. I was disappointed. I wanted IBM to benefit from Lisa and Mark's vast talents, and vice versa, but their interests took them elsewhere. Life never goes completely according to plan, but it does go, and sometimes for reasons that do not fully make sense until much later. As fate would have it, the long game evolved over time in a way that brought Lisa, Mark, and me back together again, something none of us envisioned back in 2007 and 2008. (You will hear more about our reunion shortly.)

In the meantime, I still had 199,998 other mentees to think about within the IBM Technical Community, and as with Linda, Ross, Anne, Lisa, and Mark, I wanted to help as many of them as I could. I could fill an entire book with mentoring vignettes, all powerful in their own way.

In many cases, my approach to mentoring had little to do with formal programs or assignments to mentor this person or that person. I was always on the lookout for talent, no matter where I could find it. I would keep an eye on people, stay in touch, and almost without fail, a situation would arise a month, a year, or even three years later where I needed someone for a particular situation, and sure enough, I could look to my large network for just the right person at just the right time.

> **David Carlucci:** In my case, it was an informal mentoring. This was just a guy I felt very comfortable bouncing ideas off of, and he felt comfortable enough with me to give me feedback. So if I was apt to take a position in the company, I would feel comfortable picking up the phone and calling Nick and reviewing it with him. Not only did I work with him on the RS/6000 launch, but later on, I took over the mainframe business from Linda Sanford, and I know that Nick had a lot to do with that. He approved my taking that very deep heritage and technical business, even though I didn't have a technical background.

> **Bob Samson:** He would find people that maybe the system missed or ignored, see the value in them, and begin a process with them. It wasn't like he talked to them every day, but they became a part of his orbit, and in so doing, became one of his mentees. He had the ability to see the good in people, to see the talents that they may not even be able to see themselves, and to see a spark—and maybe it's not even a spark yet, but it's going to become one—and see it early and keep that spark alive and growing through how he used everyone's strengths differently.

I think Bob's use of the word "spark" works very well. A good mentor sees that spark in someone and keeps it alive—sometimes many times over—before it can become a truly powerful blaze.

At IBM, various secretarial or assistant roles served as important stepping stones for high potential talent. In the 1980s, I had served as the Secretary of the Corporate Management Board at IBM's headquarters in

Armonk, New York. In the 1990s, both Ross Mauri and Lisa Su had served as Technical Assistant to Lou Gerstner. These were relatively short-term, rotational positions, but when well-run, they offered exposure to high-ranking IBMers and offered the potential to do important work.

Like all senior executives, I had a rotational Executive Assistant (EA) spot. Unlike many executives who might hold onto an EA for a year or two, I decided to use mine to advance the cause for women and underrepresented minorities. It was a small way of aligning my own business with what I was advocating for the Company, and I did it through quick, six-month rotations to get as many people as I could through this gateway assignment.

Lauren States

In the late 1990s, a young engineer and woman of color named Lauren States became my Executive Assistant. She had been working in Software in Chicago for a few years but made the decision to return to the Armonk area to work with me.

> **Lauren States:** For several reasons related to family and geography, I had been considering leaving IBM. One day I received a call telling me, "You're under consideration to be the Executive Assistant for Nick Donofrio." I didn't know Nick, though I knew of Nick. I knew this was a big deal, I knew it was something that might really be life-changing, and I knew that I couldn't let that go. That's how I met him and moved back east.
>
> It was immediately clear to me that Nick was very different from everybody else. I felt like you could really talk to Nick, and he would treat you with respect. At that time, many of the Executive Assistants were treated like administrative staff. Some of them even had to do personal errands for their executives. That wasn't the case with Nick. When I worked for Nick, I did meaningful work. And I got exposure to parts of the business that I might not have otherwise.

He gave me certain tasks to do, in particular, on the client side. I had worked my entire career in client-facing roles, so he essentially let me manage his client portfolio directly, not as a coordinator, but as a partner. He stretched me.

I had heard good things about Lauren, which is why I had wanted to bring her on board and expose her to new areas within the Company. It did not take long, though, for me to determine that she truly was outstanding, and I began thinking about what she might do after her quick rotation with me.

Lauren States: Several months after we were working together, I went out to California with him for a meeting. While we were driving back from Silicon Valley to San Francisco, Nick all of a sudden asked me, "What do you want to be?" This was appropriate for him to ask me at that time, because my EA assignment was winding down, but I replied, "I don't want to think about it." He said, "You can be anything you want once you decide," which is probably one of the most important things anybody ever said to me.

By this time, we had grown close, and I understood that Lauren had a lot of inner emotions swirling about what to do with her life and what was possible for her. As a woman, as a mother, and as a minority, she felt there were limitations on her. I wanted to challenge her way of thinking. I wanted to turn the spark I sensed within her into a blaze.

Lauren States: It wasn't that I didn't think I was capable. I already knew that. I knew that for a really long time, because I had had a really excellent career from the time that I was a Junior Systems Engineer. I was at a point where I was trying to decide what direction I wanted to go. There were not a lot of minority female executives in the company. Many people were telling me what to do: "You should be head of an industry." "You should be this." "You should be that."

Deep down, I wanted to be a technology executive, but many
other people were encouraging me to be a sales executive, and that
was part of my reticence. I didn't want to go out of the lane of who
I was and what I enjoyed to do something that everybody else felt I
should do and to follow a strategy of what they felt in my particular
case—as a female minority executive—I should be doing.

I was a working mother with an eight-year-old daughter. I was
unsure that I wanted to enter the executive ranks. Ultimately, it was
because of Nick Donofrio and Nancy Stewart, who was the CIO at
the time, that I gave myself permission to go for it. Nick, because of
his belief and advice that I could achieve anything I wanted once I
decided, and Nancy, because of her counsel to pursue what I wanted,
not what everyone else wanted for me.

I knew what she could become, but she had to be willing to overcome the
external resistance that she would face as a female minority executive, and
she had to overcome the internal resistance that she created for herself as a
working mother if she was going to accept the challenge.

Lauren States: "You can be anything you want once you decide."
You have to understand that people don't say that to people like me.
Of course, my parents did, and probably some of my teachers, and
I always felt like I had access to plenty of opportunity, so don't get
me wrong. But like many women, and particularly minority women,
I think I operated with a sense of muted expectations to protect
myself from what I knew was not something necessarily offered to
somebody like me. Because why should I be hurt by things that I
can't control—which is different from: why shouldn't I do the best
job that I can? Why shouldn't I protect myself emotionally? And I
think what Nick was doing—or maybe what he did and wasn't aware
of it—was forcing me to lower that protection to take more risk.

If nothing changes, nothing changes. Lauren went on to become IBM's Chief of Technology and then Vice President of Strategy and Transformation for IBM's Software Group Division. She retired from IBM in 2014 after thirty-six years with the Company. That same year, she was inducted into the Women in Technology International Hall of Fame. She was named one of *Savoy Magazine's* 2017 Power 300: Most Influential Black Corporate Directors. She met my challenge, and then some. She and I remain colleagues and friends, and I remain available for her as a mentor.

When you find people willing to accept the challenge, and you watch them go out and succeed, often beyond your wildest expectations, that is a very satisfying feeling. The fact of the matter is, I took as much out of each relationship as the so-called mentee, and maybe more.

This give-to-get concept is very powerful. What I did was take the time to get to know them and think about how I could position them to leverage their top skills and hone additional skills, all while helping IBM to prosper. Many of these people rose quite high within IBM. They did the work. They earned their success. My job was to believe in them and to keep pushing and nudging them through the inevitable frustrations that arose along the way until they fully believed in themselves.

MENTORING WITH NON-IBMERS

As others have been kind enough to say, I do care about people. I cannot tell you if I am above, below, or average in this regard, but people truly do matter to me. As a result, I have mentored not just people working for me or with me at IBM, but teaming partners, clients, and others.

Bernard Charles: We would be talking about strategy. I would be explaining to Nick about the future strategy of my company. I would go to him. First, he would listen. Then he would reformulate what I said in a better way. He would share with me new ideas. Those things cannot happen if the person is not fully immersing himself in your role to help you and giving you his knowledge, know-how, and incredible vision. As the years went on, Nick was always there for me, even if he now had a different IBM role or if I was dealing with another division run by someone else. Nick would always oversee things, and he would never let me down. This is his power. And when I needed advice, he was there.

Guy Chiarello: When I think about Nick, three things come to mind—our shared Italian heritage, our shared love of the Yankees, and our shared love of technology. When we first met, we talked about all three of those things. Clearly, we were both strongest in technology and business, from a partnership perspective, and that was valuable. But I think our sense of family, our heritage, and our interest in New York City were important, too.

I remember early on asking him if he would be the Executive Sponsor for Morgan Stanley from IBM. Not long after, I remember we were at a dinner, I think it was at a restaurant called Daniel in New York City, and I asked him if he would be my godfather, even though I already had a couple—we accumulate them as Italians—just because I felt such a really strong personal bond and connection with him. If you talk about "love at first sight," this was kind of "partner at first sight." It was just a very natural and tight connection.

He's fifteen or so years older than me, and when you're a guy rising up through the ranks, and somebody who's at the pinnacle of their career takes you under their wing, especially such a discerning and disciplined guy, it's kind of like when you get to be the young quarterback under the tutelage of Joe Namath. It's both an honor and a privilege, and when I'm sitting in my rocking chair someday, I will think, *Look at how much he taught me, and look at how much I learned, and look at how much I have tried to imitate him in a positive way in my own life.* That's almost the best form of flattery

I can give to somebody in my own life, to embrace what they've done and try to improve on it.

There are people like Guy whom you directly serve as a mentor, and there are people like Lauren States whom you carefully prod to be more and to think bigger. But as I mentioned at the beginning of the chapter, if you have the opportunity in your life to be a leader of anything, recognize that you are a role model, whether you want to be or not.

It can have a greater impact than you might realize at the time, as was the case for me with Jon Rubinstein, a well-known engineer who played a key role at Apple in the development of the iPod and iMac, as well as webOS. I first came to know Jon when he was working for NeXT, the company Steve Jobs founded after being fired by Apple and prior to his triumphant return. Jon went to Apple after NeXT, and I continued to work with him there.

Jon and I had a great relationship, but the thing I did not fully grasp at the time was that he was drawing inspiration from the hybrid business leader/technologist role I played for IBM. You might say he was instinctively T-Shaped.

Jon Rubinstein (*Longtime Electrical Engineer and Senior Executive; Instrumental in Developing iMac and iPod while SVP of Apple*): I grew up at Hewlett-Packard originally, and HP basically had a management track and a technical track. If you went into the management track, you lost your technical chops, which is part of the reason why I left HP. I didn't believe you should separate those two. I believed that really good engineering management should both be technically capable and a good manager. So I went on to try to learn how to do both over the years. When I met Nick, he was a role model, because he was someone who had actually done that—sort of an existence proof of the concept. He had stayed technically very capable, but at the same time was managing large organizations. By the time we met, I was running a reasonably large

engineering organization, and then continued running much larger
organizations when I got to Apple. He represented how I already
knew I wanted to evolve, and it was great to see an existence proof in
Nick. I was well on my way down that path.

It is humbling to know that someone who contributed to multiple game-
changing innovations drew inspiration from the way I went about my profession. It is perhaps an overused sentiment, but nonetheless true: we stand
on the shoulders of those who went before us. Jon became what he had intuited he could be, in part just by witnessing the example I was setting with
my own career.

Jon Rubinstein: I always thought the combination of keeping your
technical chops, growing your management chops, and getting your
business chops is a really special path, and a very valuable path that
I've tried to follow in my career. Nick was just a really good example
of that. It's very rare. There are a handful of guys like that in this
industry, but not many.

*   *   *

So many of the people that I have mentored were already remarkable in
their own right. But we all need someone who has perspective and experience to help unlock our potential. When it was my turn to be that someone,
I accepted that challenge, too.

Mentoring came naturally to me, and I did it to help people and to help
IBM. The law of unintended consequences is funny though. As these mentees went on to do big things in IBM and elsewhere, they never forgot me,
and sometimes, when I needed them, they were there for me, even when—
especially when—I had no formal authority over them.

Ross Mauri: I've known the word "authentic" for a long time, of
course, but I don't think it's been used in the context of leadership

until the last five years or so, but I recognize, that's one of the reasons why everyone was attracted to Nick, even though we didn't use that word at the time. What's really interesting is that in his later years, when he was Senior Vice President of Technology at Headquarters and didn't even really have any more line management roles, all the people who looked up to Nick—and it wasn't just a few hand-picked managers, it was thousands and thousands and thousands of people—felt we still worked for Nick, even though we didn't. If he wanted us to do something, we would just go do it. I don't know what to call that kind of magnetism, but he had a legion of followers that was remarkable.

Bob Samson: Nick captured my imagination. He really did. Here was a guy that was so passionate about what IBM could be and so articulate, and who defined it in terms that we didn't use before, that I was inspired by what he was doing. In my case, I never worked directly for Nick. I worked around Nick. I never reported to him, but I had a mindset of "When Nick calls, I drop everything." I would do anything Nick asked, not because of the management hierarchy, but because at the end of the day, Nick would always raise you up and thank you and appreciate you and value what you did. And not what you did for him, but what you did to help change the world. The power of that sort of motivation transcends any organizational hierarchy, and that power was built over decades. People observed him, saw how he would thank, value, inspire, and raise up people, and modeled that behavior.

It was my privilege to encourage, engage, and enable these tremendous people, along with so many others, to be anything they wanted once they decided. And nothing made me prouder than watching them do just that.

12
CHANGING IBM'S TECHNOLOGY

Technology, the marketplace, and the global economy changed drastically from the time I joined IBM in September of 1964 to the day I retired, or graduated, from IBM in October of 2008. IBM had to constantly change to keep pace with client needs and competitive offerings and to maintain a workforce that could not only adapt but also rise to the challenges these changes necessitated.

I joined IBM at a time in which the company was ascending to market leadership as the world transitioned away from vacuum tubes, ferrite cores, wire contact relays, and TO-5 can transistors. The integrated circuit, which IBM leveraged to build the System/360 mainframe family of fully compatible computers and peripheral devices, made the mainframe more powerful than anything on the market, but at the same time, less expensive.

Maybe more important, because it was a *family* of computers—from very small to very large processors—with consistent software across the entire range, clients did not bump up against compatibility issues each time they needed to upgrade. That extended out to any and all periphery devices as well, including display terminals, communication controllers, hard disk drives, tape drives, punch-card readers, and printers.

Tremendous value was created for the customer, but Watson, Jr. and IBM had taken tremendous upfront risks to do so. The considerable market position that enabled IBM to become Big Blue was *earned*, as was the expertise in hardware, software, sales, and services that was required to launch the mainframe business, keep it advancing year after year, and give the company the ability to optimize all of the pieces in the technology "stack."

While at some level it must have felt to many IBMers like the good times would never end, those feelings were offset some by the antitrust suit that lingered over the company from 1969 until 1982. The suit was indeed a distraction, but the greater threat to the future of the mainframe and IBM was the simultaneous rise of smaller companies offering pieces of the stack, the UNIX open-environment operating platform, and the closed Intel/ Microsoft stack.

Slowly but surely, IBM's market share was being chipped away from within its stack and from the rise of the new stacks. Equally concerning, the power of the IBM name—the Big Blue aura—seemed also to be in decline.

And here is where things get very interesting, as far as my own career goes. I mentioned earlier that my journey within IBM could not have been scripted nor predicted, but somehow, experiences across my entire career set me up to be on the right side of history on more than one occasion and to be a driving force within a company where different entrenched interests resisted change at every turn.

Despite the resistance, my teams scored some important victories that then gave me the IBM-wide credibility to drive my own Innovation Agenda into the culture of the company. While you have read about these victories in previous chapters—from the hard-fought battle to turn Burlington into the industry's leader in both CMOS memory and logic, to the RS/6000, to the reinvented mainframe, to the ASCI family of high-performance computers—my purpose here is to explain the interconnectedness of each win, and why that interconnectedness was so key to IBM's innovation renaissance during the Sam Palmisano era when the concept of *integration* allowed us to make great leaps with Blue Gene, Watson, and in some ways most notably of all, our services-centered Globally Integrated Enterprise, which spearheaded an academic and business concept known as Services Science, Management, and Engineering (SSME).

That is a lot of territory covered, so let me take you a few steps back, all the way back, in fact, to my first East Fishkill assignments following graduation from RPI. Right out of the gates, I was a "memory" guy. As Luis Arzubi mentioned earlier, you have memory—the "stuff" that remembers—and logic—the "stuff" that makes the decisions on the data that is remembered.

At that time, IBM's East Fishkill facility was all about semiconductor technology based on bipolar devices, which were fast, hot, expensive and complex. While bipolar devices and applications were common in the marketplace at the time, IBM and the world were pursuing something known as FET, or field-effect transistor technology. They were not as fast, hot, expensive, or complex as bipolar devices. That was my niche. I was charged with designing bipolar circuits for the sensing and driver chips needed by FET arrays.

Over time, East Fishkill became more focused on IBM's logic mission, so to make more room for logic design and manufacturing, memory people like me were asked to move to Burlington, where IBM's overall mission to develop and manufacture memory was housed. My team relocated, and we continued our work on memory, producing a string of products that established IBM's leadership in the industry with conventional FET technology and new-and-improved versions of CMOS FET technology.

Under Luis Arzubi's steady hand, we soon qualified CMOS (the new and improved version of FET technology), first with a 1 MB memory chip and then 4-megabit CMOS. Still, we were pretty much on our own up there. While IBM Research was tremendously helpful in establishing CMOS, they were not totally aligned with our goals and what we were doing. We were literally changing IBM and changing our entire industry in its wake.

Over time, however, we became aware that the logic team back in East Fishkill also was experimenting with CMOS.

Luis Arzubi: The technology was not there yet. Nonetheless, the company spent incredible time and effort, because it understood that CMOS technology for logic could be of paramount importance if they could make it work.

As I moved in and out of a few more assignments, I was becoming a true believer in the potential of CMOS not just for memory, but for logic as well. I kept my eye on the progress being made in East Fishkill. The problem was that the team in East Fishkill did not want to let go of bipolar technology even as the case for CMOS grew stronger and stronger.

Why change what was working? Well, because if nothing changes, nothing changes, that is why. If they were not going to change and leverage CMOS for logic, I figured I would go ahead and do it *in Burlington*. That is when I really began to push my ideas hard with more senior leaders.

When I returned to Burlington to oversee the transition to CMOS for logic, nothing was going to stop us. Despite our success with CMOS for memory, we understood that for Burlington to survive, we needed more. We needed logic, too, which meant we would have to challenge East Fishkill's long-held stranglehold on the technology.

Mark Papermaster: Nick forced the change to the new technology. As Lab Director, he was the top executive in Burlington, and he was very influential to us and to IBM as he drove that technology change.

With Luis and his team's help, Burlington would establish itself as the world's leader in CMOS logic. Remarkably, we were delivering the second generation of CMOS (CMOS2) when I left Burlington and were working on CMOS12 when I left IBM years later.

Luis was rewarded by succeeding me as Burlington Lab Director and ultimately Site General Manager. He did a brilliant job cementing the future and the success of IBM Burlington as the company's internal CMOS experts and source.

Luis Arzubi: Eventually we got it to work and qualified, and I got a few awards. What we did was used in all the IBM systems.

Burlington was on the right side of history. IBM East Fishkill fought for what they thought was right, but they ended up on the wrong side of history. Ultimately, East Fishkill was retooled to satisfy IBM's global CMOS technology needs.

Despite the fits and starts, despite the need to fight East Fishkill and to fight with IBM leadership to shake up the status quo, we had made it happen.

We had changed IBM's technology.

Not long after, I was off to Austin to lead the RS/6000 business. The RS/6000 was crucial to IBM's ability to compete in the burgeoning UNIX open-source operating platform, but we had fallen far behind Sun, Digital, and others despite having created the RISC-technology that enabled workstations in the first place.

Our initial entry into the workstation field, the RT/PC, was generations behind in technology, architecture, design, and software. It simply was not a competitive system. CEO John Akers was willing to bet everything we had to make a better second impression with the RS/6000, since we clearly had blown it with the first one.

He was expecting the RS/6000 to be a major and bold system that would reposition IBM in the marketplace, in the minds of our clients, our partners, and our competitors. We could not do it without CMOS.

CMOS was not a nice-to-have for the RS/6000. CMOS was *the* must-have, which underscores why Burlington's willingness to part directions from East Fishkill was so important. We needed to produce a high-performing, competitively-priced system that did not simply take the lead for a fleeting moment, but instead set the competitive bar for all others to follow. Without the support of Burlington and the CMOS processor chip set that they built for our system, my team in Austin could not have succeeded.

When we finally got the RS/6000 into the marketplace, it became a billion-dollar product line for IBM in less than a year, putting Austin on the technology map, and sending a clear message both inside and outside of IBM that Burlington was the leader in CMOS technology. The IBM

RS/6000 (now IBM System p) took the market by storm in the 1990s, made history, and left an impression that was final and lasting.

Once again, CMOS was at the heart of a major victory for my team and for me. But I was still fighting. Even as the RS/6000 and Burlington's CMOS technology were challenging competitors and winning in the marketplace, I still faced a big challenge within IBM, because many influential insiders did not want to be part of the emerging "open" technology world.

Sam Palmisano: In the UNIX world, you had to work with Oracle. They were the large UNIX database provider at that time. And you had to get the app guys to go over, and they were mostly working with Sun and Solaris. So, you had to be willing to participate with an industry-standard approach, and Nick had to be persuasive because there was business pressure as well as cultural pressure to maintain the proprietary world status quo. He had to be able to navigate both.

We did manage to make both happen. As with CMOS in Burlington, our CMOS-enabled RS/6000 put us at the forefront of the open-technology workstation world. A connective thread in my career was emerging, as I worked with others to change IBM's technology, our position in new marketplaces, and our culture.

My reward for yet again breaking the status quo? I was sent back to Poughkeepsie to lead the mainframe business at a time when its very survival, along with that of IBM itself, was in question. One of the first decisions we had to face was transitioning the mainframe from East Fishkill's bipolar technology to Burlington's CMOS technology. *Again*, the CMOS connection. And *again*, the fierce internal resistance to what we wanted and needed to do.

For me, this decision was easy and obvious, yet equally hard and gut-wrenching. It was an imperative of clients such as Larry Kittelberger at Tenneco and many, many others that we make the mainframe more cost-competitive against the mini-computers that were taking market share even as they failed to meet the needs of our biggest *Fortune* 500 and government clients. CMOS was the answer.

As mentioned, Mike Attardo, who was leading all of IBM's global packaged semiconductor products and technologies, including the East Fishkill, Burlington, and Endicott locations, played a vital role at this time. He supported my decision to move to CMOS, but there were incredible consequences on *his* business, and he shouldered tremendous responsibility when it was announced that we would pull the mainframe plug on bipolar and make the move to CMOS. With this one decision, we basically shuttered large parts of East Fishkill, Poughkeepsie, Kingston, and Endicott operations.

With anyone other than Mike as a partner, this could have easily gone another way. Mike deserves great credit and admiration, along with a tip of the cap and a victory lap for his willingness to do what he believed was right, even though it created incredible challenges for him. Mike was responsible for delivering all the CMOS technology we would need then and for the foreseeable future. That is leadership. What a partner!

Amidst this painful backdrop, I had to get my team to believe, too. They were the ones who were going to make it happen.

Linda Sanford: Nick brought the team along through very, very open dialogue. He was very collaborative. He listened to us: "What do you think?" And in listening, he actively helped us to bring out our own thoughts and ideas. That was a very unusual leadership trait way back then, but he used that trait to align the team around CMOS. Not everybody necessarily agreed with what we were doing, so those people who didn't went on to do something else. Making that shift in that moment was a monumental decision and it was absolutely the right decision. He had his own opinion, that the mainframe had to go to CMOS, but he also knew that he needed to bring the team along.

Getting the team to understand the benefits of CMOS versus traditional bipolar technology in the context of the competitive challenge we faced with the minis was relatively easy. The bigger challenge was helping Linda and the rest of the team defeat two tough opponents that easily could have derailed us. The first was a collective opponent I will call the external critic. At that time, *every* newspaper and magazine in America, and many around the world, was talking gloom-and-doom about both the mainframe and IBM. It can be very hard to focus in an atmosphere where the world seems against you.

> **Ross Mauri:** We just kind of blocked the world out around us. We just said, "Failure's not an option," borrowing from NASA and the Apollo Mission, and we determined, "We can do this." If we had been too distracted, I think we might not have made it. But through Nick's and Linda's leadership, we all believed. I think when you have strong hope and belief like that, you can do a lot of things, and that's what Nick stimulated in everyone.

> **Linda Sanford:** In that type of situation, you have two types of individuals, and they deal with these times in two different ways. One is with fear. You're going to hide. You're not going to make noise. You're just going to quietly go about and hope and pray that things will be okay. The other is to see a time like this as an opportunity to make a difference in the world. Nick certainly saw it that way, and I saw that in him, and I thought the same way. To so many of us, that gave us purpose. It wasn't a fear that was put into us. It was an exhilaration, it was a challenge, it was a goal that we all wanted to be a part of on that team.

The other kind of opponent one faces during a time like this is the internal critic—by that, I mean the little voice each of us has that tells us we are not going to make it. These were difficult times, and I had to keep the team's confidence high and focused on where we were headed.

Linda Sanford: He made them believe in themselves, trust themselves, and work together as a team. It could have turned into a real disaster if everyone had put their heads down in the sand. We would have been gone. But they didn't. And a big part of that was how Nick drew out the fears of people and gave them the mindset where they just said, "We can do this, and we will do this."

Ross Mauri: He stayed close through all of this time, guiding us and pulling the strings to make sure the decisions were the right ones for IBM. People were recognized or moved out of the way who were inhibitors as we transformed the organization structure and the technology of the mainframe.

The team did a tremendous job. Just watching our engineers and looking at and listening to what they were seeing in terms of capabilities, and how quickly we could move up the CMOS scale, was exciting. We were progressing more quickly than we had with bipolar, because times had changed—technology capabilities had changed—so they were excited about what was happening.

The reinvented mainframe met the needs of the day for our customers, but it did so without losing what made it unique. Even though competition was coming at us from multiple angles, they still could not do what we could do. They still could not do what the mainframe could do. We were hearing that from clients, and that reinforced our resolve. But we had to change our technology to make that happen, and with the time pressures we were under, there were no guarantees.

Ross Mauri: This was the biggest transformation of technology that I have ever heard of and quite frankly saved the company. Everyone worked phenomenal hours for years to bring out these machines. Starting in September 1994, we began bringing out a new generation of mainframe every year for the next six years. That's how fast we were turning the technology and trying to get it to be robust enough to run the world's biggest banks and businesses. Through those years, we had hope, because our leader convinced all of us that "We can do this." Nobody was doubting the technology, but he helped us see that with that technology we could save the mainframe and save the company.

Linda Sanford: It was the most exciting time in my whole career. We were up against the wall, but Nick showed us that we had an opportunity to make a difference and to make a lasting impact.

This time our willingness to change IBM's technology had played a critical role in saving the company. The point here again is to draw that thread from the original fight for CMOS in the 1980s to launching the RS/6000 and to saving the mainframe. Each step along the way, I had to fight and fight and fight to make the change happen.

By this time, the Burlington facility had turned itself into the CMOS logic chip engine IBM needed so that we could be the center of progress for the entire computer industry and we could restore the lean, mean, retooled, iconic mainframe to its critical place in the information processing industry. And that set the stage for still more change, as ASCI, Blue Gene, and ultimately Watson were RS/6000-based and/or derivative systems that relied heavily on CMOS.

Of course, this was not just a technology story. It was about leadership, too. Everything you have read in this book contributed to my ability to *lead* different groups of great IBMers to do what needed to be done to change our technology.

I led with the IBM Values, which happened to be my values. (Chapter 8)

I led by driving change that our clients in the marketplace needed—whether new clients in the RS/6000 space or our longstanding clients in the mainframe space—not by creating products and then looking for demand. (Chapter 9)

I led by encouraging change and innovation at every turn that was oriented around multidisciplinary collaboration that sought input from around the world to solve the problems at hand. (Chapter 10)

I led by enabling and mentoring the gifted, dedicated IBMers that made up some of the hardest-working, most pressure-resilient people you could ever meet. (Chapter 11)

And I could not have changed IBM's technology across multiple fronts without *integrating* all of those elements with my own leadership style and in a collaborative way that brought out the best in a wide variety of talent across all of IBM.

And that notion of integration leads to the next big jump in where my IBM journey was headed. While my team and I were solving the mainframe challenge, Lou Gerstner was keeping the entire company intact, even if not yet necessarily knowing how he would return a new IBM to leadership once the company had been stabilized.

That is when Lou met a longtime IBMer named Dennie Welsh, who ran a small, wholly-owned subsidiary known as the Integrated Systems Services Corporation (ISSC). The ISSC existed as a subunit of the sales force, and more or less performed product maintenance for our clients.

I knew Dennie as a colleague and a friend going all the way back to our days together when I was running the technology side of IBM Manassas. At that time, Dennie led the Federal Sales Division side. When he convinced IBM under John Akers to start ISSC, I was put on his Board of Directors. We remained friends forever.

On that board, I came to understand IBM Services and its value. Dennie was developing a bigger concept of Services, and he shared some of those thoughts with me. I knew that he was onto something.

Dennie believed that a true Services company within IBM would be less about just performing IBM product maintenance and more about helping clients understand all aspects of their IT footprint. Where necessary, it would build systems, define architectures, or even manage IT for the client. The focus would be on solving a client's business problems—even if it meant recommending products that we did not manufacture.

As with the cultural need to get the RS/6000 and the mainframe to market, this would be a difficult sell within IBM, but it was a concept that was aligned with the direction of the industry. When Lou heard Dennie's vision for Services, he immediately understood its power. He had run huge companies with complex IT infrastructures like American Express and RJR Nabisco, so he deeply felt the value that a trusted advisor who could see the whole picture and make recommendations could provide. As the CEO of IBM, he equally could see the business opportunity inherent in playing that trusted advisor role.

As Lou wrote in his autobiography, "I was thrilled that I had discovered a base from which we could build the integration capability our customers so desperately needed—and in so doing, provide the raison d'être for keeping IBM together...that this services model was IBM's unique competitive advantage."

If Services could provide that integration capability to our clients, someone had to shape the IBM Technical Community to be able to deliver this much different offering. I think that is where Lou saw my ability to understand both IBM's technology portfolio and the business landscape of a more competitive, more open world and created that next chapter in my career for me.

He understood that we would need to continually change our technology, leverage existing technology more creatively, innovate, and collaborate to carve out a new type of market leadership with Services facing the client. I understood, and I pushed these ideas as hard as I could within the Company.

David Yaun: Lou's legacy at IBM, of course, is keeping the company intact, because what he saw was that the strength of IBM was the range and diversity of its portfolio. And Nick was one of the few executives that was in a position where he could force the business into accepting, or yielding, to the benefit. He had the clout, he had the influence, he had the gravitas to get the various divisions to work much more closely with one another—to collaborate, to integrate.

Vijay Lund: The biggest strength that both possessed is that they understood integration. Integration always creates value if done correctly. When Lou Gerstner decided not to split up the company, to keep the company together, that's an integration thought. When Nick retooled the mainframe, that came out of an integration thought. That became his driving force. Integration of quality. Integration of performance. Integration of customer service.

This was a whole new way of looking at changing IBM's technology. We tend to think of things in terms of hardware or software, but the fact that we also created the Science and Technology of Services is perhaps the most impactful change of all.

We started down this path with Lou, and when he retired, it is perhaps not surprising that Sam Palmisano succeeded him as CEO. Sam had not only worked in Services for Dennie, but he later ran the business following Dennie's untimely passing.

Sam clearly embraced this future of new technologies and new management styles, and he took the integration vision that Lou had heralded and began to turn it into reality.

Sam Palmisano: Lou did a phenomenal job both strategically and financially righting the ship, but we hadn't yet quite dealt with integrating IBM. We still had these lines of business—Advanced Business Systems, the Mainframe, the RS/6000, Storage, Printers, Services. They were still self-contained in how they went to market, had their own development organizations, and so forth. If you believed that technology would continue to commoditize and that you had to be in the solutions space, then the only way that we could uniquely differentiate ourselves was by integrating IBM.

Sam gave me a lot of room to move, and over the next six years, we continued to evolve and extend IBM's technology—particularly in the Enterprise and Supercomputing space—and to create the Science of Services.

David Yaun: IBM had a little bit of a market renaissance from 2006 to 2011 or 2012. The front-end of that renaissance was driven by innovation, with Nick in charge. With the most severe pain of the turnaround in the rearview mirror, Sam sought to turn IBM into an innovative leader in enterprise computing.

We made our mark not only on the bottom line but on society as a whole. Some of these ideas are just beginning to make their impact fully felt today. Innovation was at the heart of it all.

Let us start with Blue Gene.

BLUE GENE

You will recall from Chapter 7 when Vic Reis and the Department of Energy came to us to build a supercomputer powerful enough to safeguard the nuclear stockpile following the testing moratorium initially signed into law in October 1992 by President George H. W. Bush and then extended by his successor Bill Clinton through September 1996. Our computer, known as ASCI White, was stage three of the Accelerated Strategic Computing Initiative (ASCI).

Built in Poughkeepsie and completed in June 2000, it was transported to specially-built facilities in California at the Lawrence Livermore National Laboratory, and officially dedicated on August 15, 2001. ASCI White was a computer cluster based on IBM's commercial RS/6000 SP computer.

To give some idea of the accomplishment, 512 nodes were interconnected for ASCI White, with each node containing sixteen 375 MHz IBM POWER3-II processors. In total, ASCI White had 8,192 processors, 6 terabytes (TB) of memory, and 160 TB of disk storage. The computer weighed 106 tons and consumed 3 MW of electricity with a further 3 MW needed for cooling. It had a theoretical processing speed of 12.3 teraflops (TFLOPS).

IBM had done very important work here. We innovated to meet America's needs and then used what we learned to push further into supercomputing.

While ASCI White was not finished until June of 2000, we knew some time before that we were on the right track and going to succeed. That is why in December 1999, we went forward with a $100 million, five-year research initiative to build a massively parallel computer that would be applied to the study of biomolecular phenomena such as protein folding.

And in the process, we set our minds on creating a petaflop scale super-computer before anyone else, particularly the Japanese manufacturers.

We were looking for real innovation and breakthrough thinking with Blue Gene. We wanted to use this platform to effectively meet its scientific goals, to make massively parallel machines more usable, and, importantly, to achieve performance targets at a reasonable cost, through novel machine architectures. And we did it with Blue Gene/L and kept right on going.

Tilak Agerwala: After Blue Gene/L, there was Blue Gene/P, which was roughly the same, and then Blue Gene/Q, in the 2010–11 timeframe, after Nick had retired. Blue Gene/Q took us to 20 petaflops (a petaflop is 10 to the power of 15), a long way from Nick's once seemingly impossible goal of one petaflop. But it all started with Nick's burning desire to get us to that first one.

Tilak's team delivered a paradigm shift, but here's the thing—they did it with pedestrian technology! That's unheard of! That's not how you build the world's fastest supercomputer! Or at least that's not how the rest of the world thought you made the best computer. The assumption was that you make the best computer with the best technology.

Not really.

You make the best computer with the best minds thinking better about the problem, and that is what we did with Blue Gene. They went back to the problem—getting to a petaflop—and rethought the problem and tried to understand exactly what problem they were trying to solve.

Remember, I believe that real innovation begins when you "start with the problem." With Blue Gene, we had a real problem. It was an easy problem to understand. It had a roadmap, it had a path forward, and we understood everything. We saw it all in front of us.

> **Tilak Agerwala:** Throughout this, all the way through, Nick was our champion. He was constantly helping us, protecting us, and fighting for us, even when he wasn't directly responsible, because by then he had moved on to the Executive VP role. But he was constantly there as the champion.

I was their champion, but I had to continually force them to think rather than wait for a technology miracle to get them there. I knew they could get there with the technology we already had if they just kept going back and reworking what they already knew.

When they had hit a roadblock, their answer always would be, "Dial up a new node. Dial up new technology."

I'd tell them, "No, that's not the answer. We're not doing it. We're not going there. You can't have it. Semiconductor technology is not going to save your behind every minute of every day."

So that's what was underneath our breakthroughs. I'd keep driving people back to, "Why are we doing what we're doing? You created these computers. Don't tell me you don't know how they work. Go back and study how they work. Go see how they actually operate. Go back and do something different. And then come back and tell me what better things you can do as a result."

They had to go back to the basic building blocks of computing. In a very real way, they were not unlike my father making that old hand-me-down power mower work with some copper tubing and a saltshaker. They had to get to a petaflop with what they had.

They changed the architecture. They changed the instruction set. They proved that they could do it.

We built Blue Gene out of pedestrian technology. We built *the world's fastest supercomputer* out of N-2 technology. By this I mean that we did it with technology that dated two generations back from what was currently available!

Tilak Agerwala: Blue Gene/L shipped in 2005. It brought supercomputing leadership back to the United States from Japan. It was another major paradigm shift, and IBM won the 2009 National Medal of Technology and Innovation for the Blue Gene development and its application.

Paul Horn: I'm very proud of the technology that went into the Blue Gene computer, because that brought supercomputing leadership back to the United States from Japan at the time. That really required rethinking how you made a computer. The initial idea was, "Why shouldn't we be building the fastest supercomputer?"

Blue Gene/L was the first supercomputer ever to run over 100 teraflops sustained on a real-world application, namely a three-dimensional molecular dynamics code (ddcMD), simulating solidification (nucleation and growth processes) of molten metal under high pressure and temperature conditions. This achievement won the 2005 Gordon Bell Prize, commonly referred to as the Nobel Prize of Supercomputing.

In June 2006, NNSA and IBM announced that Blue Gene/L achieved 207.3 teraflops on a quantum chemical application (Qbox). At Supercomputing 2006, Blue Gene/L was awarded the winning prize in all High-Performance Computing Challenge Classes of awards.

In 2007, a team from the IBM Almaden Research Center and the University of Nevada ran an artificial neural network almost half as complex as the brain of a mouse for the equivalent of a second (the network was run at 1/10 of normal speed for ten seconds).

Blue Gene/L Supercomputer was unique in the following aspects:

- Trading the speed of processors for lower power consumption. Blue Gene/L used low frequency and low power embedded PowerPC cores with floating point accelerators. While the performance of each chip was relatively low, the system could achieve better power efficiency for applications that could use large numbers of nodes.

- Dual processors per node with two working modes: co-processor mode where one processor handles computation and the other handles communication; and virtual-node mode, where both processors are available to run user code, but the processors share both the computation and the communication load.

- System-on-a-chip design. Components were embedded on a single chip for each node, with the exception of 512 MB external DRAM.

- A large number of nodes (scalable in increments of 1024 up to at least 65,536)

- Three-dimensional torus interconnect with auxiliary networks for global communications (broadcast and reductions), I/O, and management.

- Lightweight OS per node for minimum system overhead (system noise).

We finally got to a petaflop with Roadrunner, a supercomputer we built for the Los Alamos National Laboratory in New Mexico, USA. It achieved a sustained performance of 1.026 petaflops on May 25, 2008, thereby becoming the world's first single petascale system.

David Yaun: The concept of getting to a petascale computer in a seven-to-eight-year period was a huge undertaking. The initial investment was over $100 million, and I'm sure over time it was far more than that, but it yielded a lot of the technologies that exist today. It won a National Medal of Technology, and deservedly so. I think the world's first petaflop scale computer clearly is a highlight of Nick's leadership.

We were on a roll. Around this time, I greenlit work on Watson, which became not only an important player in the burgeoning field of Artificial Intelligence, but also part of pop culture history.

WATSON

Watson was a half-baked idea around machine learning when it was first presented to me, but its potential was clear immediately. Did we see everything that IBM would eventually do with Watson? Of course not. But we saw enough to know that it was a winner.

> **David Yaun:** Nick was in the last few months of his career, and the Research team came to him and said, "We've got this thing..." And he got it immediately. It's the last major decision he made as executive vice president, and, boy, what a dramatic way to step off the court.

Watson was created as a question answering (QA) computing system built to apply advanced natural language processing, information retrieval, knowledge representation, automated reasoning, and machine learning technologies to the field of open domain question answering.

QA technology is different from document search. Document search takes a keyword query and returns a list of documents, ranked in order of relevance to the query (often based on popularity and page ranking). QA technology, on the other hand, takes a question expressed in natural language, seeks to understand it in much greater detail, and returns a precise answer to the question.

Watson was incredible. Initially, it was using over 100 different techniques to analyze natural language, identify sources, find and generate hypotheses, find and score evidence, and merge and rank hypotheses.

In a way, from my perspective, it was ASCI all over again, though in a more fun-loving way. QA technology was a field we knew we were going to be pursuing, and our researchers had this idea that competing on *Jeopardy!* would provide a proof of concept that literally *everyone*—from teenagers to senior citizens—would remember, giving us an advantage when we went to market.

> **David Yaun:** He saw it not only for its technological implications, but he also realized that taking on Jeopardy! was a great public relations coup. He was the type of executive who would see both sides of that. I'm sure he wouldn't have greenlit the investment in Watson if he didn't believe the technology was worth exploring, but his savvy in terms of seeing the potential of taking on *Jeopardy!* champions four or five years out and knowing how great it would be for IBM's image was part of it. Watson is part of his legacy, even though he barely worked on it, because he saw all sides of its potential.

Today Watson can understand all forms of data, interact naturally with people, and learn and reason. And all at scale. Its impact on business, government, healthcare, crime fighting, and just about everything else is about to explode.

In a nice bit of full-circle magic, in 2013, it was announced that my alma mater, Rensselaer Polytechnic Institute, would be the first university to receive a successor version of Watson, which would be housed at the Institute's technology park and be available to researchers and students.

That is another way to say that my journey sometimes has this other-worldly feel to it. The fact of the matter is, there are elements to Watson that connect all the way back to the decision to move to CMOS and everything that came after in my career.

> **Tilak Agerwala:** Blue Gene and Watson are connected—as are the RS/6000 workstation, IBM's Unix servers, and the 200 petaflop Summit supercomputer. They have a common DNA—the

original POWER architecture developed by the RS/6000 team and implemented in CMOS. These computers were successively architected to handle increasingly complex workloads. We went all the way from using the POWER chip to build the RS/6000 workstation and then, used that same technology to build our highest-performance servers and supercomputers, and now, over 30 years later, we have scalable POWER-based computers that excel at modeling, simulation, analytics, and machine learning.

CMOS is key to where the world is now, but having lived in a world where we started with vacuum tubes, ferrite cores, wire contact relays, TO-5 can transistors, and finally LSI, MLSI and ultimately VLSI technologies, I know that it will not be forever. That change from bipolar to CMOS, as critical as it was, was simply a point in time on the continuum of technological possibilities and change. I was in a position to fight for that change, which I did over and over.

As the predictable and comforting steady stream of nearly forty years of CMOS advances slows and ultimately stops, the continuum of technology possibilities will continue. The world will again know what I saw, felt, and thrived on over sixty years ago, when everything changed almost year-by-year, if not day-by-day.

When I consider the fact that there are basically only four computer system architectures left in the global IT world such as it is—i86, ARM, POWER and S/360—IBM has two out of four, and I was there to enable and nurture them both. That is a professional legacy to which, I do believe, my father would have said, "You did a good job, son."

This legacy stems from understanding—along with Lou, Sam, Linda, Paul and many others—that IBM had a *responsibility* to do big things and that our financial success also was tied to doing big things. Our mainframe customers needed us. The world's businesses and governments ran on IBM mainframes. They were counting on us. We had reacted late, but in the end, we innovated to meet their needs and restored IBM to a place of technological leadership.

And yet there remains one more element to changing IBM's technology and reviving IBM's role as an innovator, and that circles back to my friend Dennie Welsh and his vision for Services. Once again, the haunting—if not taunting—theme of "Why did things happen for me this way?" can be expanded around services.

SERVICES AND THE GLOBALLY INTEGRATED ENTERPRISE

From our days together in Manassas and my tenure on the board of Dennie's ISSC, I always retained in the back of my mind this constant thought about IBM as an integrated enterprise that was much stronger than simply the sum of its parts. Lou also understood the vision and saw it as the way to provide the integration capability our customers craved, as did Sam. But to bring an integrated capability to our customers, we had to create an integrated IBM, or what Sam dubbed "The Globally Integrated Enterprise."

> **Sam Palmisano:** Why a Globally Integrated Enterprise? Because we had to integrate IBM on a global scale. That was the strategic point of view, and we all shared that point of view. You can argue that we shared that point of view because we grew up in an IBM that was integrated at one point in time, when we all started. If you go back to the late '60s/early '70s, that's how it worked, so you can call it déjà vu if you want. People said, "These guys are going back to the past," but what drove it was really this point of view that the way that we would continue to differentiate ourselves and be unique in enterprise computing was through an integrated IBM.

My job, as has been discussed, was to reintegrate the technical work-force no matter where they were or who they were or what they did or where they came from. In doing so, we conceived the "Science and Technology of Services," and in some ways, this may be the most impactful change of all, because it was really difficult to pull off.

In building a Globally Integrated Enterprise, we were not talking about managing nine ballplayers on a diamond. We were not talking about a few hundred or even thousand people spread across a few offices and laboratories. We were talking about 400,000-plus diverse talents around the world.

I thought about my teams and what had made them work, and I came back to the multidisciplinary concept. The people I loved to work with most knew their roles, but usually saw the bigger picture, too. How could we scale that capability?

The question frustrated me to no end because I realized that through no fault of their own, too much of IBM's talent knew next to nothing beyond their specialties. They could do great work, but it was almost as if they did it with blinders on.

Real innovation, though, requires some knowledge of areas outside our specialties. The broader our frame of reference, the more material we have to work with, as we identify problems, evaluate solutions, and provide value to a general population. I came to understand this sort of person as the "T-Shaped Individual."

Picture the "T," with its long, vertical leg, but also its horizontal arms. The vertical leg equates to one's focus, one's deep level of expertise. The horizontal arms represent a breadth of knowledge that enables greater and easier interaction and collaboration. How you develop and deploy such people at scale requires insight, experience, and intuition.

I had intuited the "T-Shape" in people such as Linda Sanford and Ross Mauri long before I had ever heard of the concept, and I moved them into roles that ran counter to their IBM training to shake up the groupthink that could sometimes take hold within any particular IBM subculture.

We wanted to see this mindset, encourage it, and build it in, well, *everybody*. Good. We had identified a problem. Now we had to try to solve it.

I started seeking out thought leaders who could help me better understand where I could go with this line of thinking. One was an academic named Rick Miller, President of the Franklin W. Olin College of Engineering.

Rick Miller (*President, Olin College of Engineering, 1999–2020*): I
first met Nick in the early 2000s at a small group meeting sponsored
by the National Academy of Engineering. The meeting focused
on the gap between what industry needed in innovation and what
universities were teaching in engineering and in general. Nick
explained to me that at IBM, they were frustrated. At that point, they
had a hardware business, they had a software business, and they had
a services business. So they had three different pieces, and people
became siloed in their area, and they were known as specialists who
were good at those particular things. Nick wanted one integrated
technical workforce, and that started the beginning of the T-Shaped
Movement, in which the broader the staff members became, the
more valuable they were to the business.

Rick and I talked through my frustration, and he was able to not only
articulate it back to me, but to share some initiatives that gave a framework
for what I was hoping to build.

Rick Miller: In Nick's view, as people moved up the food chain, he
didn't want them becoming more narrow and more specialized. He
believed that the broader and the more integrated you were in your
thinking about the whole business, the more valuable you were.
So maybe you grew up in the hardware business, and you got to a
certain point where you were managing a team. Nick saw value in
relocating you to the software business, where you knew nothing.
You would have to gather from your new peers how things worked
and figure out on your own how to make sense of it and how your
work in the hardware business could be integrated.

The National Academy had a number of initiatives that related
to Nick's struggle, and they related to what we called mindsets.
The first one is what I will call a Collaborative Mindset, and that's
the horizontal bar in the "T" of the T-Shaped Individual. It's a

mindset that predisposes people to not want to eat alone, but to want to meet people who are new, who have ideas, and who have expertise different from their own. These are people who are comfortable collaborating with others on a team. Another one is an Interdisciplinary Mindset, represented by people who don't define themselves so narrowly by the title or the description of the program that they got their bachelor's degree in.

We think of this in the following way: your academic discipline is like your hometown. It's where you grew up. Now, in today's world, it's pretty easy to understand that very few people have a thriving career if they never leave their hometown. Very few academic disciplines have the ability to support your career for the rest of your life, either. You need to have an interdisciplinary mindset where you just basically say, "This is the starting point on a long journey. I'm going to continue to learn things all through my whole life, and a lot of the things that my company is going to make five years from now don't even exist today, so I'm not bound by my discipline."

These two mindsets were at the very heart of what we needed to see more of at IBM—people who wanted to work across silos and who had the mindset to develop a breadth of knowledge to enable them to do so. Three other mindsets enhance and unleash these first two and were as critical at IBM as they are most anywhere.

Rick Miller: Add to those first two an Entrepreneurial Mindset, which is really important. Two ingredients—a belief that there could be a better world and that it's up to you to make it happen—are the heart of entrepreneurial thinking. The next ingredient is an Ethical and Empathetic Mindset. It's caring about others and doing things that make a positive impact in the world, not doing whatever you can get away with in order to get wealthy. The final one is a Global Mindset, or understanding the world from the perspective of other countries, which is a real big challenge for Americans. Most of us have no clue that there is anything on the planet west of San Francisco or east of New York.

Obviously, we already were well aware of the Global Mindset at IBM. We had reshaped our IBM Values through the ValuesJam to reflect this mindset, but we knew we had a long way to go to bring that mindset out in everyone. Without it, though, we could not solve for our primary challenge—becoming the world's first truly Globally Integrated Enterprise.

GLOBAL THINKING AND INCLUSIVENESS

Global Thinking is an inclusiveness mindset. Global Thinking is a diversity mindset. Global Thinking is an equitable mindset. As a result, Global Thinking is an innovation mindset. You do not know *a priori* who does or does not have the last piece of the puzzle, and therefore, it is critical that you keep an open mind, that you are inclusive, that you understand diversity, and that you think globally. That last puzzle piece is out there somewhere, and you need to capture it.

I probably was more open-minded about diversity and inclusiveness than most white men my age in the early 2000s, but I definitely came from a background where these things were not thought about or discussed. Still, I understood change, so my walls were movable, and over time, my wife and kids opened my mind even more.

So did a young man by the name of Frans Johansson, who, like Rick Miller, had managed to articulate the way I thought in ways that helped me as I sought to integrate my global technical community.

Frans coined the term "the Medici Effect," referring to Renaissance Florence, where highly intelligent, creative people—Italian, no less—drew on each other's work to form some of the finest art and writing known to civilization. Very briefly, the Medici Effect sees that innovation happens with the sharing of ideas and information across functions, areas of

specialization, and diverse groups of people—again, exactly what I was trying to achieve with the IBM of the early 2000s.

> **Frans Johansson** (*Author and Speaker on Innovation, Leadership,*
> *Diversity and Inclusion*)**:** Back in 2004, Ted Childs, the Chief Diversity
> Officer for IBM, read *The Medici Effect* and really took to my message.
> Ted asked me to come to IBM to speak on the topic, specifically on
> how diversity drives innovation. It was really something they hadn't
> seen before. I didn't realize at the time how well it fit how Ted saw
> things. A few years later, Ted said, "Look, there's a couple of people I
> want to introduce you to at IBM," and one of those people was Nick.
> It was just terrific because Nick really fascinated me. It wasn't just
> all of his background and success, but it was how well he was able to
> articulate his feelings for the ideas of why he was doing what he was
> doing. In other words, it wasn't just about execution or operations for
> the IBM Company, it was having a perspective on why certain things
> were successful and his own internal theories.

We talked about being open, about collaboration, about T-Shaped
Individuals, and about global thinking as it related to the still-evolving integrated IBM and the comprehensive enterprise computing we sought to provide. The lens Frans brought helped me to better articulate what I already
believed deep down.

> **Frans Johansson:** In *The Medici Effect*, I outlined an idea about
> the intersection of different fields and cultures and industries
> and disciplines, and how that becomes the heart that keeps
> driving innovation, and Nick saw it in the same way. And what the
> conversation really centered around was, "Well, let's focus on the
> diversity piece in terms of not just industries and disciplines and
> functions and backgrounds, but also in terms of culture and gender
> and country and race and so on."

I don't know if I ever had had that type of conversation with somebody that was that immersed in innovation who thought, *Wow, this guy Frans gets it,* but I really do feel that it left an impression on Nick. After that first lunch, I did a few other minor things with IBM, until finally Nick said, "Look, you need to come to our Corporate Technical Recognition Event. I want you to speak to them."

That's a 500-person event where all the IBM Fellows (and others) come together, and I think that was what really made the connection. We had a chance to really talk and learn about each other's work, what was interesting him at the time, and how he thought about where IBM needed to go.

I had driven the idea of being open and collaborative into the technical community, but here we were now adding the idea of breaking down not only traditional business silos as a means of fostering innovation, but adding race, culture, and nationality to the mix.

Frans Johansson: I think for Nick this has been intuitive, probably for his whole life, where it's obvious that if you're going to innovate in this part of the business, you have to get new ideas into it. Where are you going to get them? Well, the easiest place to start is right over there, right down the hall. So why don't we start with that? So when I speak "diversity," I very much include that way of thinking about it.

That's basically the heart of innovation. And I think Nick understands that at a level that is very, very deep. It goes beyond that of most executives that I've talked to that are actively engaged in innovation. But those dimensions of diversity like gender, race, and nationality also are very important, very topical these days, and where a lot of the discussion focuses. I also happen to believe that a company that has structured that out has a huge advantage, and Nick agreed.

Even then, a lot of multinationals were creating programs around diversity and inclusion. But I saw another wrinkle. It is equity as well. You need to have that broad-based thinking. It is not enough to salute diversity, but then have inequity and not be inclusive. Otherwise, your diverse talent will either leave or they will tune out and see your actions on their behalf as style over substance.

Innovation involves seeing the world as it is and where it is going and changing so that you can leverage your strengths to create value in that new world. Historically, IBM has been able to do that, and our attempt to create the Globally Integrated Enterprise in the first decade of the 2000s was part of that history.

> **Frans Johansson:** Is IBM an American company? Yes, but it has been open to looking at innovation and growth and new concepts and new ideas from all kinds of different places around the world.
>
> I've often been asked the question, "Who do I believe to be the most innovative company in the world?" The answer people expect for me to give would be Apple or Google or Amazon, but one of the definitions I have for great innovators is, "Has the company been able to reimagine who they are over and over again?"
>
> In IBM, you've got a company that has done that, from mainframes and hardware and then pivoting into services, and from there they went into software. Now IBM is heading into AI and cognitive computing. There's a perspective that every one of my conversations with Nick hits upon. He thinks, *This is how the world is evolving. IBM has to evolve the same way.*

Eventually what we were doing took on the name Services Science, Management, and Engineering (SSME) to describe an interdisciplinary approach to the study and innovation of service systems. More precisely, SSME has been defined as the application of science, management, and engineering disciplines to tasks that one organization beneficially performs for and with another.

Services Science is now a growing field of focus, attention, and investment with an ever-growing following outside IBM. SSME is a call for academia, industry, and governments to focus on becoming more systematic about innovation in the service sector, which is the largest sector of the economy in most industrialized nations and is fast becoming the largest sector in developing nations as well.

This idea is easy to understand: the more people participating, the better. It is diversity, inclusion, and equity for everyone—not just women, not just underrepresented minorities—the people who practice a different religion than you, the people from a different country than you, the people who have different political beliefs than you. There is a totality here that says, "We are stronger together than alone." That power of inclusion, diversity, and equity built into an enabling environment is what gives you the better anything.

I am thankful that this science evolved out of our efforts to create the Globally Integrated Enterprise, because with the heightened tension around diversity currently roiling America and the world, we need it badly. The topic of diversity inherent to SSME is so timely in 2021 that I have chosen to devote an entire chapter to insights around diversity during my career at IBM.

13
EQUITY

I am a proud American. In many ways, the story of my life epitomizes the classic "American Dream": a poor kid from Beacon, New York rises to the top technology position in one of America's most storied companies. I am very proud of my accomplishments, but aspects of my tale have long given me pause.

I have written with reverence of my parents, Nick and Beatrice Donofrio, and all that they did to help me achieve as close to my full potential as possible. I also look back fondly on the lives that they lived, and I see those lives very much as positive examples of the American Dream.

They emerged out of the early twentieth century immigrant experience to carve out a middle-class lifestyle that enabled them to own a home, raise a family, educate their children, and eventually enjoy membership at the Beacon Country Club. It wasn't easy for either of them, with my father working multiple jobs so that we could afford that modest middle-class lifestyle, but they did it. There were ups and downs and joys and sorrows, but most important to them, they sacrificed to enable a path out into a much bigger world for their children. For all these reasons and more, it is hard for me to qualify either of their lives as anything but a success.

And yet, what might have been.

My dad was very smart, and he had a softer side to him, too. As a kid he played the violin. But in the 1920s and 1930s, in a dirt-poor Italian community, there was little room for those softer things, and at age fourteen, my father put school and the violin aside, went to work, and largely assumed the role of leader in his family.

His father had come to America, and now Nicholas Donofrio was going to make his way in that America. My father was there for his brothers, he was there for his father, and he was there for his stepmother when they needed him. He was a very bright kid and a very wise kid, but he went with the flow, and what the flow did during those times was leave school and step out into the working world of the Beacon economy. He accepted this fate, and he never complained.

My mother, meanwhile, had been a great student—she earned her high school degree when she was only sixteen. She had doubled down, taking two grades in one year at one point, and she had risen to the occasion. She was fluent in French as well as Italian, and if she had had the time, space, money, and opportunity to go to college and out into the world, she could have done *anything*. Instead, she went to work in a hat factory. She accepted her fate, and she never complained.

As my career unfolded at IBM, my American Dream emerged in bold Technicolor. Like them, I worked hard. I made sacrifices. I was rewarded. But I also would think about my parents and say to myself, "God only knows what they might have achieved in this day and age."

Meanwhile, I kept accepting the challenges that came my way. I always did what I thought was best for my family. In fact, we bet our lives on my career. My wife Anita and I had nothing when we started our life together, other than each other and a great deal of confidence and optimism. With love and hope, we made our way forward.

Anita and I were the first in our respective families to move away from the Mid-Hudson Valley. We moved physically nine times, the first two times as husband and wife, then with one child, and then two, as I climbed the corporate ladder with IBM. Anita and I, and eventually our children, discussed every career decision. Even when I received two serious job offers outside IBM, both from Silicon Valley-based companies, and both providing strong opportunity and growth potential, the options were discussed.

I carefully chose the operative words here: "were discussed." Sadly, as I reflect on those major decisions, the discussions were simply lopsided. My family had little choice. What could they say, but "yes"? I thought I knew what I was doing, as we were optimizing my career, but in some sense, the risks we were taking on my career were nothing compared to the risks that we were taking on each other.

Anita never really was given the opportunity to become the amazing leader she is now until later in life. I should have seen that earlier. Clearly, I was looking, but not seeing. My wife's talents as a force for good and for change should have been nurtured years earlier, as they would have blossomed much sooner. I have no doubt that the world would have been a different and better place for that. Michael and Nicole, too, experienced childhood differently than they likely would have chosen so that *I* could pursue *my* dreams.

What I am getting at here, of course, is that I believe wholeheartedly that America is the land of opportunity. But for whom?

So much has happened since May 25, 2020, the day that George Floyd, a forty-six-year-old Black man, was killed in Minneapolis, Minnesota, while being arrested. In the immediate aftermath, Floyd's death triggered worldwide protests against police brutality, racism, and lack of accountability. But at a broader level, the tragedy again brought that same question to the forefront of the national discussion: how do we make America the land of opportunity for everyone?

It is a question I have thought much about over the years, and one which I tried to answer during my time at IBM. When I joined IBM in 1967, the Women's Liberation and Civil Rights Movements were in full swing. I confess that in those early years of my career, I was very focused on my work and my young family, but I believe that IBM was in many ways a progressive company, and like many major corporations at the time, they stepped up their efforts to recruit women and Blacks, and eventually Hispanics, too.

While I was not necessarily thinking deeply about these movements, and in some ways was a creature of my times, I was happy to work with anyone capable, regardless of race or gender. By the early '90s, though, I was a rising executive thinking far more deeply about the so-called War for Talent, our increasingly global technical community, and innovation.

Around this time, I met Ted Childs. Ted and I started working full-time for IBM within a week of one another in 1967, and we knew many of the same IBMers in the Mid-Hudson Valley. Ted was the executive responsible for IBM's Global Workforce Diversity Programs, and as we came to know one another and he shared his points of view with me, I was more than willing to engage.

> **Ted Childs** (*Thirty-nine-year IBM Veteran and VP, Human Resources*): In the '60s and the '70s, coming out of the Civil Rights Era, there was intense focus on the part of the major corporations to recruit women and Blacks. The message was, "Come join us and be like us." That was the moral motivation: it's the right thing to do. But by the time we reached the '90s, we recognized a flaw in the "Come join us and be like us" message, because there was a growing recognition that if we didn't allow people to be themselves, number one, they weren't going to be happy.
>
> And number two, depending upon the business that you were in, you were increasingly going to be selling to diverse people, so you needed them to be comfortable working for you, because people on the outside can look in and see who is there, and if they couldn't see people like themselves from the mailroom to the boardroom, they might decide not to spend their money.

I had long understood the moral side to the diversity discussion, and I could see the business side to Ted's point of view. But as I extended the diversity idea into my thoughts about products and innovation, I saw incredible possibility.

Ted Childs: I think for Nick, that transition was one of the shortest transitions of any of the executives I had to deal with. Nick moved from the moral discussion to the strategic discussion seamlessly. He came to understand, "I've got to preside over this technical juggernaut, and traditional executives sitting in a room cannot conceivably always come up with the best decision or the best assessment of a problem. I need more diverse thinkers. And I've got to go to places where they're not currently coming from to get them on my team." So he became a champion for recruiting women, minorities, and disabled people into the technical family.

As I came to better appreciate the challenges that faced women and minorities in the largely all-white, all-male labs and research facilities, I felt a kinship with them, despite my own race and gender. While I had been raised by incredibly supportive parents, we were far from wealthy. They could not have fully funded my education, but there were scholarships and programs I was able to access to help me get a leg up when I needed it and to create the supply of talent that American industry needed at that time.

I realized that many young women, minorities, and disabled people were no different than I had been. They needed that same leg up, and I knew that if they had the qualifications, they could help me in the IBM Technical Community. Yet because of cultural, financial, and prejudicial barriers to entry, the supply of talent was limited.

So as always, start with the problem.

The first thing I wanted to do was to understand it. One way I was able to begin to do so came when I joined the Board of the National Action Council for Minorities in Engineering (NACME), where I met a passionate champion of the cause in Dr. Diana Natalicio.

Diana Natalicio *(President of University of Texas at El Paso, 1988–2019)*: I was immediately impressed with two things about Nick when I first began to know him. One was that his commitment to the issue of minorities in engineering was truly sincere. It wasn't just to be trendy. It was earnest. Second, he was a no-nonsense guy. He was the kind of guy who, if he was serving on the board, he dedicated his talent, his time, his energy, his expertise—everything—to that assignment. He was highly engaged. He was really very, very sincere, but also, I think, highly constructive and eager to make his time on the board worthwhile and to have meaning. He just seemed to know so much about so many issues, both on the technology side and on the human resource side.

By the time I met Diana in the early 1990s, I was well-informed about historically Black colleges and universities. However, UTEP was a Hispanic-serving institution. These were the RS/6000 days, and I was spending a lot of time in Austin in those days, and I wanted to better understand what motivated Hispanic students, and what Diana and her team were doing to create opportunity. If they could help IBM in Austin, and elsewhere, I was all for it.

Diana Natalicio: He came to visit UTEP for the first time in the early 1990s. He was sincere about wanting to learn more about the university and Hispanic students in engineering, in particular engineering in computer science. He gave a talk that was very well-received. He then visited a couple of our facilities where the students were working using technologies. In those early days of my tenure, what we had wasn't very impressive, but it was not bad for that time. I think he was impressed with UTEP—we were larger, more active, more engaged in science and engineering than he might have expected, partly because we began as a mining school. Our traditions were always in Science & Engineering. Nick left with a much more complete sense of UTEP than most visitors might, because he asked a lot of questions and spent time talking to students, faculty, and staff members. He has unbridled enthusiasm about just about everything, which is very endearing, because I think that is what makes us all human, to be curious. He absorbed a lot of UTEP in a short time.

I saw that these were amazing students and that Diana was an amazing leader. She had a vision to develop not just a university, but the university that her community needed. Most of her students worked, many of them had families, and over 80 percent of UTEP's more than 23,000 students were Mexican-American, with an additional 5 percent coming from nearby Ciudad Juárez, Mexico. She built the types of programs that her students could manage along with their other responsibilities. She and her team had started with the right problems and built solutions that could help their community get a leg up in a way that was doable for them.

I saw similar innovative approaches being developed at historically Black colleges and universities, too. As time went by, I became more and more committed to diversity and inclusiveness, eventually becoming Board Chair for NACME.

John Slaughter *(Electrical Engineer, Former President of Occidental College, Former IBM Board Member)*: Nick was not just interested in the Harvards and the Purdues and the Wisconsins and the big universities. He also had a strong interest in helping those institutions that do a great job in supporting underrepresented minorities in the study of engineering. Nick even supported my initiative at NACME to develop more young people in the junior high and high schools—and not wait until they were in college to learn about engineering. Nick encouraged me in this regard, and that was important.

Diana Natalicio: He had a hard-driving, passionate determination to make NACME play a critically-impactful role in ensuring that we could increase the participation of African Americans and

Hispanics in engineering and science fields. Nick never lost his passion for the mission, and in fact, it probably grew a little when he became board chair. He was in charge and even more determined, and he was a tough taskmaster. Nick didn't just sit on the board and rubber stamp things. Far from it. He was extremely determined to make a difference.

I had no problem advocating that IBM give more opportunities to the graduates from these programs. More and more, I believed it was imperative to our future.

John Slaughter: Nick and I share a very strong opinion that diversity drives innovation, and that in the absence of diversity, innovation can falter or not be present. So we shared not only a common interest, but a common belief, about the importance of diversity in any institution.

Of course, for IBM to benefit from our inclusive approach, we not only had to recruit women, minorities, and disabled people to join us, we also had to create an environment where they would want to stay and to build their careers. Ted Childs had continued pushing hard in this direction in the years since I first met him, and by 1995, he was ready to take a big step forward.

Ted Childs: In 1995, I got approval to form eight Task Forces: Asian, Black, Hispanic, Native American Indian, Gay/Lesbian, Disabled, Women, and White Men. Each Task Force would be led by executives from a different constituency and was going to have an executive sponsor. And each Task Force was going to have to answer the same four questions: (1) What's required of your group to be welcomed and valued at IBM? (2) What can the company do to improve the productivity of your group? (3) What can the company do to make our products and services more appealing to people from your group? (4) What outside organizations that represent your interests should the IBM Company have a relationship with?

While Ted had Lou Gerstner's approval, he needed to generate buy-in from some tough senior leaders if he was going to convince them to head one of the Task Forces. He called a meeting to make his pitch.

Ted Childs: There was a critical meeting with all the Senior Vice Presidents in attendance. I have to present to these guys, and they've got to buy in. I put up a chart that had down the left-hand column the names of the eight Task Forces. The middle column had the names of the Executive Co-Chairs of each Task Force. The right-hand column had the names of the guys in the room and which Task Force was their assignment.

Well, one of the most influential Senior Vice Presidents in the room spoke up against this initiative, and I immediately knew the likelihood of this getting done had plunged. He felt we were doing enough already, and perhaps more importantly, he worried that we were going to make promises to people that we couldn't keep. He just railed against it.

Here was an "If nothing changes" moment if I had ever seen one. By this time, I had been championing the recruitment of minorities and women for a few years. I believed in not only the moral but the business logic of a more diversified workforce, and I did not think we were doing enough.

Ted Childs: Nick Donofrio speaks up and says, "I respectfully disagree. I think Ted's got something here. We've got to think differently. The world's changing. Look at the people he has in the middle column—the people who are going to lead the Task Forces— they work for us! They already manage thousands of people and hundreds of millions of dollars of resource. Do we trust this? Do we think they're now going to become Civil Rights leaders and try to destroy us? We need to trust this." Well, you could have heard a pin drop. Here was Nick, the youngest Senior Vice President in the room, standing up to one of his mentors. And he carried the day.

I'm no saint. The fact of the matter is, I was not born some wonderfully enlightened soul. My parents raised me with a very good, but to some degree, limited way of looking at the world. I was a mischievous kid, but my parents held me to a high standard, and over time, I came around. Through their Catholic faith, they held me to the Golden Rule, particularly my mother, and so I tried to think about what was best for people. And my father enforced in me that notion of change, and change I did, and that is why I was unafraid to speak up in these sorts of meetings. Even as thick-headed and as stubborn as I could be, I was willing to listen, I was willing to learn, and I was willing to change.

> **Ted Childs:** So we did the Task Forces, with Nick as the sponsor for
> the Hispanics. Nick was embedded in the full array of our diversity
> work, particularly in terms of the fundamental blend of fairness
> and strategic responsibility for the work. And over time, every
> constituency group—the Black people, the Hispanic people, the gay
> people—came to understand that this guy's door is closed to no one.

In another example in and around that same 1995 timeframe, IBM bought Lotus Development Corporation, the first major US company that had offered employees same sex partner benefits, which they implemented in 1992. Immediately, IBM's gay and lesbian employees hoped this meant that IBM would follow Lotus's lead. At the same time, Lotus employees worried that IBM would take their benefits away. Ted again found himself with a difficult situation to manage.

I realized we had to have this debate at the top of the company, and I stood behind Ted. In a staff meeting that included Lou Gerstner, many of my colleagues were opposed to adopting the Lotus same sex partner benefits offering. When I had the opportunity to speak, I put forth my own beliefs about how inclusiveness and innovation were intertwined.

I said, "We don't know who the next person is that will help us create the next big thing. We're just not that gifted. Anyone might have those skills, so we need to welcome everyone at IBM and to allow them to be exactly who they are. If somehow you think a gay or lesbian person doesn't have those skills, then don't grant same sex partner benefits. But if we want to stay focused on what matters—like making sure we have the talent we need to drive our company forward and win in the marketplace—we have to allow people to be who they are, and to support them for who they are. It's always been that way at IBM, and we should continue to live by those values and practices."

Everyone agreed with that logic, and that gave Ted a boost. While many other people played important roles, too, I am glad that I contributed to IBM's 1996 decision to grant gay and lesbian partners of IBM workers benefits.

Lauren States: Nick is someone who thinks in terms of equality. There had to be something in his life that made him either consciously or unconsciously think with a mindset of equality. There are examples of people like Nick throughout the history of our country, in all different contexts. Unfortunately, they're not the majority. But what was unique about Nick was the fact that he accumulated enough power in his accession at IBM that he could create change.

While my thoughts around diversity were always well-intentioned—both for IBM and for the talent themselves—it took some time to get it right. Like a parent at Christmas trying to make sure that each child was treated equally, Ted and I had sometimes operated on the fly, both figuratively and literally.

Ted Childs: There was so much going on, it was hard to keep it all straight, and there was an element of politics to it, given the many different constituencies. For example, we had a piece of work going on with a group called NSBE—the National Society of Black Engineers—the largest student-run organization in the United States, founded at Purdue. The NSBE kids had a survey every year, and one of the questions was along the lines of, "What company would you most like to work for?" And for seven consecutive years, they had picked IBM!

Well, we had one of our Black executives serving as a liaison to NSBE, and to his credit, he worked hard on the relationship. One day I called him and said, "Seven years at number one is really impressive, but it's going to be worthless if you don't get ten in a row." And he looks at me and says, "Man, do you understand how hard it is to get one at a time?" I said, "Yeah, but it doesn't matter anymore. You got seven. If you can't get three more, then this is all useless. But I'm going to help you. We're going to put up $500,000 and call it your NSBE SWAT Team Strategy."

So, Ted and his NSBE executive came to see me, and I came up with the money to keep building that relationship. We wrote a letter to NSBE with some guidelines around how the money would be distributed and how it could be used.

Ted Childs: Meanwhile, around the same time, Nick ends up as the recipient of the Rodney D. Chipp Memorial Award from the Society of Women Engineers. Nick and I flew down to Birmingham for him to get this award. I'll never forget this, but while we were on this plane home from Alabama after he'd received this reward from SWE women, and not long after he's approved the $500,000 for the NSBE, I tell him, "You know, we just put up this three-year bill for NSBE. We have to do the same thing for the Hispanics to keep things fair." Nick asks, "Well, what do you have in mind?" I say, "Another $500,000." Nick has never said no to me, and he says, "Okay."

Of course, even as he's committing to half a million for the Hispanics, I say, "But these women just gave you this award. We have to do something really big for women, and it's got to be bigger than what we're doing for the Black and Hispanic interests!" Nick says, "Why?" I say, "There's more of them!" He says, "What do you have in mind?" I say, "How about a million dollars?" He looks at me and says, "A million?"

I say, "The Hispanics have SHPE—the Society of Hispanic Professional Engineers—the women have SWE—the Society of Women Engineers. They gave you this award, so we'll make our initiative global and we'll have women co-chairs. It will give us global vision and credibility." We found a technical woman in Nick's organization and put her on a Leave of Absence so that she could work with SWE on implementing their strategy.

Ted makes everything seem very back-of-the-envelope, but in truth, what he was saying made sense, because this really was about building the IBM name as a talent magnet across diverse groups, which was crucial to my innovation goals. We ended up with three SWAT Teams—one for NSBE, one for SHPE, and one for SWE—and we ended up with a cover story in each of their magazines, which contributed tremendously to our ability to attract the best talent from these three key groups.

Over the course of a decade or so, between my role at NACME and the work that Ted was doing, we began to get traction. Ted had been around IBM as long as I had, and he knew how to operate within the large bureaucracy to cobble together an effective program. As with Ted's anecdote about our expensive plane ride together, there were many similar occasions where I would come up with a half a million here or a half a million there for various projects. I realized this piecemeal approach was not the way forward, so I called him in to create a true strategy around Global Diversity.

Ted Childs: Around 2004 or 2005, after years of what I called "Tin Cupping," Nick said to me, "Ted, we need another approach." We

were both approaching retirement age, so we wanted to create
something that would outlast us both. We came up with the idea
of creating a Global Diversity Strategy. My staff and I would work
on the plan, and we'd take it to Nick. He'd coach us, and then we'd
go back and do more. We got it to a point where we invited Sam
Palmisano to come to a meeting with Nick and me in my War Room,
and we took him through all the details on the strategy. We ended
up with a six-year Global Diversity Strategy, with $300 million in
funding over that time, to be spread around the world.

John Slaughter: So much of the global diversity effort at IBM
depended upon the fact that Nick, behind the scenes, made it happen,
and gave Ted the support from the top administration that nobody
else provided. Nick ran interference for Ted in many, many cases.

Lauren States: With Nick, the confluence of his core values, his
power, and his influence significantly changed our careers. He
had a gift, and we were recipients of that gift. With that gift came a
responsibility to act on behalf of others in order to multiply it. That
force-multiplier will be his legacy. I went on to manage large global
teams and to create opportunities that would not have happened if it
weren't for me, meaning, as well, that if it were not for Nick.

I trust history will judge me as an agent of change at IBM, and yet here is
an area where I feel in my heart that I did not do enough. That said, I have continued to work on the diversity initiative in other ways in the years since I left
IBM. The events of 2020 prove that those efforts remain as necessary as ever.

Driving large-scale change is incredibly difficult—whether in a massive corporation like IBM or a complex nation like the United States of
America—and in both examples, we obviously are not yet where we need to
be in regard to maximizing the potential of every single person who is willing to work hard and who wants to make a difference.

Lauren States: In some of my more recent communications with Nick, I kind of thought I heard Nick say he wasn't sure he did enough or wasn't sure that the things he wanted most in terms of enabling others, particularly people who are diverse, was effective enough. And I just don't want him to believe that, because, whether he thinks of it this way or not, he's up against 400 years of history, and the most important thing that he could have done was to be an enabler and a force-multiplier, because that's the only way to achieve what I know he wants to see happen. He did that. He did so many things for me and for so many other underrepresented people that continue to ripple into the world today. Nick Donofrio activated Lauren States, and so to this day, every small thing I might do to advance the cause, Nick did. That's the force-multiplier effect in action. When you add up the actions that Nick did for us, and those so many of us have since done in our own small ways since he touched our lives, millions of people have a different life. And so, yes, he's done enough—more than enough—and more than most. I really want him to know that.

John Slaughter: This belief that diversity drives innovation is one that I carried when I was on the board at IBM and first met Nick, and it's a belief that I carry and continue to attempt to foster here in 2021 at the University of Southern California. Nick would be frustrated if he felt that the emphasis on diversity at IBM or at any institution was failing. I know that he continues to feel that way.

14

MY WAY

Few people begin their careers thinking about their legacies. Yet through hard work, creativity and, yes, a little luck, over time many of us find that we can point to milestones and accomplishments that can rightly be considered a legacy of making a difference. The scale of these contributions can vary greatly and take many forms, be it business success, societal impact, or the influence that we had on others. Taking time to appreciate such accomplishments can prove to be a rewarding (and inexhaustible) retirement dividend.

While I am obviously biased toward technology, I believe that some of the greatest advances of the past few generations are directly predicated on what we were doing at IBM (and in the information technology industry as a whole). The company's focus on having an impact, harkening back to the days of Thomas J. Watson, Sr., created a culture that helped revolutionize industries such as banking and retail, put men on the moon, made nuclear arsenals more secure, and unlocked life-saving discoveries in medicine. The work we did was important, and together, I believe we made the United States and the world better places, raising the standard of living for generations of people.

As I look back over my IBM career, I feel a great deal of pride in what we accomplished and pleasure in the people whom I came to know. I have enjoyed reliving all that we did in these pages. If I were to try to summarize what we accomplished at IBM during my years into some enduring high-lights, I would offer the following:

- We Saved the Mainframe
- We Created a Culture of Innovation
- We Molded a Generation of Future Leaders
- We Drove Industry-Changing Technologies to Market as Part of a Company We Loved

WE SAVED THE MAINFRAME

By now, you have come to understand just how important saving the IBM mainframe was to my career and to IBM at that pivotal juncture when its very survival was in jeopardy. From a legacy perspective, though, I take tremendous pride in the fact that the mainframe remains vital to IBM, the global economy, and the world today—even if it may no longer garner flashy headlines.

A few years after we transitioned the mainframe to CMOS, a Mainframe 30th Anniversary Celebration was held at the Computer History Museum in San Jose, California—the heart of Silicon Valley. We invited the three IBMers who had won the US Medal of Technology for their leadership work on the System/360 to be part of the big event. They were Erich Bloch, who developed and manufactured the technology, Bob Evans, who was the system architect and product developer, and Fred Brooks, who wrote the mainframe software. Unfortunately, Erich's wife was ill, so he could not come, but Bob and Fred were there.

I had them on stage with me as part of the celebration, and as we walked down memory lane, at some point I said, "What did you guys think you were doing when you built the mainframe? What did you think the life expectancy of the 360 was going to be?"

Bob looked at me, and he said, "I don't know about you, Fred, but I figured at most they could get twenty-five years out of it. Nick, I have to tell you, the last five years are completely on you."

I still remember those words, and they made me feel good, to be honest. I had played my small role in IBM history, which was what being a career IBMer was about in my mind. The decision to move to CMOS and a new system structure, while preserving the same code that ran the first time the system was released in 1964, is one of the things I am most proud of in my career and in my life.

But now System/360 Mainframe has celebrated fifty-seven years and it is still the same code! Can you imagine that? These were brilliant people telling us, "The best we thought you could do was twenty-five years," and now, as the IBM Z System Family, we are at fifty-seven years and counting, with many of the largest and most important institutions in government and the business world still relying on the IBM mainframe to make the world turn.

That is the legacy of System/360, and part of the legacies of some of the heroes from my team, including Linda and Ross, who each went on to run the business. I am proud to be a part of that legacy.

Ross Mauri: I run the mainframe business nowadays, and people ask me, "How can you have a product that's more than fifty years old, Ross?" And I say, "Well, it's easy, because none of it is five decades old. All the hardware is state of the art. A lot of the software was written in the last few years and much of this is based on open source technologies. Yes, some of it was written twenty or thirty years ago and is maintained and updated still to this day, but that's one of the values. There's no other system in the world that brings their client and ISV applications forward untouched generation after generation. That's called investment protection. Do you want to use modern languages like Go, Python, or Java? Do you want to use modern platforms like Apache Spark or Ignite? Or do you want to use something tried and true for business logic (e.g., COBOL) that's been running the world's economy for over five decades? That's your choice, they all run well on IBM Z."

David Yaun: Many of the technological advancements, the innovations, the societal advancements, and business advancements of the past few decades would not have happened if IBM had discontinued or disinvested in the mainframe. So ironically, Nick's greatest accomplishment was keeping alive a dinosaur, but a dinosaur that to this day helps drive tremendous revenues and profits for the IBM Company. I've seen estimates that say roughly $3 trillion—trillion!—in commercial transactions flow through mainframes every single day. There is no doubt in my mind that the mainframe would have been dead if Nick hadn't been where he was at IBM at the time. And because IBM maintained its investment in the mainframe, advances in certain core technologies happened at a much greater pace than they would have if IBM had abandoned it.

Bob Samson: We purchased a brand new IBM mainframe for the State of New York in 2019. You can't run the State of New York without an IBM mainframe. In fact, much of our modern way of life would grind to a halt without IBM mainframes. It's really that simple.

Personally, its rewarding that people who matter in my line of work know full well what my team accomplished and what it meant for IBM and the industry. Most people in highly-competitive professions will tell you that having the respect of their peers is one of the greatest rewards you can receive, and I definitely agree. They understand how what we did in the early to mid 1990s continues to influence the technology world to this day.

WE CREATED A CULTURE OF INNOVATION

Over and over and over and over, I told the IBM Technical Community that "If nothing changes, nothing changes." The more we accepted that we could use change to enable ourselves, the better we did. We became true innovators. We became problem-focused. We became increasingly open and collaborative. We became multi-disciplined. We embraced global thinking and inclusivity.

This evolution reflected itself inside of IBM through a revitalized energy and culture, through the popularity and success of our Jams, through the dissemination of our new values throughout the world. And it was reflected outside of IBM through market performance, patent leadership, and innovation metrics.

> **Bob Samson:** Nick illustrated for people that the power that IBM has is not in a vertical silo. It's a horizontal play. In other words, how do we stitch together multiple different components from different organizations to create a more profound value proposition for a client? At the core of what he was doing, that was it—forcing organizations inside the company to think horizontally—because that's what unlocked the value of IBM. There was individual value in the silos, don't get me wrong, but the paradigm shifts came from horizontal collaboration. Before Nick, you'd have a guy that sells a server. He goes home. He's happy. He sold a server today, that's a good thing.
>
> But wait a minute. When you sell the server, the customer is going to buy all kinds of other things. They're going to buy some services. They're going to buy some software. Do they need some consulting around the side of it? Do they need storage? Taking all of that into account just got people to begin thinking differently. In a broad sense, it was a way for IBM to figure out in a more profound way how to connect outside of measurements, because that's where true innovation occurs.
>
> Without him there, I don't know that they've broken through that old paradigm. I don't think they would have, probably. Nick was our biggest cheerleader, because he would bring different people into a room from different organizations and their different silos and say, "Here's a problem we have to solve," and things happened.

And things happened because he operated equally well in three dimensions. The first one was the technical dimension, and he had incredible relationships deep into horizontal technical organizations. The second one was working very closely with the sales organizations. When I ran our Federal business, he would come down and speak to our team often. The third part of this was what I would call an "Ideas Warehouse." He would solicit the best ideas—the wisdom of teams, the wisdom of the group—and fuel the first part (manufacturing, development, and research) and the second part (the sales engine). So it became a complete architecture for how you not just create, but succeed, with an agenda of innovation.

Paul Horn: Well, there's no question Nick's a special person. The way he connects to people. The way he can project excitement and caring is no doubt unique. He was able to take that ability and help the IBM Company transition in a way that I think very few people could have accomplished. We talk about how IBM has kept reinventing itself through the years, and one of the key pieces each time was very strong innovative leadership, and he certainly played a huge leadership role in several crucial chapters of our story. When he pursued his Innovation Agenda, he said, "We need everybody to pull together. This is a huge transition for the future of the company. If we work together as a team, we're going to kick some butt." And we did.

We are stronger together than alone. If you go back through history—not just IBM's history, but all of history—you will find that the best work has been done in an environment that enabled total open collaboration. That is what I tried to do. We broke down the silos, we embraced diversity, inclusion, and equity, and we went out looking for the best ideas for our clients and for the world.

WE MOLDED A GENERATION OF FUTURE LEADERS

You have read of the many people I mentored. You have read of what I was passionate about—IBM's Values, putting the customer first, change and innovation, building talent, new technologies, collaboration, and equity. In evangelizing on these matters and modeling them through my own behavior, many bought into my message and took elements of what they saw in me to become incredible leaders in their own rights. I am grateful to IBM and my many advocates—from John Akers to Lou Gerstner to Sam Palmisano—for giving me the platform to be myself and to encourage people.

Whether lifelong IBMers such as Linda, Ross, and so many others who became leaders within IBM; or IBMers such as Mark, Lisa, and so many others who went on to greater success beyond IBM; or clients and partners such as Guy, Bernard, and many others who today are leaders of some of the great organizations of the world, I am deeply honored to have contributed to their development. The thought that some of them still mention me while they mentor the next generations of leaders is humbling, to say the least.

> **Terry Milholland:** I think the legacy of most good leaders is not
> in what they did—that is, in the jobs they held—but in the people
> they nurtured and influenced along the way to make into leaders
> themselves. Certainly for Nick, that's true. People who would
> comment to me about him would mention his personal style and
> relationship with them. They wouldn't say, "Oh, he was the one who
> did CMOS." Or, "He was the one who did the RS/6000." No, it was,
> "Here are the people that he helped groom for leadership." Or, "Here
> are the people he helped to get better in their jobs." I think it was the
> people that he shaped that matters most, and they probably are too
> numerous to count.

Ross Mauri: From technology and business decisions to one-on-ones, people still hold Nick up as a role model, and ask, "What would Nick do?" For those of us who worked with him for so many years, he's still here, because we still think of him every day. I reference him, and I know others do, too, because I hear it. He was an extraordinary technologist who had vision and business savvy, but he also really knew how to relate to people and thus could get us to do amazing things.

Bob Samson: He created this whole next generation of leaders that led in his image, where it's not about hierarchy, it's not about silos, and it's not about organizations that compete with each other. It ultimately gets back to the client and what they need and what they want and how you can you best figure out a way to deliver it. And if you were one of his people, then your job was to do your part in helping the client, and I think that's why the whole next generation of IBM leaders so often reflected his way of looking at the world.

WE DROVE INDUSTRY-CHANGING TECHNOLOGIES TO MARKET AS PART OF A COMPANY WE LOVED

Obviously, IBM had done countless incredible things before I joined, and my contributions to the company built off of what had come before. What we did, from CMOS to the RS/6000, from System/390 to ASCI, from Blue Gene to the Science of Services, made a mark on IBM and on the industry. We learned from our mistakes, and we kept getting better. Now, others are building on what we did, which is just as it should be.

I was ambitious in my career at IBM. I wanted to be successful as an individual. I was driven. But I truly loved—and still love—IBM. I loved being a part of IBM. I loved seeing what IBM could do for its employees, for the United States, and for the world. I loved the teamwork and the collaboration.

During my career, I faced almost all of the challenges an employee, manager, executive, and senior executive could face to help IBM succeed and to help solve some big problems. The price was high, but so was the reward.

Rick Miller: I don't think Nick had a job or a career. I think Nick had a calling. He saw purpose in life through making innovation and change. He was gifted with the opportunity to have this platform at IBM to work from, and he could see how important the outcomes were that IBM was creating and he was influencing. It was almost as if this was a calling from the supernatural to dedicate his life to making change and making the world a better place.

Vijay Lund: He was a gentle hand. Nick is a gentle soul who was asked by the IBM Company to do hard things, from the first layoff, to all the time away from his family, to the high-pressure assignments he accepted. He took on so much to help IBM, and he did it with style, grace, and that gentle hand.

Lisa Su: I would say that Nick is an incredible technology leader who has led the industry through a number of key technology transitions. He's not just a great technologist—he's a great person and a compassionate leader overall.

Jon Rubinstein: Nick is a gentleman. He's a very strong technical guy. He's a great manager. He's incredibly well-respected by everyone who has worked for him and around him. Nick usually is behind the scenes, and he's very quiet, but I think he's one of the giants of the industry. He's not well-known outside of the industry, but inside of the industry, he's very well-respected and very well-known.

Many technology leaders have become figures within pop culture. That was never my goal. I cared more about the work, the innovation, the progress, the people and clients, and how IBM was helping to change the world. I was able to do that every day for over forty years at one of the greatest companies the world has ever known, and that was always enough for me.

> **David Yaun:** Nick never achieved the type of fame that Jobs, Gates, or others achieved, but in his own way, he had some of the influence that those people achieved, though he did so more quietly. Our clients, some of the biggest, most complex and most influential companies in the world, trusted and valued Nick's perspective; they sought out his expertise in the same way they would any one of those other guys. Nick could have been a CEO of any number of companies, but in some ways, his incredible loyalty to IBM, for better or for worse, kept him from ever doing something like that. There's no doubt in my mind, he could have been CEO of one of the larger tech companies in the world and would have been very successful, but for a variety of reasons, all of them truly noble, he spent his entire forty-four-year career at IBM.

> **Mark Papermaster:** I don't think Nick's ever sought out "fame and fortune," so to speak. His passion and his commitment have been about technology and people. It has never been about him and his ego or public persona. That's another reason why he was trusted, admired, and followed by those that had the opportunity to work with him.

> **Sam Palmisano:** Nick cares about society and institutions more than himself, and he's usually a faceless partner. He cares about what happens in society. He cares about the institution called IBM, even to this day. He cares deeply about IBM. And he's faceless. He won't take any credit. I've never seen Nick do a big victory lap. He's happy being a great team player and a great partner. That's Nick. He cares

deeply what happens in our world, what happens to the institutions he's fond of, and put family in there as well. Society, business, and family—and IBM's business side.

Even though I graduated from IBM more than a decade ago, I stay involved with the company. I remain an IBM Fellow Emeritus and am often invited back to talk with employees about the work and technology.

When I look at IBM over recent years, like many former IBMers, I admit that I sometimes can get frustrated and angry. Some of it is to be expected. Any company that endures for 110 years will make and miss signals, make and miss markets, capture and miss value. IBM often knew better and often forgot what it had learned. IBM did all of that and more.

But IBM is remarkable and unique because over 110 years, it has completely reinvented itself more than a half dozen times. They no longer sell scales, time clocks, or meat slicers, right? Somewhere there is a warehouse full of tons of punch cards that never got used. Yet, with each transformation, the company grew bigger and more relevant.

Now, we are witnessing another IBM transformation—as I write this book, IBM is splitting into two separate companies, one focused on the cloud, the other on traditional IT services—and the jury remains out on whether this move will be the catalyst for a vibrant and meaningful future. Believe me, I hope it is. And I am willing to help leadership of both the companies in any way that they choose, if they should so choose.

I am very familiar with new CEO Arvind Krishna as well as Martin Schroeter, who is heading the spinoff company, Kyndryl. Arvind was a strong and accomplished member of IBM Research and a leader in our technical community, especially when he ran development and manufacturing for IBM's Systems and Technology Group. He has an inquisitive and analytical leadership style and is willing to battle-test and adjust his preconceptions. As long as he stays keenly self-aware of his strengths and weaknesses, IBM can reinvent itself again. The same goes for Martin, a career IBMer with deep experience in finance.

They both know that change is afoot at all times, and even more change faster will be needed if IBM is to reassert itself again. I guess this all circles back to a characteristic that I think marks IBM and IBMers as a whole: we are always digging to understand who and what we are at our core. *What got us here? Is it still relevant? Does the world still want it? If not, how do we change?*

Linda Sanford: There is just something that's deep inside the core of the company, or deep inside our values, that drives the behavior of employees. These values have stood the test of time. And, yes, we changed the wording a little bit—modernized it—but it was basically the same: you've got to bring innovation that matters to the world. It's all about trust and confidence with your employees. And it's about listening to your clients—at the end of the day, that's why you're in business. Lou Gerstner said, "A company has to be able to change everything about itself, because the world is continuously changing, except its core values." I think that's embedded deeply into the soul of IBMers. So while over time IBM may become a completely different business than it was before in terms of what it sells in the marketplace, it will always be true to those values. And those values are what will enable it to transform and to remain successful.

Ross Mauri: The founders of the company instilled in us this culture of excellence—in particular, technical excellence and business excellence—but we're not solely rooted in one way to do things. We can adapt. IBMers have a great culture, but there are always parts of it that we need to leave to start anew. Our commitment to our clients and our commitment to our quality—those are things we want to keep and never lose.

I made my career at IBM, and always will want IBM to succeed. Times are different today, both for IBM, and for young people trying to decide what to do with their careers. Careers like mine—forty-plus years with one company—are no longer the norm, that is for sure. If nothing changes, nothing changes, right?

I still want people to believe they can create for themselves a wonderful career at IBM, whether that be for ten, fifteen, twenty years or more. Recently, I was asked what I would say to a group attending IBM's Technical University. I thought this would be appropriate:

We have always lived in a world where everything is knowable, but now the time for knowledge is shrinking because of technology. Since the key to knowledge is data, how do we know what we are knowing is authentic? We can deal with data volume, we can deal with data velocity, we can even deal with data variety; but what can and should we do about data veracity, data validity, and its provenance? Is the data you are training your AI and ML systems on and making all those critical business decisions with more authentic or synthetic?

Technology got us here, and technology will get us out of here. Technology does nothing on its own. But in the hands of the right folks, it has, can, and will do amazing things.

IBM still has so many great people. I hope that continues. To be certain, there are so many more factors to consider these days when making career decisions. When I started, choices certainly seemed more binary—you did what the company asked, or if you did not, your career would stall. Accomplishment—and presumably satisfaction—was often measured by how far up the ranks you rose.

That is different from how those now entering the workforce do the calculus and plan their careers. Some seek a portfolio of interesting and diverse experiences; others are more socially-minded and want to have societal impact. The COVID-19 pandemic of 2020 and beyond is upending norms even further, especially as a generation of workers grow accustomed to working from home or embrace other nontraditional work arrangements, including the so-called "gig economy."

What remains consistent, however, is that successful leaders must embrace change, and even more so, adjust to an accelerated pace of change.

I have spent my career extolling how much technology matters. But people matter more; they always have and always will. For me, the bottom line is that there are no people more important in your life than your family. Mine enabled me to do all that I did. They sacrificed and perhaps suffered in silence as I advanced in my career. For this and more, they are the loves of my life. For this and more, I see now they deserved better of me.

Being remembered—whether within IBM's storied history, or for the changes we helped drive in industry and across society—is interesting, and of course, gratifying. These concerns never drove any decision that I made during my career. Being on the right side of history ultimately mattered more. That said, it is not a bad compass to follow as you travel through your career, whatever form it may take or wherever it may lead you: What will be your legacy? How will what you are doing now be judged later?

My way. No regrets? Now wouldn't that be nice! I have a few. Realistically, there is always a better way!

PART IV

EXTENDING
CHANGE AND
INNOVATION
TO SOCIETY

While my work at IBM was important, in many ways my real focus was in service of a greater mission: to extend the understanding and embrace of science and technology into broader society. Since my graduation from IBM, I have focused my energies on helping to lead businesses, nonprofits, and individuals to what I call our shared Technological Future.

We live in an age of ever-more rapid change, and businesses, organizations, and people must embrace and use the newest technologies to keep pace with that change or be left behind. And by that, I do not limit my thinking to the latest digital technologies—today's innovators must understand and stay abreast of the latest developments in life sciences, physical sciences, and even the social sciences. You do not need to be an expert on everything, but to be T-Shaped is to be facile on a wide range of technological and societal developments and is foundational to success.

I have been privileged to work on national and global initiatives related to technology and science, both before and since I left IBM. I have served on multiple boards of directors of large and small companies, both within and outside of the technology space. I have consulted with businesses and governmental entities about the critical issues facing them. I am exposed to many thinkers and doers, and in each of those settings, two interrelated themes repeatedly emerge:

1. The world's leading organizations, regardless of size or age, embrace change, innovation, and the future of technology.
2. The people driving meaningful progress in business and society openly embrace change, innovation, and new technologies, both professionally and as individuals.

These benchmark organizations and individuals:

- Understand the meaning of what *real* change and innovation represent.
- Recognize that effective change and innovation begin with a problem to be solved, not with the desire to simply create something new.
- Think about how individuals and groups fit into the new world being created and ensure that no one is left behind for lack of opportunity.
- Move quickly to capture the innovation that is happening now and to understand what is on the horizon.

Unfortunately, for a variety of reasons—shifting political winds, misplaced emphasis on shareholder return over all constituencies, an unprecedented global pandemic—I also see fewer and fewer organizations displaying these characteristics. In fact, I believe the biggest problem we face now as a society is a lack of political will to identify, define, address, and solve the many real challenges that accompany the inevitable march forward of technology.

This lack of vision results in lost opportunities, most notable in the lack of trained and knowledgeable people to fill technology jobs, innovate using technology, and solve societal issues. And it facilitates the misuse of technology, whether through identity theft, cybersecurity violations, loss and misuse of data, cyberbullying, or many other challenges we have yet to address satisfactorily.

I see so many opportunities and threats ahead as the new Technological Future advances—large, complex, global opportunities and threats—and I want to be part of bringing the good to life and sending the bad to the trash heap. I am still my father's son. His voice from the porch still reminds me, "If nothing changes, nothing changes. If all you do is what you have been doing, then all you will get is what you have been getting."

These words ring as true today as they did in Beacon, New York in the late 1950s when he first spoke them to me. Part of me wishes I was that young kid still, looking out at a world of potential, ready to make my mark. But where I sit today is pretty good, too. With all I saw and did at IBM, I believe that I have been gifted a unique take on life, leadership, and innovation. And as long as people want to hear from me, I am going to keep making my points, and I am going to keep rolling up my sleeves to actively help the world to understand and embrace innovation and change.

One of the ways in which I have most enjoyed extending my footprint has been through numerous opportunities to serve on boards of directors. Boards can be tremendously vital, not only from a governance standpoint, but from the opportunity they provide people like me to push, enable, and encourage new generations to reach their potential, to create enduring organizations, and to solve the problems of their age.

As part of a board, I bring some, if not all, of what I learned in my four decades at IBM to the table to help dynamic companies and organizations both large and small. At the same time, I get to collaborate with so many incredible women and men from many walks of life who make up these boards and enterprises. These leaders help me to learn, to stay current, and to maintain my edge, as we work together to try to do good and significant work. Each role has been different, and as much as I hope I have given to those organizations, I know I have gotten back just as much.

15

SERVING ON BOARDS OF DIRECTORS

T oward the end of my IBM career, I started receiving numerous invitations to join corporate boards. I found it a humbling experience, but challenging as well, in that I had to carefully consider the pros and cons of accepting or declining each offer. I took each opportunity I did accept very seriously and have learned a great deal in the process. While I have been on many boards over the years, I will focus on only a handful here, as they each contain valuable lessons.

Perhaps it would be helpful to first share some of my fundamental thoughts about this crucial form of governance. I have well over 150 total years of board experience, so these thoughts on what a director should be and what they should know in order to make a lasting contribution have been earned the hard way.

It is clear to me that a director's duty of care and duty of loyalty extend to their duty of knowledge. Directors simply must engage in *all* matters critical to the success of the enterprise they represent and serve, and that begins with some basics:

- They must be able to read a balance sheet and accounting profile.
- They must understand enterprise risk.

- They must understand business models and value propositions.
- They must understand the talent needs of the enterprise, including the creation of next-generation leadership.
- They must understand the impact of technology on the enterprise. While no one expects them to be the expert, a reasonable expectation is that they are knowledgeable and savvy on technology matters and on topics that matter: cybersecurity, the internet, data, artificial intelligence, machine learning, modeling and simulation, quantum computing, automation and robotics, life sciences, genomics, and more.
- They should demand of themselves relevance to the enterprise they represent. They must commit to lifelong learning and change and then find the change happening around them which they can influence.
- And more than anything, they must make it *personal.*

These ideas evolved and hardened over the past twenty years, and they will continue to do both as long as I can remain active. This journey of mine began over twenty years ago when I joined a board of historical significance.

BANK OF NEW YORK

In 1999, I was invited to join the Board of Directors of the Bank of New York. What an honor! Bank of New York is one of the three oldest banking corporations in the United States, and among the oldest banks in the world, having been established in June 1784 by a group that included both founding father Alexander Hamilton and his rival Aaron Burr. I was brought on board by then-CEO Thomas Renyi, a distinguished leader in the financial services industry and an equally distinguished man.

Thomas Renyi *(Chairman and CEO, Bank of New York, 1998–2007)*: The Bank of New York had a history of having an IBM executive on its board. I approached Lou Gerstner in the latter part of the 1990s, and we discussed the history of the two organizations and their relationship at a board level. Lou was very kind and forthright in saying, "Tom, I've got the exact right person for you, given the business model you're creating at the Bank of New York. He is a rare combination of a propeller-head and a blue suit." He meant Nick, of course, and what Lou was implying was that he was a rare individual who had an in-depth understanding of technology, but also was a businessman who took a businesslike view of the application of technology to a business model. I think Lou couldn't have been more right about Nick.

Tom had been CEO for about two years at this time, and he was accelerating the evolution of the bank through a series of mergers and acquisitions and other strategic initiatives. I believed I could help. I initially was assigned to the Audit Committee, where I began to get a good overview of the organization.

Thomas Renyi: The Audit Committee delved into the intricacies of the organization and provided a great opportunity for Nick to understand the bank, its business model, and its approach to doing business. I think what we both found very clearly was that Nick's understanding of technology and being able to think in abstract terms was precisely what we needed. Most people would think that the analysis of lending money or the analysis of a corporation in terms of its ability to repay us is pretty straightforward, but as we all know, banking was becoming much, much, much more beyond that.

The grounding experience with the Audit Committee set the stage for a more strategic assignment as a member of a newly-formed Risk Committee. By this time, I had learned a great deal about operational risk. From managing the complex RS/6000 turnaround and launch, to my role in the overall

IBM turnaround that hinged on the mainframe, to my then-new strategic role with Lou, I had seen enterprise-risk from many different angles. And, of course, I understood change.

> **Thomas Renyi:** We began changing the business model from a traditional commercial bank to one specializing in securities servicing. That activity entailed significant operational risk. A Risk Committee was a relatively new phenomenon within our businesses, which is somewhat surprising, since as far as a prototypical bank is concerned, risk-taking is its product. That's how it makes its money.

I greatly appreciated that Tom gave me something to sink my teeth into that took advantage not only of my deep technical background, but my business and strategic know-how as well.

> **Thomas Renyi:** He understood precisely, very quickly, the issues that we faced in providing some fairly abstract risk-taking activities including the creation of collateralized mortgage obligations, collateralized debt obligations, and our foreign-exchange trading. All of those activities of the bank entailed risk, and he was able to add an enormous amount of value in terms of understanding the risk and seeing things where maybe other board members would not. Nick was instrumental in identifying how we should look at operational risk, understanding the risk that we were taking, and dealing with it at an acceptable level. He was able to take the outline of what I thought we should be doing to quickly understand the risks we were taking on and how we might better manage that risk. He wasn't so much advising me on what sort of technology we should be utilizing—although he did do that separately with our CIO—but more from a business perspective in understanding what we were trying to accomplish, what kind of risk we were taking on, and how we were going to manage that risk.

While we were working to create processes for managing operational risk, Bank of New York and Tom were managing a different sort of risk scenario that had begun even before his tenure as CEO. In 1996, US federal investigators had uncovered a money laundering scheme related to post-Soviet privatization in Russia. The illegal operation involved two Russian émigrés, one of whom was a vice president of the bank, and they had moved over $7 billion via hundreds of wires.

Back during the mainframe crisis, when adverse media coverage was a daily occurrence, when I personally received death threats, and when the continued existence of IBM literally was at stake, it would have been easy to get sucked into the abyss and lose focus on the true task at hand. While the circumstances at Bank of New York were different, I applied this experience to help Tom and his team keep perspective and take a measured approach to what they did. Not that they couldn't have done so without me, but as an external board member, I could more easily bring perspective and help them step back to see the bigger picture.

Thomas Renyi: The US Attorney's Office was all over us and really caused us some severe issues that we had to deal with. There was one Russian émigré who accused me personally, and the Board had to put together a special committee to look into his claims. It was a time where you could look at the allegations and say, "This is horrific and horrendous. We've got to deal with this quickly." Yet Nick was level-headed, understood the issues exceptionally well, and took a very rational approach to the challenge, which ultimately was solved very, very satisfactorily from my position. The individual was deported, and any allegations were rejected and refuted, but it was not a very pleasant time for me, personally. I felt very comfortable and confident with Nick's leadership on that particular committee, during which time I think he gained a better understanding of us, and of me personally, and there was an empathetic relationship that emerged.

As I had with IBM, I embraced the fact that I was making contributions to a company of historical significance and took my board responsibilities seriously. Then came 9/11.

Thomas Renyi: The events of 9/11 impacted the Bank of New York very severely. We literally were taken out of business. A board member generally interacts with the company episodically, and during periods of crisis like 9/11, they are there to provide counsel, support, and encouragement, but not necessarily to be hands-on. But since we literally were taken out of business by the collapse of the towers, we had to recreate our business literally overnight around the city. Nick understood that precisely, and he grasped our form of crisis management and our ability to recreate our data centers and our communications network. We benefited dramatically from his experience in that crisis.

I was motivated to contribute as much as I could during these days of intense crisis. While my efforts did not require the sort of courage found at Ground Zero, the Pentagon, or many other locations, the knowledge that we were keeping this important institution up and running during a time when any semblance of normalcy greatly helped the American public and economy was gratifying.

Like the country, Bank of New York weathered the storm and went back to work. In fact, they hardly skipped a beat.

A few years later, in 2007, the bank and Mellon Financial Corporation announced a merger creating the world's largest custodian bank and asset servicing company, The Bank of New York Mellon Corporation. During this period of time, I became Chair of the Risk Committee, a role that stretched me in many ways. Of course, timing is everything, as they say. A year later, with the global economy headed toward the financial precipice following the collapse of both Bear Stearns and Lehman Brothers, the role took on particular importance.

Thomas Renyi: We were lucky to have Nick as Chair of the Risk Committee, especially after the credit debacle. Banks were not only being encouraged, but required, to seek out board members who had some risk-taking experience and could understand the business of financial technology. That was the advent of FinTech and Nick was really at the forefront of that.

I believe that our risk management efforts contributed to the results of the February 2009 "stress test" conducted by federal regulators, in which BNY Mellon was one of only three banks deemed able to withstand a worsening economic situation. And while the company had received $3 billion from the Troubled Asset Relief Program, they paid it back in full by June 2009, along with an additional $136 million to buy back warrants from the Treasury in August 2009.

By 2013, the company's capital had steadily risen from levels of the financial crisis, and during the Federal Reserve's Dodd-Frank stress test, when hypothetical extreme economic scenarios were run, the bank was shown to be the best prepared institution. BNY Mellon remains a high-performing and trusted brand today.

I enjoyed my time with the BNY Mellon board. The experience also served as a fine training ground for the many boards I have served on since. I had led strong-willed people at IBM before, but leading board committees for BNY Mellon refined those skills in new and important ways.

DELPHI AUTOMOTIVE SYSTEMS

Right around the same time that I graduated from IBM, I joined the board of Delphi. Delphi had been formed as Delphi Automotive Systems by General Motors in the mid '90s to better market their technological advantages for the automotive and commercial vehicle industry.

The Chairman at the time was an incredible man by the name of John "Jack" Krol. Jack had come up through the managerial ranks at DuPont, holding just about every position imaginable there, before eventually becoming Chairman and Chief Executive Officer. Jack had seen me speak at National Association of Corporate Directors (NACD) meetings, enjoyed my thoughts around technology, and introduced himself. We bonded instantly.

> **John Krol** (*Former Chairman of Delphi and Chairman and CEO of DuPont*): Delphi was with General Motors, but then in 1999 they were spun out. By 2005 or so, it went bankrupt, and remained in bankruptcy for at least four years. In 2009, it worked out a deal to come out of bankruptcy, and there were big investors that put money into it. They asked me to be Chairman of the Board, and I told them, "I'd like to get eleven board members, and here's what I want: three CEOs, two people from finance, and three from technology. The other three can be for whatever else we might need on the board."

I was one of the technologists Jack brought on to the board, and I was excited to be part of the revitalization effort, as it reminded me of the turn-arounds I had contributed to at IBM. At the same time, as a lover of both technology and cars, I felt right at home. Most importantly, Jack had vision and he had me earmarked for a concept he had been considering that went beyond just board membership.

> **John Krol:** I wanted to create an Information Technology Committee for the company, and I had in my mind that Nick was the right person to chair it. I created the committee because while we had this new board, we would have a meeting, and we'd go around the table for an hour or two with everybody talking about technology—what they think, what's right, what's not right—but it was a waste of time. That's when I decided to create a committee and put a person in charge of it who knew how to assess and

commercialize technologies at scale. There was no other person there that I would have put into something like this.

The first thing I told Jack was that he needed to think more broadly— that what he was really seeking was innovation enabled by technology. So we called it the Innovation and Technology Committee (ITC) to make that specific point. I was blessed with gifted, talented, and broad-thinking board colleagues on the ITC. I also asked Jack to review our committee's performance and review its mission and purpose annually. I only wanted the ITC to exist if we were adding value to Delphi.

Of course, before I could create much value for Delphi, I had to better understand the business and the role of innovation and technology within the business. The only real way to do that was to get out and observe, so I traveled the globe with the ITC and brought my observations back to the board.

> **John Krol:** Nick traveled all around the world to each place where Delphi had technology work going on, and he would take the other two or three guys on his committee with him. I went with him a couple of times, too, because I wanted to see how things were going outside. As far as Nick was concerned, it was not our job to tell them what to do. It was our job to figure out what they were doing, and then have a discussion with the board and the CEO about it. I liked how he interacted and learned from everyone, and people liked him.

I was committed to creating real impact with Jack's Innovation and Technology Committee, and after a few months of travel, we started going to the board, and I would talk about where I had visited, what I was seeing, and where the people in the field thought we should be going.

In many ways, what I was doing for Jack and Delphi was the same thing that I had spent so many years doing for Sam Palmisano at IBM. I helped

him put their technology work in the context of the overall business strategy as well as the macroeconomic trends that were impacting Delphi. And
as always, once I felt informed, I was not afraid to offer my opinions or
recommendations.

> **John Krol:** Nick hit the ground running. He thought in terms of the
> business of technology, so he'd be asking, "Okay, the technology
> we've got now, how do we make it work better and more profitably?"
> He's always thinking about the future, too. When he was looking at
> technology, he would look way out. But at the same time, he never
> forgot about what was going on in the present moment. Some leaders
> forget about what's going on today and start spending all of their
> time on the moon. Nick wasn't like that. Nick knew technology, but
> he also dug in on finance and the business.

Jack was trying to bring the company out of bankruptcy, so number one,
he had to get Delphi in shape for the investment community. That meant
getting the right people in the right places within the company. He also
had to look at the business and where it was going. He wanted to know,
"Where is the technology going in the cars? Is it going to be growing?" and
"How's the money? Are you creating value that could generate revenues for
a long time?"

He also wanted to know what Delphi was selling and why. What was
Delphi's real value? Was it in the pieces and parts it sold to its clients or was
it in the integrated solutions that it provided to them?

Delphi had already chosen its path forward with its "Green, Safe, and
Connected" slogan. What we were able to do was focus its efforts on delivering the innovative value that made dollars and cents out of that slogan.
Clearly electrification was high on our list, as it was the obvious technology
of choice for Delphi Automotive, the Green, Safe, and Connected Company.

We honed in on what pieces were growing and making money and win-
nowed down from 122 to 32 pieces and really focused. We told the world,

"We're going to be in safety. We're going to be in radio and anything with electricity flowing through it."

Wall Street jumped right onto that message, and Delphi came out of bankruptcy in two years, going from $9 billion in revenue to $16 billion in just five years. Jack also moved the work around the world closer to where sales were growing. Jack was all about technology improvement and change that could drive growth, and I was glad to be a part of the turnaround he led.

> **John Krol:** Nick wanted to learn everything that he could learn about our technological options, but then when it came time to pick—"What's the option that fits here for us? How much value is it going to create?"—he was decisive. That's him. I just thought he was somebody who could really make a difference for Delphi, and I believe that time proved me and Nick to be correct.

Over the course of the next decade, Delphi continued to make steady progress. In 2017, following the spinoff of a powertrain group, the remaining company became Aptiv, a name created to represent knowledge, adaptiveness, and drive. I remain on the Aptiv Board of Directors to this day and just recently passed the chair of the Innovation and Technology Committee on to my successor.

Today, Aptiv is one of the world's largest providers of components and technologies to the automobile equipment manufacturing industry. In fact, in 2021, Harvard Business School completed a business case that details the history of the turnaround, dating back to Jack's recasting of the board in 2009. You can find the case on the Harvard Business School website.

Additionally, it is with great humility and honor that I mention my recent induction into Aptiv's Innovation Hall of Fame—the first non-Aptiv employee to be so honored. Aptiv CEO Kevin Clark and his team saw fit to recognize my commitment and contribution to the company in this way. There have been so many incredible changes at Aptiv over the past twelve years, and I am proud to have helped enable them.

ADVANCED MICRO DEVICES (AMD)

In November 2009, around the same time I joined the Delphi board, I was appointed to the Board of Directors for Advanced Micro Devices, or AMD.

AMD was founded in 1969 as a Silicon Valley startup focused on leading-edge semiconductor products, grew quickly, and went public in 1972. By 2000, at the height of the tech-stock bubble, AMD was trading at a split-adjusted price of about $46 per share, with a market capitalization of over $55 billion. However, over the next eight years, the stock plunged to less than $2 per share, with a commensurate decline in market cap to just over $2 billion.

By the time I joined the board in late 2009, this fallen angel had bounced back to about $7 per share. Nevertheless, a lot of work was going to be needed to reposition the company to compete with their market rivals.

I knew a lot about AMD before I ever joined the board because their history was intertwined with that of IBM. And that of Intel. Intel had introduced the first x86 microprocessors in 1978, and when we created our PC at IBM in 1981, we wanted those processors for it, but only under the condition that Intel provide a second-source manufacturer. AMD became that second source, a decision that really put them on the map.

Over the course of the next decade or more, we came to understand AMD. We watched their business ebb and flow several times, and we worked with them when they started to take some share from Intel in the server market, including assigning researchers to their business. At one time, they had a lot of the server market because their processor was better than Intel's. Intel had decided to build a noncompatible 64-bit version of the 32-bit processor, thinking it could manage its way with a new architecture. It was a costly decision, and AMD capitalized on it. They built a compatible version, and their business took off like a rocket.

But they could not sustain themselves. They had their own set of issues. They were a fabricator, but they had to get out of the fabrication business. They had to get focused. They experienced a lot of bumps along the way.

I was never deeply involved with the relationship with AMD, but I understood it. Over my years with IBM, I engaged with Intel on more than one occasion. I truly understood them, along with their strengths and weaknesses. But that was the extent of it for me, at least until I graduated from IBM in 2008.

Not long after, I received a call from Bruce Claflin, a former IBMer who eventually became CEO of 3Com. At the time, he was the chair of the AMD board, and he asked me to join. By this time, they had already sold off their fabricators to Global Foundries, who not only was a major partner of AMD, but an activist shareholder on their board.

I said to Bruce, "Why on earth would I do that? They're a gang that can't shoot straight, and I don't like their direction."

But Bruce and I were friends, and he persisted. He said, "Well, you really don't know that. Why don't you come here and help me, and let's see what we can do together?"

So, I said, "Alright, I'll give it a year. That's it."

I spent that first year on the board getting a deep understanding of what was taking place, and while I could see so much potential, I also became convinced that I had been right in my initial assessment. The clincher for me came after we worked for an entire year to build a new strategy, but the leadership team did not want anything to do with it or to change anything they were doing.

Bruce now clearly understood my concerns and asked me to partner with him to fix things. We knew we needed new leadership, and we knew we needed to flip everything around and turn everything upside down. The business was sagging and lagging. AMD was only getting what the market would give them—the low end of the marketplace. We needed an infusion of new talent, and I took the lead, while the rest of the board helped and stayed engaged.

To be fair, I made things worse with some of my initial moves. But I am my father's son, and I set out to fix these issues. Luckily, I also had made some good decisions along the way.

Remember Mark Papermaster and Lisa Su? They were the two IBM pro-
tégés of mine who had left to pursue other opportunities right around the
time of my retirement. Well, I brought them back into the fold, only this
time with AMD.

Getting the two of them to come to AMD more than made up for my
earlier miscalculations. I started with Mark, who joined AMD in October
2011 as Chief Technology Officer. A few months later, I recruited Lisa to be
Product Manager.

> **Mark Papermaster:** Nick called me and I said, "Nick, I can't take
> that job. I'm not going to look at AMD." He said, "Mark, you have an
> opportunity to be the Lead Engineer, the Chief Technology Officer,
> and head development here. It could be the biggest technology
> impact in your life. And if you don't take it, I think I'm going to have
> to step out of retirement, and I'm going to have to take it. And by the
> way, if it were earlier in my career, I'd already be doing it!"

Mark knew from my words that I was as serious about turning AMD
around as anything he ever witnessed me do at IBM. Even though Mark had
done big things at Apple and Cisco, I believed this could be a monumental
opportunity for him, though not without risk.

> **Mark Papermaster:** I had such immense respect for Nick that sure
> enough, I saw the opportunity, felt I really could make a difference, and
> took it. Anyone other than Nick, and I never would have considered
> this position. I could see that even though Nick was now operating from
> a board role, not an operational role, Nick was still Nick. It was still
> personal. I loved that about him when I was with IBM, and I felt good
> knowing that was still the case as I considered this new opportunity.

Getting Mark to join AMD was important to me. I knew I could trust
him to run the tech side of the business and to listen to my guidance while

still being his own man. Mark understood the vision I articulated, but he needed to convert it quickly into a plan of action. Speed matters, and he needed to show he could lead the technology side of the business quickly.

Mark Papermaster: When I came in, one of the first questions I was asked by the board was, "Mark, should AMD exit the server market?" My position was very strongly, emphatically, "No." We had to rebuild ourselves and go after the server market, because the industry was moving toward a greater and greater demand for high-performance computing. Nick saw that, and he saw the kind of impact that AMD could have if it regained its microprocessor competitiveness. We just needed the right strategy. When I first joined the company, I had to show that technology strategy within two months. What I came up with and showed them was that we needed to go after high-performance computing and change the engineering approaches so we could achieve that goal. The board's reaction was mixed.

I had faith in Mark. I believed in him in a way the board could not yet, so I went to bat for him hard.

Mark Papermaster: Some people were technology-savvy, but most weren't—it's a board of directors, they come from all walks of life— and Nick was incredibly articulate to the rest of the board in support of what I brought in with that technology strategy. He explained why it made sense. He had spent time with me privately to make sure he understood, and in fact, to help guide it. He proposed forming an Innovation and Technology Committee of the board, and I was the AMD Lead Executive for this committee.

Every quarter, when we had a board meeting, we would have a breakout with this committee, where we would take Nick and the other members in detail through our technology strategy and execution as we proceeded with this turnaround. That was his idea, because he realized that as a technology company, AMD needed a smaller group that could really make sure that there was alignment on these tough decisions and tough actions that AMD was making along with our progress toward our goals. Nick then would report that back to the rest of the board of directors on a regular basis.

With the technology plan beginning to take shape—and yes, inspired by my Delphi experience, I created an Innovation and Technology Committee at the board level to stay focused on and engaged in what mattered—we now needed a CEO who could drive the strategy across the entire business and into the marketplace, while rebuilding the confidence of the investment community in AMD's ability to execute. That person was Lisa Su, and in 2014, she was named CEO.

Lisa Su: I had observed AMD from afar. I knew AMD well as a company. I knew the technology well. Of course, I wanted to discuss the potential opportunity with Nick before joining the company. Nick was very persuasive. His point of view was, "You want to make a difference? Come to AMD. You can make a difference. You can make a huge difference." My combination of business and technology skills was the way to reconnect with Nick.

With this dynamic duo in place on both the tech side and the business side, my job was to simultaneously build them up and buy them time with the board. They rolled up their sleeves and went to work.

Lisa Su: Nick was always about playing the long game, and he knew from the beginning that this was going to be a long game. He knew that we had to redo our development roadmap and capabilities, which was primarily Mark's responsibility, and that we had to also refocus the business markets and business execution, and that was primarily my responsibility. Nick was incredibly, incredibly helpful on our board, because as often happens when you have a diverse board, people have different experiences. Some are more technical, some are more business-oriented, but few have the insight that spans all of that, and Nick did. So I found that during those first few years, he was always helping the board understand what the long-term vision was, and it was always, "We've got to build our technology assets such that we can address these large, wonderful markets that we are in." He was very clear that it was going to take time. Although the company went through a period of decline in revenues and decline in profitability and financial losses, Nick was clear to the board, "This is what it takes, and you guys have got to give these people time."

I made sure that Mark and Lisa knew I would be there for them for advice, counsel, and support. They both had experienced that support from me at IBM, but it was important that they understood that they would have it here in this different context, where I was a board member.

Lisa Su: When I took over as CEO, Nick was incredibly supportive. He would talk to me any time, because as a new CEO, sometimes you do need a little bit of reassurance, primarily with how to handle the board. He was clear to Mark and me, "I am buying you the time. You guys gotta go execute what you said you're going to do." We knew what the strategy was, we just knew it would take time.

Make no mistake, Mark and Lisa had and have very difficult jobs. I had sold them on the potential at AMD, but that is what it was—potential. To realize that potential would take execution on their parts.

They had to push AMD's technologists with the same innovation theme that I had preached to them at IBM: "The answer isn't technology. The answer is you. How do you make it work? How do you make it work faster? Go back and look at the architecture and see what changes you can make."

The approach worked just as well at AMD as it had at IBM. But it was a long journey. They each had a lot of work to do and a lot of weight on their shoulders.

By October 2014, with Lisa and Mark fully in charge, things started to move. They met commitments to customers, made a few bold bets on chip-manufacturing technologies, and now lead the chip market at nearly every price point.

Lisa Su: Where I was quite capable of managing the day-to-day, Nick was very good about always reminding me about the future and what we were trying to do in the long term. It's quite interesting. If I go back to what we said we were going to do—whether it was in 2012 or in 2014 when I took over as CEO—we're pretty much on that path. It's a path that we've laid out, and although it's a multi-year path, you accomplish that quarter by quarter, and we've stayed very true to that.

Mark Papermaster: It's been quite the journey. It's been tumultuous, to say the least. It's been a phenomenal challenge to turn around a Fortune 500 company. We've had any number of challenges. Now it's seven years later, and we've been a great team. Lisa and I have been very successful in turning around the company. It's on a very, very successful path. None of that would have happened without Nick. You can look at this AMD turnaround, with the CEO and the CTO each Nick mentees, and it's quite the story.

The stock has gone from roughly $2.75 per share when Lisa took over to over $155 per share by late 2021, a return of 5,600 percent. Market cap has grown from the $3 billion range to nearly $188 billion during that time.

Along the way, AMD earned the distinction of being the top-performing stock on the S&P 500 for both 2018 and 2019. I cannot tell you how proud I was when the respected investing weekly *Barron's* named Lisa one of the World's Best CEOs for 2019 and placed her on the cover. The accolades continued to roll in across 2019, including *Fortune's* #44 "Most Powerful Women in Business", *Harvard Business Review's* #26 "The Best-Performing CEOs in the World", and *Bloomberg Businessweek's* "The Bloomberg 50."

In 2020, she was named *Fortune's* #2 "Business Person of the Year," received the Semiconductor Industry Association's Robert N. Noyce Award, was elected to the National Academy of Engineering and the American Academy of Arts and Sciences, won the Technical Leadership Abie Award, and won the Global Semiconductor Association Dr. Morris Chang Exemplary Leadership Award. Lisa also just received the highest IEEE Robert Noyce Medal for groundbreaking semiconductor leadership.

> **Lisa Su:** Nick continues to remind me, "Hey, don't get ahead of yourself. Don't let the company get ahead of themselves. Stay humble and stay true to what you believe." I think that's the way that I lead the company. We share a very common set of values in terms of how to run a tech company. But he also wants to know, "How are you going to beat Intel?" and "What's the next five-year architectural strategy?"

No matter how good Lisa and Mark have become, their competitors are not going away. They have to keep their heads about them and keep doing the same things they did to turn the company around in terms of innovation. Equally important, they need to focus on talent.

> **Lisa Su:** I cannot even begin to count the number of times he has talked to me about people development and "How are you developing your next generation of talent?" and "How are you making sure that you have enough diversity within AMD?" He is interested in all of those people-related things. It's the combination—strategy and talent—that makes him quite genuine and quite lovable. Our Fellows and Senior Fellows love talking to him, because he just imparts so much insight from his many, many

years of experience. As it relates to my own management style, I'm not Nick in any way, shape, or form, but I try to adopt that style of "what you see is what you get" and be very sincere in how I approach every situation.

The competition remains fierce. They have much more to do. But always accepting the challenge can be like that sometimes. It has been very rewarding to have the opportunity to lead them both again and to see such fantastic results.

Mark Papermaster: Nick is Nick. He has been by and large the same man we both knew at IBM. What he drove at AMD was a penchant for action, a penchant to build the talent of the company, to build focus, and to get a winning game plan in place. That's what he's been doing his whole career. It's just from a different chair.

Lisa Su: Mark and I almost think of it as, "We're finishing the story." We started the story at IBM. And we're finishing the story at AMD. Whatever success we have, Nick deserves a lot of credit for that. He's been with me, and with us, through a lot of challenges, and he's never once wavered in his support, his advice, or his ability to advise without telling us what to do. He always will be a trusted and dear friend, and it's the same today, even now that he's retired from the board. I know he's always thinking about us. And you need that sometimes. I know he cares about AMD—he cares very deeply about us as a company—but more than that, I think he cares deeply about Mark and me, and felt some responsibility in bringing us to this particular place.

Today, AMD is a global company of 15,500 people, achieving many important industry firsts, with many more to come. Lisa, Mark, and their team are positioned to lead the semiconductor industry with high-performance computing and graphics solutions that transform the world. I am proud of them. I know they are just getting started.

I should mention that there is an added bonus for me—they continue to use the same approach to innovation that we pioneered at IBM. They are doing far more than their competitors with far less.

They do not have the same technology—they may have even *less* technology. Yet, they are winning in the marketplace.

You do not need technology every day of your life to save your hide. There is a difference. Instead of semiconductor technology, it is *thinking* technology, it is the *architectural* technology. Go study what problems you are solving.

I would push them by saying, "You mean you can't do better? You can't architect this thing differently? You can't figure this out? Of course you can. You're all very smart people." Lisa and Mark are pushing their talent that same way.

They are doing it, and I love it, because AMD is now leading and no longer following. They believe in themselves and focus on the market problems they are committed to solving.

MITRE CORPORATION

For the past eleven years, I have served on the Board of The MITRE Corporation, a large nonprofit entity dedicated to solving problems for a safer world. MITRE does significant work in such areas as defense and intelligence, cybersecurity, and government systems. It also does significant work in education around the sciences, engineering, and technology. Obviously, MITRE has a mission that I feel passionate about—and so does its CEO, Jason Providakes.

Jason Providakes (*President & CEO of The MITRE Corporation and Thirty-Year MITRE Veteran*): I first met Nick when he arrived as a new board member in 2010. The previous CEO was looking to bring on some new board members who weren't necessarily former four-star generals or secretaries of defense but were knowledgeable in the national security space. Nick was, having worked the IBM side of the house that dealt in national security for many years. He also was somebody with a strong technological bent, and MITRE is a deep technical company. But Nick's contributions quickly went beyond that. He was a voice that helped move the board to broaden its thinking and its mindset, which impacted the officers of the company, like myself and others, and became a real ally. Nick thought we could contribute a lot, and he was right.

When I looked at MITRE's expertise, my first thought was that there was so much more that they could do with their people and their capabilities. I asked, "Why doesn't MITRE focus on some of these big national problems, beyond defense?"

In fact, MITRE is a classic "If nothing changes" story. They had created a great niche serving the Department of Defense and the Intelligence agencies, but they were leaving on the table so much opportunity to make a difference in the big problems of the day. I pushed them hard to expand their footprint.

Jason Providakes: One example would be the healthcare work that MITRE was pursuing. We began competing for work, and Nick helped our Pursuit Team to think differently about how to understand what differentiates MITRE from others and how to price our value proposition correctly. That really helped, particularly in the healthcare space, but as we explored new areas, other more traditional board members would question why MITRE was broadening into a new area. It was always Nick who would press forward and ask, "Why not? If it's important, why shouldn't MITRE pursue it?"

And that leads me into a second area where Nick really helped us broaden our thinking, and that was in terms of partnering with others.

For instance, when we became involved with the topic of climate change, and we were pursuing some work in that area, Nick chimed in, "This is an important topic—a big system-engineering problem."

As with my collaboration efforts at IBM, I pushed them to take a step back and see the whole end-to-end picture of some of these challenges, which is something they do well.

Jason Providakes: The discipline of Systems Engineering—all of the interdependencies and implications—resonates with Nick. He asks people, "Are we working the right problems? Did we define the right problem? Are we bringing other partners in?" Nick always questions those organizations who say, "It's got to be the IBM way," or "It's got to be the MITRE way." Nick would say, "There are other people in this world who you could benefit from by partnering with and interacting with. You can bring new ideas to a problem and help accelerate solutions." That is one area where Nick really pushed the organization, and to this day, we have a significant strategic initiative in partnerships, and that's new. That's a big cultural shift for us, at a company where we took great pride in that "We don't need anybody else—we do it ourselves" mindset. Nick broke that paradigm, and that broadened our thinking about what MITRE could contribute and our view of how we do our work. By bringing others in, we not only really enrich our solutions, we actually get to the answers faster.

And as far as innovation goes, I wanted to push them to take some risks and act boldly. I would tell them, "If you're going to invest money, is it going to lead to something big?"

Jason Providakes: MITRE spends about $120 million annually on research; that's the R&D of the company, and when Nick was on the Technology Committee of the Board, he felt very vested in the question, "Is MITRE leveraging that $120 million every year? What are you doing with it that really is creating new future capabilities or insights that are going to pay dividends back in new potential solutions or new capabilities to apply to problems which we see coming down the pike?" He was very good at asking very penetrating questions about how we were investing the money.

Publishing papers is great. Thought leadership is great. The work they already were doing was great. But I wanted them to think first and foremost about doing even more significant work and in even more areas, which led to a great program at MITRE that already is leading to significant breakthroughs.

> **Jason Providakes:** As I became CEO, Nick said, "Don't take $120 million and do 120 different million-dollar little projects. Think of two or three big projects." And that's what basically became our "Moonshots." A couple years ago we launched three "Moonshots." They had to do with looking at a particular problem and putting some significant resources on it—more than 10 times as much as we had ever done in the past—a $20 million-plus investment to us is big.

That is change. That is organizational innovation. In a way, my work with MITRE reminds me, at the organizational level, of my work as a mentor with individuals at IBM. Whether it was a Lauren States or a Ross Mauri or any number of others, these were already strong performers who I was trying to get to see themselves at that next level of greatness. In a sense, I was trying to do the same at MITRE.

> **Jason Providakes:** We launched the Oncology/Cancer Moonshot, which really looked at a new paradigm of looking at clinical trials, particularly for breast cancer, that leveraged advances in information technology. There is so much data that exists with cancer patients

which is never tapped into or looked at. So we partnered with half a dozen or so really major hospital systems like the Mayo Clinic, Brigham and Women's, and others. Partners played huge in this Moonshot, and to this day—after two and a half years—we just had a large national conference on this new data set, and it's going international, and that really has advanced some new therapies in breast cancer. It's been the same thing in quantum computing. Everything is about quantum computers these days. Well, MITRE's been doing quantum science for the last twenty years, and we had some ideas about a new approach.

The breast cancer data set and subsequent national conference represent just one example of the way that MITRE can lead change in our complex world. While I obviously am a fan of capitalism and the profit motive, some roles can be better played by hybrid-type organizations such as MITRE.

Jason Providakes: MITRE is a very trusted organization, not just in government, but also inside industry. It goes beyond the fact that we don't make a profit and we aren't necessarily in it for ourselves, but how we treat data and how we treat partners and how we share information and not share information is really important. So over the past sixty years as a company, we've established strong, trusted relationships. And it was Nick who said, "You guys need to leverage that as a national, if not global, convener. People will come to MITRE, feel safe, and get into a dialogue on these topics. You can really help advance some of the thinking collectively on a set of problems."

As MITRE evolves and plays this expanded and expanding role, they need to ensure that they have the right leadership and talent in place to meet the challenges. So you can bet I prod Jason and his team to pay attention to talent and next-generation leadership.

Jason Providakes: He cares about the institution and how we grow and develop leaders in the company for the future of MITRE. Nick's certainly been involved in that sort of topic in terms of developing future leaders, and what should those future leaders look like, and what should their attributes and character be, and how should they behave? He is really passionate around ensuring we take care of the employees and how we think about our employees, too. They are our number one asset. And as it evolves, ensuring that we continue to see the value of diversity and inclusion. That's another accelerant in seeing the world differently, discovering new things, and creating new opportunities.

Each opportunity to be part of a board is special to me, but what makes MITRE so special is that it almost feels like an extension of my personality at this stage of my life and career. I am all about technology, innovation, collaboration, and the urgent need to make serious dents in some of the major problems plaguing America and the world. So is MITRE.

There is a part of me that can never rest until every major problem—education, healthcare, the environment—is solved, but I also recognize my own limitations as one person. Through MITRE, I can work to solve those problems, and at the same time, help shape this organization so that it can keep working those problems long after I've moved on.

Jason Providakes: Nick, not so much explicitly but implicitly, laid the foundation to think differently about MITRE going into the future. I think he saw that with MITRE, he could almost scale himself into an institution. Even to this day, I think there are some areas I think Nick would want us to go, and we haven't gone there yet.

I am very excited about the direction that MITRE is headed. They have unlimited potential to contribute to the solving of major problems if they continue to focus on moonshots and ways to innovate in their approach. As long as I can, I will keep pushing them to solve big challenges, in the same way that I push myself.

> **Jason Providakes:** Nick can be contentious. You know, Nick's a lightning rod. He will ask the difficult questions. And he doesn't do it out of spitefulness. He doesn't do it because he wants to be a jerk. It's important to opening up the eyes, and pausing, and getting people to lift their heads up and say, "We have an issue here. This is important." And in the best possible way, he's relentless. When we would have program reviews with Nick, as part of the board meeting—the highlights, accomplishments, and the like—Nick would challenge everything. He'd never settle. That's one thing about Nick. He would say, "Gee, that's a great result. You guys really nailed it. But could you do more? How would you have done more?"
>
> At the same time, he's been a great mentor to me as CEO. He's been really instrumental in helping me look forward. Particularly, what do you do with a company like MITRE twenty years from now? How do you position it properly? At the end of the day, it comes down to people and leaders, and developing them is really important, whether in government, places like MITRE, or commercial institutions. Nick understands that very well.

SMALL COMPANIES

While I made my name at a large, iconic, global corporation and have served on the boards of many large, publicly-traded firms, I have great interest and belief in early-stage companies with ideas just beginning to make their mark. When the right situation appears, I jump in and give it the same attention and passion that I give to the marquee names.

> **David Yaun:** Nick is taking on a lot of smaller companies that allow him to play more of a mentor role. He's sort of a grown-up

for companies that are growing up, which I think is a fantastic role for him. It allows his passion and his desire to mentor and teach to shine through.

Atlas Research

One of the small companies I currently am mentoring is the brainchild of two dynamic guys named Ryung Suh and Mark Chichester. They are both highly intelligent yet scrappy individuals, and their story inspires me.

When you stay busy, enjoy people, and get out and about into the world as much as I do, sometimes unexpected, unplanned things happen that prove to be a great blessing. Such was the case for me about a decade ago when I was attending a MITRE board meeting and Ryung, then the Chair of the Department of Health Systems Administration at Georgetown, was giving a presentation to us on healthcare reform issues.

> **Ryung Suh** *(CEO and Co-Founder of Atlas Research)*: I had heard of Nick Donofrio, but I had never met or even seen him before that MITRE board meeting. That day, I had an opportunity to really see Nick in action. He has such facility with big, strategic governance issues, and I could just tell the values and integrity that were reflected in the way that he approached all issues, and the way he recommended solutions and ways to navigate things. I could just tell that he was a very effective and collegial strategic advisor. I had just started a consulting firm called Atlas a couple of years before. We were a tiny, tiny firm, and just watching Nick, my initial reaction was that I was a little bit envious that large organizations like MITRE had access to the great strategic advice that Nick could offer, while small organizations like mine did not have access to such perspective.

Later that night, at the board dinner, I happened to be seated at the same table as Ryung. Just in chatting, I learned that in addition to his responsibilities at Georgetown, Ryung had recently founded this consultancy he called Atlas Research, along with his co-founder Mark Chichester. He told me his vision for the company, and I was impressed not only with him, but with what he was hoping to accomplish and with the dash of audacity he displayed.

> **Ryung Suh:** During the course of that discussion, I rather boldly asked him to join my advisory board, fully expecting him to decline. I was very reluctant to ask him to help us, because we were such a tiny firm dealing with relatively mundane and trivial issues compared to the things that Nick normally deals with, but to my great surprise and utter satisfaction, he said, "I don't normally join a lot of small boards, but I do try to set aside some of my time to help small businesses approach their growth. I like the vision you have for Atlas Research, so let me think about it." I just thought he was being polite, but Nick being true to his word, did in fact follow up after the dinner. He approached me and said, "I checked with IBM to make sure there were no conflicts of interest, and there are not, so I'd be happy to join your Advisory Board."

> **Mark Chichester** (*President and Co-Founder of Atlas Research*): Ryung and I don't kid ourselves. It wasn't the overall business promise of Atlas that initially resonated with Nick and led him to agree to come on the Advisory Board of this very young company. It was our mission, it was the work, it was the communities that benefit from our work—specifically veterans—that I think resonated immediately with Nick.

Ryung and Mark had been in business for about three years when I met them, and they had done very well, going from nothing to several million dollars in revenue and about forty-five employees serving their government clients. Then, as it almost always does, adversity struck.

Ryung Suh: One of the very first things that he did came when we were faced with a moment of existential crisis, as all small businesses just starting out do. In our case, it was an economic downturn and government shutdown, and contracts we had been counting on were delayed and did not go out before the end of the fiscal year.

Mark Chichester: After a really successful run out of the gate, we had gone about three and a half quarters without a new contract win. We had a budget sequester that had come in and had locked in, and essentially, we had so much concentration of our contract portfolio with just one or two clients that overnight, we went from roughly a six-or-seven-million-dollar company to a two-million-dollar company with a six-million-dollar payroll.

Ryung Suh: We essentially were faced with a decision about whether to double down and keep continuing to drive ahead or to transition out of the market altogether. For us, it was such a dramatic, heart-wrenching thing, because we felt like we were in the midst of building a good, solid startup company, and now it looked like it was coming to an end.

Mark Chichester: Ryung and I engaged with our staff and had what we called a Jimmy Stewart kind of moment. If you remember the movie It's a Wonderful Life, when the run on the banks hit and everybody came to the bank and Jimmy Stewart jumped behind the teller station and to everyone he says, "Well, how much do you need? I can't give you all of your savings, but how much do you need to make it to next month?" Ryung and I had that exact conversation with our team.

Ryung Suh: And we gave Nick a call and said, "This is what we're facing," and gave him the summary. In his characteristic upbeat, succinct, and simple way, Nick told us, "You have to have the courage to stand up when things go bad. Business cycles go up and down. You have a solid vision and talented people. You either believe it or you don't. If you believe it, stand up and be counted. Don't be afraid to drive on no matter what the ups and downs of any normal business cycle might be." It sounded like very simple encouragement, but frankly, for a young, brand-new business, that simple encouragement gave us a great deal of confidence to drive through our challenges and ultimately prevail.

Everybody needs a boost sometimes. These were smart, experienced guys, but they had never had *this* type of experience before. I had been telling engineers for decades, "Check your assumptions when all else fails; go back to the beginning since something there is likely wrong." Here, I was telling Ryung and Mark that nothing was wrong *if*—and it is a big if—they had the courage of their convictions. I believed that they should, but only they could decide if they would.

Ryung Suh: I think he's been through enough challenges and ups and downs, that none of these things really fazed him much. He just kind of listened to us and said, "What's the big deal? If you think you've got the right solution, don't be afraid." We knew we had a good advisor when he could help us harness the courage we had in us.

Here, I was more the father figure, helping them to, as Ryung says, "harness the courage" I believed they possessed. The next time they really needed me, though, was as a seasoned tech leader, because these guys were about to have another existential crisis, this one of their own making.

Mark Chichester: We came out of that rough patch, had some good fortune in having our portfolio turned around by providing management consulting services to help the VA figure out how to end veteran homelessness (or at least significantly reduce it), and then began to try to determine where else we ought to be looking to create client and portfolio diversification. We have flirted almost from our inception with the notion of building an IT capability here at Atlas. While IT contracts came with huge dollars and were attractive in that respect, it's largely commoditized work where you compete on price. Still, we had a vision where we could take our more upmarket, professional services consulting capabilities and wrap an IT capability into it. Nick was very polite. He let us talk through our presentation, but then he said, "Guys, let me just put this very simply: health IT is the road to hell. Don't go down that road. It will burn every bit of cash you have. The road is littered with small and big businesses that placed that bet. Stay off it." We honored his advice, and that's a story that's told over and over in Atlas Business School.

Ryung Suh: Obviously, given his background, we asked if we should turn from our core, traditional professional services and expand into information technology. I think that was an occasion where we were thinking Nick would say, "Hey, yeah. Drive on, and here's some advice," and instead, he said, "Frankly, without sufficient resources, both in expertise and capital, IT is the road to hell. I wouldn't go into starting up an IT business, because it requires a lot of investment and a lot of expertise and a lot of experience that you guys frankly don't have." I think Nick saved us from making a poor choice going into a sector that we didn't really know anything about and instead guided us on a good path. We didn't go into the commodity information technology services capability, but we did invest in digital, and we did invest in a proprietary platform build, and we did invest in healthcare-related clinical informatics. All three of those were direct suggestions of Nick's, and they've been excellent investments for us, and they've really helped us increase the value that we can offer our clients.

SERVING ON BOARDS OF DIRECTORS

I try to observe everything and take in all the data that I can, and I knew just from being around as long as I have been, that building an IT capability was the wrong move for them. I cut through the clutter and reminded them of who they were and how they could hone what they were thinking into offerings that better fit the Atlas brand.

With MITRE, it made sense to take their strengths and expand them to other areas of focus. With Atlas, at that stage, I did not want them to lose sight of their core strength—high-end client service—because they had gotten starry-eyed over a niche they were ill-suited to serve. Ryung and Mark knew how to serve federal agencies, which is no small skill to possess, and because I understand that, I think I have been able to advise them appropriately.

Mark Chichester: Typically, technologists who come from the private sector can have a tendency to drip with a bit of condescension when they deal with public sector folks—almost a resentment of the inefficiency of government, the lack of understanding in government of how to leverage technology, and the sense that the culture of government is broken and needs to be torn down and fixed. Nick was, and is today, different. He seems to occupy a unique space as a "translator," as opposed to someone who sits outside and drops ideas and recommendations like manna on these lowly bureaucrats. He's able to translate between government and tech in a way that is really unique, and I have to believe that that is attributable to his orientation as a bridger-connector type. He just seems wired that way. When you have done some of the things Nick has done within the Intelligence Community, rather than look at government as this inefficient, enemy-of-the-people kind of thing, he takes it on to translate back and forth across the transom between government leaders and technology leaders.

It is a balancing act. Think back to what IBM did with the Department of Energy's Accelerated Strategic Computing Initiative (ASCI). The government is not always hidebound. There are times when they go along to get along, but there are times when they enable innovations that the private sector is not yet willing to fund. You have to read the situation with nuance, and Ryung and Mark both understand that, and we look for our spots.

> **Mark Chichester:** At critical moments, Nick will remind us, "Hey, here's an opportunity to introduce something that is different, to introduce a different way. You can demonstrate to them how technology can be leveraged—not in and of itself—but with the translation that Atlas can do between government and the technology expertise or technological solution. And here's how you might approach it." He's been enormously valuable to us. I would contrast Nick's approach with some other people who have been advisors to us over the years. We've had folks coming from the private sector who are tremendously successful and smart people, but not able to sit at that nexus point and to be able to translate and to speak to folks in the language and the terms that move them.

Ryung and Mark built their business with the right balance of patience and aggressiveness, and even with their successes, they have stayed humble and grounded. And they keep asking questions.

> **Mark Chichester:** Around 2014, Ryung and I posed to the board the question of whether we had reached the end of our potential to lead the company on its continued growth trajectory. What we were asking is, "Hey, do we need to be thinking right now about avoiding the trap that so many founders fall into—that they can't let it go, that they can't recognize when they have to bring in folks who have 'been there, done that, grown it'?" In other words, we wondered if we needed to be thinking about bringing in a growth-minded CEO who could build the systems and infrastructure and bring a growth framework that gets us to maturity as a small business, and

ultimately, out into the middle market as a successful company competing on bigger engagements.

I remember the first time they asked about bringing in a "professional" CEO, I told them, "I love you guys. I appreciate that you have the humility and the confidence to ask the question, but as I look around the table, I think I can speak confidently for all the other members of this Advisory Board: No. Not now. You're doing just fine."

Mark Chichester: We had the same conversation about a year and a half later, in the 2016 timeframe, when we now were at a point when we were moving into a pretty high-growth phase of the business. And we asked the question again.

I still did not think so, so I told them, "No. Not yet. We'll know it when we get there, but the company needs you right now. The things that have allowed you to weather the adversity, to keep people motivated and focused, to keep an eye on the mission and making sure that that remains at the forefront of what drives the business—the business needs you to do that."

Ryung Suh: I think when we reached maybe $50 million in annual revenues, and the company really began to compete head-to-head with the large consulting firms, we asked the same question again.

This time I said, "Yeah, I think it's the right time. You guys have done a tremendous job. You've built it to this stage. But now you're making a strategic pivot. You're going head-to-head with multi-billion-dollar companies, and if you're going to really go at it, this is a good time to bring in somebody with that experience."

Mark Chichester: That conversation, and that sort of turn in terms of his sense of timing for thinking about adding to the leadership team translated into our being able to attract the former Chief Growth Officer of Booz Allen, Robin Portman. She ultimately retired from Booz, went over to Georgetown University for a while, and then came to Atlas as the President and CEO. Nick was instrumental in encouraging us to pursue her, to think about the opportunity we had if we could get her on board, and then he was instrumental also in speaking with her and sealing the deal.

Ryung Suh: Robin has been phenomenal in terms of laying on a big-business mindset, building an incredible capture engine, and really driving our leadership to thrive in the middle market. Again, I don't think that that's something that Mark and I would have been able to do, or to time it at the right time when the business actually needed us to make that type of decision, had it not been for Nick really being there to be a good sounding board for us.

Leaders get to the top by being self-assured, no doubt about it. But true leadership requires being self-aware, too—having confidence in one's strengths and finding others to offset one's weaknesses. Mark and Ryung complement each other very well in that regard, and I think it has been a big part of their success to date.

Mark Chichester: I think Ryung and I realized early on that neither of us alone could have had the success, steered through the adversity that we faced, and gotten to whatever level of success we've had without each other. Nick recognized that explicitly and encouraged it. While it's challenging for some people who work with and for us at times to "get it," having Nick encourage that really was important to the successful evolution and the growth of the business. Having someone like Nick, who clearly understood and could sense these dynamics in terms of Ryung's and my relative strengths and weaknesses, was a huge boost for me. He seemed to just pick up on that and had a really subtle, but effective way of nurturing and encouraging that, and at times, when Ryung and I asked whether we were up to this, Nick said, "You're absolutely up to it. Look what you've done."

Look what they have done, indeed. On August 24, 2021, Customer Value Partners, Inc. (CVP), a business and technology consulting firm that helps organizations prepare for a culture of continuous change, acquired Atlas Research, broadening their Healthcare Strategy and Consulting & Research offerings and validating the special contributions Ryung, Mark, and the entire Atlas team bring to the government workspace.

*   *   *

These few are just some of the boards that I have had the privilege to serve. While it would not make sense to go into such detail on all of the boards I have been on, I would like to acknowledge them. I currently am the Chairman of the Board of the PeaceTech Lab in Washington, DC and the Chairman of the Board of Quantexa, a UK-based company. I am a member of the board of National Association of Corporate Directors (NACD), ACD, Aptiv PLC, HYPR Corp., Sproxil Corp., Security Score Card, and Ravenpod, Inc.

Additionally, I serve as an advisor to ASTIA, Mitchells, HBI Solutions, TeraGroup, Grey Market Labs, Bold Start VC, and StarVest Partners.

In the past, I also served as a board member at National Action Council for Minorities in Engineering (NACME), InRoads, Rensellaer Polytechnic Institute (RPI), Syracuse University, TopCoder, O'Brien & Gere, Liberty Mutual, and the US Secretary of Energy's Advisory Board.

In each case, I bring my experiences as a technologist, leader, and person to the table and look to drive change and innovation. Ultimately, though, as a board member, you are not the leader. You are an advisor.

The best leaders—from a Sam Palmisano to a Lisa Su to the team of Ryung and Mark—combine self-assuredness and self-awareness in order to combine the advice of the board with the courage of their own convictions. I do not think many men or women can reach the top of an organization without a strong sense of self-assuredness. Without that skill, too many forces will undo the leader before he or she ever reaches the top.

Without self-awareness, however, the leader will almost always succumb to hubris when problems present themselves, as they inevitably will in the world we inhabit. Too many boards fail to prod their leaders to become more self-aware.

Any and all leaders have weaknesses. If they acknowledge those weaknesses, they can improve upon them, but perhaps more importantly, they can leverage other leaders from the board and executive ranks to fill in for the gaps in their skill set, whether temporarily, until the skill is fully honed, or permanently, if the leader just does not possess that particular skill.

If the leader is not self-aware, board members all too often have to end up shouldering the responsibility for plugging those weaknesses. Equally often, they do not want to engage in this difficult work. I am not afraid to prod, but in the end, it is up to them.

> **Jason Providakes:** You know that godfather you love who is
> also a pain in the rear end? Look, Nick and I have had plenty of
> disagreements. I keep telling him, "Nick, you're not the CEO, I am.
> You don't know the business as well as I do." But that doesn't mean I
> don't stop and talk and listen, and Nick does the same, and at the end
> of the day, Nick says, "Jason, you're the CEO. It's your decision. I'm a
> board member. I just have governance responsibilities." I tell you, for
> the uninitiated, Nick can be pretty daunting to deal with. For some
> on the board, they probably find it difficult coming in and having
> Nick be that voice who wants to keep going when all you want to do
> is end the meeting or put something else on the table. It depends on
> who you are. For me personally, I grew up that way. I'm sort of old
> school. I like to be challenged. I like what Nick brings to the table,
> and you don't always have to agree with Nick, nor does he expect

you to. What he wants you to do is listen to his perspective, think about it, and then do what you believe is right.

I think the issue I am really pointing at for the leader is that it all stems from you. As the leader, do you fully understand yourself, and are you fully willing to admit who you are, both the good and the bad? Too many confuse being self-assured, which is necessary to reach the top, with being self-aware. Many think that being self-aware is a weakness and will erode their self-assuredness. It does not have to be that way. You can change.

I had to do that in my career. I was and remain fully willing to admit that I am highly opinionated. I have thoughts about everything. I was and remain willing to admit that I talk too much. I was and remain willing to admit that I need to learn a lot more on a lot of different topics and that I am not the smartest person in the room. I think that many leaders are unable to do that.

One the reasons I champion certain young leaders like Jason Providakes at MITRE is that he is willing to bring self-awareness into play and build upon the self-assuredness that got him to the top but will not necessarily keep him there.

Jason Providakes: He helped me think through some of the leadership changes that all CEOs have to make, which was quite valuable. He also reminds me to remember what got me here and to spend time with and engage our people. That's important. It's easy to lose sight of those things when you start to get consumed by other things. Nick always reminds me, "Get down to the lunchroom. Sit with the staff. Have lunch. Get out to the sights. Meet the employees. Meet the sponsors first-hand, don't count on everything coming up to you from others in the system." I think Nick has always been a high-touch person. He would always tell me, "Keep a high touch on the pulse of the organization," and that's been very valuable to do.

Even when leaders and their boards work in great harmony, they have to constantly adapt in anticipation of and in response to the significant technology shifts that...just...keep...coming. The ability to think about and communicate on these complex shifts in a simple manner has been a major secret to my ability to drive change. In the next chapter, we will take a look at understanding these shifts.

16

SIGNIFICANT TECHNOLOGY SHIFTS

O ne of my driving purposes at this stage of my life is to help as many people as possible to understand the changes that are happening today in the world. As much as I love helping the Bank of New York create the technology infrastructure necessary to advance their business model or strategizing with Lisa Su and Mark Papermaster at AMD in ways that have created billions of dollars in shareholder value, I equally enjoy taking a step back and speaking to science and business associations, universities, educational bodies, governmental groups, and science-based organizations about the seismic technological shifts underway.

Sometimes I talk about technology and about how technological changes will affect all of our lives.

Sometimes I talk about what we have to do to build society in a technological age.

Sometimes I talk about my values and the lessons I have learned throughout my life, which tie closely to the need to embrace the flow of technological innovation so that it can contribute to the most progress for the most people possible, rather than creating tiers of winners and losers by default.

The pace of change can be exciting, and we all enjoy some of the perks of that change—whether that comes from seeing a beautiful photograph of a grandchild posted to a social media site, using an app to help us better monitor our fitness and health, streaming a movie that makes us laugh or cry, or staying in touch with friends and loved ones via Zoom during the COVID-19 pandemic.

The pace of change can also be terrifying. What, as some alarmists ask, if those same efforts ultimately lead to our jobs being destroyed? To our national security being compromised? Or at the extreme, to AI-powered robots taking action of their own accord? These are the fears each of us harbor to one degree or another.

That is why the most important thing I have learned when speaking is the need to be very clear about complex things. The issues and technologies have gotten so complicated that many (even the most highly educated professionals) do not understand them. As a result, the general public has trouble finding explanations and information that can help them to make valid decisions about their lives and futures. I try to fill that gap.

David Yaun: Nick always has been able to see above the technical mumbo-jumbo and get very quickly to what the implications of the technology are. He could see what the application might be and the potential for the technology and then convey it in terms that his mother would understand, your neighbors would understand, or even someone from another century might understand. I think that is one advantage he has over people who arguably are deeper on the technology. His ability to translate it into applicability and relevance and implications is a huge advantage that he has, and he understands this gift of his.

Paul Horn: The New York Academy of Sciences focuses very heavily on global STEM educational programs aimed at kids from around the world. A few years ago, some high school kids came from around the world to visit and brainstorm about things related to the UN Global Sustainability Goals, or how you can make a better planet and solve problems of all sorts. Nick gave a talk to a group of about 100 of those kids. He talked about T-Shaped Individuals and T-Shaped Experiences. He made it personal. He talked about his family. These were kids from around the world, but they immediately related to him. Somehow, he has always had the ability to talk to a disparate audience and connect with them, and the stories he tells connect with them. He can do that with a young kid from Africa or a young kid from the Middle East as much as he can a young kid from the United States.

I try to help audiences understand what I believe is vital for them to know to be successful in the years to come—no matter what their age might be. So in the case of those kids, I wanted them to understand that the key for each of them to one day participate in solving those sustainability problems was to get a T-Shaped Education, so that they will have not only the STEM skills they will need, but also the well-roundedness to excel as a collaborator. I could dazzle them with tech gadgetry, but I would rather plant the seed that will help them one day to help us all.

Keeping it simple comes somewhat naturally to me by now. Since I am an engineer, I think like one. Engineers are problem solvers. They follow a disciplined thought path. They always are willing to separate variables and make assumptions in the hopes of solving a problem.

They rarely are the purest thinkers in the crowd.

They are more likely the most practical in the crowd.

When their work does not yield the expected answer, and they have checked all of their actions every step along the way, they are the first to go back to the beginning to check the initial assumptions that led them to expect a particular outcome. They know that when all else is right and the answer is wrong, the assumptions made at the beginning must therefore have been wrong.

Let me give you a concrete example. At one point in the 1990s, IBM had fallen from number one to number four in the Storage business, so Lou

Gerstner put Linda Sanford in charge of the business, and she, along with her sales leader Bob Samson, set out to recapture the top spot.

> **Bob Samson:** Lou Gerstner had said, "This is ridiculous. We've got to go back to being number one." Nick asked me, "How are you going to measure yourself?" I said, "I don't know, I'll have to think about this."

I tried to help Bob think along a disciplined thought path. He had a big challenge to solve, but I wanted to help him simplify it.

> **Bob Samson:** Nick said, "Measure yourself against two things. The first one is market share." Well, I knew I could track how much market share IBM had in the storage business, because it's widely tracked and reported.

That was the obvious answer, but I also wanted Bob to be able to look at his competitors to determine the magnitude of our move. So, I gave him another metric.

> **Bob Samson:** Nick said, "Who's your biggest competitor?" I told him. And he said, "Measure yourself against their market cap decline." I thought, *Who thinks of that?* But if I'm going to go after a competitor, what better way to think about it than how much market cap I'm going to knock out of them as I beat them in the marketplace. Well, as we clawed our way back, my competitor's market cap was cut by 75 percent!

Keep it simple. Use a disciplined thought path. Solve the problem.

> **Bob Samson:** It was just a different way of stripping away all the complexity. You could look at customers that we won or any number of measurements, but he knew to bring it back to just two things. I

remember him saying, "Those two things, Bob. Those two things." And that became our mantra. Later I looked like a genius, because Lou Gerstner sat me down one day and asked, "How are you going to measure yourself?" When I told him, Lou, who didn't suffer any fools, had this big grin on his face, and I thought, *Yes!* But that's what Nick was so good at, because big companies with a clear mandate to go do something big can easily get ground up in minutiae and things that are meaningless. Nick could strip all of that away and get to the core of the essence of the challenge.

If you use this type of thinking for any and all problems and issues you face, you will find yourself not only speaking more clearly but also *thinking* more clearly about complex problems and issues. While you must keep track of your assumptions and simplifications to ensure you understand the limits of your thinking, simplification generally leads to explanation, which leads to understanding. That is always my goal, and yes, sometimes to a fault, as my friends remind me.

David Yaun: Having served as Nick's "comms guy" for many years, I admit that sometimes when I heard him say something like, "Horsey-horsey, ducky-ducky," I cringed a little bit. I mean, the man holds seven patents and has accumulated innumerable engineering and business honors. But his secret power is that he insists on making everything simple for people to understand. There's a unique skill there, and it is such an asset, and it helped IBM enormously that we could put a person out there who had the combination of the ability to explain things simplistically, to draw audiences in, and to charm them. It works. I've seen him make comments at his local library or to groups of young girls being encouraged to envision careers in technology, and he makes everyone present feel like he is having a one-on-one conversation with them. To me, that is very different than so many people in the technology industry who feel like they have to impress their audience by getting into all the arcane, technical mumbo-jumbo. He is unique in that he realizes that his strength is connecting on a personal level.

I think about simple explanations as the wrapper around everything else. As Dr. Seuss says, "Sometimes the questions are complicated, and the answers are simple."

When I speak on the tech landscape of today, I often start by discussing basic, significant technology shifts, whether they be the growth of robotics and artificial intelligence and the ways these technologies affect our workplaces and homes; the coming post-silicon move to magnetics, optics, quantum, or some hybrid form of technology; or how technologies are getting smaller and bigger at the same time.

To illustrate that last point, I have recreated a table I first saw years ago in the New York Times that I have referred to ever since and that is shown on the following page.

People often are stunned when they see the range of measurements in this table and try to contemplate what these mean in terms of what they experience. Small gets smaller, but big gets bigger? What does that mean?

Think about it. The technology devices we carry get smaller and smaller, while their output and capabilities—computing power and storage—get bigger and bigger. The phones we carry in our pockets and purses now are more powerful than those original IBM mainframes I worked on when I began my career in the 1960s. While at some level this fact is mind-boggling, a simple explanation of Moore's Law and Dennard's Scaling puts it all in perspective.

Moore's Law, as mentioned earlier, observes that the performance of electronic chips doubles every eighteen months or so. Dennard Scaling, meanwhile, is a scaling law documented by the late IBM Fellow Robert H. Dennard which roughly states that as transistors get smaller, their power density stays constant, meaning that the power use stays in proportion with area; both voltage and current scale downward with length. Combining the observations of both laws means that performance per watt doubles roughly every eighteen months.

Orders of magnitude: Things are always changing; small gets smaller, but big gets bigger.

In words (long scale)	In words (short scale)	Prefix	Symbol	Decimal	Power of ten	Order of magnitude
quadrillionth	septillionth	yocto-	y	0.000,000,000,000,000,000,000,001	10^{-24}	−24
trilliardth	sextillionth	zepto-	z	0.000,000,000,000,000,000,001	10^{-21}	−21
trillionth	quintillionth	atto-	a	0.000,000,000,000,000,001	10^{-18}	−18
billiardth	quadrillionth	femto-	f	0.000,000,000,000,001	10^{-15}	−15
billionth	trillionth	pico-	p	0.000,000,000,001	10^{-12}	−12
milliardth	billionth	nano-	n	0.000,000,001	10^{-9}	−9
millionth	millionth	micro-	μ	0.000,001	10^{-6}	−6
thousandth	thousandth	milli-	m	0.001	10^{-3}	−3
hundredth	hundredth	centi-	c	0.01	10^{-2}	−2
tenth	tenth	deci-	d	0.1	10^{-1}	−1
one	one	-	-	1	10^{0}	0
ten	ten	deca-	da	10	10^{1}	1
hundred	hundred	hecto-	h	100	10^{2}	2
thousand	thousand	kilo-	k	1,000	10^{3}	3
million	million	mega-	M	1,000,000	10^{6}	6
milliard	billion	giga-	G	1,000,000,000	10^{9}	9
billion	trillion	tera-	T	1,000,000,000,000	10^{12}	12
billiard	quadrillion	peta-	P	1,000,000,000,000,000	10^{15}	15
trillion	quintillion	exa-	E	1,000,000,000,000,000,000	10^{18}	18
trilliard	sextillion	zetta-	Z	1,000,000,000,000,000,000,000	10^{21}	21
quadrillion	septillion	yotta-	Y	1,000,000,000,000,000,000,000,000	10^{24}	24

Even laypeople can understand just how rapidly performance has improved over the last fifty years and how it explains the power we now hold in our hands with our smartphones. More important, they begin to see just how far we can expect to go in the next fifty if these laws continue to reasonably endure.

Society now sits on these foundational "laws" of technology, and I see innovations in technology as driving how society will operate and advance going forward. It is a marriage of sorts, and like all marriages, it exists for better or for worse. Achieving more "better" and less "worse" requires technological literacy.

It is a never-ending loop of give-and-get that I believe drives progress. I need both to maintain my position in the world, and I believe everybody else does, too. Now more than ever.

Over the past twenty years, I have had the privilege of working on major projects that studied significant technology shifts and made recommendations on bringing technology to society. Two were the Council on Competitiveness's National Innovation Initiative and the National Academy of Engineering's Making Value for America Initiative, the latter of which I led.

The reports that were written at the conclusion of these projects can be found respectively at:

- *www.compete.org/component/content/article/11/202* and
- *www.nae.edu/19579/19582/19649/129940/Making-Value-for-America*

The work of these projects was solid and the recommendations valid. The recommendations are broad, covering business, the workforce, education, and the individual. This breadth was necessary, because the changes cover all areas of our lives and will affect how we work, conduct our lives, pursue our interests, and build our communities going forward.

The issue becomes: How do we get the recommendations implemented? How do we engage people, businesses, and governmental entities in the conversations leading to the understanding of what is happening in the technology world, so they can change to keep up with the innovation that is taking place?

I am concerned that without the necessary conversations and without following up on the recommendations, we will find ourselves with tiers in society of those who know enough to keep up with the change and those who do not.

In the coming chapters, I will attempt to explain simply the findings from these projects, along with other beliefs I have come to embrace in my give-and-take experiences with the world. Combined, my hope is that they will help you to understand where I think the world is going, and how I believe we must respond to ensure that as many people as possible participate in the Technological Future.

17

THE NEW WORLD OF WORK

f nothing changes, nothing changes.

Except some things *never* change.

And one of those things that never changes is the impact of new technologies on the workplace. *That* has been a *constant* since the invention of the wheel.

When I started at IBM in 1964, only highly-trained professionals were allowed to use the cutting-edge Selectric typewriters and Xerox copy machines, let alone program the computers. By the early 1990s, almost every professional at IBM and across much of the workforce had a personal computer on their desk, and before long, they would have laptops to take everywhere with them.

New technologies emerge that make it even easier to automate and make more efficient the work that we do. Ever new technologies emerge that fuel innovate business models, transform the ways in which we work, create entirely new job categories, and make others obsolete. That has not changed.

But something *has* changed, of course, and that is the *pace* of change enabled by new technologies. There is no real metric to measure these developments, but we all know it is happening. And as in every era, whether from the point of view of a worker, manager, or executive, it is natural to feel anxiety about these developments, or perhaps even to fear them. But as I have made abundantly clear throughout these pages, I believe in embracing change and finding—even making—opportunity in the disruption.

That is certainly what happened in the late 1990s and early 2000s, when more ubiquitous access to technology—especially through the World Wide Web and, ultimately, handheld devices—flattened access to ideas and markets in ways we had never seen. While these trends caused great disruption, particularly for employers and employees in mature economies, they also created opportunities for organizations to restructure to take advantage of global talent, new ways of doing business, and reduced costs.

More important to the path forward is the fact that the very nature of work itself has changed. We were already witnessing the explosive growth of the "gig" economy and the radical redefinition of "employee" that ensued, increasing automation, and the rising impact of artificial intelligence, when the global pandemic—literally over the course of less than two weeks—shuttered just about every office building and every storefront in the world, while simultaneously bringing travel of any distance to a virtual halt. Is it any wonder that the National Academy of Engineering estimates that 50 percent of existing jobs are ripe for disruption through these and other means?

For many existing companies and organizations, fewer traditional employees will be needed, office interaction will be greatly reduced, and those who remain will need to vigilantly advance their skills in order to keep up with the new demands of the workplace. While even that may not be enough to enable an individual to protect a particular role or job, it should ensure that the individual remains upskilled and employable.

Just to be clear, I am not saying that employment will go away. Rather, jobs will take completely new forms—some that will be familiar, many that we would not immediately recognize. Some may lament these changes— every other era has had its lamenters—but let us be honest, we have adapted to the loss of obsolete jobs such as elevator operator or tollbooth collector in the past, and we will adapt to the loss of existing jobs that no longer drive growth in twenty-first-century economies.

Of course, the upside from these changes benefits us in many ways, too. We need look no further than the many new ways in which consumers and marketplaces interact. Developments in software and data collection now enable businesses to carry out big data and analytics projects to better meet customers' needs, discover new market opportunities, and optimize design and production processes. Digitally literate talent with unique new skills carry out this work—and the best of them are in high demand and very nicely compensated.

But back to this pace of change idea. I believe that most of us, even as we experience and witness these changes, fail to fully grasp how much and how fast the entire business ecosystem is being disrupted. Tech disruptions affect all industries. The same technologies that are transforming manufacturing and high-tech services are in the process of transforming energy, healthcare, financial services, and education. As all of this happens around us, most of us say our prayers and do the best we can to stay a half-step ahead of the disruption.

I believe we must find a better way, and in this section, I will attempt to explain in simple language the changes necessary to thrive in a "New World of Work." This world will offer everyone the opportunity to succeed and at the same time, be better organized around not just principles of free-market competition, but also around solving some of the major problems threatening America and the entire world.

First, let us take a look at the micro-level, or the individual companies and organizations looking to not only survive, but thrive, in this new world. To get in front of disruption, manage it, and benefit from it, leaders need to answer some critical questions:

1. How do people (executives, managers, and employees at all levels) act and work in the business world being created?
2. How can they drive the growth and success—or even rebirth—of their organizations?
3. How should they lead for innovation and for the Technological Future?

4. How do they build and maintain technological literacy for themselves and their organizations?

5. How can people and their businesses create new ecosystems that allow them to continuously create new skilled jobs and establish their place in the Technological Future?

For organizational leaders who ask themselves these questions, there tends to be a focus on analyzing their entire system to ensure that they are "making value" for their customers and therefore less likely to be disrupted in the short run by competitors or new technologies.

These leaders also examine their business models to search for missed opportunities. They strive to create practices that boost productivity and enable continuous improvement. Their analysts further investigate and codify best practices and make sure these best practices flow throughout the entire organization so that optimization follows.

Next, these leaders carefully examine their abilities to innovate and capture the benefits of that innovation. Just as I experienced in my final decade at IBM, collaborative actions are needed to encourage the development of new businesses across manufacturing and high-tech value chains and to stimulate innovation and job creation.

The talent that will succeed in this new world of work is different, too. The generation that has entered the workforce over the past decade has absolutely no illusions about what I took for granted when I joined IBM—lifetime employment with one company. Their expectations are to be mobile and to shift jobs quickly, and they certainly do not believe that their employers will shower them with generous benefits packages.

So, what should leaders consider when hiring talent for the new world of work?

First of all, they should look for talent with a belief in the philosophy, culture, goals, and processes of their organization. Roles change too fast today to hire individuals just because they can perform a particular job. People who truly want to be part of your organization will be far more resilient and adapt to the needs of the organization because they *want* to be there, be part of your mission, and succeed, not just because they need to collect a paycheck until the next disruption eliminates their role or makes them unsuited to fill it anymore.

These are the same employees who will proactively seek out training, even if that means finding it on their own through the rapidly developing online education industry. While self-learning is on the rise, and absolutely crucial, businesses still should establish training programs to create the workforces they need. Through job rotations, selected classes and training, as well as formal and informal mentoring, your talent can keep pace, opt in to your mission, and find meaning in their work while doing more than they believed possible.

As far as tangible and intangible skills, technological literacy is a must. In later chapters, I will present ideas around enabling experienced workers, who might not have grown up in today's digital reality, to achieve technological literacy later in their careers, as well as ideas for shrinking the digital divide that for myriad reasons, leaves some talent with less access to the technologies and experiences taken for granted by many others.

As I have used the term technological literacy several times, I should define what I mean by it. To me, technological literacy means keeping yourself current and relevant with what is happening in all the sciences of the world: physical, life, social, political, economic, educational. It does not imply anything about your skill and ability. It does mean that you know enough to engage with an informed opinion. Given that value migrates, your technological literacy will determine your ability to keep up with that value, and hopefully, capture it if not create it.

Equally important for talent is a bias toward action and problem-solving skills that embrace collaboration and speed. While there may always be some roles that can be done in relative solitude, today's fast-paced economy favors individuals who work well in teams—including virtual teams—and care only that the work gets done and gets done well. These collaborative skills are ever-more essential as employees are no longer co-located and able to interact next to the proverbial water coolers of the past.

The demands on today's managers are different, too. For starters, very few people will simply "manage"—everyone will *do*, even within hierarchies.

I also believe that in these volatile times, trust has never been more important for managers. When managers focus on their own work ethic, do quality work, do what is right by their staff, and do it with transparency, trust follows. And just as they earn trust, they need to then extend it to those whom they see doing the same. While I personally may have been a little ahead of the curve in this area, in large part thanks to what I learned from both of my parents, we are currently in a much more skeptical and cynical era, so trust is an even harder—and more valuable—commodity for today's managers to earn.

In a trusting atmosphere, people will collaborate and be willing to bring their full self to the effort, rather than presenting inauthentic versions of the type of person they think they need to be in order to keep their jobs. They also will be able to handle peer reviews and constructive criticism from a positive position of trust rather than a defensive position, and thus be able to forge ahead to quickly get work done creatively and correctly. What is more, feedback needs to be constant and multidirectional—no more annual reviews given the pace of change in today's world and no more reviews given only from the top down. In an atmosphere of trust, talent must advise upward to maintain speed.

When we revisited our values at IBM, in many ways we had just this sort of atmosphere in mind, but at a global level. While we did not get it all right and no organization ever will, we reestablished in our minds just what type of talent could help us create the Globally Integrated Enterprise. My experience is that these people are harder to find and retain than you might think. And when you find your type of person, treat them well. You do not want to lose them to one of your competitors.

With operations and talent positioned for collaborative performance, leaders can begin to consider how effectively an organization is positioned to innovate, which in my opinion is and will remain the single most important factor for success in the coming decades.

As you have read in these pages, I lived innovation for over thirty years in my many roles, culminating with the Innovation Agenda I implemented for IBM in the early 2000s. In that final role, I began thinking about the importance of innovation in much deeper and more nuanced ways.

Around this time, Sam and I, along with others, began to ponder the significance of what we were learning in the macro-context of America's competitive health, particularly in the shadow of the dot-com boom and post-9/11 bust. As the nation began to emerge from those jolts, we began again to hear encouraging talk about technology, new inventions, and the latest products. Yet by our estimations, the concept of innovation was not factoring much in the overall mix.

IBM, led by Sam, was a member organization of the Council on Competitiveness, which consisted of leading business leaders and thinkers. Sam, Chris Caine, and I put some ideas on the table, went to them, and emerged as the sponsors of what became known as the Council on Competitiveness's National Innovation Initiative.

Our idea was to try to take the national conversation in a different direction that we believed could lead to a better future for America. Sam served as a co-chair along with Wayne Cough, who was then the President of Georgia Tech.

> **Chris Caine:** The Council on Competitiveness was a Washington, DC-based nonprofit made of companies and universities. It had been around for maybe ten or fifteen years before this timeframe. Half the members of the National Innovation Initiative were CEOs and half were university presidents. There were about twenty-five members. Nick was the private sector leader, basically, of the entire working level of the Commission.

Chris Caine and I began to steer this impressive group of business and higher-ed leaders into some new territory. Perhaps not surprisingly, we concluded that innovation would be the single most important initiative determining America's position in the twenty-first century. Beneath that headline, though, came a significant finding. We observed that innovation *only occurs at the intersection of invention and insight,* and only then results in the creation of social and economic value.

With this nuanced observation in mind, we recommended three specific and actionable initiatives be undertaken to reposition America to maximize its innovative potential. These recommendations focused on the **talent** required to innovate; the **investment** required to fund a renewed focus on innovation—particularly "Frontier Research" such as the space program—that leads to major breakthroughs that bolster national economies; and finally, on **infrastructure**, or how the federal government, along with other participants, can foster an environment to unleash America's immense potential to innovate. We presented our findings to President George W. Bush in November of 2004.

Nothing that has happened in the subsequent seventeen years changes these fundamental findings—not the rise of Amazon, nor Tesla, nor Google, nor the revitalization of Apple. While all these innovators have contributed mightily to our economy, our consumers, and the world, the fact remains that our nation is not aligned to help maximize the number of these companies nor the innovations they generate. Nor have we effectively reoriented to produce the Frontier Research we need. Briefly, then, let me outline these recommendations, which still await true implementation.

Our recommendations on **talent**—or how to create the leaders, managers, and employees for the Technological Future—began with the concept of creating a National Innovation Initiative Education Strategy. Too much of our primary and secondary educational system remains oriented around the needs of the Industrial Era and not the needs of the tech-led Knowledge Economy.

To remedy this gap, we recommended:

- Establishing tax-deductible, private-sector, "Invest-in-the-Future" scholarships for American science and engineering undergraduates

- Encouraging, incentivizing, and empowering young American innovators through the creation of 5,000 new portable graduate fellowships funded by federal R&D agencies
- Expanding the reach of innovation education deeper into our human capital pool by expanding university-based Professional Science Master's and traineeships to all state university systems
- Reforming immigration to attract the best and brightest science and engineering students from around the world and providing work permits to foreign science and engineering graduates of US institutions

Beyond the National Innovation Initiative Education Strategy, we advised that we catalyze the next generation of American innovators by stimulating creative thinking and innovation skills. These skills are developed through problem-based learning, by creating innovation learning opportunities for students to bridge the gap between research and application, and by establishing innovation curricula for entrepreneurs and small business managers. More on this in the next chapter.

Our workforce is far more fluid in the global twenty-first century than it was even in the latter decades of the twentieth century. However, we have yet to fully empower our workers to succeed in this atmosphere of global competition. It is imperative that we lay better foundations to stimulate workforce flexibility and skills development through lifelong learning opportunities, by accelerating the portability of benefits, by aligning federal- and state-skills needs more tightly to training resources, and by strategically expanding assistance to those dislocated by technology and trade.

When we created our Innovation Agenda at IBM, it also required an **investment** strategy. You will recall that we were able to get more impact out of a smaller, though still very significant, research and development investment by having the right strategy. The same can apply to our national approach.

First, we must revitalize frontier and multidisciplinary research—the kind that enabled America to be first to the moon. We can do this by stimulating high-risk research through "innovation acceleration" grants and by restoring the Department of Defense's historic commitment to basic research, from which many game-changing innovations have emerged.

We also must intensify support for physical sciences and engineering to achieve a robust national R&D portfolio. Such support can go hand-in-hand with a *permanent*, restructured, R&D tax credit that extends not only to the corporate world, but to research conducted through university-industrial consortia.

America today enjoys an incredible entrepreneurial spirit focused on creating exciting products and services that the marketplace embraces or rejects. The efforts of Jeff Bezos, Elon Musk, the late Steve Jobs, and so many others prove that our ability to innovate is as great as ever before. The ability to generate significant fortunes must always remain part of the free-market equation.

That said, for efforts that relate more to the national interest and less so to the consumer marketplace, a better organized and coordinated means for harnessing entrepreneurial zeal is required. A lead agency and an inter-agency council that coordinate federal economic development policies and programs to accelerate innovation-based growth that serves the nation's interests is a logical first step.

We can further accelerate progress by building Innovation Hot Spots to capitalize on regional assets and to leverage public-private investments. Lastly, we can increase the availability of early-stage risk capital through tax incentives aimed at angel-investor networks and state and private seed capital funds that invest in initiatives of the plan.

Consider the joint efforts of NASA and Musk's Space X that have reignited the national passion for space exploration. While such relationships do form organically, we can incentivize many more of them through better structured agencies and policies that celebrate the American spirit of innovation.

Our investment community can further help by working on a challenge that has evolved over time and sometimes hinders frontier thinking. I am not the first to point out that investors sometimes focus too much on "making the quarter," which can have the unintended consequence of discouraging expensive R&D efforts. Our national competitiveness and our capacity for moonshot innovation are best enhanced by aligning private-sector incentives and compensation structures to reward long-term value creation in addition to smart balance-sheet management and desired steady growth. We did it at IBM when I had control of the R&D budget, and so I know that others can, too, especially if the environment is conducive.

It is not just Wall Street that can help. The realignment toward moonshot thinking can be better enabled through the creation of safe-harbor provisions to promote voluntary disclosure of intangible assets, through the reduction of the cost of tort litigation, and by convening a Financial Markets Intermediary Committee to evaluate the impact of new regulations on risk-taking.

Finally, we need to rethink our nation's **infrastructure** vis-a-vis innovation. For starters, we need to reject noisy voices who cling to definitions of infrastructure that are decades (if not centuries) old.

How can it be that as 2021 closes, large parts of the United States—both rural and urban—do not have access to ultra-high-speed internet, or 5G wireless technologies? Well, the answer actually is obvious—because we have no consistent national strategy in place to address these gaps. Compare that to the federal government's role in building out the postal system, the nation's rail networks, telephone networks, or even the Eisenhower highway system. Perhaps President Biden's infrastructure bill, passed in late 2021, will begin to close the gap.

We got the job done in each of those cases. How can we do the same now? For starters, we can address these gaps by creating national consensus for innovation growth strategies and then rolling them up into a Federal Innovation Strategy supported and enacted by the President. While the notion of national consensus on anything in 2021 might seem ludicrous, we must forge ahead.

For example, we *can* catalyze national and regional alliances to implement innovation policies and innovation-led growth along with new metrics to understand and manage that innovation more effectively. We *can* envision national innovation prizes to recognize excellence in innovation performance and to protect our innovators through a new twenty-first-century intellectual property regime that builds quality into all phases of the patent process, leverages patent databases as innovation tools, and creates best practices for collaborative standards setting. We *can* do so much more.

Politicians from both sides of the aisle have talked a great deal about strengthening America's manufacturing capacity, and some steps have been taken, but it is a long game, for sure. Especially in a modern era where collaboration between companies is increasingly common, I envision the creation of centers for production excellence including shared facilities and consortia, and we should foster the development of industry-led standards for interoperable manufacturing and logistics that fuel greater collaboration through trust-building ground rules in the twenty-first century.

Imagine the creation of Innovation Extension Centers that bring first-tier manufacturing partners together to pursue incentivized R&D projects established at the industry level that roll up to meet the President's Federal Innovation Strategy.

You might be reading these ideas and thinking that this guy Donofrio is talking pie-in-the-sky stuff that will never happen. Part of the reason I spent so much time describing my action-orientation not only at IBM but on many boards and committees was to establish my bona fides for standing behind these recommendations. I am an optimist, for sure, but I am driven by the desire to get real—and big—results and to get them faster than many believe possible.

Leading the Council on Competitiveness's National Innovation Agenda on the ground offered me a stimulating and important experience, one that I look back upon fondly. But I will be the first to admit that not enough *coordinated* action has been taken in the years since.

Given the challenges unleashed by the COVID-19 crisis, healthcare is an obvious test bed for getting twenty-first-century innovation infrastructures in place. There is no time to waste.

I should mention that soon after we presented our findings to President Bush, other countries began to show interest in this new economic and policy framework that the United States, with its National Innovation Initiative, had created, and began to consider whether they should be replicating it.

> **Chris Caine:** Nick, me, and others from IBM traveled the world to talk with the highest levels of government as to why Vietnam or Russia or Brazil or China should have a National Innovation Initiative comparable to or similar to that of the United States.

America out in front on what matters most—that is what I like to see. But I like to see implementation even more. These recommendations, while taken very seriously, have not been implemented. Without massive action, the exercise will have been largely for nothing.

And while I have explained all the actions needed to better organize at the national level for the New World of Work and an integrated approach to innovation that once again looks out toward brave new frontiers, the next thing that I want to do is dive into the nuts and bolts of what innovation really means today and what some of the leading thinkers are doing to create the innovators of tomorrow.

18

INNOVATION AND CHANGE

When people talk about innovation, they often are thinking about *inventions*. When I talk about innovation, I mean something much different. So does my friend Rick Miller, President of Olin College of Engineering, whom you met in Chapter 12 when we discussed the "T-Shaped Individual." Consider how he positions innovation:

Rick Miller: Innovation is not the same thing as entrepreneurship. It's not the same thing as creating a new device that has a market, either. Innovation is a new way of thinking. An innovation is an idea that is brought to bear in a process or a device that changes the way people live. A really profound innovation is one that changes the way people live so dramatically that they can't remember the way life was before it happened.

Every major innovation that you can identify—the internet, the airplane, space travel—has three characteristics, simultaneously. First, it's feasible. Nothing exists in the real world that isn't consistent with what we know about natural laws. You have to know something about natural law in order to create an innovation that works. That's where the engineering part comes from, and that's a big part of innovation.

But everything that is feasible is not an innovation. It also has to be viable, meaning that it has to be something that adds enough value to justify an investment from the consumer that generates more revenue than it takes to create it. Seen in this light, it's possible for a new product or service to be feasible but not viable. Take solar cells on houses for producing electric power as an example. We've known about solar cells for fifty years. We could have put them on the roofs of every house in America and forgotten power plants. Why didn't we do that? Well, the reason is that they were not financially viable. It's still cheaper to make power from petroleum and other sources. So it has to be both feasible and viable to change the way people live.

That leads to the third ingredient. It's possible to be feasible and viable and still not change the way people live. It has to be desirable, too. That means that when the consumer is given a choice in the free market, they'll take that one. It has the characteristics that they desire to solve a particular problem or meet a particular need. The master of understanding this in our age was Steve Jobs, who understood that of all the devices out there, the one that is intuitive, the one that builds an emotional linkage, the one that is compelling to you at a subliminal level—that's the one you're going to buy. So desirability is a really important part.

I agree with Rick, particularly on his idea that innovation is a new way of *thinking*. When I talk about innovation to audiences, I lay out what I call "Innovation Insights," and immediately, people begin to grasp why leading through innovation matters so much. Some of these insights include:

- Innovation is all about collaboration and thinking in an open, global, and multi-disciplined fashion to create value.
- Start with the problem and not the answer.
- Know the difference between innovation, creation, and discovery. Create value, not things.

- Check your assumptions when all else fails. Do this by going back to the beginning, since something there likely is to be wrong if no progress is being made.
- We increasingly will be judged more on what we do about what we do not know than on what we know. In other words, the ability to ask the right questions just may be more valuable than having all the answers. Be a lifelong learner.

To build on these insights, let us again think about Steve Jobs, who I agree is perhaps the most iconic innovator of the last forty years. Steve was a man I knew, liked, collaborated with well, and admired.

What made him such a great innovator? He was not an engineer; he did not create great products himself. What he was terrific at, though, was identifying and articulating a problem, bringing together collaborators from multiple disciplines, and together devising a solution that created great value. The iPod, the iPhone, the iPad, and so many of Apple's other products became wildly successful because they created value by solving problems.

Steve understood as well as anyone that the great and lasting innovations start with a problem and then work their way toward a solution that creates value. That is why I do not fear disruption. I *love* disruption. The very word disruption indicates problems. And only with a problem can there be an opportunity to create value through its solution.

John Chen (*Executive Chairman and CEO, BlackBerry, 2013–Present*): Interestingly enough, people like Nick and me actually look for the disruption and look for changes. That's probably the biggest part of our toolkit. Opportunities are actually created because the market is looking for change. Because if there are steady states, we can't make enough impact. We want to find a disruptor or sea change to grab onto, because without it, you can't generate enough value and energy to successfully drive innovation. We look for that discontinuity. We need the change.

That is the way to the Technological Future. When I think about Rick's positioning of innovation and align it to any organization, whether that is IBM, Atlas, or your corner pizza parlor, I simplify it as follows:

- Feasibility: Identify problems that can be solved by your organization.
- Viability: Simplify the problems that will be solved by your organization.
- Desirability: Create value in the marketplace through solutions that are different and better than those of your competitors.

That is what Google did.

That is what the iPhone did.

That is what the IBM System/360 did.

If innovation is a new way of *thinking*, then it can take almost any form, as long as value is being created through the solving of problems.

It can come through new products, new uses of old products, new types of customers, or new ways of creating value for old customers.

It can come through how or where the business operates.

It can draw on changes in society, culture, or politics.

It can take place in one area, support innovation in other areas, or take over the entire organization.

You did not think I would casually drop the words "pizza parlor" into this chapter and not come back to them, did you? Think about how creative—how innovative—restaurant owners and other small businesspeople needed to become during 2020 and 2021, perhaps the biggest disruption many of us have experienced in our lifetimes. Sure, many fell by the wayside, but at the same time others thrived and even expanded their operations. They had problems to solve, and they applied new technologies and methodologies to address them—from ordering methods to hands-free pick-up, to new delivery models.

Some of these innovations will fade to memory as the problems that they were designed to solve expire. Other developments, such as Zoom calls with groups of geographically dispersed colleagues and friends or working remotely will likely prove quite sticky, as people realize the benefits that emerged initially as end runs around COVID-19 disruption.

When I look back on what I learned leading the National Academy of Engineering effort entitled Making Value for America, I see distinct connections between the recommendations we made for manufacturing businesses around creating value and the experiences that we all have been through personally and professionally during the pandemic. These include recommendations to:

- Start by carefully examining your abilities to innovate, capturing the benefits of the innovation, and creating value.
- Reengineer your operations and management systems in ways that improve productivity and speed-to-market.
- Change the way you talk about manufacturing workflows, so you can identify new ways to create value.
- Structure strategy to make sure you capture value.
- Build a workforce that can take you into the Technological Future by:
    - Communicating and teaching about how jobs and the workplace are changing.
    - Creating opportunities for employees to change and develop futures for themselves.
- Drive active management from passionate, digitally literate people with the courage and commitment to make the Technological Future happen.

What underlies all these ways to innovate and create value is the willingness to change. I strongly believe that:

- Success in any field—in industry, in education, in politics—now requires actively seeking out change and embracing it.
- Value is migrating because the world is changing radically, and faster than we can keep up.

- Manufacturing will continue, but the *value* in making things will be somewhere other than in the product itself. The value will be found in the service's value proposition or in the business model used to deliver the product.
- Trends and changes matter because there are always ways to apply them and to capitalize on them. That is innovation in the twenty-first century.
- To find value, you must build a culture around innovation.
- To find value where it lives in today's world, you must be intelligent, which means doing something with your information and your knowledge. By itself, all of your data does no work and has no value.
- Another key to solving problems in the new economy is *inclusive thinking*. Including other people's thinking to tackle your issues—technical, business, political, educational, societal—is the way to find more valuable solutions and to find them faster.

If you want to not only survive but thrive in the years to come, drive innovation and a willingness to change into your world—whether in the office, your community, or your home. Write it down. Say it over and over. Whatever it takes.

And if you are a business or professional leader, believe this: organizations and their people cannot continue to do the same things and create the same products and expect to survive in the Technological Future. Leaders need to look at how they operate and what they know and then make the changes that will allow them to innovate and to create value.

Similarly, businesses need to understand that if nothing changes, nothing changes. Societal and economic changes mean that consumers see value differently; if businesses want to continue to provide value to consumers, they must innovate and change to create new value. They must reengineer their processes and operations to support these changes. They must make sure that their people (from top executives down throughout the business) have the knowledge and skills to perform the new work. They must keep looking for opportunities to innovate and create new value in the marketplace. That is the Technological Future you must create.

Easier said than done, I know, but because I have done it at IBM, and I have helped others to do it, from Bank of New York to Delphi to AMD, I believe my experiences have value for you.

What about today? While the notion of the need to fill gaps in STEM talent gets a lot of attention, the need to also provide students with the T-Shaped balance that fuels collaboration and innovation remains less well-known. Enter again Rick Miller and the Olin College of Engineering.

Rick and the staff at Olin have literally rethought their curriculum to create not just engineers, but innovators, who are prepared to succeed in the New World of Work. Olin creates innovators through a learning environment in which students learn to think as innovators both in the classroom and through active learning.

Allow Rick to walk you through the process and stick with him. When I write about the ways in which education needs to be rethought for the twenty-first century, here is a proof of concept that it can be done.

Rick Miller: We begin with a course we call UOCD—User Oriented Collaborative Design—a course that is built around concepts that the Design School at Stanford has used for fifty years.

We take all the kids in maybe their third semester—so they're about nineteen years old—and we put them in a class, we organize them in groups of five, and we ask each group to identify a group of people whose lives they want to change. Not someday, but in the next four months. And then we just listen.

In one group, a student had a grandmother with Alzheimer's. The student said, "We went to visit her in assisted living over the holidays, and I'd like to do something to help the lives of the elderly."

We thought that was a worthy idea, so we found ten people living in nursing homes within a ten-minute drive from campus who agreed to allow these five students to spend about two hours interviewing them over the first two weeks of class. That helped the students find out what it means to be elderly in America today, which gets at desirability—what is it that elderly people care about?

After two weeks, they came back with a bunch of notes they'd taken, and in this little cubicle in which they were working, they started putting sticky notes up on the wall—quotes of what they've heard—and they're trying to make sense of what they've heard.

One of the things that they heard was that almost all of the elderly had a friend who had fallen in the last couple of years and broken a hip. And in some cases, the hip had not healed properly, and that person was now permanently confined to a wheelchair. They were deathly afraid of this, and the students, being so much younger, were trying to understand the problem. At first, they didn't think that this was that big of a deal. People wheel you around. You don't even have to mess with walking.

But as they thought about it more, they understood that once you are in a wheelchair, you can't look people in the eye. You only look at their belt buckle. Staff and family look down on you. They assemble over your head, and they talk about you in the third person. You're essentially a non-person now. You're an object. Something that needs care. A burden. They hated that, and they would do practically anything to avoid it.

Other problems arise, too. When you can't exercise, you lose control of your metabolism, and you can't control your weight. In fact, you can't even tell what you weigh, because it's a big ordeal to have somebody lift you out of the chair in order to take your weight.

So these are the notes. Now they have to come up with two or three ideas that would change these people's lives. The students decided to focus on the weight. So they began to brainstorm. They hadn't had any of the technical courses yet, but they decided that they could possibly build a little carpet with pressure sensors on it.

You could drive your wheelchair onto this carpet, and the pressure sensors would transmit information data through a radio to your iPhone. Your iPhone could interpret it and subtract out the tare weight of the wheelchair and tell you what you weigh.

They went back to talk to these elderly people, and asked them, "Would this be something that you would care about?" They found out that all 10 of the elderly participants were excited about the idea. They asked, "Could you really do that?" The students said, "We don't know, but we think so."

By the end of the semester, they turned in their project on this idea, and then in the next couple of months, they were on fire to see if they could make a prototype. Within about four months they had built a prototype.

The next course in the curriculum? How to start and run a business. So you can see how we're just dropping breadcrumbs down a path. Now they had to confront the feasibility issues in building the prototype. They started with the desirability issues. Why bother if it doesn't have a market? The next course, about starting and running a business, is about exploring the viability issues. And when they got through with that, they had a product. In fact, they started it in their dorm room. It's called Lilly Pads Scales. It still exists to this day. You can buy them online.

Now, every kid in the school goes through this experience. There's lots of innovation sitting on the cutting room floor at the end of that class that doesn't get implemented, although often they graduate and they, or someone they know, takes ideas very similar to those they came up with to market. There's quite a record of that.

So the template that you see here relates back to the way innovation works, and they have eight consecutive semesters of this. By the time they graduate from Olin, they've done between twenty and thirty design/build projects, explored starting and running businesses, and learned the process of innovation.

They can't graduate without having a fluidity with that process. They get an exposure to traditional technical material like VLSI circuit design or RF antennae theory as seen through the context of the projects they are working on, but they're not miniature PhDs in a subarea of content. If they had one, their PhD would be in the process of innovation.

It is all there. They have to understand feasibility. They do that through traditional math and physics education. They have to encounter viability. They do that by creating and refining products that their "customers" express a desire to have, which helps them to understand how the marketplace works and whether they can meet the need economically. Finally, they have to understand desirability, which involves understanding people. But there is more, and it matters greatly.

Rick Miller: There's something else that they learn by learning it in this order. For example, by starting with people, we find out that they not only encounter all the same technical concepts that they would by reading chapters out of a book, but they learn two other things, too. The first one is empathy. They learn to listen to people, and they learn to empathize with people. If they can't really deeply feel what the concern is of the client, they won't get through this class. Secondly, they learn a sense of purpose. This is hard to explain in mathematical terms, but when they gain a deep, resonant sense of having made a difference in somebody else's life at the age of just nineteen, they've gained something that doesn't happen in most engineering curriculums. Unlike with textbook learning, where you say, "Trust me, someday this will make sense to you," this makes sense to them now.

And still, there is more, and Olin's take on this next concept is very close to my heart. These people are innovator's innovators, believe me.

Rick Miller: If you're going to create a new generation of innovators who are going to create the technology companies of the future, they better understand the desirability circle. They better understand people. But the way we've organized our universities almost prevents the creation of innovators, because we separate them into silos. It's the same problem Nick was trying to solve at IBM with his integrated workforce!

In fact, if you look at the map of most campuses, you'll see just how we organize higher education. Take the University of Michigan, for example. Somewhere in the north there is a quad called the Engineering Quad, and that's where all the engineering faculty have their offices. Engineering students spend three-quarters of their time in that quad, as dictated by the accreditation standards. Students there learn feasibility.

There's another spot on campus that has the equivalent quad for business. That's where the business school students hang out. And by standards of accreditation, all business students have to take half of their credit hours in that quad. They learn viability there, along with the ins and outs of profit and loss, market share, and revenue growth.

About two miles south of the engineering quad is the Rackham Library. This is sort of the heart of the Arts & Humanities part of the campus where students learn about desirability.

So what happens is that the students hardly encounter each other. There are physical barriers. The message we're sending them is that specialization is the key to the future. If you're going to be an engineer, be good at math, do all these technical things, produce papers, and that's how the world works.

But specialization is not the key to the future. Innovation is the key to the future. What Rick just described with his University of Michigan example runs completely counter to my entire thesis that became the IBM Innovation Agenda. To me, an innovation environment is one that enables collaboration, openness, multiple-disciplinary thinking, and global think-ing. That is how innovation works.

Let me provide a concrete example of a time in which I took advantage of a situation at IBM in order to reduce specialization and create the more globally-integrated, collaborative IBM we needed. This example dates back to our efforts to bring the revitalized CMOS mainframe to market. At the time, we had two key hardware labs in IBM—Poughkeepsie and Boeblingen, Germany—both on their own creating the design and the proposal for the new CMOS mainframe. While I wanted the best ideas from both—particu-larly in light of what we were trying to do at the time—I also was looking toward a future in which I wanted to see more collaboration.

> **Ross Mauri:** Those teams were in direct competition with each
> other. And though it was never said, I know that those teams
> believed that if their design didn't get chosen, they would get laid
> off and their whole lab would be closed. So, this was competition at
> its highest form from a technical and business point of view. And
> Nick orchestrated this process—I realized partway into it, not in the
> beginning—of having two labs competing to get the best ideas out.

While the participants thought themselves to be in an all-or-nothing competition, aware as they were of the fact that we needed to take costs out as part of the overall IBM turnaround, I saw it differently.

> **Ross Mauri:** When the "competition" was finished, Nick didn't pick
> Poughkeepsie over Boeblingen or Boeblingen over Poughkeepsie.
> He picked elements of each that were the best parts of the system.
> And then when we downsized, we downsized part of each lab so that
> those labs could no longer function on their own. They had to depend
> on each other and work together. You want to talk about three-
> dimensional chess; this was such a brilliant play because he kept the
> talent and the passion of both labs alive, but he forced them—because

they couldn't be successful on their own—to work together. So, he orchestrated a competition that in the end didn't have a loser. It had two winners, and because of that, IBM and our clients won.

Frans Johansson: The cornerstone of this idea of bringing together ideas from different places always starts with breaking downs silos inside of a company. It's the first piece. I think this is a big thing people miss about innovation in general. What Nick did with the Poughkeepsie/Boeblingen situation was brilliant. He took a negative and rethought it into an opportunity—an unexpected moment that enabled him to make a breakthrough toward creating the collaboration he wanted to see. Seeing an opportunity in everything is so important because that's how the world operates.

Ask yourself these questions: What is my openness to difference? What is my openness to diverse points of view? What is my openness to diverse people who hold these diverse points of view? These I believe are the centerpieces of how all work is interrelated and intersected and a key to sustained value creation. I think knowing your answer to these questions is crucial.

These are the thoughts of Nick Donofrio, electrical engineer, but circling back again to COVID-19, the world is demanding that we think this way again. When I started out as an electrical engineer, the digital world had not quite erupted yet. It was more of an analog world, meaning it was not just on or off. The digital world is binary. All you need to know is if you have enough energy in a circuit to flip it from a 1 to a 0 or a 0 to a 1. That is binary. It is on. It is off. That is the digital world.

The analog world says, "How did you do that? What does the wave form look like? When did it flip? How much energy did you put into it? How much voltage? How much current?" When I went to RPI, all they wanted to know was the wave form. You did not get graded on the steady state. They said, "Show me the work. Show me the wave form. How did you get from here to there?"

That is the analog world, and the irony of the Technological Future is that I see our current world more in these analog terms than I do the binary notion of "on" or "off." We have the digital world and the physical world. That we understood. But we have never understood quite how they are connected. We have always said, "I'm in one world or I'm in the other."

The fact of the matter is, they have been slowly connecting themselves through a continuum, so it is not totally on or off. It is not totally digital or physical. It can be both. It can be some different mix in between. When you participate in a Zoom call, is it digital or physical? Well, I suggest that perhaps it is both and neither. So, the wave form between the digital world and the physical world matters now. The idea of continuum, spectrum, and hybrid are what we must understand. The simple view that it is one or the other, is gone. The Technological Future is the spectrum of possibilities and no longer the simple one or the other.

The tech world is slowly realizing that there is value in the in between. The 1 or the 0 end-state is no longer the gospel truth. A lot of that has to do with technology and the way we think. But it all seems to be converging and it is truly naïve of us to think that there are only finite spaces out there. It is the blend that matters.

In the workplace, that blend matters whether you are a leader, a manager, or an individual performer. The answers matter in your community and your home, too. The type of citizen, husband, wife, partner, father, mother, son, or daughter you will be hinges on the way you see and interact in the world that is speeding our way. I encourage you to see and interact in the world as an innovator.

Which leads me back to Steve Jobs. I mentioned earlier in this chapter that I knew Steve. Given all that has been written about the man—the good, the bad, and the ugly—I wanted to write a bit about my own relationship with this complicated innovator, as well as my relationship with one of his most trusted engineers, Jon Rubinstein, whom you have met elsewhere in these pages.

It all dates back to Steve's NeXT venture—or adventure, if you prefer. NeXT, you might recall, was the company Steve started after he was ousted in 1985 by Apple, the already-legendary company he had founded with Steve Wozniak in the 1970s.

Steve had introduced the Macintosh, or Mac, only a year or so before and was seen in the business, tech, and even popular press as a genius and a rock star. He was not yet a fully-formed leader, though, and before long, John Sculley, the CEO he had lured to Cupertino from Pepsi to steer Woz and his creation into big company maturity, did what many thought unthinkable and showed Steve the door.

Barely into his thirties, Steve began his second act and had grand hopes for NeXT. His first offering, the NeXT Computer, was going to be a work-station computer aimed primarily at the higher-ed market.

At this same time, I was in Austin trying to create the RS/6000 workstation computer. We were pursuing a UNIX interface, and among my many other challenges, I was working with the Open Software Foundation to craft that interface.

As all of this was going on, John Akers, thinking he was doing the right thing, bought the NeXT interface from Steve for me for the RS/6000! Somebody told John to do it, and he did it. I think it was a several-million-dollar deal. For Steve and NeXT, this was a big deal, while IBM was hoping it would be a good deal.

We were looking for a UNIX interface, but now we had this deal with NeXT. John had negotiated a deal where we were going to have to use NeXT no matter what, so I wanted to determine what value I was going to get from him. So, Steve and I would have these meetings. I would ask him things like, "What can I do with it?" "How can I change it?" "Will it run in my UNIX environment?"

> **Jon Rubinstein:** I think NeXT was the first time I met Nick
> Donofrio. He'd come to visit us occasionally. He'd come to
> visit Steve. It was always a very positive, solid relationship. I can
> remember him coming to visit and look at the products we were
> developing and being very supportive and very positive.

At the same time, I had to negotiate the payment schedule with Steve, and at that stage in his business, that money was important to him. It was in that context that I came to really get to know him.

I understood the dynamics quite clearly. He *needed* me at that time. We had agreed to pay him a lot of money, and naturally, he wanted to get it.

And I literally had to decide, "How am I going to pay this guy? When am I going to pay him? And what am I going to get for what I paid?"

He clearly understood that I was important to him, and so he was always willing to talk to me. Steve also understood that it was a difficult situation for me to be in, that I had a lawyer strapped to my arm, and that it was a challenge I did not need. He respected all of that.

We got to know each other. We got to build a relationship. Our discussions were always thoughtful. No matter what you may have heard about Steve Jobs, he never yelled at me. If the subject was touchy, I would lower my voice, and then he would lower his voice, and we would get through it. I came to like him.

And it worked out. He got his money. We got the NeXTStep interface, and it was great. It was very fashionable. Very edgy. Very Steve.

Jon Rubinstein: I think Nick dealt with him really well over the years, and I know Steve always respected Nick. Nick was really straightforward, and I think Steve behaved pretty well because Nick was so straightforward.

All that said, we never did anything with NeXTStep. We also had the Open Software Foundation's Motif Interface; that is what the world wanted at the time, and the RS/6000 workstation became a billion-dollar business within a year after its introduction in February 1990.

Meanwhile, NeXT struggled. Still, my view of Steve was much different than everybody else's, because I dealt with him in a much different way at a much different time for a different set of reasons than most. I also came to know Jon quite well during that time frame. He was great to work with, and we became friends.

While all of this was going on with Steve Jobs and NeXT, IBM had been working with Apple. I think Lou Gerstner even thought about buying Apple, though I was not involved in any of that thinking. At any rate, we were working with Apple and their then-CEO Gil Amelio to try to get Apple to be POWER PC-based. We were trying to do a lot of different things with them.

Ultimately, in 1991, we did a POWER PC deal that was an Apple-IBM-Motorola joint venture. Known as the AIM alliance, Apple, IBM, and Motorola created a new unified computing standard based on the POWER instruction set architecture. The alliance yielded the launch of the highly successful POWER PC CPU family and Apple's highly successful Power Macintosh computer line. In fact, beginning in 1994, Apple used POWER PC chips in almost every Macintosh.

Still, Apple was struggling to find direction. Steve's third act was about to begin.

Jon Rubinstein: Now a few years go by, and by this time, Steve Jobs was advising then-Apple CEO Gil Amelio. Gil also had hired McKinsey to look at how to restructure Apple. McKinsey spent about six months doing a deep dive, and they did a great job in recommending the reconfiguring of the company from a division-based company to a functional-based company. In that transition, they needed to hire somebody to run Product Development. Steve recommended me. I interviewed, and in early 1997, they hired me to do that.

The day I joined was the day that Apple acquired NeXT. So Avie Tevanian came in to help run software, and a couple of the other NeXT people came back in as well. But mostly it was Avie and me who were the two main NeXT people who came in at that point in time. Later on we added more NeXT people. When I first got there in February, Steve still only was consulting, but then, basically, Gil got fired in, I think it was July, and Steve started hanging around more, eventually taking over as interim CEO in September.

So now Steve was back at Apple, and Jon was there with him. We stayed friends and would talk to each other. I tried to sell them things—memory, storage, displays—we had it all and they wanted it. In fact, during this period, IBM made far, far more on every iMac sold than we did on our own PCs, despite having the ThinkPad brand.

Their progress was impressive. Steve had reenergized Apple by focusing them like a laser. The first big hit was the iMac, which restored some of the shine to Apple, and by 2000, Steve was expressing interest in developing a portable music player, and it was up to Jon to figure out how to make it happen.

> **Jon Rubinstein:** By this point in time, Nick was out of the POWER PC business and was running the labs. I used to interact with him in the labs, and he basically was "open kimono." He'd tell me, "You go into any of the labs that you want. Anything you can use, we will license to you. And whatever products we make that you need, we will work it out with you." I had originally learned about the IBM Microdrive in 2000 or 2001, when I was doing the first iPod. I was trying to figure out how to do an iPod. I went to the IBM Microdrive Division and said, "We can build an iPod around your micro-drive. Here's the specifications we need." IBM didn't bite, so I found a Toshiba mini-drive, and we ended up doing the first iPod with the Toshiba drive.

Steve wanted our help, and he wanted to make it work, but we screwed it up on our end. Using the Toshiba drive, Jon and his hardware and software engineers built the first-generation iPod, and you know where the story goes from there.

Even though we screwed up, we went to the ceremony where Steve announced the iPod. He gave us front-row seats. He gave me front-row rec-ognition. He could not have been nicer.

And Jon? To this day, Jon is sometimes called the "Podfather" for his role in developing the iPod, which became one of the most popular consumer electronics products of all time and truly created the momentum from which everything else at Apple followed.

Jon Rubinstein: Now, by the time I went to do the iPod Mini, I contacted the same people, although by this time the group had been sold to Hitachi Data Systems. Of course, by now we're selling iPods like hotcakes. We basically have an exclusive deal where we're taking all of Toshiba's small-drive manufacturing. So, it's a big business. This time, when I said, "Hey, I want to do this," they said, "Done. You can have whatever you want." That's how that drive ended up in the iPod Mini. And by the way, the Mini is really the iPod that made the iPod successful. The iPod was pretty successful before that, but the Mini really took off. And then we got rid of drives completely.

Obviously, we screwed up that deal initially, but Steve stayed with me, and we continued to work well together. Eventually, in 2006, the POWER PC deal fell apart, too, and Apple moved entirely to Intel CPUs.

Jon Rubinstein: I held it off for five years, working with the IBM team. Nick wasn't as directly involved anymore by that point in time, but he was still the Godfather of the relationship, so he was always there in the background. I don't think there is anything that went wrong—our needs simply diverged. POWER PC was only being used by Apple and IBM at the end of the day. It was just the two companies. Motorola couldn't afford to keep developing. The business wasn't big enough. Apple wasn't what it is today, and IBM's business is basically minicomputers.

The whole reason for the POWER Personal Systems Division was to get really high volume, and we never got the volume we needed. As long as our requirements for our computers and their requirements for their computers were similar, it was possible to build processors that met both our needs, but our products were moving more and more toward portable products. And the power was just killing us, and IBM didn't have any low-power requirements.

So, our needs diverged—it wasn't like there were any bad guys or anything—it was just that they didn't have the need, and they didn't have the process, because they weren't developing low-power processes. So we had to switch to Intel.

So together, Steve and I had some wins and losses over the years, but because of the situations we had been in together, I know that Steve respected me. We respected each other. I was not out to try to do something stupid and disruptive or challenging. We were trying to complement each other. We were trying to help each other in different ways. If he respected you, I think he handled you differently than many of the stories that are out there. That certainly was my experience.

Jon Rubinstein: Steve tended to not treat our suppliers very well. I'm a partnership kind of guy. Steve was not a partnership kind of guy. Steve was a "win/lose" kind of guy and always had to win. We had relationships with lots of different companies, and the IBM relationship was always a really good one. That could not be said about all of these other companies, and I think part of that was because Steve trusted Nick. I think that's what it came down to. Steve never left a nickel on the table, but he wasn't that way with Nick. Steve always respected Nick. I think it really helped both IBM and Apple (and NeXT) through the years to have the two senior guys have a good relationship. I remember the opposite effect, where an executive would come to deal with Steve, and the two of them would just sit there and lie to each other. The guy would have his CTO with him, and the CTO and I would look at each other and roll our eyes, because these two guys were just lying through their teeth. I never saw that with Nick.

And here is something I do not talk too often about. Steve Jobs wanted me to go to work for him. He actually asked me to leave IBM and come to work for him as COO when he went back to Apple. And I turned him down.

I turned him down because Anita was very sick at the time. She had had major surgery. I remember Steve calling me in the hospital begging me to consider his offer to come out and join him. I said, "I can't do it, Steve. We're lucky my wife is alive. I just cannot do it. I'm sorry."

That was a tough conversation to have, and it was certainly a gut-wrenching decision for me to make. I was not happy with the way I left that COO offer with him. I actually wrote him a letter apologizing, but it never got anywhere.

Still, we would talk. Even after I left IBM, he would call me. He used to call me all the time at night. I would get a call from him at 11:00 or 12:00 at night.

And he was sick. I knew he was sick. But I did not know how sick he was. The last late-night call from Steve was very brief. He simply said, "Nick, I wish you the best," and I thanked him.

Sadly, we never spoke again. I know we lost an icon of innovation with his untimely passing. I also lost a close business colleague.

Perhaps these anecdotes are unnecessary to my story, but because these sides of Steve rarely see publication, I wanted to share them. What is necessary to my story is the fact that he helped me understand innovation greatly. He was a tinkerer. He would always take things apart. He did not just want to find a better way. He wanted to find the best way.

A lot of my thinking around innovation came from him. He understood innovation like few others. He started with the problem.

The whole iPod story is a great example and is well-understood. MP3s, Napster, and everything else came first, but everybody screwed up. Steve was late to the market, but he figured it all out and did a much better job than everybody else at creating the solution that customers needed, because he just worried about the problem.

I give him a lot of credit, and if in a different place and different time I could have gone to work for and with him, who knows how it would have worked out. Even so, I had a lot of interactions with him over the years, and I always came out better for it. We need more leaders like Steve today.

19

LEADERSHIP AND TALENT

While in many ways this is a book about "innovation," and one man's journey to understand it, define it, and capture it, it is just as much about "leadership" and the qualities that separate truly great leaders from the rest of the pack. Some leadership qualities are innate—you are born with certain instincts and abilities—while others, including analytic capabilities and empathy, have to be developed, molded, and constantly refreshed over the course of a lifetime.

My journey has led me to develop a firm set of convictions and core ideas about leadership, particularly the leadership of technology initiatives and technology startups. The first speaks to the innate quality of so many leaders—be yourself, stand up, and be counted. As Dr. Seuss once wrote, "Why fit in when you were born to stand out?"

Beyond that, I also believe:

- Leaders set clear expectations—they must be real and they must be hopeful.
- Leaders cannot know everything—and they only undermine themselves when they pretend that they do. That is why the best leaders surround themselves with experts who can go deep on specific subjects of importance.

- Leaders understand risk—when to take it, how to take it, and what the rewards and trade-offs may be.
- Leaders understand the fundamental and significant difference between enabling and empowering.

For executives and managers, this last attribute is crucial. "Empowerment" is an HR buzzword that entered the corporate vocabulary more than two decades ago, and it is as specious a concept now as it was then. It may sound good, but no employee is ever truly "empowered" to do things autonomously or outside their scope of responsibility. Rather, I believe that a leader's ability—and willingness—to *enable* their people is the fulcrum on which success or failure for an organization or team will be determined. Simply put, your job is to put your team in position to succeed by giving them the tools, information, feedback, and encouragement they need.

In earlier sections of this book, you learned of my journey from something of a young tyrant in Burlington to that of a true collaborator, even as—or *especially* as—I earned more influence within IBM. While that influence was exerted with senior leaders, board members, key clients, or my peers in IBM, the reality is that the key to my success really could be found in talent that I was leading and pushing toward IBM's Innovation Agenda.

So often when you read books about successful leaders, very little ends up being said about the talent who made those leaders winners and the way in which the leader enabled them to do so. That is a *huge* oversight if trying to accurately analyze and portray leadership.

In my case, particularly in my last major role at IBM, I *needed* our talent to rise to the occasion by understanding and accepting the need to collaborate to a much greater degree across functions. The nature of business and competition had changed so much that this was very much a make-or-break proposition.

I was frustrated at the beginning, however, because I realized that through no fault of their own, much of our talent knew next to little beyond their core specialties. They could do great work within a familiar domain, but to a large degree, they were doing it with blinders on.

I am not oversimplifying by that much when I say that we basically had people in Rick Miller's three camps—feasibility (the labs), viability (finance and other purely business functions), and desirability (marketing and sales). They were not organized physically, nor were they incentivized via compensation or recognition, to understand much about any part of the business beyond their field of work.

Out of this frustration came the T-Shaped Movement, which you have read about already. Of course, some of our people already had the T-Shaped Qualities needed to collaborate. I was wired to recognize those skills in people such as Linda Sanford and Ross Mauri, and, as a result, I gave them important roles during my operational career.

But how do you *create* and then *enable* a T-Shaped Workforce for a massive company such as IBM? This was a true test for my executive leadership capabilities, as it would be for any senior leader looking to organize around innovation.

I began to beat the drum. During my days at IBM, and ever since, I have talked to as many people as I can to learn more about how to build T-Shaped Individuals in organizations. I believe, if anything, that it is even more vital now than it was at the beginning of the twenty-first century. Collaboration across an entire business, including the nooks and corners, leads to the sharing of ideas that are generated by people who think differently from one another.

I took that thought another step further, and I began to actively seek out diverse talent—not so much for the sake of equity (as discussed in Chapter 13)—but for the sake of collaboration and innovation.

I took these ideas to people I knew across academia and the thought leadership spectrum and found that many people shared my thinking. Take Diana Natalicio, President of the University of Texas at El Paso (UTEP) from 1988–2019, whom you met earlier. She built a tremendous institution around the needs of her predominantly Hispanic community, but always with a broader context in mind.

Diana Natalicio: I think that people are more valuable when they are capable of communicating effectively what they are working on and are not just monomaniacal about a particular narrow technical field. In order to have an effective organization, you have to have people working together and communicating well, and I don't think that you do that if everybody goes into their independent cocoon.

The notion that we can't be as creative as we should be if we're not open to a broad range of ideas, perspectives, backgrounds, and histories of people is a valid one. The perspectives they bring to the table can totally change the way you think about something, but there has to be an open environment in which people feel comfortable expressing those ideas and sharing their thinking about them. That is a very important premise.

Commitment to diversity isn't about doing anybody a favor at all. It's about enriching the dialogue and the work that we're engaged in through the range of perspectives that people bring to it. And the benefits accrue to everyone. This is not a unidirectional kind of favor-giving.

Or take my good friend Dr. John Brooks Slaughter, an electrical engineer, former president of Occidental College, and the first African American director of the National Science Foundation (NSF). Throughout his storied career, his work focused on development of computer algorithms for system optimization and discrete signal processing, but his mind was often wrapped around social issues, too.

Even in his eighties, John remains incredibly relevant, having joined USC's Rossier School of Education in 2010 as Professor of Education, with a joint appointment at the Viterbi School of Engineering. He, too, advocates the T-Shaped Concept.

John Slaughter: None of the big problems that the world is facing today—in terms of issues like climate change and the need for getting rid of CO_2 in the air and the need for clean water in places that don't have it—can be solved by science and engineering alone. They require an understanding of the human and social issues, too.

Nick and I share that opinion, and that's the reason that this idea of collaboration is so exceedingly important, because no longer can we continue to progress if all we do is focus on a narrow field. It's going to require that engineering become much more understanding of social and humanistic issues. I think that's one of the things that Nick was driving at—not just across technology fields—but integrating engineering with areas that it has not collaborated with in the past, including the arts and the humanities and the social sciences. That's the kind of collaboration that he believes is going to be increasingly important if we're going to solve the problems that face the world today, and I share that belief.

While I am not formally an educator, I certainly share the concept of the T-Shaped Individual when I have the opportunity to speak with students or anyone concerned with the future of the United States (not to mention, all humankind). My IBM client, friend, and mentee Guy Chiarello recalls a time when he brought me to Syracuse University to speak in front of a group of students and local professionals.

Guy Chiarello: I had invited Nick to Syracuse University, where he was loved, to do a sort of interview. I was fond of Syracuse, and I wanted to talk to him and interview him in front of students, as well as professionals. I asked him to leave all the students and professionals with something that they could take with them to their classrooms or their offices that really would mean something, and he talked about something called the "T." We spent maybe twenty minutes of that forty-minute interview in front of hundreds at Syracuse on the importance of the T, and how to really make sure that your career had both depth of specialization in some key areas, but also the breadth of a range of capabilities and experiences that really allows you to stretch and be valuable to a lot of companies in a lot of ways.

Guy's story is important, because I was telling his audience at Syracuse the same thoughts I had shared with him when advising him on his own career. He had incorporated my advice and the T-Shaped Concept into life-changing decisions he had made.

Guy Chiarello: That T-Shaped Individual Concept really was the core of the conversation that we had when I decided to leave Morgan Stanley for JP Morgan. I had been at Morgan Stanley for twenty-three years when I decided that I wanted to do something different. I sat with Nick and said, "Look, Steve Ballmer talked with me several times. A number of other tech companies have talked to me several times. I've got Jamie Dimon to speak to. My old boss Vikram Pandit is now the CEO at Citibank. Dick Fuld is a friend of mine at Lehman. I have all these people who are pursuing me, but I'm thinking about Microsoft as the lead opportunity. What do you think?" He was really, truly instrumental in my thinking. We talked about the T. We talked about long-term perspective of where I wanted to be. It was great advice and free therapy from a friend who had known me, and joining JP Morgan was probably one of the best decisions I ever made in my career and in my life, because I met people and worked with people who influenced me. I rose to the top of my profession at JP Morgan. And I give Nick a tremendous amount of credit for that, because he got me to see some things that I couldn't really see clearly at the time.

Leaders with fortitude and courage must convince people of their vision and then enable them to get there. This is hard work. My thesis has always been that great leadership calls for 2 percent Aspiration, 3 percent Inspiration, and 95 percent Perspiration.

When Sam, Linda, and I set out to create the Globally Integrated Enterprise, my aspiration within that vision was to launch the Innovation Agenda. As you have read in other chapters, I had the ability to inspire the IBM technical community. I told them over and over that "If nothing changes, nothing changes." I told them over and over again that they had step out of their silos and listen to others within IBM, as well as the client. They bought into my vision.

Next came perspiration, as I pushed to break down silos, coaxed—sometimes forced—T-Shaped Behaviors, enabled collaboration, and enabled an approach to innovation that started with the problem.

John Chen: A great technology leader has to have the ability to see both macro and micro. And when I think micro, most of us were engineers—Nick's one and I'm one—and we tend to be very data-driven. We tend to be very fact-driven, numbers-driven, statistically-driven, and even probability-driven. But technology is really an imperfect science. In order to make a technology business work, a technologist has to both understand the data and the facts and figures, and the imperfectness of the data. That's a really big part of it. As a tech leader, you have to feel comfortable with the imperfectness of the data—there's sometimes incomplete and sometimes contradictory data—and formulate a decision. You see it in a macro way. Nick has that combination of macro- and micro-vision, which is what makes businesses successful. He talks about both technology and strategy with equal skill.

Great leadership is authentic because it knows how people feel, what the actual situation of the day is, and how to create the hope of a better tomorrow. In business, if you can inspire a talented workforce to see beyond their respective areas of specialty and embrace your vision of the bigger picture and how they can contribute to the achievement of that vision, then the organization can set out for new frontiers. In life, it is the same way.

While incremental progress matters, I am guessing your people, and even your family, want to be part of big swings and game-changing break-throughs, too. I believe that is very important today, and given the challenges we face as global citizens, perhaps more important than ever before. In the next chapter, I will talk about my vision for Frontier Research in the Technological Future.

20

NEW FRONTIERS IN INNOVATION, COLLABORATION, AND EDUCATION

A few years ago I wrote an article for IBM's annual Corporate Responsibility Report entitled, *"Creating a New Frontier of Innovation,"* in which I made my case that we—governmental agencies, educational institutions, corporations, citizens—must maintain our commitment to Frontier Research, those seemingly impossible big swings that change the world forever. If you would like to read this article in full, you can find it at: *www.ibm.com/ibm/environment/annual/ibm_crr_061505.pdf*

In 2019, we saw the fiftieth Anniversary of America landing the first astronauts on the moon. The moon landing arguably was the crowning legacy of President John F. Kennedy, who had won office by creating an inspiring vision of a New Frontier. Kennedy said, "We stand today on the edge of a New Frontier—the frontier of the 1960s, the frontier of unknown opportunities and perils, the frontier of unfilled hopes and unfilled threats... Beyond that frontier are uncharted areas of science and space, unsolved problems of peace and war, unconquered problems of ignorance and prejudice, unanswered questions of poverty and surplus."

His vision set in motion myriad actions across business, government, research, and academia that enabled America to be first to the moon. But as a nation, we still stand on the edge of that New Frontier in all other aspects he mentioned. And then some.

We need to get that spirit back again.

We need more moonshots.

We need to seek out and find new frontiers.

Indeed, investment in Frontier Research has always been a bedrock of innovation. It is rarely the invention itself that creates the revolution—it is the people who figure out how to apply it and, better yet, apply it in multiple and diverse ways. That is what innovation is all about—taking a great invention or idea and making it pervasive by applying it in a way that literally transforms institutions, enterprises, or society as a whole.

An environment must be created to foster this sort of research, and it begins with our government. As I have written already, the will to create that environment is sadly lacking in most of our elected leaders today—not just in the United States, but across Europe and Asia, and more or less much of the "developed" world. We simply cannot assume that established public policies are adequate for the new challenges that lie ahead.

Future prosperity lies in placing innovation at the heart of multiple policy areas and in fostering collaboration. In order to create my dream of innovation-driven prosperity, we must:

- Address the growing tensions between universities and industry around the transfer of technologies.
- Create a balance between the protection of intellectual property and the encouragement of the "open" movement.
- Critically reexamine and optimize our regulatory and legal systems to better support innovation, entrepreneurship, and flexibility in labor markets, while protecting society as a whole.
- Improve our education systems by fundamentally transforming and realigning them.

Because I have invested a great deal of my time on that fourth challenge, I want to focus there, but the other three are equally important. It takes more than intentions to create innovative, digitally literate businesses, executives, and employees. We, as a society, need to look at how we are educating students and providing ongoing education and training to people in the workforce.

As mentioned earlier, in the Technological Future, people will be judged not by what they know but rather by what they do about what they do not know. That is a fair exchange, as the pace of change constantly increases!

We all receive formal educations through traditional schools and other forms of training and courses. Informal education, though, is becoming increasingly important, as we find out what we need to know and then go about gaining that knowledge. A larger and larger part of our knowledge will come from the education we gain for ourselves, while less and less will come from the education given to us through traditional schooling.

I wrote in the previous chapter about the need for T-Shaped Individuals in our organizations. We need to drive that concept down into our educational system as well. Formal education is too often deep, rather than wide. We major in a subject in college and get degrees in specific areas. That may have worked in the industrial era, but it is no longer sufficient today. Dare I suggest that in addition to "liberal arts" curricula, we need to embrace a similar concept for "liberal sciences" degrees? We are inching that way, as John Slaughter can attest to with his efforts at USC.

John Slaughter: One of the things that I'm very pleased about is that USC has developed a new set of general education courses which introduce social analysis into all areas, including engineering and science. I teach a course called "Technology and Society" which gives me an opportunity to introduce to freshmen the importance of including social issues in every field of technology. And that's being replicated in a lot of areas across the university. So, it's beginning to happen, even though it's taken a long time.

During my IBM career and in the years since, I have worked closely with many leaders in education. These leaders include several you have heard from already such as Rick Miller, Diana Natalicio, and John Slaughter. Another is Yvette Melendez, former Vice Chair, Connecticut Board of Regents, whom you will learn more about shortly.

Each has influenced my thinking. Each has made and is making significant contributions to the creation of a Technological Future that is open to all who are willing to keep working and keep learning.

How do we infuse our educational system with a T-Shaped Mindset that will drive twenty-first-century innovation? Well, there is the direct approach of Rick Miller and Olin, where they intentionally redesigned the curriculum to get at this very idea. And while for many reasons, not all educational institutions (nor businesses) will take such a direct approach, all—and at all levels—should consider new ways to create the talent needed for twenty-first-century vitality and the renewed pursuit of brave frontiers. Examples include:

- Partnerships between organizations and colleges/universities.
- Partnerships among organizations, colleges/universities, and governmental entities.
- Continuing education programs run by professional organizations, associations, and colleges.
- STEM initiatives which aim at getting more students (especially more women) into the sciences, engineering, and technology.
- Programs run by businesses to support education.
- New programs and initiatives recommended and developed to meet evolving needs.

When I participated in the US Council on Competitiveness's National Innovation Initiative (NII), each recommendation around talent, investment, and infrastructure related directly to the need for formal and informal education to create a technologically literate and innovative workforce.

Many of the NII recommendations fall across society or are driven by various levels of government. A single organization cannot carry them out in full, although it could implement its own version of some of the recommendations. I work with many educational and nonprofit initiatives to help them do just that.

I believe so strongly in the need for technological literacy and education that I make sure to accept almost every invitation to speak at universities, colleges, and other institutes that I receive. In recent years, I have given major presentations at Columbia University, University of Vermont, Southern Vermont College, University of Delaware, and University of Dayton, among others. (My presentations often can be found on the websites of these schools.)

Without fail, I talk with students about how they can enable their careers by building their technological competence. (And you just know that I am not talking about mastering the intricacies of TikTok or helping their grandparents set up their Wi-Fi.) I believe that people need to build their own success and future, and since the future will be a technologically-driven one, this means continuing to build digital knowledge and expertise. There are many programs being developed that help enable the development of digital and technological competence; far too many to mention and many of which I probably am unaware. However, I will point out just a few here for consideration:

- **MITRE Corporation's Social Responsibility Programs:** MITRE conducts a number of activities, such as sharing technology experiences with the next generation of science, technology, engineering, and mathematics (STEM) professionals; holding an annual Robot Day program for high school students; and encouraging underrepresented groups (such as women and minorities) to become engineers.

- **PeaceTech Lab:** A global network of professionals from the technology community, academia, and government, PeaceTech Lab fosters cross-discipline, cross-generational collaboration to resolve conflicts. The Lab acts as a data hub, forming partnerships with social media and big data companies to develop tools for early warning, decision-making, collaboration, and evaluation.

- **New York Academy of Science's Science, Technology, Engineering, Mathematics (STEM) Initiatives**: When I give presentations to educational or general audiences, people often ask me what they can do at home to build the level of science knowledge within their families. I mention the many programs run by science museums and my work on STEM and mathematics programs at the New York Academy of Sciences for starters, as referenced earlier by Paul Horn, and which were created in conjunction with the New York Hall of Science. But there are many opportunities out there if you are willing to do just a little bit of looking.

- **Maker Movement**: I also suggest families look for activities that are part of the Maker Movement. This once-rapidly growing network of technology-focused do-it-yourself communities provides activities, fairs, and publications aimed at nurturing creative and intellectually curious people who want to create new products and build value in their communities. While this movement seems to have lost some momentum, it remains a valid idea that is alive at local levels.

I believe the Technological Future can be a great one, but we need to continually infuse young people with energy and belief that this is so and the skills to make it so. Kids are inundated with fear and negativity in both the real and virtual worlds, but I want to leave young people with messages of hope and possibility, because there *is* so much hope and possibility out there if they achieve technological literacy and develop a mindset for continual learning and action.

I also believe that parents can help to mitigate their children's fears and the impact of so much negativity, regardless of their own current digital literacy. In fact, I believe that they have certain responsibilities, including the:

- Responsibility for developing and supporting their children's interests in science, engineering, and technology subjects. They need to expose their children to science. They need to work with schools on promoting science.

- Responsibility to push their school systems to support the interest of girls in science. Even in 2021, teachers too often assume that female students are less interested in science than male students. This is dinosaur thinking and must be changed.

- Responsibility to promote technological literacy by getting involved with what their children are doing digitally, and by exposing their children to interesting technology work and projects. Parents tend to worry about how much time their children spend "on screens," but the bigger concern might be with *what* they are doing on screens. Screen time that enhances technological literacy is not only valuable, it gives children an advantage over their peers.

- Responsibility to take advantage of programs aimed at building students' interests in science, engineering, and technology through such programs as National Engineering Week, the aforementioned Maker Movement, robotic competitions like FIRST, and local, regional, and national science fairs.

Of course, I believe parents need to build and maintain their own technological literacy and knowledge of science in order to best guide their children and prosper themselves in the Technological Future. As with my own life, lessons for the future can often be found in the past. A parent need not be an expert in technology to be informed enough to help guide their children. My parents certainly were not technologists, but they understood where the world was headed and encouraged me greatly to go in that direction.

Likewise, John Slaughter's parents provide an inspiring example. Back in the 1930s and 1940s, there were very few African Americans pursuing engineering. That did not stop John Slaughter's parents from encouraging him.

> **John Slaughter:** I grew up in Topeka, Kansas, prior to the *Brown v. Board of Education* decision, so I attended segregated elementary schools. I liked to build things and tear things apart to see how they worked. I would take my bike apart once a week and put it back together again. Had it not been for the fact that I always had a lot of curiosity, I might not ever have gone into engineering, but I was lucky. I had the encouragement of my parents. Even though we certainly weren't a family of wealth, they encouraged me to do things, and they made it possible for me to pursue my interests.
>
> I would take *Popular Mechanic* magazines, and if there was something in there that I thought I might be able to build, I'd try it. I would find the parts and build cameras and radios and things of that sort. I just became interested in mechanical and electrical things, and my parents encouraged me to pursue those interests. That's how I think my desire to become an engineer came about. That encouragement was crucial, because I think back upon the time when I graduated from college, where I was the only African American in my engineering class, and the year that I got my doctorate, where I was the only Black PhD in the country in engineering who graduated that year.

Despite the times John was born into, he not only became a PhD engineer, he achieved so much throughout his lifetime that he is today a member of the National Academy of Engineering (NAE) and the Hall of Fame of the American Society for Engineering Education. He is a Fellow of the American Academy of Arts and Sciences, the American Association for the

Advancement of Science, the Institute of Electrical and Electronic Engineers, and the Tau Beta Pi Honorary Engineering Society. He is the founding editor of the international journal *Computers & Electrical Engineering*. He holds honorary degrees from more than twenty-five institutions, and has received numerous awards, including the Martin Luther King, Jr. National Award, the UCLA Medal of Excellence, the first US Black Engineer of the Year award, the NAE Arthur M. Bueche Award, the UCLA Distinguished Alumnus of the Year, and the NSF Distinguished Service Award, among many others.

John's story is an inspiration. Today's young John Slaughters are everywhere. Our challenge is to ensure all of this raw potential today is steered into situations where their youthful curiosity is given direction and support, and where they have an understanding of just what is possible if they believe in themselves and the future. As I once said to Lauren States, "You can be anything you want once you decide."

We all have a part to play in creating this reality, including, of course, the individual. John's parents encouraged him, despite the odds, but it was John who stayed the course. He took ownership of his future at a time when a good percentage of the world did not much care what his future would be. I believe we all need that same mindset, and I am not just talking about kids and young adults. I am talking about *everyone*.

I have increasingly come to believe that professionals cannot rely on institutions for their education and training for the Technological Future anymore. It is hard to find programs that address the needs of executives and managers or that give employees the information they are looking for as quickly as they need it. The idea of digital literacy is too new in our rapidly changing world for training and educational programs to be developed around it as quickly as is needed, although innovative efforts are underway to help close the gap.

Rather, individuals need to develop their own education programs to gain their set of skills for the Technological Future. These skills should fall in the T shape—with deep expertise in one area and complementary learning across a number of areas.

I have put together some of my own recommendations to help individuals prepare to operate in the Technological Future. The recommendations vary, depending on the stage of life and role in life one is in at any given time. As people move into new roles, I recommend they acquire further skills, so they can carry out increasingly broad and complex tasks. The need for ongoing education applies throughout all of our lifetimes, as we work to increase our value in the evolving workplace, and even after we retire, in the evolving society.

In terms of technological literacy, employees need to acquire or develop:

- Sufficient knowledge to see the path of future employment.
- Skills useful to employers, both at their current company and at different organizations throughout the economy, should mobility be desired or necessary.
- A willingness to embrace technology-driven initiatives and learn how to work with new technologies.
- The knowledge and aptitude to identify, simplify, and innovate to develop solutions to problems. They also need to own the ability to communicate their solutions throughout the organization.
- The realization that they are often in the best position to make productive decisions for their organizations.
- Continuing education, through programs they identify that teach new skills that will ensure employability in a rapidly changing digital economy.

As for managers, they need to acquire or develop:

- Sufficient knowledge to implement technology projects.
- The ability to perceive pending digital disruptions in their areas of responsibility and to suggest valid solutions.
- The ability to simplify problems in their areas of responsibility so that they can innovate to develop solutions.

- The ability to recognize solutions that already exist in the company, often in the customer-facing positions, and bring those solutions to the rest of the company.
- The ability to distinguish among uses of technology and to make decisions about what would be productive in their areas of responsibility and to make those recommendations to leadership convincingly.
- Continuing education programs to keep themselves informed about trends, innovations, and developments across all areas of business on the way to the Technological Future.

Meanwhile, board directors and executives need to acquire or develop:

- Sufficient knowledge to make productive and timely decisions.
- The ability to see across the company to drive large-scale initiatives.
- An informed sense of the ways to perceive and handle digital disruption.
- The ability to understand proposals from IT departments and internal/external consultants.
- The ability to make decisions about productive, valid uses of technology, along with the equally important ability to determine what is not valid or useful.
- The ability to simplify problems for the enterprise so that they can be solved through innovation.
- The ability to recognize solutions that already exist within the company, often in the customer-facing positions, and drive those solutions throughout the company. Many times, the most important decisions are made—and the best solutions devised—at lower levels of an organization but not expanded across boundaries for maximum leverage.
- Continuing education programs to keep themselves informed about trends, innovations, and developments for their business,

the business ecosystem, and society in general on the way to the Technological Future.

Increasingly, the workforce is composed of entrepreneurs and intrapreneurs for whom digital literacy is essential. Here are recommendations for such talent as they carve out their careers in the digital world:

- Figure out how, whether as an entrepreneur or intrapreneur, you can provide value and position yourself accordingly as a founder, full-time employee, consultant, or contractor.
- Identify yourself as someone who can make things better, and understand the tools, information, approaches, and network you need to make that happen.

I also have done a lot of thinking about the personal skills and attitudes people need to support their digital literacy. It's not going to be enough to know about technology and functional areas. The people who will succeed going forward, at all levels in the business world, will demonstrate certain skills, attitudes, and mindsets that allow them to deal with digital transformation and disruption, while simultaneously building their own future and that of the world.

My initial list of these attributes includes:

- Orientation to problem-solving, including an active involvement both in defining problems and in their possible solutions.
- Trustworthiness, which one earns and then extends to others.
- A focus on quality, both in terms of productive activities, results, and in doing what is right.
- A strong work ethic.
- An attitude of collaboration and willingness to enable others.
- A belief in the philosophy, culture, goals, and processes of the organization.

- A passion for innovation.
- A primary focus on what people know and do, as opposed to an over-emphasis on "official" credentials.
- An interest in tapping into the global community for ideas and talent, since the best of both are out there and everywhere.
- An ability to work in teams and to participate on leadership teams.
- An interest in working with peers to get work done correctly, including participation in an iterative process of focused discussions that lead to the right decisions.
- The ability to decide when you need to create your own rules to get the work done right (as long as you are prepared to deal with the consequences).
- The courage and conviction to know when you must put your career on the line.

You may recognize in these attributes the lessons I learned from my parents, as well as behaviors I displayed throughout my career. These are ideals I have strived to meet, and while I succeeded more often than I failed, I came up short many times, and will continue to do so. Perhaps you would add additional attributes to this list or disagree with some of my thoughts. Regardless, I think we all need a list like this to measure ourselves against, because the future is coming, and the people and organizations that will succeed in it are those who understand the need for change, ongoing learning, and a spirit of innovation.

I am seventy-six years old as I finish writing this book. You have heard many say, including me, how hard I still work today. That is where I find fulfillment, and through the organizations I support and the educational opportunities I seek, I try to ensure I remain relevant in the Technological Future. That is my choice. Others, having worked hard throughout their entire lives, choose a life of retirement and the pursuit of hobbies, family, and other noble or less-than-noble uses of their time. That is their choice.

I frequently meet people from a third group, though. These are people who retired from their primary careers and would like to continue contributing to society but are unsure of how to retool for the Technological Future in a comprehensive way. A simple suggestion is to connect with Columbia University's Center for Technology Management. I did!

For many years now I have worked with Dr. Art Langer at the Columbia University Center for Technology Management. Art is the Center's Director and a Professor of Professional Practice at Columbia University. I serve as a member of the Center's Executive Advisory Board, an Executive Mentor, and also a Lecturer.

I knew Art originally through his work at Workforce Opportunity Services (WOS), where he founded an organization that is committed to developing the skills of untapped talent from underserved and veteran communities through partnerships with organizations dedicated to diversifying their workforce. This includes people of color, first-generation college graduates, and early-career aspirants. Seeing all the good that Art and WOS did, it seemed natural for me to engage with him at Columbia and the Center.

In fact, the Center actually encouraged me to self-document my career and learnings through this book. Several of its early chapters can be found on the Center's website. Having now been through the process, I would encourage you to "knowledge capture" yourself by documenting your story so that others can learn from your life's experiences.

Programs at Columbia University's Center for Technology Management allow you to remain a lifetime learner by honing or improving your skills to satisfy your own standard of currency and relevancy. The Center uses the simple driving thought that while you are never too young to learn, you also are never too old to learn either. For folks like me, having an environment that lets me update and refine the skills needed to continue to contribute to the business world, the global economy, and society in general by keeping current and relevant on emerging technologies—including subjects such as cybersecurity and infrastructure needs, artificial intelligence and data, and other technology-related matters that affect and impact our world—cannot be valued enough.

You can learn more about the Center for Technology Management's programs and work through our website: *ctm.columbia.edu.*

The overall vision is quite simple. We need to revamp the educational system for primary and secondary school students. We need to rethink continuing education for today's workforce, including the need for the individual to "own" that commitment to a far greater degree than ever before, regardless of company offerings. We need innovative educational approaches such as the one I am spearheading at Columbia to enable senior executives and other talent to reinvent themselves so they can carve out new roles in a world where traditional retirement is not always feasible or desirable.

The point of this cradle-to-grave focus on constant learning is not only to help the individual maximize opportunity, but to create the total human capital required to create more moonshot innovations.

There is more, though. Much more.

Technology is dominating our workplaces, our society, and our lives. Therefore, we need to make sure that everyone in our workforce, our society, and our lives has access to the education, programs, and opportunities that will help them to achieve technological literacy. Everyone has something to contribute, and everyone needs to be able to use their abilities to participate in the technology-based world that is being created.

As our economy changes, and as traditional skills are being automated or moved overseas, we need to make sure that we are providing access to training for people who have been displaced from their roles so they can regain access to jobs with as little "friction" as possible. We need to develop training and education programs to meet the skills requirements of the new jobs being created. Unless we develop solutions for the future for all workers, we are fooling ourselves that we can meet this gap.

Our government understands this, of course. Back in 2005, US Secretary of Education Margaret Spellings announced the formation of a Commission on the Future of Higher Education, often referred to as the Spellings

Commission. The nineteen-member commission, of which I was a member, crafted recommendations for a national strategy to reform post-secondary education. In particular, we focused on how well colleges and universities are preparing students for the twenty-first-century workplace. We released our report in 2006, with a focus on access, affordability (particularly for nontraditional students), the standards of quality in instruction, and the accountability of institutions of higher learning to their constituencies, including students, families, taxpayers, and other investors in higher education.

As far as affordability goes, everyone needs help sometimes, and we must figure out how to break down financial barriers. One positive program that exists today is ALICE, which stands for Asset Limited Income Constrained Employed. As the United Way (a supporter of ALICE) puts it, "ALICE cares for our children and aging parents, fixes our cars and works in our local grocery stores, retail stores, and restaurants. ALICE is our friend, neighbor, coworker, and family member. We lean on ALICE for support, yet many ALICE households are one emergency away from a financial crisis impacting their ability to feed their family, heat their home, maintain their housing, and ensure their medical care."

By supporting hard working families, ALICE enables kids to gain the education and opportunities they need to start their careers. ALICE, along with other programs, strives to make it possible for families across the economic spectrum to prepare their children for the Technological Future. But many still fall through the cracks.

Sometimes the help relates to representation, and we must keep breaking down those barriers, too. Women are currently underrepresented in the technology industry, and I have supported initiatives to both provide science, technology, engineering, and mathematics (STEM) educations to women, and to support women in technology, both as entrepreneurs and as employees of technology companies.

Larry Kittelberger: Nick is probably one of the people who pushed diversity in management more than anybody I ever met. He would chastise me, because I'd come in to IBM each year with all these male CIOs. I didn't have a woman leader. He gave me a hard time. He said, "What the heck is this?" And in manufacturing, sometimes it's hard to get that one to stick. But I said, "Look at their passports. How many of them are US citizens? They're from all over the world." That's diversity, also, but Nick is really big on women in business and giving them the opportunity.

Linda Sanford: When I joined Nick on the mainframe team, Nick just wanted me to be myself. He trusted me, and it had to do with what he saw as my abilities, not whether I was a man or a woman. He also believed that the team, while they might be skeptical of me since I didn't know mainframes, didn't have a problem with my being a woman. I've been very fortunate maybe, or maybe it's unusual, but that just was not an issue for me, even though there were so few women in technology or technology leadership at the time.

Anne Altman: Nick is such a passionate individual about diversity in the workplace and leadership. He looks for talent. I don't believe that he creates an environment where he takes anything less than the best and nurtures the best, but he's always been an advocate for women, and he's very proud of that. What was challenging for me as a female was the fact that I ran the Federal Government Division. It's less so today, but if you go back to the year 2000, there were almost no examples of women running federal government businesses at all. In 1994, when I went out to Manassas, Virginia, to run the Commercial Services Business, they called me a "skirt." It's amazing that IBM put a woman in that role at that time to run the business when the federal government itself and the federal market was so male-centric. But Nick always let me do my thing. Always. I can't think of a time when he did not. He never, ever said things to me that might even hint at me being female. He just knew I had the talent to get the job done.

Linda and Anne were incredibly skilled and both had the T-Shaped Aptitude that would enable them to handle their respective environments. Always accept the challenge? That was Linda. That was Anne. I was happy to give them chances—they were ready for them—and they definitely made the most of them.

Everyone deserves a chance. Like John Slaughter's parents, my parents encouraged my drive—sometimes *forced* that drive—and I did the work. But we needed help, too. Luckily, because of the paper route I had as a kid, I was able to apply for and win a Gannett Scholarship that helped my parents send me to RPI. By ourselves, we could not have afforded it. As I advanced in my career, I looked for opportunities to advance traditionally under-represented groups, both within IBM, in terms of talent development, and without, in terms of certain boards I chose to join or programs I chose to support to encourage inclusiveness.

Diana Natalicio: When I joined Nick as a member of the Board of the National Action Council for Minorities in Engineering (NACME), I was immediately impressed with two things about him. One was that his commitment to the issue of minorities in engineering was truly sincere. It wasn't just to be trendy. It was earnest. Second, he was a no-nonsense guy. If he was serving on the board, he dedicated his talent, his time, his energy, his expertise—everything—to the assignment. He was highly engaged. Nick had a hard-driving, passionate determination to ensure that NACME played a critically-impactful role in ensuring that we could increase the participation of African Americans and Hispanics in engineering and science fields. Nick never lost his passion for that mission, and in fact, it probably grew a little when he became board chair. Then, when he was in charge and even more determined, he was a tough taskmaster. He was extremely determined to make a difference.

I *was* determined to make a difference, and I learned everything I could from people like Diana, who had developed tactics to make a difference that could be rolled out in all directions. Consider, for example, that from those days when I first met Diana in the late 1980s to late 2019, when she finally retired as president, she had built the nearly 100 percent Hispanic UTEP into a major research institution, growing research dollars from $6 million to more than $90 million annually. Innovation and inclusiveness—that is Diana's legacy. And while her achievements are monumental, the challenge nationwide is daunting, as she could explain as well as anyone.

Diana Natalicio: I think the real common denominator, because of the high correlation between being an ethnic or racial minority and being poor, is that most of these students come from backgrounds of very modest means. They are not at all financially prepared to take on college education. They work while they go to school. They have elder-care and child-care and a lot of other kinds of things for which they have responsibility. So I think Hispanic and African Americans certainly share a great challenge, and that is that they are typically first-generation in college, they come from low-income households, and so socioeconomically, they are very, very challenged. We worked hard to develop a strategy at UTEP that would work for any low-income student, whatever their ethnicity, race, or gender.

The common denominator is this socioeconomic challenge, and data on bachelor's degree attainment in any area of study in the United States over the past fifty years is so absolutely discouraging. Begin with the lowest socioeconomic quartile, and ask, "What is your probability of getting a baccalaureate degree?" Well, in the 1970s, the probability was 6 percent that you'd get a baccalaureate degree if you came from that socioeconomic background. At the same time, in the 1970s, if you were in the highest quartile, it was 35 percent. So there was a gap between six and thirty-five based on money. If you fast-forward forty years to the 2000s, the lowest quartile moved up from 6 to 8 percent, a two-percentage point gain, while the highest quartile doubled to 70 percent. The gap between the have-nots and the haves has widened dramatically over the past forty years.

That is just a recipe for disaster, and it does not matter your ethnicity or race. If your probability as a low-income student to get a college degree is that low, then what do you do? What are your options?

What would my options have been as a kid back in Beacon had I not been able to go to RPI?

What would John Slaughter's options have been had he not gone to Kansas State University?

What would Diana Natalicio's options have been had she not gone to St. Louis University?

Diana Natalicio: I was a first-generation college student myself, and the importance of ensuring that first-generation students do have a chance at success matters, because talent is distributed equally across all boundaries, and what we are doing is squandering it selectively by socioeconomic background or race or ethnicity. Nick and I both grew up in similar backgrounds in which our parents were committed, even though they themselves had never had the opportunity to get a college education, and even though the resources were thin. They managed to get us through by all sorts of means, but not the least of which was encouraging us to have high expectations. They knew that if they just invested in us there would be success. I tend to resonate with people with those attitudes and find myself always more comfortable with people who come from the kind of background that Nick and I share. These people tend to be humble about their education and about the opportunities that they had. They're not entitled. I'm better with them than I am with entitled people.

TIME could not have been more correct when they named Diana as one of their 100 Most Influential People in the World for 2016, and former HUD Director and presidential candidate Julian Castro could not have been more correct when he wrote for *TIME*, "Brainpower is the new currency of success in the twenty-first-century global economy. And that currency is even more precious—and sadly elusive—for far too many first-generation low-income college students. No one understands this better than Diana Natalicio…Natalicio was ahead of her time, seeing the future of America in the faces of her students."

We have already seen how John Slaughter also was ahead of his time as a pioneering African American engineer and college president throughout the second half of the twentieth century. When I first met him in the 1990s, he was a member of IBM's Board of Directors.

> **John Slaughter:** When I was on the Board at IBM, I stayed at the Rye Town Hilton. One morning for breakfast, I went downstairs, and I was sitting in a booth, and in the adjacent booth was Nick Donofrio talking to a young man who IBM was attempting to hire. Nick apparently had the responsibility for convincing this young man that IBM was the place to go, and I could not help but overhear the conversation. As I thought about it later, if I already didn't have a job, I would have applied after hearing Nick describing it! Nick and I became friends shortly after that, because he would appear before the Board from time to time, giving presentations. I found out that he was committed to some of the same things I believed in, and we would share our feelings about diversity and the importance it played and why it should be emphasized at IBM.

Among many opinions John and I share is that diversity drives innovation, and that in the absence of diversity, innovation cannot be maximized.

> **John Slaughter:** We shared a common interest, and a common belief about the importance of diversity in any institution, and it's

a belief that I carry and continue to attempt to foster here at the University of Southern California. But I also knew that Nick was not just a man of beliefs, but a man of action. Within IBM, Nick has supported people, particularly some of my African American colleagues including Ted Childs. Ted was the Vice President for Global Diversity for IBM for a number of years, and Nick gave Ted the support from the top administration that nobody else provided, running interference for him many, many times. Another person that I recall Nick was very, very supportive of was Rod Adkins, who was the first Black Senior Vice President at IBM. Nick had a lot to do with Rod's ascendancy to a senior position. Again, Nick's role was not heralded, but certainly was recognized by those of us who were aware of what was going on.

John and I saw eye to eye, but I also had a great admiration for the life this man had created for himself against incredible odds. When it looked like we might be able to collaborate outside of our IBM relationship, I was very excited.

John Slaughter: A few years after I met Nick, the position of President of NACME opened up. Nick was the NACME Chairman of the Board at that time, and I expressed an interest in the position to him. Nick played an exceedingly important role in convincing me that that would be a position that would fit my interests and where I might be able to make a contribution.

I convinced him alright. I threatened to abandon him on the other side of the planet if he did not take the job!

John Slaughter: That's the truth. In 2000, the IBM Board went to China, and that was the same time when Nick and I were talking about the possibility of my becoming President and CEO of

NACME. I was somewhat reluctant, frankly, because I wasn't sure whether I wanted to leave California to go back to New York. I remember Nick and I were having breakfast, and I said, "Nick, I'm not sure I want to do it." And Nick said, "Do you want to return to the United States on the IBM plane?" I could see myself being left in China, so I immediately agreed to become President of NACME! Nick has a unique way of convincing people, I find.

Humor aside, John and I both are passionate about drawing underrepresented minorities into STEM education, and working together through NACME, we had the opportunity to really roll up our sleeves together and make some things happen.

John Slaughter: We talked about the importance of not just recruiting minority engineers, but of their development via their educational programs. Nick was a strong believer in supporting the historically Black colleges and universities and the Hispanic-serving institutions. Nick encouraged me to spark the fire in junior high and high school kids, too, and that was important. At NACME, Nick was a strong chairman who supported the initiatives that I proposed.

Women and men like Diana and John see the nuances that lead to misallocation of so much potential talent away from not only higher education, but from STEM degrees. If seeing is believing, too many young people fail to *believe* because they never *see* anyone like them in the careers they might otherwise pursue.

John Slaughter: In order to change the situation in higher education, I'm thoroughly convinced that the biggest problem is the absence of underrepresented minority faculty. Our predominantly white colleges and universities have engineering programs where at most, 2 percent of faculty are from underrepresented minority classes—African American, Latino, or Native Americans. That has a significant impact, I believe, on getting more underrepresented minority students into engineering and succeeding in their education, because they seldom have the opportunity to see that there is a person that looks like them who can be a success in the field. I sometimes say that I was the first Black engineer that I ever saw, and that's true. I had never, ever seen a Black engineer before I graduated. And the fact that that remains the case for too many young Black students today is the reason why, in my opinion, we've done such a poor job of increasing the numbers.

The education-related challenges that African-American, Hispanic, and Native Americans face are daunting, as Diana showed with the discouraging data of the last fifty years. Yet, as she pointed out, the true common denominator today is socioeconomics, which creates challenges everywhere, including right here in my own backyard of Connecticut, where I have also tried to make a difference.

CONNECTICUT REGENTS

Whether within a company, a community, a country, or even the world, the ultimate goal is to lift as many people as possible into a position to contribute their best for the greatest benefit of all. Life is not fair, and we do not all start from the same place. We also all meet roadblocks at certain points along the way. In America, state university and community college systems can play a key role in helping people from all walks of life to build initial and advanced tools—and periodically retool—with offerings that propel them forward.

A great challenge and opportunity came to me in 2016, halfway through a four-year appointment I was serving with the Connecticut Board of Regents when Connecticut Governor Dannel Malloy asked me to become the chairman. He only had recently reorganized the board to have oversight of both the community college and state university systems, and he was offering me not only a new challenge, but a very hands-on opportunity to impact higher education. Always accept the challenge.

My key collaborator in this endeavor was an amazing woman by the name of Yvette Melendez, who lucky for me, had thirty years of experience in public sector, education, and higher education arenas.

> **Yvette Melendez** (*Vice Chair, Connecticut Board of Regents; Board Member, MITRE*): I first met Nick when then-Governor Dannel Malloy made an executive decision to merge the community college and the state university systems into one board. Nick and I were part of that inaugural board. I also was named as vice chair to the chairperson of the board. Within a year or two, the governor decided to name Nick as the board chair. Nick asked me if I would remain vice chair and work alongside of him. Quite honestly, it was a very difficult time in the organization with lots of turmoil at the top and public controversy. To say there were challenges would clearly be an understatement. Mergers of any kind are difficult and often controversial, but when you undertake a merger within the public sector, it's fraught with difficulty and countless obstacles. And when you attempt it in higher education, most people run for the hills, because it is extremely arduous! Higher education is not known for being nimble.

I understood the challenges, but I saw a great opportunity, too. Public education, especially in Connecticut, is pretty unique, but I see such opportunity in it, and I wanted to make a difference if I could. I wanted to make a difference not only for the state of Connecticut, but for the thousands of individuals in different stages of their lives looking to advance themselves and achieve their full potential. Luckily for me, Yvette agreed to stay on to help me.

> **Yvette Melendez:** He and I both share a deep-seated commitment to higher education, so that made it easy, but we truly just really

worked side by side. There was not one decision—and this is his style of leadership—where he did not involve me, engage me, or ask me my opinion and seek my advice. So from the very beginning, his sense of how he would exercise his leadership as chair was made clear. It's one that is very inclusive and very collaborative but ultimately focused on decision-making. At the same time, he also ensured that whatever knowledge or whatever expertise he could pass on to me, he did.

Across a massive economy, we need a massive amount of technologically literate talent. There will always be those people with the will and drive that no one and nothing can stop. They will find a way, and I admire people like that. Many of the people you have heard from in this book are those kinds of people. But to get the raw numbers we need to drive global innovation, we need to bring as many people into the fold as possible.

Yvette Melendez: He sees higher education as the vehicle by which we will innovate, the vehicle by which we will be competitive, the vehicle by which we inform citizenry, and the vehicle by which we get to the greater social good and within those walls, create thoughtful citizens who then exercise their individual power outside to contribute to the economy or to the well-being of the state. I think that's at the crux of his commitment to higher ed, and that's what we shared.

That is why the Connecticut Board of Regents was so special to me. I had served on a variety of higher-education boards, a couple of those being private institutions, but here, in particular, I felt a passion for the mission of community colleges and the role that community colleges play at the ground level. These are the foot soldiers in terms of developing talent and preparing or retooling people for the workforce.

Yvette Melendez: The more he became knowledgeable about the individual community colleges in Connecticut and the work that was being done on the front line with not just young, traditional eighteen-year-olds coming out of school, but heads of households and single moms and dads, the more excited he became. These people were turning to community college as a way to become trained in twenty-first-century skills, to be able to adapt to the changes in their immediate working environment, to get a better opportunity, and to provide for their families. So he became particularly enamored with the role that community colleges could play in Connecticut.

I focused on workforce development by forming partnerships between community colleges and employers. If we knew the types of skills particular employers needed, and in what volume, we could work with students to steer them in those directions.

I also facilitated, enhanced, and "moved the ball"—because it had been a topic for many, many years—on the issue of individuals who had completed a community college degree being able to seamlessly move into a four-year institution to complete their bachelor's degree. That was something Yvette and I spent a lot of time working on with our executive staff and the academic leadership of the state schools.

Yvette Melendez: I know that it sounds like something that makes sense to do and wouldn't be hard, but believe me, it was a major challenge. Nick was passionate about making sure that we met our commitment to students by facilitating that process. To him, it was a great victory in human capital creation if a community college student discovered that what they really wanted was a four-year bachelor's degree. He worked with both academic leadership at the four-year institutions as well as all of the community colleges to make that transition as easy and seamless as possible.

Our community colleges are so critical, because they give a person that first foot in the doorway toward the Technological Future. The individuals have to do the work, of course, but then, if the program is well-designed, it feeds them into the local economy to meet a need or sets them off to two more years of education to build out skills even further. If the process is flawed, the individual, already distracted with other responsibilities, can become discouraged and lose the momentum necessary to progress. They deserve our best so that we can get their best.

In my lifetime, I have seen the global talent ecosystem from so many angles. I particularly loved being able to make a difference with this one. That is because going all the way back to the lawns I mowed and the gardens I planted, I never did anything in life just to check a box. I was raised to do jobs the right way. Once I came to understand and commit to making the community college system work better, it was no different. Once I was in, I was all in. But it took time and there were many elements to it. I believed it was not only the right thing to do, because it represented another form of inclusiveness, but it was good business, too, because Connecticut's employers are desperate for talent ready for the Technological Future.

Yvette Melendez: I think for Nick, what makes a difference is that he truly believes that inclusiveness is the way it's supposed to be. He just believes that in order to be better, in order to be responsive—whether it's to consumers in terms of a product you're trying to sell, whether it's a higher-education institution, whether you're a nonprofit—if you want to reach as wide a base or market as possible, or negotiate a deal in India or Latin America, you can't do that if you haven't been built inclusively from the ground up. So he approaches it, one, from a business perspective, and two, because it's inherently part of a core value that he deeply holds.

I'm no saint. I am not completely comfortable with the plaudits laid upon me in these pages, although I am deeply humbled. The fact of the matter is, I was not born some wonderfully enlightened soul. I was a mischievous kid, but my parents fueled my academic ambitions and held me to a high standard. Through their Catholic faith, they also held me to the Golden Rule, my mother in particular. But these were hard-scrabble Italian-Americans preparing me for the world, while fighting to find and maintain their own place in it.

What I am trying to say is that my parents raised a good son. They raised me with a very good, but to some degree limited, way of looking at the world, but because my father enforced in me that notion of change and my mother pushed me to be good to people, they gave me the tools to expand my viewpoint beyond what they could see in their time and place.

I changed every step along the way. After all of these years, maybe my strongest feature is that I am willing to change. Maybe that is why I am who I am. I can change. I am willing to change. I am willing to listen. I am willing to learn. Even as thick-headed and as stubborn as I can be, I am willing to listen, I am willing to learn, and I am willing to change.

Sometimes I will tell people, "My parents raised a good son. My wife raised a good husband. My kids raised a good father. I didn't do this on my own."

I changed, and they changed me. That is why, so far anyway, I have not been left behind. I do not want anyone else to be left behind, either.

I have often said that the best talent always wins in the end, but when institutions directly or indirectly discourage that talent from pursuing certain paths, we all lose. The cost goes well beyond the social justice implications and in fact gets to the very heart of innovation and the world of tomorrow.

Getting everyone equipped for the Technological Future requires new ways of thinking and doing on the part of our corporations, governments, and educators. It requires effort on the part of all us to take personal responsibility, too.

New frontiers remain and await our willingness to change and rise to the challenge. Many of those new frontiers deal with well-known and longtime challenges known to us all for a very long time, and optimist that I am, I believe we can meet these challenges. But it will take as many of us as possible, wherever we are in life, to skill up and work together.

21

ON LIFE AND LIVING

n writing this book, I have been reviewing the many presentations I have given over the past ten years, and I find that I keep repeating certain points, which I consider Life Lessons. They are so important to think about and apply, whether eighteen or eighty-one years of age:

- Observe everything; constantly take in all the data you can. Again, I quote Dr. Seuss, who said, "You'll miss the best things if you keep your eyes shut."
- Change is your best friend.
- Lifelong learning is essential for everyone.
- Time works against you. Speed is important.
- Value migrates, and you do not control it.
- Education must be T-Shaped: deep in one area and broad across the top.
- If nothing changes, nothing changes.

Always, when presenting, I tell stories and give examples. Stories and examples help to make the complex issues simple.

Sam Palmisano: I'm sure no communications genius would look at any particular presentation by Nick and say, "This is how you do it," and yet he is such a good communicator. And he cares about the people he is talking to, whether they were customers or the technical community in the IBM days, or a group of students today. It doesn't matter. He sincerely cared about those people then, and he cares about the people he is working with and inspiring today. And that's why he is so good.

It has taken me hundreds of pages to tell you my life story and to spell out the things I remain passionate about today. But if it has been a long story, I think it is in many ways a simple one, too, and perhaps no surprise, it all ties back to my father.

To this day, I have a desire to solve problems—to figure things out. Growing up, I tended to take things apart. I still do. But I was no John Slaughter taking apart his bike and putting it back together each week. If my mom and dad were still alive, they would say, "Yeah, he takes things apart, and often times he never put them back together."

As a matter of fact, after my mother passed and we cleaned out her house, we found a pile of things that I had tried to fix. I took them apart, tried to figure out exactly what was wrong with them, and just did not stand a chance of putting them back together! But I know I have that shortcoming, so I try to be careful. I try not to take apart things that I cannot put back together. To this day, Anita tells me all the time, "Don't touch this, don't touch that."

It is all part of the learning. My father taught me to tinker, but he was better at it than me, maybe out of necessity. He had to be better at it than I was, because if he took something apart and could not put it together again, we did not have a backup or a replacement. He had to make things work, like he did with that lawnmower. Craziest thing I had ever seen—but we could mow the lawn to his exacting standards with it.

So I learned a lot from him. He gave me my inquisitive mind. He gave me that sense that problems could be solved, that I could say, "If we don't have it, make it. If we don't have it, go build it. If we don't have it, go solve that problem and figure out why we can't have it."

It is why I knew from the get-go that I would be an engineer. It is why I applied "early decision" to RPI and passed up a lot of other schools.

I do think that it all fits together. I think I am true to myself. I am who I am.

It is why I have a small car collection now. It is why I have the garage. I need to tinker. I want to be there, and I want to do everything myself, but I have to stop myself. If something is leaking, I call people who actually know what they are doing, because God only knows what I would do!

I mention these things in humor, but at the same time, I am very serious. I do have an inquisitive mind. That is why I want and need to stay involved with companies and challenges bigger than myself. I want to solve problems. I want to fix things. I want to make the world better for people.

And honestly, I want to prove to *myself* each day that I still matter.

Jason Providakes: He's a great example for someone like me. If I have half his energy at seventy-six, I'll be happy. But Nick is driven. Leaving his mark is really important, and how he pays it forward. That's why I think for an organization like MITRE, we feel pretty honored to have him, because we know his time is very valuable to him. For him to spend the time with us means a lot. He's really a technological giant in the sense of seeing the evolution of technology and the value it brings. But I also would call him a leader in the area of social innovation. He truly understands humanity and the value technology can bring to make this a better world. And you always know where you stand with Nick. It's refreshing in this day and age. That doesn't mean he's always right, but his intentions are always good.

Yvette Melendez: He's all in. He's one of those people that regardless of age, just has boundless high energy, but there are lots of ways that people choose to burn off that energy after their primary career has ended. For him, though, I think he wants his legacy to be that he's made a difference. So he's been part of public and mission-driven entities and what he's accomplished has made a big difference and is part of a legacy. He believes that he can make a significant contribution by being present on boards. He talks about culture, he talks about the impact of AI and digital, he talks about diversity and inclusion. All those things together are the things that leaders, trustees, and board members of companies need to master if we are going to remain competitive. He cares about ensuring America's competitiveness in the world and believes it comes from making darn sure that we've got the best possible leadership in the board room.

Ryung Suh: You hear a lot of really accomplished people who talk about being willing to give back, but a lot of them don't mean it. I think in his case, there's probably an element of him that likes giving back, but the other thing is that he's been a doer all of his life. Just because you've accomplished all the things that you want to accomplish, or you have all of the material wealth that you want, your inherent character doesn't change. He remains a very strategic, impactful guy, even when he's not running a business day-to-day, so I think he enjoys being engaged and sharing his knowledge. I think it's just built into who he is, and I don't think that's going to change no matter where he is in life.

I still feel like I have something to prove. Even at seventy-six, I still think I am worth my weight in something semi-precious, if not precious. I still feel like I want to learn. I have not stopped learning. I have not stopped doing.

I still have that same desire that I grew up with as a kid. Back then, I woke up every day to make a difference—not just to "be nice" as my mother would say—because my father's question of "What difference did you make?" had gotten deep into my makeup. That still goes through my head every day. I get the greatest amount of satisfaction seeing something through to its end.

Bob Bedard (*President and CEO, deFacto Global; Former IBM Director*)**:** If you sit with Nick, you never think of him as being retired. I don't think his mode is any different now than it was twenty, thirty, forty, fifty years ago. He's always pushing forward, which is cool, at least in my mind. He has a vision for things, and I think he pushes his agenda forward. I think he sees the path forward that he would like to take, and he pursues that aggressively. He uses resources that he has available to him to achieve the goals he wants to achieve.

I still always accept the challenge, at least most of the time, but there is a method to my madness even today. For example, in 2020, I received a request from the Royal Academy of Engineering to judge a piece of work on the "Beyond Silicon" future, a topic that is a great passion of mine. Now, before I could render a professional opinion about a highly-technical topic, I would have to do a deep dive. The way I see it, if I am going to be opening my mouth on a topic, I need to be committed to learning as much about it as I can, so I said to them, "Of course I will engage," thereby putting the pressure on myself to prepare.

Bob Bedard: He continually retools himself and keeps himself current so he can continue to be part of the conversation and contribute to the thinking and the doing as we move through these eras of big technological changes. Think about that in the context of what he wants to do at Columbia. The whole point of what he wants to do at Columbia is say to his peers, "Don't just sit there and rest on your laurels and look back and say, 'Wow, I was there when the cell phone was invented, and that was cool.' No, you have to look forward. You have to retool yourself for a new era so you can continue to participate in what's happening." It's the same world, it's just a new phase of what we're going through; he wants to remain a valued member of that community, and he wants his peers to do so, too.

So I think it is a combination of a few things. And maybe it is just being seventy-six, too. Maybe it is just realizing that the end is coming. I do not know how much time I have. I do not know when my final day will come. And I do not know the time or place, as the Bible says.

My suspicion is that it is not any one thing that drives me. There are many. They motivate me and keep me moving.

I am changing in the here and now, though. I have become more self-aware. I challenge myself every day. I think the variety of things that I am involved with gives me vitality. My days can go from talking to MITRE about a government program, to talking to Aptiv about a set of auto electrification and or self-driving issues, to talking to the PeaceTech Lab about Racial Justice and Equity or Global Voter Suppression issues, to talking to one of the cybersecurity boards that I am on about a recent hack, to talking to one of the AI boards that I am on about the issues of data and model provenance, to talking to one of the academies about participating in the next leading issue. I go from one end to the other. It expands every day, and it fills the horizon.

It is science in every form. The science of life. The science of politics. The science of education. The science of engineering. The science of technology. The science of the physical world. The science of the digital world. I enjoy being everywhere on the continuum, and that is what makes me do what I do. That is why I keep saying "yes" to offers as opposed to saying "no." I suspect that I fear if I ever say "no," it may be the end, to be honest.

I feel like every day I get slightly better, not slightly worse. In some ways I am physically healthier than I have ever been, and I keep my mind healthy, as well. I stay engaged, and I still reach out and try to make a difference.

Perhaps another sign of age is that I have become more opinionated. I do not always see it the way other people see it. I am no longer a go-along to get-along person. Not that I ever really was that way completely, but I *really* am not that way now. With that said, I want to close this book with a few observations, particularly as they relate to free will, self-awareness, and what we all have gone through with the COVID-19 pandemic.

I have been doing a lot of thinking about the concept of free will lately, particularly as technology becomes a greater part of our lives. My thinking goes like this:

More or less, everyone wants more freedom. And yet, we all forget to use the most important freedom we have as human beings: free will, or the freedom to choose.

We make so many choices every minute of every day, often without knowing it. If you choose to be told what to do, you are clearly not exercising your free will. If, on the other hand, you decide, after being told what to do, that it makes sense to do it, you clearly are exercising your free will. If you give up your free will, you need to understand that you made the choice to do so.

For me, this line of thinking goes all the way back to my early struggles with my father. At first, I met his demands out of fear. As I grew into a teen, I began to understand at some level how he was molding me. I also began to see all that he was *teaching* me. I came to take pride in the work I did, even though it was work he *made* me do and work that kept me from hanging out with my friends, playing organized sports, or enjoying some of the other typical teenage pleasures.

While I was never going to find all of the freedoms I sought while under his roof, I learned to work within the program. I found ways to be active within my high school. I found ways to participate by choosing activities that fit with my schedule. I had no after-school time, because he had me working, so I could only join activities that met at night or on weekends. The Debate Club fit that bill, so I joined. I became a member of the thespian group, and I had lead roles in two plays. I joined the yearbook staff. I was active in community support and work groups. I played baseball and basketball on the weekends, as my schedule allowed.

In other words, while I was too young to think much about concepts like free will and self-awareness, both figured into the solution I crafted to enjoy my teenage years as much as I could within the constraints of my particular situation.

I started with the problem.

I created a solution that worked for me. I took the best that my dad had to offer, and benefited greatly from it, but I also bobbed and weaved to create my own identity, too.

That is what I have been doing ever since. I have been an organization man—primarily with IBM, but also, as you have seen, with many other companies and organizations—sometimes out in front, but perhaps more often in the background. I kiddingly was called "the Godfather" by some at IBM, because I was known for making things happen behind the scenes. I used that method of exercising my free will within the constraints of organizations to build a worthwhile life and to make the world a better place, too.

Where am I going with all of this? Well, throughout history, those with power often have used force overtly to suppress free will. We would all like to believe there is less suppression now than ever before. And that is likely true. But there are ways to get people to suppress their free will without force, to get them to give it up without a fight, to get them to give it up unwittingly and unknowingly.

As technology demands more and more of our lives, we must remember our own free will. As I did with my dad, we must take the good from technology, but remain aware enough of what is going on to not let it suppress us. It is tricky.

Technology is rarely developed for the purpose of doing bad things. But history has shown us over and over again that technology, as agnostic as it is, in the hands of bad people can and will be made to do bad things, evil things, and unthinkable things.

The internet, social media, life sciences, artificial intelligence, and machine learning—to name just a few—bring a lot of joy to people across a spectrum wide enough to include sharing pictures of puppies and babies to identifying genetic markers for diseases that allow for early intervention and the saving of lives. Yet these tech tools also have proven capabilities to alter our willingness to give up our free will. We become oppressed not by force but by more subtle and sometimes insidious forms of persuasion, innuendo, and suggestion. Along the way, we become influenced into giving up the most precious gift we have—free will.

While we each need to take ownership of our ability to exercise free will, leaders have an even more critical role. All leaders need to find ways to do more.

They need to understand the threat and prepare themselves and their organizations for how technology may impede free will. They need to enable systems and processes where free will is cherished, valued, and protected. When there is no more free will, there will soon no longer be anything.

This is yet another reason why I consider technological literacy for everyone so crucial. We must be aware of what is happening in order to act and react in relation to the expansion of the influence of technology. We need to have discussions as a society about the effects of technology on our cultures, institutions, and lives. We can only do so if we have taken the steps to make ourselves, our families, and our communities digitally literate.

During the bizarre and often tragic 2020–21 timeframe in which I have been finalizing this book, my thinking here has only deepened and at the same time, expanded. Perhaps during this timeframe, you have used technology in new ways to maintain a semblance of normalcy: You "gathered" for happy hour with friends via Zoom rather than at your favorite restaurant, bar, coffee shop, or park. You played online chess with your best friend rather than at one another's homes. You visited the doctor via a video-enabled appointment rather than in person. The list is endless.

Technology has helped us to weather the storm. We used tech tools in ways we never had before and to our benefit. You could have done most, if not all, of these things prior to COVID-19, but the pandemic made them mainstays, at least temporarily. Now, I am guessing that while you will gladly go back to your old face-to-face habits as soon as possible, you will hang on to these new ways of doing things, too, whether to make do in a pinch or by choice. At the macro level, companies are reconsidering mobility policies, real estate trends are shifting rapidly, and innovative companies are popping up left and right to cater to our blended world.

That is the new balance, and there is so much more to come. There are so many other things that are going to happen. But not all of them are good. And remember, I am a huge tech advocate. I am a huge tech cheerleader. Still, there are moral and ethical concerns to everything, including science and engineering. There are adverse consequences to everything, including science and engineering "breakthroughs."

I am not just talking about all the secret activity that occurs on the dark web, either. As we all know by now, the activity that goes on through publicly-available platforms can take terrible turns. It is shameful the attacks that go on with no basis in fact, and where are the business leaders when they occur? They have moral and ethical policies in place, they just do not *enforce* them. Where are the moral compasses?

These companies are creating tech for the good, and with worthy intentions, but we have to question the bad. This is not new. The Law of Unintended Consequences has been proving itself since the dawn of humankind.

Think about the people who created the Atom Bomb. They knew what they were doing. While they were working to try to end a horrific war, they were deeply worried about the full scope of damage that could be done with their creation. They understood fully the consequences of their actions. I am waiting for many in the tech industry to step up and take responsibility for the consequences of *their* actions. When are they going to make the leap?

Today, lying via social media platforms is a big problem. Fake news is indeed a big problem. While everything known is knowable, there are plenty of people out there with agendas and something to gain by trying to make you believe something that they know to be false.

Currently, at the end of the day, I do not think the leaders of the tech industry are owning up to their responsibilities to their users and to society in general. Eventually, they will step up, but in the meantime, your moral fiber and moral compass are in play. I am not saying we should not have these platforms. I am just asking if each of us understands our own actions and the potential consequences.

This brings me back to the concept of self-awareness and change. I have spent much of this book linking the need for change to the business career I built, to the innovations I drove and drive, and to my belief in a better tech-enabled tomorrow for *all* if we work for it.

Perhaps it has been the undercurrent of my entire life. Maybe that is the binding force here. Maybe the title of this book, *If Nothing Changes, Nothing Changes,* has even more meaning and is even more powerful than I already believed. Looking back to that night on the porch through my now seventy-six-year-old eyes, I know that when my dad said, "If nothing changes, nothing changes," he in many ways was saying, "Don't be like me. I'm not just telling you to be better than me. I'm not just telling you to change everything around you and stop trying to conform. I'm telling you to learn every minute of every day and change *yourself* along with the world."

So yes, he started me down this path, but I would be so wrong if I did not give credit to *everyone* who has been there for me along the way. I have already given credit to my mom, my dad, my wife, and my kids, but you could probably make a case that *everyone* who touched me—many of whom have spoken in these pages—and everyone whom I touched, changed me in some way.

I think history will show that the types of events we have seen over the past few years—from COVID-19 to Black Lives Matter to the Fake News crisis—will bring about long-term seismic change. They will force us to think about everything differently and to start to *do* things differently or risk being left behind. That was evidenced in 2021, as the COVID-19 Delta variant and the subsequent controversies over whether to be or not to be vaccinated brought the idea of being left behind into the public dialogue.

While these and other events force us to change the physical world itself, they also force us to *think* differently about what is going on and what really matters and who really matters. More than ever, I think to myself, *Did I do enough? And what am I going to do differently going forward?*

On the political-will side, I do not know. We will see. I do not know if COVID-19 will be enough to bring about the changes I have advocated earlier in these pages. It is not just an American problem, either. What is going on in the United States is going on in other countries. We have a bigger magnifying glass over us, and at a higher magnification level, but it is not really much different in Italy or England or China or even India, truth be known.

There is a backlash movement everywhere, because people feel adrift and lack confidence in their leaders. A pandemic such as COVID-19 wakes you up, grabs you, gives you a kick in the butt, and says, "Come on, this is about *all* of us. This isn't just about some of us."

The Delta variant extended that wake-up call still further.

Any one of us can be a carrier.

Any one of us can become infected.

It does not matter who you are, your age, or your politics. You could be toting a gun or not toting a gun. You could be a Republican or a Democrat. You could be a conservative or a liberal. You could be Black or White. You could be a man or a woman. You could even be the President or First Lady of the United States of America.

COVID-19 did not know the difference. That is the humbling experience of something like COVID-19, and yet, we did not do well managing it, particularly early on, whether in the US or, for the most part, anywhere else.

And yet everything known is knowable. When I speak to boards or board members who long to turn back the clock, I say, "What do you mean go back? Go back to what? You have no idea what you are going back to."

You cannot go back. You have to prepare to keep changing. That is why the continuum thought, the spectrum thought, is a change thought.

It is not an either/or world these days. It is not a binary world anymore. We have to worry about every spot in between, too. That is the way things are going. That is what is possible now. It has probably always been possible; it just never was needed. It was never where we were as a society at any previous time.

I take the sciences seriously, and in my heart of hearts, I think engineering is just the application of science to everyday problems. But I take the science of life, the science of politics, the politics of education, the politics of society, and the politics of the physical world very, very seriously, too. It is my view of these sciences that continues to change me, continues to challenge me, and continues to drive me. I just wish I saw more people thinking that way, to be honest. I do not mean that people should necessarily draw the same conclusions that I do. I just want them to *think* and to look forward.

And that is why my recommendation to you remains: maintain an open, collaborative, multidisciplinary and global perspective. If you do, then your life and your free will always be just that—*yours!*

It will require you to think more broadly. It will require you to change the way you think, to think differently, and to work more closely with others, in the T-Shaped fashion. You start to understand and appreciate the fact that you cannot be alone and you are not alone. Do you want to live as a hermit and avoid the new realities? Do you want to live in isolation? Do you live with just your own nuclear family? Or do you want to change?

COVID-19 has proven to be a complex systems-engineering problem, and I am not trying to trivialize any of the lives that have been lost or any of the dislocations that have occurred, but we have to be more honest, and we have to be more candid with ourselves.

Yet we are not.

We are simply not honest brokers.

And the fact that we now can propagate fake news and lies easily, almost at will, means that there are going to be more opinions considered, and leaders are going to have to be stronger, be braver, and be more outreaching. It does not mean that the task is impossible. It just means that it is changing.

The good news, I think, is that in the end, dictators are doomed. I think they know this in their heart of hearts. They are not going to admit this of course, but their time grows short.

I believe in free will. The choices belong to the individual, no matter what, and that is going to continue.

To impose your will is a fool's errand in the end. I learned this at IBM. It did not get easier the further up I went. It got harder. I will never forget remembering the lectures I was given as I studied Communication Theory and why people listen and why people learn. They have to be *convinced*.

Telling people to do something lasts for a very short period of time, and it only works in limited cases: I have got a powerful piece of equipment. I am going to tell you the way to use it, and if you use it differently, I am going to fire you. Okay, fine. That was the way things worked when I first joined IBM, and of course, it was not just there, but across most of the business world. That was the command-and-control leadership approach that had emerged following two world wars and the Great Depression.

But it got me in trouble in Burlington, and it would have ruined my career if I did not change. I was then, and we all are even more so today, in a *creative* environment. When I was leading engineers and scientists and professionals, I could not just tell them, "Now, I want you to invent today. By the end of the day, you have to *invent* this solution for me."

That does not work. That makes no sense.

But *leading* does work—explaining *what* needs to be done and *why* it needs to be done—and listening to the ideas of others about how to accomplish the goal. That is the way that the impossible became possible for my teams more than once.

A leader can outline all the tasks that need to be performed along with some boundary conditions, and that "what" that we are working on is not done until those tasks are performed. But I am not doing it for you, and I cannot tell you how to do the work. In the end, you have to do it.

That is how I built environments fused with trust and confidence. I was not perfect. I made many, many mistakes along the way, and I continue to make mistakes today, but I built cultures—in Burlington, in Austin, in Poughkeepsie, and around the world—built around the leadership principle of, "I will be forthcoming if you will be forthright."

By that I meant, "If you tell me the truth, I will be there to help you."

And the faster you tell me the truth—the faster you tell me you are getting it done or you cannot get it done—the faster we will collectively get it done, the faster we *will* get it done, and the faster I will be able to help you.

I believe very much in this approach to building a culture of trust—be forthright, be forthcoming. I do not believe in a "Keep your mouth shut. Loose lips sink ships" environment. That is the environment that a dictator mandates and that is just a doomed environment today. Over time, you are not going to get it done.

It may work in wartime. It may have worked in other cultures and at other times, but it is not going to work in the multigenerational, multicultural world of 2021 and beyond.

I do not believe might will make right over time. The fact of the matter is, logic will prevail. Honesty, integrity, and truth will prevail.

That is my hope for the future and that engineering and science—and innovation—will aid and abet so that truth can prevail. That is my deepest feeling, and everything I have been saying throughout these pages all comes together here, in my mind. The circle does square. Everything converges here in my mind.

That is what keeps me going. After all, if nothing changes, nothing changes.

ACKNOWLEDGMENTS

My journey to complete this book, much like my career, could not have happened without family, friends, and colleagues to guide me and redirect me along the way. In particular, I am deeply grateful for the encouragement of my entire extended family of Donofrios, Fulvios and Berners. At its heart, this is indeed a book about the power of family, and I continue to learn and gain energy from them each and every day.

I want to thank all of the incredible leaders who agreed to be interviewed for this book, and who helped me not only throughout my career but most recently, to advance this narrative in powerful and insightful ways. This story would not have happened without you, and this story could not be fully told without you. Sadly, three of these leaders have left us in the time since I began this effort. Dick Gladu, Diana Natalicio, and Jim Onalfo all made big impressions on my life, and more importantly, on the world in which they lived. They live on in their family members and in the marks they left in their professions.

There are thousands of amazing and talented people that I have had the pleasure of working with throughout my career who are not named in this book. My fervent hope is that you still see yourself in the stories and lessons shared. It has been my honor to be one of your colleagues.

And finally, my co-author Michael DeMarco and our editor David Yaun. You have brought fresh perspective and new insights to a story that I thought I already knew so well. I appreciate the combination of professionalism and passion that brought so many of these lessons to vivid life.

CONTRIBUTOR CHAPTER INDEX

Agerwala, Tilak: Chapters 4, 7, 8, 11, 12

Altman, Anne: Chapters 7, 8, 11, 20

Arzubi, Luis: Chapters 3, 12

Bedard, Bob: Chapter 21

Caine, Chris: Chapters 7, 17

Carlucci, David: Chapters 4, 11

Charles, Bernard: Chapters 4, 9, 10, 11

Chen, John: Chapters 18, 19

Chiarello, Guy: Chapters 9, 11, 19

Chichester, Mark: Chapter 15

Childs, Ted: Chapter 13

Gladu, Dick: Chapters 2, 3

Horn, Paul: Chapters 7, 10, 12, 14, 16

Johansson, Frans: Chapters 12, 18

Kittelberger, Larry: Chapters 9, 20

Krol, John: Chapter 15

Linton, Dick: Chapters 2, 3

Lund, Vijay: Chapters 5, 6, 12, 14

Mauri, Ross: Chapters 5, 8, 9, 11, 12, 14, 18

Melendez, Yvette: Chapters 20, 21

Milholland, Terry: Chapters 9, 14

Miller, Rick: Chapters 12, 14, 18

Natalicio, Diana: Chapters 13, 19, 20

Onalfo, Jim: Chapter 9

Palmisano, Sam: Chapters 4, 5, 6, 7, 9, 10, 12, 14, 21

Papermaster, Mark: Chapters 3, 5, 11, 12, 14, 15

Providakes, Jason: Chapters 15, 21

Reis, Vic: Chapter 7

Renyi, Thomas: Chapter 15

Rubinstein, Jon: Chapters 11, 14, 18

Samson, Bob: Chapters 4, 6, 7, 10, 11, 14, 16

Sanford, Linda: Chapters 5, 6, 9, 10, 11, 12, 14, 20

Slaughter, John: Chapters 13, 19, 20

States, Lauren: Chapters 9, 11, 13

Su, Lisa: Chapters 10, 11, 14, 15

Suh, Ryung: Chapters 15, 21

Yaun, David: Chapters 6, 10, 11, 12, 14, 15, 16

BIBLIOGRAPHY

Gerstner, Jr., Louis V. *Who Says Elephants Can't Dance?* New York: HarperBusiness. 2002.

Johannson, Frans. *The Medici Effect*. Boston: Harvard Business School Press. 2004

Maney, Kevin. *The Maverick and His Machine*. Hoboken: Wiley. 2003.

Watson, Jr., Thomas J. and Peter Petre. *Father, Son & Co.* New York: Bantam. 1990.

REFERENCES

Columbia Center for Technology Management. https://ctm.columbia.edu/

Council on Competitiveness National Innovation Initiative Report: *Innovate America: Thriving in a World of Challenge and Change.* 2005. https://www.compete.org/component/content/article/11/202

Harvard Business School: *Aptiv PLC Board of Directors (A).* Lynn S. Paine and Will Hurwitz. May 2021. https://www.hbs.edu/faculty/Pages/item.aspx?num=59440

IBM Corporate Responsibility Report: Creating a New Frontier of Innovation. Nicholas M. Donofrio. p 4. 2005. https://www.ibm.com/ibm/environment/annual/ibm_crr_061505.pdf

National Academy of Engineering Report: *Making Value for America.* 2015. https://www.nae.edu/19579/19582/19649/129940/Making-Value-for-America

CPSIA information can be obtained
at www.ICGtesting.com
Printed in the USA
BVHW051653160922
647245BV00013B/91

9 781544 531342